BEFORE

BEFORE

Children's Memories of Previous Lives

Jim B. Tucker

ST. MARTIN'S
ESSENTIALS
NEW YORK

First published in the United States by St. Martin's Essentials,
an imprint of St. Martin's Publishing Group

BEFORE. Copyright © 2021 by Jim B. Tucker. All rights reserved.
Printed in the United States of America. For information,
address St. Martin's Publishing Group, 120 Broadway,
New York, NY 10271.

www.stmartins.com

The Library of Congress Cataloging-in-Publication Data
is available upon request.

ISBN 978-1-250-78177-2 (trade paperback)
ISBN 978-1-250-78178-9 (ebook)

Our books may be purchased in bulk for promotional, educational,
or business use. Please contact your local bookseller or the
Macmillan Corporate and Premium Sales Department at 1-800-221-7945,
extension 5442, or by email at MacmillanSpecialMarkets@macmillan.com.

Life Before Life was originally published by St. Martin's Press in 2005.
Return to Life was originally published by St. Martin's Press in 2013.

First Edition: 2021

10 9 8 7 6 5 4 3 2 1

For Chris and our children,
Alex, Ben, Jake, and Meghan

CONTENTS

INTRODUCTION

Young children sometimes say they remember a different life before their current one. Many of them give enough specific details—the area where they worked as an incense maker before being hit by a bus for instance, or the name of the aircraft carrier their plane flew off of before it crashed—so that this other life can be identified.

What do we make of that—can past lives be real?

At the University of Virginia, we've spent the last sixty years trying to answer that question, trying to figure out the best way to explain this phenomenon. The work started with Ian Stevenson, an iconoclastic physician who was chairman of the psychiatry department at the medical school. He became intrigued by such cases in the early 1960s and ended up giving up his position and prestige as chairman to focus on the research. After setting up a small research unit, now known as the Division of Perceptual Studies, he spent decades studying cases from all over the world. He also got others involved in the research, including me.

I was a child psychiatrist with a busy private practice when I got interested in the work in the 1990s. At the time I met Ian, he was a dignified man—often wearing a three-piece suit to work—who was approaching eighty while still publishing papers and books prolifically and traveling halfway across the globe to investigate cases. I enjoyed seeing patients—and I still do—but here was an opportunity to also be part of something bigger, to explore in a completely serious-minded way the question of life after death. I soon left my practice and joined the effort.

With this new two-in-one edition, you can assess the results of our labors. *Life Before Life* is an overview of the work, examining the different aspects of the cases, as well as a greatest hits collection of sorts, with summaries of cases ranging from Asian ones Ian studied in the 1960s up to American cases in the 2000s. Then in *Return to Life*, I recount my investigations of a number of recent cases, including what are probably the two best known American cases: James Leininger, who remembered being a World War II pilot, and Ryan Hammons, who remembered being a Hollywood extra.

Those two cases show that in addition to documenting the veracity of the children's reports, part of what's exciting about this work is how the cases give clues about what survival after death might entail. Some of the children provide intriguing descriptions of events from their time between lives, sometimes including verifiable information. Both James and Ryan gave startlingly accurate details about their parents' activities around the early time of the pregnancy. The cases also indicate that with multiple lives, some aspects of one life carry over to the next. This carryover often includes traumatic memories of a violent death, but it can also include warm, positive emotions, as some of the children voice great affection and sometimes longing for loved ones from before. Along with knowledge about past events, love and attachment appear to survive as well.

Toward the end of *Return to Life*, I try to include our cases in a more general exploration of the ultimate nature of existence. In the penultimate chapter, I venture into quantum physics territory in order to make the argument that consciousness is the core of reality that the physical world grows out of, not the other way around. If that's true, it should not be surprising that an individual consciousness can survive after the physical brain dies, and in our cases becomes associated with a new brain and starts a new life.

There seems to be consensus among the people who have read *Return to Life* that this chapter is either the best or worst in the book. If it's not your cup of tea, feel free to skip it. But I do think quantum physics offers insights that are relevant to questions about Mind and reality. There's a reason why Max Planck, the founder of quantum theory, said he regarded consciousness as fundamental and he regarded matter as being derived from consciousness.

Our work contributes to the evidence for such a position. If our cases are what they appear to be and children really do have past-life memories, they cannot be mapped onto a materialist view of reality. If the materialist view—that physical matter is all there—is correct, then it's impossible for children to remember previous lives. Yet some children do.

I've now been engaged in this research for twenty years, and I continue to be impressed by new cases. A while back, I met Grant, a little boy who, from a very early age, told his mother that she was not his only mommy. When he was five, he asked his parents if they remembered when he was in the war. He said he was in the army and described being on the beach and in the jungle. He said it was 1969, and when his parents asked him if he was talking about Vietnam, he told them he was. He said he had died in an explosion when he was twenty-one. He gave the state he was from and his last name, an unusual one I'll call "Slaven," which occurs with similar frequency in the United States.

His mother went to the Vietnam Memorial website and was shocked to see that a soldier named Slaven from the state Grant had said was killed in the war when he was twenty-one. She showed Grant pictures of various men on the site, and when they got to Slaven's, he said, "Oh, that's me." His mother then contacted our office and agreed to an interview.

Before meeting the family, I joined a virtual newspaper archive site and accessed Slaven's obituary. Following leads from it, I was able to obtain certain details about his life, including his family's address when he was in high school.

I met Grant and his parents in their spacious home near a city in the middle of the United States that is rich with history.

His parents came across as totally reasonable people. They are Catholic (though non-practicing), and his father in particular had initially been quite skeptical about a past-life connection. I brought along pictures to use as tests for Grant, who was still only five years old. I showed him pairs of photographs, one from Slaven's life along with a control picture, one that had nothing to do with him. When I showed Grant a picture of the Slaven family's house along with a control picture, Grant said he didn't remember either one. Of course, I don't know how the appearance of the house may have changed over the last fifty years. I then showed him a picture of the house across the street from the Slaven home along with a control, and he pointed to the correct one and said he remembered it. Slaven went to a Central High School, and when I showed Grant pictures of two large Central High schools, he pointed to the correct one and said he had been to it.

After the meeting, I continued searching online for information about Slaven. I was eventually able to access his high school yearbook from 1968, the year he graduated. I emailed electronic copies of pages from the yearbook, along with pages from the 1968 yearbook of a different Central High School, to Grant's mother. I sent three pairs: pages showing the school's administration, ones showing teachers, and ones showing students. I did not tell Grant's mother which pages were the correct ones. Grant picked the one from Slaven's school for all three pairs. When I told his mother the results, she replied, "Oh wow, that is absolutely crazy!!! Again, wow, I am blown away that they were all right, he was so casual about it."

After doing some more internet sleuthing, I wrote to Slaven's sister, and her daughter sent me some family photographs. I sent Grant's mother pairs for each of Slaven's parents. Again, I did not tell her which pictures were correct. At that point, Grant asked why he had to keep taking tests. He didn't make a choice for the mothers, although he did ask if we had a better picture of the second woman, which was Slaven's mother. For the fathers, he picked the correct one.

Altogether, we showed Grant eight pairs of pictures. For the ones he made a selection on, he was six out of six.

This is what our work involves. We approach each case with an open mind and then work to determine, as carefully and methodically as we can, whether there is evidence to support the child's claims about a past life. Adding together the evidence from case after case after case, it starts to look undeniable. And it will only become more so. We have upped our profile in recent years, and with the help of the internet, more and more families are finding us. Over a hundred parents have contacted us in the past year after their children reported memories of a previous life. And more are contacting us when the children are still young and still remembering. I was able to give picture tests to another little boy recently as I did with Grant, and that boy was five out of five. So the evidence continues to grow.

William James, the famed philosopher and psychologist, said that if you want to upset the law that all crows are black, you don't need to show that no crows are. It's enough if you produce a single white crow. In these two books you'll find a flock of crows that look awfully white to me. They are telling us that there is more to reality than just physical matter. And there is more to us than just physical matter. And more to the story than you live once and then you die, the end. Instead of the end, the cases tell us we can have a return to life.

How about that?

LIFE BEFORE LIFE

A Scientific Investigation of
Children's Memories of Previous Lives

Jim B. Tucker, M.D.

With a Foreword by
Ian Stevenson, M.D.

For Chris

CONTENTS

Numerous authors have written about reincarnation, nearly always affirming it, some of them even purporting to describe its processes; a few writers dismiss the idea of reincarnation as absurd. Few of these authors seem interested in the question of evidence for or against reincarnation.

Jim Tucker has written a different kind of book. For him evidence has become central. Does it, he asks, support or even compel a belief in reincarnation?

One can easily think of objections to reincarnation: the paucity of persons who actually claim to remember a past life, the fragility of memories, the population explosion, the mind-body problem, fraud, and others. Jim Tucker discusses these, one by one and thoroughly. His book resembles no other, because it has no predecessor of its type.

I found particularly impressive Jim Tucker's guidance of his readers. He asks, almost requires, them to reason along with him as he describes and discusses each objection to the idea of reincarnation. He writes so well that he may beguile a casual reader into thinking he or she has no work to do. Read on, and learn that evidence may answer—sooner than you expected—the most important question we can ask ourselves: "What happens after death?"

Some young children say that they have been here before. They give various details about previous lives, often describing the way in which they died. Of course, young children say a lot of things, and we may simply think that they are fantasizing as children often do. But what if, in a number of instances, people listened to the children and then tried to find out if the events they described had actually happened? And what if, when those people went to the places the children had named, they found that what the children had said about the past events was indeed true? What then?

The Case of Kemal Atasoy

Dr. Jürgen Keil, a psychologist from Australia, listened as Kemal Atasoy, a six-year-old boy in Turkey, confidently recounted details of a previous life that he claimed to remember. They were meeting in the boy's home, a comfortable house in an upper middle class neighborhood, and with them were Dr. Keil's interpreter and Kemal's parents, a well-educated couple who seemed amused at times by the enthusiasm that the little boy showed in describing his experiences. He said that he had lived in Istanbul, 500 miles away. He stated that his family's name had been Karakas and that he had been a rich Armenian Christian who lived in a large three-story house. The house, he said, was next to the house of a woman named Aysegul, a well-known personality in Turkey, who had left the country because of legal problems. Kemal said that his house had been on the water, where boats were tied up, and that a church was behind it. He said that his wife and children had Greek first names. He also said that he often carried a large leather bag and that he only lived in the house for part of the year.

No one knew if Kemal's story was true when he met Dr. Keil in 1997. His parents did not know anyone in Istanbul. In fact, Kemal and his mother had never been there, and his father had only visited the city twice on business. In addition, the family knew no Armenians. His parents were Alevi Muslims, a group with a belief in reincarnation, but they did not seem to think that Kemal's statements, which he had been making from the time he was just a toddler at two years of age, were particularly important.

Dr. Keil set out to determine if the statements that Kemal had given fit with someone who had actually lived. The work that Dr. Keil had to perform to find out if such a person even existed demonstrates that Kemal could not have come across the details of the man's life by accident.

When Dr. Keil and his interpreter went to Istanbul, they found the house of Aysegul, the woman whom Kemal had named. Next to the house was an empty three-story residence that precisely matched Kemal's description—it was at the edge of the water, where boats were tied up, with a church behind it. Dr. Keil then had trouble finding any evidence that a person like the one Kemal described had ever lived there. No Armenians were living in that part of Istanbul at the time, and Dr. Keil could not find anyone who remembered any Armenians ever having lived there. When he returned to Istanbul later that year, he talked with Armenian church officials, who told him that they were not aware that an Armenian had ever lived in the house. No church records indicated one had, but a fire had destroyed many of the records. Dr. Keil talked with an elderly man in the neighborhood who said that an Armenian had definitely lived there many years before and that the church officials were simply too young to remember that long ago.

Armed with that report, Dr. Keil decided to continue his search for information. The next year, he made a third trip to the area and interviewed a well-respected local historian. During the interview, Dr. Keil made sure he did not prompt any answers or make any suggestions. The historian told a story strikingly similar to the one Kemal had told. The historian said that a rich Armenian Christian had, in fact, lived in that house. He had been the only Armenian in that area, and his family's name was Karakas. His wife was Greek Orthodox, and her family did not approve of the marriage. The couple had three children, but the historian did not know their names. He said that the Karakas clan lived in another part of Istanbul, that they dealt in leather goods, and that the deceased man in question often carried a large leather bag. He also said that the deceased man lived in the house only during the summer months of the year. He had died in 1940 or 1941.

Though Dr. Keil was not able to verify Kemal's statement that the wife and children had Greek first names, the wife came from a Greek family. The first name that Kemal had given for the man turned out to be an Armenian term meaning "nice man."

Dr. Keil could not confirm that people actually called Mr. Karakas that, but he was struck by the fact that, even though no one around him knew the expression, Kemal had given a name that could easily have been used to describe Mr. Karakas.

How did this little boy, living in a town 500 miles away, know so many things about a man who had died in Istanbul fifty years before he was born? He could not have heard about the man Dr. Keil had to work so hard to learn anything about. What possible explanation could there be? Kemal had a very simple answer: he said that he had been the man in a previous life.

Kemal is not alone in his claims. Children all over the world have described memories of previous lives. For more than forty years, researchers have investigated their reports. More than 2,500 cases are registered in the files of the Division of Perceptual Studies at the University of Virginia. Some of the children have said they were deceased family members, and others described previous lives as strangers. In a typical case, a very young child begins to describe memories of another life. The child is persistent about this and often demands to be taken to his other family in another location. When the child has given names or enough details about the other location, the family often goes there to find that the child's statements fit the life of a person who has died in the recent past.

Were Kemal and the other 2,500 children remembering what they thought they were remembering—events from lives they had previously experienced? That question has occupied researchers for years, and this book will attempt to answer it. Previously, we have only written for a scientific audience, but now that we have forty years' worth of data, the general public deserves the opportunity to evaluate the evidence as well. I will try to present it in as fair a way as possible so that you can judge for yourself. The phenomenon of young children reporting past-life memories is fascinating in and of itself, and as you learn about it, you can gradually form an opinion about what it means. You can eventually decide whether you think that children like Kemal really have come back after having previous lives—and whether the rest of us may be able to come back, too.

LIFE BEFORE LIFE

CHAPTER 1

Children Who Report Memories of Previous Lives

John McConnell, a retired New York City policeman working as a security guard, stopped at an electronics store after work one night in 1992. He saw two men robbing the store and pulled out his pistol. Another thief behind a counter began shooting at him. John tried to shoot back, and even after he fell, he got up and shot again. He was hit six times. One of the bullets entered his back and sliced through his left lung, his heart, and the main pulmonary artery, the blood vessel that takes blood from the right side of the heart to the lungs to receive oxygen. He was rushed to the hospital but did not survive.

John had been close to his family and had frequently told one of his daughters, Doreen, "No matter what, I'm always going to take care of you." Five years after John died, Doreen gave birth to a son named William. William began passing out soon after he was born. Doctors diagnosed him with a condition called pulmonary valve atresia, in which the valve of the pulmonary artery has not adequately formed, so blood cannot travel through it to the lungs. In addition, one of the chambers of his heart, the right ventricle, had not formed properly as a result of the problem with the valve. He underwent several surgeries. Although he will need to take medication indefinitely, he has done quite well.

William had birth defects that were very similar to the fatal wounds suffered by his grandfather. In addition, when he became old enough to talk, he began talking about his grandfather's life. One day when he was three years old, his mother was at home trying to work in her study when William kept acting up. Finally, she told him, "Sit down, or I'm going to spank you." William replied, "Mom, when you were a little girl and I was your daddy, you were bad a lot of times, and I never hit you!"

His mother was initially taken aback by this. As William talked more about the life of his grandfather, she began to feel comforted by the idea that her father had returned. William talked about being his grandfather a number of times and discussed his death. He told his mother that several people were shooting during the incident when he was killed, and he asked a lot of questions about it.

One time, he said to his mother, "When you were a little girl and I was your daddy, what was my cat's name?" She responded, "You mean Maniac?"

"No, not that one," William answered. "The white one."

"Boston?" his mom asked.

"Yeah," William responded. "I used to call him Boss, right?" That was correct. The family had two cats, named Maniac and Boston, and only John referred to the white one as Boss.

One day, Doreen asked William if he remembered anything about the time before he was born. He said that he died on Thursday and went to heaven. He said that he saw animals there and also talked to God. He said, "I told God I was ready to come back, and I got born on Tuesday." Doreen was amazed that William mentioned days since he did not even know his days of the week without prompting. She tested him by saying, "So, you were born on a Thursday and died on Tuesday?" He quickly responded, "No, I died Thursday at night and was born Tuesday in the morning." He was correct on both counts—John died on a Thursday, and William was born on a Tuesday five years later.

He talked about the period between lives at other times. He told his mother, "When you die, you don't go right to heaven. You go to different levels—here, then here, then here" as he moved his hand up each time. He said that animals are reborn as well as humans and that the animals he saw in heaven did not bite or scratch.

John had been a practicing Roman Catholic, but he believed in reincarnation and said that he would take care of animals in his next life. His grandson, William, says that he will be an animal doctor and will take care of large animals at a zoo.

William reminds Doreen of her father in several ways. He loves books, as his grandfather did. When they visit William's grandmother, he can spend hours looking at books in John's study, duplicating his grandfather's behavior from years before. William, like his grandfather, is good at putting things together and can be a "nonstop talker."

William especially reminds Doreen of her father when he tells her, "Don't worry, Mom. I'll take care of you."

The idea that research could actually support the concept of reincarnation is surprising to many people in the West, since reincarnation may seem foreign or even absurd. People sometimes joke about their past lives or about their next one. The media document people dramatically describing lives from ancient times after being hypnotized. Reincarnation conflicts with the view of the majority of scientists that the material world is all that exists, and with many people's religious beliefs.

Although some people find the idea of reincarnation to be ridiculous or offensive, others accept it on faith. The idea of reincarnation has appealed to many throughout history and into the present day, including Plato and the ancient Greeks, Hindus and Buddhists in Asia, various West Africans, many Native Americans in northwest North America, and even some groups of early Christians. Today, people in the world who believe in reincarnation may outnumber those who do not.

Such beliefs are not restricted to distant places. A surprising number of Americans believe in reincarnation—between 20 and 27 percent, depending on the poll—and a similar percentage of Europeans do as well. They cannot base this belief on the evidence for reincarnation since most people do not know about this research done at the University of Virginia. They often do not base it on formal religious doctrine since many believers attend churches that do not hold such a view. In fact, a Harris poll in 2003 found that 21 percent of Christians in the United States believe in reincarnation. The work described here may give such individuals support for their beliefs, but the researchers have not operated from the perspective of any particular religious doctrine or bias. Our goals have been to determine the best explanation for the statements by the children and to see if science should consider reincarnation as a possibility.

Most people probably hope that the answer is yes. After all, the idea that we cease to exist when we die is unsettling for many of us. Though many in the United States may not be comfortable with the concept of reincarnation, the idea that part of us continues after we die is certainly appealing. If a deceased individual can survive death in some form and be reborn, then this means that we can continue on. Perhaps we can stay close to loved ones as they continue their lives or perhaps go to heaven or to other dimensions or who knows what. If these children are correct when they report that they lived before, then a part of us can survive the death of our bodies.

More specifically, the concept of reincarnation is compelling because the idea of being able to come back to try again may appeal to a lot of people. We cannot change the mistakes we have made in the past, but being able to try to do better the next time would certainly be a comfort. If we get to live repeated lives, then perhaps we can make progress across lifetimes and become better people.

As much as we might wish to come back ourselves, we also wish that the people we love could do so. Surely, William's mother must have been thrilled and comforted by her impression that her adoring father survived death and was reborn as her son. She had to deal with the horror of knowing that her father was murdered, and the idea that he was reborn as her son undoubtedly helped her change her grief into acceptance. We will meet others in this book who have dealt with similar losses: for example, a mother who watched her toddler die from cancer and a man whose father was closed off from his children before he died. In such situations, people would love the possibility of a second chance, of another opportunity to love and to share moments with the person who died. When any of us grieve for loved ones we have lost, we would certainly be comforted to know that those people have continued in some form and that they may come back into our lives.

Believing in that possibility may seem like wishful thinking and nothing more. But could life after death be more than wishful thinking?

Even though it may seem hard to believe, evidence might exist that life after death is actually a reality. *Life Before Life* will describe the cases researchers have collected that suggest that some people can survive death and be reborn into another life. This is not work that we have undertaken lightly. Researchers have addressed this issue with the same open-minded analytical approach that we would use with any question. We have approached the work rationally instead of emotionally, so it is analytical rather than emotional. In addition, we have done this work with clearheaded care, not with religious zeal. Of course, many people believe in life after death based purely on their religious faith. Though I mean to take nothing away from faith, religious belief need not keep us from looking for evidence that supports the idea. Faith should not prevent us from trying to gain a better understanding of the nature of life, and we have made this a scientific endeavor rather than a religious one.

Life Before Life is therefore analytical rather than emotional or religious. I will not try to convince you that these cases prove that reincarnation occurs, to promote a theory. Instead, I will present the cases so that you can assess them and reach your own conclusions about what they mean. I will give my analysis of where I think the evidence leads us, but you should also be forming your own opinions along the way. In doing so, you should not be too quick to make a judgment, either that the cases are nonsense or that they are definitive proof of reincarnation. Instead, I would encourage you to take the same analytical approach that we have used in doing the research.

These cases are not about "proof," they are about evidence.

Since this work has taken place in the messy real world rather than a tightly controlled laboratory, proof is not possible. This is often the case in science and medicine. For example, many medications are judged to be helpful, because evidence indicates that they work even though they have not been absolutely proven to do so. Our work also involves an area, the possibility of life after death, that does not easily lend itself to being researched. Some people even say that researchers should not try to study the subject of life after death scientifically since it is so far removed from usual empirical areas of investigation. Nevertheless, there is no bigger question in the world than whether we can survive death, and researchers have attempted to collect the best evidence possible to answer it, evidence that I will share with you.

Each case of course has its unique aspects, but we can discuss typical features found in many of the cases. In later chapters, we will then examine in depth a number of cases that include each of these features.

Predictions, Experimental Birthmarks, and Dreams Before Birth

Sometimes, the case begins before the child, the *subject* of the case, is even born. One situation involves an elderly or dying individual, the *previous personality*, making a prediction about his or her next life. Such cases are rare, but they do occur with some frequency among two groups. One is the lamas of Tibet. Though their predictions can be vague or unclear, others use these predictions to identify young children as the lamas reborn. In the case of the current Dalai Lama, his predecessor apparently did not make any predictions, so other clues such as meditation visions after his death were used to find the boy identified as his rebirth.

The Tlingits, a tribe in Alaska, frequently make predictions about rebirth. Of forty-six cases there, the previous personality made a prediction about his or her subsequent rebirth in ten of them. In eight of the ten, the person gave the names of the parents to which he or she wanted to be reborn. For example, a man named Victor Vincent told his niece that he was going to come back as her son. He showed her two scars he had from minor surgeries and predicted that he would carry those marks to his next life. Eighteen months after he died, she gave birth to a boy who had birthmarks in the same spots. One of them even had small round marks lined up beside the main linear mark, giving the appearance of stitch wounds from a surgical scar. The boy later said that he was the previous personality, and he seemed to recognize several people from Victor's life.

Some cases involve another feature that occurs before the child is born. In several Asian countries, a family member or friend may mark the body of a dying or deceased individual in hopes that when that person is reborn, the baby will have a birthmark that matches the marking. This practice is known as experimental birthmarks, and we will look at it in detail in Chapter 4.

An announcing dream can occur before the birth of the child. With this feature, a family member, usually the subject's mother, has a dream before or during the pregnancy in which the previous personality either announces that he or she is coming to the expecting mother or asks to come to her. Such dreams usually occur in *same-family* cases, ones in which the previous personality is a deceased member of the subject's family, or in cases in which the subject's mother at least knew the previous personality. Exceptions do occur as we will soon see. Cases from all the various cultures have included announcing dreams, which have occurred in approximately 22 percent of the first 1,100 cases in our computer database. They are much more common in some places than others, and they also tend to occur at different times in different places. In Myanmar, families generally report that the dreams occur before the child is conceived, whereas among the tribes in northwest North America, they tend to occur at the very end of the pregnancy.

Birthmarks and Birth Defects

Many of the subjects in our cases are born with birthmarks or birth defects that match wounds on the body of the previous personality, usually fatal wounds. One case that includes both an announcing dream and a birth defect is that of Süleyman Çaper in Turkey. His mother dreamed during her pregnancy that a man she did not recognize told her, "I was killed with a blow from a shovel. I want to stay with you and not anyone else." When Süleyman was born, the back of his skull was partially depressed, and he also had a birthmark there. When he became able to talk, he said that he had been a miller who died when an angry customer hit him on the head. Along with other details, he gave the first name of the miller and the village where he had lived. In fact, an angry customer had killed a miller with that name in that village by hitting him on the back of the head with a shovel.

Many of the birthmarks are not small discolorations. Instead, they are often unusual in shape or size and are often puckered or raised rather than simply being flat. Some can be quite dramatic and unusual in appearance. In Chapter 4, I will discuss the case of Patrick, a boy in Michigan, who had three distinct lesions that matched those of the previous personality. There are several cases in which a small, round birthmark matching a typical bullet entrance wound and a larger, more irregularly shaped birthmark matching a typical exit wound were both present. Other examples include cases with birthmarks in such unusual places as wrapping around an ankle and cases with deformities like missing or malformed limbs or digits.

In these cases, the birthmarks and birth defects can provide a concrete indication of a connection between the subject and the previous personality. Since they remain on the body, birthmarks and defects are not dependent on witnesses' memories to be part of the case. When an autopsy report or a medical record of the previous personality is available, as it was in Süleyman's case, researchers can objectively compare it to the birthmarks to see how well they correspond.

Such birthmarks and birth defects are not rare among our cases. A third of the cases from India include birthmarks or birth defects that are thought to correspond to wounds on the previous personalities, with 18 percent of those including medical records that confirm the match. I should note that the actual percentage of all children reporting past-life memories who have birthmarks might be much lower. We often have to make decisions about which cases to investigate, and since we are particularly interested in the birthmark cases, we are more likely to pursue them than other types of cases. Thus, we end up registering more of them.

Past-life Statements

The key feature in our cases, of course, is the statements that the children make about a past life. As an example, when Suzanne Ghanem of Lebanon was less than a year old, her first word was "Leila," and she would pick up the telephone and say, "Hello, Leila." She began telling her family about a previous life that ended when she went to the United States for heart surgery. She talked about this life a great deal, but her family was not able to track down the previous personality until Suzanne was five years old. At that point, Suzanne met the family of the woman who she thought she had been, and she convinced them that she was the woman reborn when she knew details about that life. The woman, who died at a medical center in the United States after heart surgery, turned out to have a daughter named Leila, who was not able to join her there because of passport problems. Before the woman died, her brother at the hospital tried to telephone Leila for her but was unsuccessful. In all, Suzanne made forty statements about the previous life that were verified as accurate, including the names of twenty-five people.

The children make these statements at a very early age. Most who talk about a past life begin doing so between the ages of two and four. Some parents say that their children made detailed statements about a previous life at a surprisingly young age, but as we will discuss later, psychological testing has now shown that many of these children are very intelligent. The early advanced language skills necessary to make such statements would be consistent with the testing. The children almost always stop talking about the past life around the age of six or seven, and they seem to go on to lead normal lives after that.

During the time that the children are talking about the past life, some do so in a very matter-of-fact manner while others show great emotion. One example of the latter is a boy in Seattle named Joey. He talked a number of times about his other mother dying in a car accident. One night at dinner when he was almost four years old, he stood up in his chair and appeared pale as he looked intently at his mother and said, "You are not my family—my family is dead." He cried quietly for a minute as a tear rolled down his cheek, then sat back down and continued with his meal. The fact that his mother had a dinner guest that night did not help the awkwardness of the situation, though she proved to be quite understanding.

Some children only make a few comments about the past life and only talk about it at certain times, often during relaxed periods, while others talk about it almost constantly and make many statements. In general, the children tend to talk about people and events from near the end of the previous life. A child who describes a past life that ended in adulthood is likely to talk about a spouse or children rather than talking about parents. Seventy-five percent of the children describe the way that they died in their previous life, and the mode of death is frequently violent or sudden.

The lives that the children describe tend to be very recent ones, and in fact, the median time between the death of the previous personality and the birth of the subject is only fifteen to sixteen months. Exceptions certainly exist, as Kemal's case in the Introduction shows, but most of the children describe very recent lives. Few report having been famous personalities, as almost all describe ordinary lives, often ending in very unpleasant ways.

When the children give enough information so that one particular deceased individual can be identified as the previous personality, we say that the case is *solved*. If the previous personality has not been identified, we say that the case is *unsolved*. A colleague told me that he objects to the term "unsolved" in this instance, because it implies that the child is actually remembering the life of one unique previous personality who could be identified if the case could only be solved. This is not what we mean when we use the term. We can all agree that an unsolved case, or a solved one for that matter, does not automatically indicate a case of reincarnation.

With only rare exceptions, almost all of the children describe only one previous life. In addition, though most children do not talk about the time between lives, some occasionally do. Their statements can involve either events that took place on earth, for example the funeral of the previous personality, or descriptions of other realms. An example of the latter is a boy named Kenny who, though his case was unsolved, gave numerous details about the life of a man who died in an automobile accident. He said that after he died, another spirit, probably the driver of the vehicle, took him by the hand, and the two of them were with other spirits in what seemed to be a huge hall. He said another spirit he took to be God told him that there were people wishing for a child and that he had been chosen to go down to be born.

Past-life Behaviors

In addition to the statements, many children show behaviors that seem connected to the past-life memories they are reporting.

Many show strong emotions related to their memories. In some cases, the children cry and beg their parents to take them to their previous family until their parents finally relent. In a case in which the previous personality was murdered, the subject may also display an immense anger toward the killer. I will discuss a case later in which a toddler tried to strangle the man he said had killed him in his previous life.

The children often demonstrate unusual play. For instance, Parmod Sharma in India became wrapped up in his play as a shopkeeper of biscuits and soda water, the occupation of the previous personality, from the ages of four to seven. This caused him to neglect his work when he started school, and he never seemed to fully recover. His mother blamed his poor school performance and subsequent limited vocational opportunities on his preoccupation with his past-life memories and his shopkeeping play as a young child. That case is an extreme example, but the play can be excessive. In these cases, the children repeat the same play over and over, and it is play that is not seen in the other children of the family or modeled after an adult family member or close family friend. Most commonly, the child mimics the occupation of the previous personality as Parmod did, and the drive that some of these children demonstrate in wanting to engage repeatedly in the play can be quite striking. Other children have repeatedly acted out the death scene from the previous life. This can be similar to the post-traumatic play of children who have been through difficult experiences, only in this case the trauma is thought to be from a previous life rather than the current one.

Phobias seem to be linked to the past-life memories at times. Many of the children show intense fear related to the method of the previous personality's death. Often, these fears will show up before the child has begun to report past-life memories. For example, a very young child may show an intense fear of water. As a baby in Sri Lanka, Shamlinie Prema always had to be held down by three adults in order to be bathed, and then later told of having drowned in the previous life.

Some children are also unusually fond of certain things, including foods the previous personality especially enjoyed or even alcohol or tobacco products. Though the use of alcohol and tobacco is common in various cultures, consumption is not considered appropriate for three-year-olds. Parents have been amused and appalled by their children's attempts to get alcohol. As for foods, one particularly prominent example is the request to eat raw fish from Burmese children who say they remember lives as Japanese soldiers.

When unusual play, phobias, and preferences are present along with statements or birthmarks or other features, the impression of a link between the subject and the previous personality is strengthened. Such cases are often about more than possible memories or statements; they suggest that behaviors and emotions have carried over as well.

Past-life Recognitions

Sometimes subjects recognize, or are thought to recognize, people or places from their past lives. Frequently, when the subject's family takes the child to the home of the previous personality, the subject seems to recognize members of the previous family. At times, the previous family is hoping that their deceased loved one has returned, so they may be open to interpreting anything the child does as evidence that he recognizes them. Others are much more skeptical, and some suspect that the subject's family is hoping for financial gain in making the claim, even though this seems rarely to be the case. Some will engineer such informal tests for the child as having him identify objects that belonged to the previous personality before deciding whether to accept the claims.

In a much smaller number of cases, subjects have been tested under more controlled conditions, and we will review some of these in Chapter 7. The strongest examples add to the impression that something is going on that cannot be written off as simply wishful thinking or childhood fantasy.

In summary, cases from all over the world can include birthmarks that match wounds on the previous personality, statements that are accurate for the life of that person, behaviors that appear to be linked to the person—strong emotions, unusual play, phobias, and unusual preferences—and situations in which the child was judged to recognize something or someone from that life.

CHAPTER 2

Investigating the Cases

The story of this research at the University of Virginia begins in 1958. By any standard, Dr. Ian Stevenson had achieved a successful academic career at that point. After graduating at the top of his medical school class at McGill University, he had initially studied biochemistry before becoming interested in psychosomatic medicine, the study of the connections between emotions and health. He had written extensively, almost always in medical journals but several times also in *Harper's Magazine* and *The New Republic,* and by 1958, he had seventy publications to his credit. A year earlier, he had become the chairman of the Department of Psychiatry at the University of Virginia at the unusually young age of thirty-eight.

Along with these accomplishments, Dr. Stevenson was interested in paranormal phenomena—ones beyond current scientific explanation. When the American Society for Psychical Research announced a contest in 1958 for the best essay on paranormal mental phenomena and their relationship to life after death, he submitted the winning entry, entitled, "The Evidence for Survival from Claimed Memories of Former Incarnations." In this essay, he reviewed forty-four cases that had previously been published of individuals from various parts of the world who had described memories of previous lives. The reports came from a number of sources—books, magazines, and newspapers. Almost all of the most impressive cases involved children who were under the age of ten when they first reported the memories, and in many of them, the children were three years old or younger. Dr. Stevenson was struck by the pattern of children from very different places making similar statements about past-life memories. As he said later, "These forty-four cases, when you put them together, it just seemed inescapable to me that there must be something there." He ended the paper by saying that the evidence he presented did not permit any definite conclusion about reincarnation, but he felt that more extensive study was justified.

After the paper was published in 1960, Dr. Stevenson began to hear about new cases. After learning of four or five cases in India and one in Ceylon (now Sri Lanka), he took a trip to investigate. Once he got to India, he was surprised by how many cases he found. In four weeks, he investigated twenty-five cases. Likewise, he visited Ceylon for one week and found five or six cases. He concluded that children reported memories of previous lives much more frequently than anyone had previously known.

One person who read Dr. Stevenson's essay was Chester Carlson, the inventor of the photocopying process that formed the basis for the Xerox Corporation. His wife, Dorris Carlson, had gotten him interested in parapsychology. After reading the essay, he contacted Dr. Stevenson to offer financial support. Dr. Stevenson initially declined the offer, because he was busy with his other work, but as he collected more cases and became increasingly intrigued by what he found, he accepted funding support from Carlson.

In 1966, he published his first book on the topic, *Twenty Cases*

Suggestive of Reincarnation. Dr. Stevenson had worked hard to verify independently what the twenty children had said and how well their statements matched the lives of the individuals the children were thought to remember. The book consisted of very detailed reports of cases from India, Ceylon, Brazil, and Lebanon that included lists of every person Dr. Stevenson interviewed about each case, along with lengthy tables in which each of the child's statements about a previous life was listed along with the informant for that statement and the person or persons who had verified that the statement was correct for the life of the deceased individual. Dr. Stevenson presented the cases in an objective, evenhanded manner, and he discussed their weaknesses as well as their strengths.

A number of journals, including the prestigious *American Journal of Psychiatry,* gave the book positive reviews, with reviewers often noting Dr. Stevenson's painstaking work and objectivity, and it has continued to be well regarded over the years because of those features.

With the help of assistants, Dr. Stevenson was soon finding cases in a number of countries, and he made trips to India, Sri Lanka, Turkey, Lebanon, Thailand, Burma, Nigeria, Brazil, and Alaska. After publishing *Twenty Cases,* he also began to learn of occasional cases in this country.

With Carlson's funding, Dr. Stevenson was able to step down as chairman of the Department of Psychiatry in 1967 to focus full-time on his research. The dean of the medical school, who did not approve of the work, was happy to see Dr. Stevenson step down, and he agreed to allow the formation of a small research division, now known as the Division of Perceptual Studies, where the work would take place.

The following year, Chester Carlson died suddenly of a heart attack. Since the division was dependent on Mr. Carlson's funding in order to operate, Dr. Stevenson assumed that he would have to try a return to more routine research. Carlson's will was then opened, and he had left one million dollars to the University of Virginia for Dr. Stevenson's work.

At that point, controversy broke out regarding whether the university would accept the money, given the unusual nature of the research. Universities are not in the habit of turning down million-dollar gifts, but the situation clearly made some people uneasy. The university eventually did decide to accept the money since it had been given to support scholarly work, and the work continued.

Dr. Stevenson wrote more books about the cases, and these continued to be well received by at least some in the field. In reviewing one, Lester S. King, the Book Review Editor of *JAMA: The Journal of the American Medical Association,* wrote that "in regard to reincarnation [Stevenson] has painstakingly and unemotionally collected a detailed series of cases from India, cases in which the evidence is difficult to explain on any other grounds." He also added, "He has placed on record a large amount of data that cannot be ignored."

In 1977, the *Journal of Nervous and Mental Disease* devoted most of one issue to Dr. Stevenson's reincarnation work. It included a paper by Dr. Stevenson and commentaries on it from several others. Dr. Harold Lief, a well-respected figure in the field of psychiatry, wrote one of the commentaries. He described Dr. Stevenson as "a methodical, careful, even cautious, investigator, whose personality is on the obsessive side." He also wrote, "Either he is making a colossal mistake, or he will be known . . . as 'the Galileo of the twentieth century.' "

Dr. Stevenson gradually got others interested in investigating cases. Satwant Pasricha, a psychologist in India, began assisting Dr. Stevenson on the cases there, and she continues to research them today. Erlendur Haraldsson, a psychologist at the University of Iceland who had a long history in experimental psychology, became interested in the cases in the 1970s, and he has studied them ever since. Antonia Mills, an anthropologist who received her Ph.D. from Harvard, began assisting Dr. Stevenson on cases in northwest North America, and she has since investigated cases independently there and in India. Jürgen Keil, who investigated Kemal's case in the Introduction, is a psychologist at the University of Tasmania who was able to establish new contacts in Turkey, Thailand, and Myanmar in order to study cases in those locations. In addition, he and I made two trips to Thailand and Myanmar to study cases together, and I will be describing some of those later in the book. Dr. Stevenson investigated most of the cases from Asia that I will discuss, and the end notes at the back of the book list the references for his detailed reports of the cases.

He became particularly interested in cases in which a child was born with a birthmark that matched a wound on the deceased individual. He believes in strength in numbers, so he held off publishing any of these cases until he could publish a series of them in a book. After several delays, he published *Reincarnation and Biology: A Contribution to the Etiology of Birthmarks and Birth Defects* in 1997. The work is massive—2,200 pages long in two volumes—and it includes detailed reports of 225 cases along with pictures of the various birthmarks. Dr. Stevenson published it as he approached his eightieth birthday. Though *Reincarnation and Biology* in some ways represented the culmination of his decades of work, he was still not done and continued to write and research cases.

I came onto the scene in 1996, and I eventually left my private practice in psychiatry to pursue this research. Recently, I have been focusing on American cases. Though they are harder to find here, American cases occur without the cultural factors that some critics hold responsible for cases in other parts of the world. I will use a number of these American cases to illustrate the various aspects of the experiences. When I do, I will change the names of the children and other identifying details. I will do so for the international cases as well unless a case report has already been published that used the child's real name.

As for Dr. Stevenson, he has continued to show enthusiasm for the work. He retired in 2002, perhaps with a reluctance that few people in their eighties would feel toward retirement, partly to focus more on his writings but also to spend more time with his wife, Margaret. He had talked about cutting back on the research trips for years but had failed to do so. Even after he retired, he took one final "final trip" to India. Margaret once said that she did not mind his taking the trips, but she wished that he would stop referring to each one as the last. He wrote yet another book in 2003—*European Cases of the Reincarnation Type*—and continued to work on other papers and book projects. His publications now number more than 290.

The Investigations

Before we investigate cases, we have to find them. We have done so wherever we have looked for them, but cases are easiest to find in areas with a general belief in reincarnation. This includes India and Sri Lanka, where Dr. Stevenson made his initial trips, along with other countries with similar beliefs, including Thailand, Myanmar (Burma), Turkey, and among the Druses in Lebanon. The geographical pattern of cases is determined to some extent by where we have people looking for them. We have been fortunate to have assistants in each of these countries looking for cases for us. They find them through a variety of means, some from occasional newspaper articles but most through word of mouth. We go where they find them. That does not mean, of course, that cases do not occur in areas where we are not looking for them. We have many cases from Thailand but essentially none from Vietnam, and this may simply be because we have no connection in Vietnam.

In fact, we have found cases on all the continents except for Antarctica, and no one has looked for them there. In some ways, looking for cases here in the United States is harder than in other countries. In Thailand, we sometimes seem to hit areas where we cannot stop to ask for directions without hearing about another case. In the United States, on the other hand, we cannot just walk into a convenience store and ask if anyone knows of a child talking about a past life. That does not mean that the cases are not here. When I give talks, people often speak to me afterwards to mention a family member who at one point talked about a past life. Since we set up our Web site in 1998, www.healthsystem. virginia.edu/personalitystudies, we have received e-mails from dozens of American families describing a child who reported past-life memories.

We tend to use the same general methods when we investigate a case. We usually conduct the interviews through a translator, since few of the families in the international cases speak English. Though this may introduce a potential source for error in the process, the native translators are able to understand the informants with ease. We often clarify any potential misunderstandings with the translator until we are sure that we have understood what the informants are trying to tell us. After working with us a while, our translators come to understand what we are trying to learn in the interviews, and they are careful to ask whatever questions are necessary to gather a clear understanding of the events that have taken place. All of this means that the interviews sometimes proceed very slowly, with us repeatedly making sure that we understand exactly what has happened, but the families usually tolerate us quite well. We never pay them, since doing so could lead people to make up cases, but they are almost always hospitable during our visits.

Most of the time, we get to a case after it has been solved. This means that the child gave enough details about the previous life to enable the family to find and meet the family of the previous personality. This meeting has occurred a few weeks before our arrival in some cases and years before in others. Sometimes, the case is unsolved when we arrive, and the two families have not met. Though this is obviously our preference, it is most often not the case, and our job becomes an effort to reconstruct as accurately as possible what was said and done in the case before we got there.

We usually start our investigation by interviewing the subject's family. We begin all the interviews by explaining the research so that all those involved can agree to participate in it. We then start out with general open-ended questions about the history of a case. This interview is usually with the parents of the subject, but grandparents or other family members can participate as well. We do not begin with the subjects. Often, they have little or nothing to say about the case. If they are quite young, they may be too shy to talk with us, or they may not be in the right frame of mind to discuss the case. If they are older, they may not remember anything about the case. We attempt to talk to them, but we place the greatest emphasis on what the adults can tell us about the child's statements or behaviors when the case was beginning. If the family has met the family of the previous personality, we are most interested in what the subject said before the two families met, since his or her statements after the families met could be colored by information learned from the previous personality's family.

If the case involves a birthmark, then obviously we ask to see the birthmark on the child. We then photograph it and note its location and appearance on a human figure drawing, since our photography at times can lead to disappointing results. The parents sometimes say that the birthmark moved as the child grew older, so we note their description of the location of the mark when the child was born.

Some children only tell their parents about their memories, but others tell any number of people. In the latter situation, we attempt to interview as many additional witnesses as possible. What we do not accept is hearsay testimony. If a villager says that he or she heard that the subject made a certain statement, we do not accept it unless we can talk with someone who actually heard the child firsthand.

After we get as much information as possible from the subject's side of the case, we move to the previous personality's side. We talk to the family members to verify how closely the child's statements matched the life of the previous personality. We also find out their impressions of their first meeting with the child.

Since the child is often said to recognize members of the previous personality's family or belongings of the previous personality at this meeting, we want to get the testimony of both families about it.

When Dr. Stevenson has published reports of cases in his books, he has included a list of all the statements that each child has made about a previous life. Each statement is then followed by the name of the informant who heard the statement, whether the statement was verified as accurate for the previous personality and if so by whom, and any additional comments. By seeing all the statements, the correct ones as well as the incorrect ones, readers are able to judge the cases in their entirety without worrying that the child may have had one or two lucky hits in a sea of misses.

In addition to the statements, other aspects of the cases often need to be investigated as well. When the child has a birthmark that is thought to match a wound on the body of the deceased, we then attempt to determine how close that match actually is. In the best of circumstances, an autopsy report exists that records the wounds on the body of the previous personality. If the birthmark matches a nonfatal wound on the previous personality, then medical records may also be helpful in assessing the match. In the case of a violent death, a police record may be available even if an autopsy record is not, and it may document wounds.

Since no written record of any kind is available that documents the wounds in the case of many of these villagers, eyewitness testimony then becomes the best evidence available. Family members have often seen the body of the previous personality at death or have helped prepare the body for funeral. A number of people may have noticed wounds, and we try to talk to them so that we can be as sure as possible about what wounds were present and where they were located. Dr. Keil and I published a case in which the subject's family thought that the birth defects on his hands corresponded to wounds that the previous personality suffered during a fatal parachuting accident. Through persistent effort, Dr. Keil eventually determined with some certainty that the previous personality did not actually have any major wounds on his hands.

In many cases, the investigators have conducted follow-up interviews in subsequent trips to the area. This serves several purposes. One obviously is to learn if any new developments have occurred in the case. Another is to find out if the testimony of the witnesses stays consistent over time. Lastly, the subject's subsequent life and development can be assessed. Dr. Stevenson has followed some cases for decades, so he has seen the subjects grow up.

After a case is investigated, it is registered in our files at the university if it meets certain criteria. These involve many of the features we have discussed, and according to the criteria, a case has to have at least two of the following:

1. Prediction of rebirth—not just "I will be reborn" but with some specifying details; for example, selection of next parents
2. An announcing dream
3. Birthmarks or birth defects related to previous life—not just any nevus or other blemish; also the birthmark/birth defect should be noticed immediately after birth or within a few weeks
4. Statements by the subject, as a child, about a previous life—the record of these should not depend on the

subject alone: at least one other older person (for example, a parent or older sibling) should corroborate that the subject spoke about a previous life as a child

5. Recognitions by subject of persons or objects with which the previous personality was familiar

6. Unusual behavior on the part of the subject—that is, behavior that is unusual in subject's family and that apparently corresponds to similar behavior shown by the presumed previous personality or that could be conjectured for him/her (for example, a phobia of firearms if the previous personality was fatally shot)

No criteria are perfect in all situations. One concern I have is that a case could have enough impressive statements by the child so that we would want to include it even if none of the other features were present. Other situations could certainly arise in which a case would meet these criteria, but we would choose not to include it in the collection. Overall, these criteria have served us well, and I hope they make clear what is required for us to include a case in our series.

These criteria show that a wide diversity in the strength of cases can exist. Some cases offer compelling evidence that something unusual has happened, while the evidence is far less convincing in others. The strength of these cases often lies in the eye of the beholder, but we think that collecting as many as possible is important so that the beholder has the best information on which to base a judgment.

With each case, the investigators fill out a registration form, which is an eight-page form that asks for various details about each case. The file also includes notes of the various interviews along with any photographs or records that have been obtained. At some point, all of this information is then transferred onto a coding form so that it can be entered into a computer database. It includes 200 variables that are assigned values that can then be entered into the computer. These range from the subject's country of origin to the parents' initial reactions to the child's statements, the distance between the subject's family and the previous family, and dozens of other minute details. By entering such information into a database, we can see features of the cases as a group that we cannot observe from just the individual cases. For instance, when I said that 18 percent of the Indian birthmark cases include medical records that confirm the match, I knew this because we have all 421 Indian cases entered into the computer, and I can simply look at the frequencies for that item. This process is labor intensive, and getting all the cases into the database is years away. At this point, we have entered 1,100 out of the 2,500 cases into the computer database. It includes all the Indian cases but as yet includes virtually no cases from Thailand and Myanmar, even though those two countries have combined to produce hundreds of cases. I will give figures from time to time based on these 1,100 cases, but we should remember that these are not necessarily representative of all 2,500 cases. As we get more cases coded during the next few years, we can expect to learn more about the phenomenon, even about the cases that researchers investigated years ago.

CHAPTER 3

Explanations to Consider

Abby Swanson, a young girl who lives in Ohio, was four years old when she began talking to her mother one night after having her bath. "Mommy, I used to give you baths when you were a baby," she said. "Oh really?" her mom replied. "Uh huh. You cried," Abby responded. "I did?" said her mom. "Yep," Abby said. "I was your grandma."

"And what was your name?" her mother asked her. She remembers her hair standing on end as Abby considered the question, tapping her mouth with her fingers.

"Lucy? . . . Ruthie? . . . Ruthie," she finally said. Since this was Abby's great-grandmother's name, her mother tried to ask her more questions, but Abby did not say anything else.

Abby's great-grandmother died in 1985, nine years before Abby was born. She had twenty grandchildren, and unlike most of the others, Abby's mother lived nearby and was close to her while growing up. They had some conflict when Abby's mother was a teenager but then got along well when she became an adult.

Abby's mother would occasionally mention Abby's great-grandparents to her children, but never by name, and she had not talked about them for at least six months before that night. In addition, Abby's grandmother lived on the West Coast and could not have been a source of information for Abby to learn about her great-grandmother. Later, her mother did check with Abby's grandmother to confirm that Abby's great-grandmother had in fact given her mother baths. Abby's grandmother also said that her mother cried a lot when she was given baths as a baby.

Abby's mother is certain that Abby had never heard her great-grandmother's name. In fact, when she asked her a few days later what the name was, Abby did not know. Whatever knowledge, or memory, was available to Abby that night was not available to her after that.

What are we to make of this? Much stronger cases exist, as we will see, but Abby's is a succinct one that we can use to explore the possible explanations for cases of children who report past-life memories. We approach the cases with an attitude of scientific curiosity. Our job is to explore this phenomenon and to try to determine the most likely explanation for each case. In particular, the question of whether or not a case represents a paranormal event—one that is beyond current scientific explanation—is always present and in many regards is the most important question in our work. This question is often impossible to answer. A child may claim to remember a previous life but does not give any information about that life that he or she could not have learned through normal means. In such a case, we cannot say that the child is the reincarnation of the person whose life he or she claims to remember. At the same time, we cannot say with certainty that the child's statements are false, even if we conclude that no evidence exists to support them.

We approach each case with an attitude of wanting to learn as much about it as possible. We do not approach a case with our minds already made up about it. We are open to all possibilities, including that a paranormal link may exist between the child and a deceased individual or that a link may not exist.

This attitude is necessary for scientific inquiry, which is different from the two extremes. On one end, believers in reincarnation may be quick to accept any claim of rebirth that supports their firmly held beliefs. On the other end, individuals convinced that the material universe is all that can possibly exist—including so-called "professional skeptics"—will dismiss any claim that challenges their views. Though many people in scientific fields hold views that can be just as dogmatic as those of an intensely religious person, judging from firmly held beliefs does not make for sound scientific inquiry.

Therefore, we are open to all possibilities. This means that when a child claims to remember a previous life, we think that he or she may be telling the truth. On the other hand, the child may be engaging in fantasy, or the adults may have misinterpreted the child's statements. We are trying to determine what scenario is most likely. Though this is our attitude, I will not, in writing this book, always say that the past-life memories of a child are "alleged" or "claimed." This would be cumbersome and irritating to writer and reader both, and unnecessary, since I have already been explicit about our approach to the cases. I could put "past-life memories" in quotation marks every time I use the term, but that would grow tiresome as well.

I will speculate at times about what a situation might mean if the memories are in fact past-life ones. Though this does not mean that I have concluded that the memories are actually memories of past lives, I do not want us to avoid intriguing areas of interest because we do not yet have final proof of one possibility or another.

As for the possible explanations, there are two basic types. Cases are caused either by a normal process or by a paranormal one. The following list touches on a variety of explanations we should consider.

Normal Explanations

FRAUD

This would mean that Abby's mother intentionally lied to us about what happened. This is theoretically possible. Abby did not remember that night when we met her two years later, and no other witnesses were there to confirm the story. Someone could make up such a story if she had a reason to do so, which is why we only report cases in which we have interviewed the families ourselves. When we interview them, we try to judge how reliable they are.

The problem with the explanation of fraud is that for the vast majority of the cases, the family has absolutely no reason to make up such a story. Abby's mother certainly did not. The only thing that she got out of contacting us was having her home invaded by a psychiatrist and psychologist who asked a lot of questions, so unless she was badly in need of attention from two strangers, she would have no motivation to lie to us. Though she believed in reincarnation, her husband did not. He did not seem thrilled to have us in his home, so any potential unhappiness on his part would have presumably made her even less likely to invent a story when she contacted us. Similarly, the people involved in the cases in other countries get no material benefit. Though families have on rare occasion tried to get gifts from the families of the previous personality, almost all of them have appeared to be ordinary, decent people who happened to have children who said some extraordinary things.

In addition, Abby's case is unusual because there is only one witness. In many of the others, numerous family members and friends have heard the child talk about a previous life, along with several family members of the previous personality who later heard the child as well. For fraud to exist, a conspiracy would have to be responsible, and though the cases may bring the families some brief notoriety, the absence of any meaningful benefit to all the people who would have to be involved in this elaborate undertaking makes this scenario very unlikely.

The other possibility for fraud is that the investigators have made up the cases. We know that we have met these children, but you do not. Nonetheless, the field notes packed in the file cabinets in our offices document that the interviews have taken place. In addition, anyone who reads Dr. Stevenson's write-ups of the cases, in which he highlights the weaknesses of the cases along with the strengths, will understand that he has not committed fraud, even if he is mistaken about the significance of these cases. Another practical objection to investigator fraud is that six of us have published cases, so the fraud would have to involve a number of professionals who have never shown any tendencies toward dishonesty in their work.

Though the possibility exists that Abby's mother made up this story, the chances that fraud is responsible for this case, and for the cases as a group, are quite small.

FANTASY

In this scenario, Abby made up a story when she said that she remembered giving her mother baths. We need to consider this possibility in cases in which the child's statements are unverified, meaning that the cases are unsolved. In many of our American cases, the children have talked a lot about when they lived before, but since they have not given any names, their statements remain unverified. We might think that a young child fantasizing in this way is odd, particularly if the parents dislike the idea of reincarnation, and even odder if the child becomes emotionally wrapped up in the stories, but unless the child demonstrates knowledge that can be verified as accurate, fantasy cannot be ruled out.

Of course, many of these children, including Abby, seem to have shown knowledge that they could not have acquired through normal means, so coincidence is then added to fantasy as part of the explanation. In Abby's case, this would mean that she came up with her great-grandmother's name purely by chance. She did need two tries to get the right name, doubling her chances of success, but considering all the possible names that she could have said, even doubling the chances still makes the odds of successfully picking the correct one quite a long shot.

Proponents of coincidence would say "Not so fast." They argue that we are fooled about how unlikely an event is unless we consider the number of tries it takes to produce it. In this case, the idea that Abby could have correctly guessed her great-grandmother's name seems incredible, but we only heard about the case because she came up with the correct name. A million-to-one shot only seems amazing if you do not know that a million other shots took place along with the successful one. As an example, the fact that anyone ever wins the lottery may seem incredible, given the long odds of winning, but people win every week because so many people are playing. If the odds are twenty million to one and over twenty million people are playing, we should not be surprised when someone wins.

The odds of guessing a name correctly are clearly better than that, since hundreds of names exist but not millions, but this argument runs into serious trouble when we see its eventual conclusion: hundreds of American children have told their parents that they were their great-grandmothers, but the only family that our group heard from was Abby's, because the others came up with an incorrect name. That may be happening all across America, but such a possibility seems preposterous.

Then there is the case of Suzanne Ghanem that I mentioned in Chapter 1. She accurately gave the names of twenty-five people from the previous life and their relationship to the previous personality, while giving only one incorrect name. The odds of her getting that many right by coincidence are so small as to approach zero unless we think that there are millions of children who give twenty-five proper names in describing past lives to their parents, and Suzanne just happened to be the one who was lucky enough to give the correct ones.

Cases with proper names make the coincidence argument seem absurd, but some cases clearly might be due to coincidence. If a child gives general statements about a life but does not give a location, the number of potential matches would be very high, and a deceased individual might be found whose life was similar to the one described by the child simply by coincidence. Even if the child does give a location, coincidence could be a possibility if there are few details given. If a child says, "I was a man who died in California," then a lot of individuals would obviously fit that description.

As we will see, these cases involve a lot more detail than that.

KNOWLEDGE ACQUIRED THROUGH NORMAL MEANS

In this explanation, the child has learned the information about the previous life through normal means but has simply forgotten the source of that information. So, in Abby's case, this means that she heard her great-grandmother's name at some point, later forgot that event, as her mother did, but did not forget the name. This argument has a certain logic. We often know facts but do not remember when we learned them. In this case, her mother was certain that Abby had not heard her great-grandmother's name, and she was too young to have read it in any family document. The idea that she would know the name of her great-grandmother who died nine years before she was born does seem unlikely. Most four-year-olds do not know the names of their deceased great-grandmothers, and a lot of us do not even know them as adults.

Compared to cases involving strangers, the possibility of knowledge being acquired through normal means is greater in cases like Abby's in which the child and the previous personality are in the same family. Being certain that the child has not overheard something about the previous personality can be difficult. Even if Abby had heard her great-grandmother's name at some point, this scenario does not explain why she later thought she had been her great-grandmother and why she developed the memory of giving her mother baths. We know that young children engage in fantasy play, but that would be an unusual game of make-believe.

More importantly, we have to explain the cases in which children have given many specific details about deceased individuals who lived many miles away. Often in those cases, the children appear to have had no possible opportunity to learn the information. On top of that, we must then try to imagine what could have possessed them to think that they had been these strangers in a previous life.

In Abby's case, this scenario is unlikely but possible, since she could have heard her great-grandmother's name at some point, despite her mother's certainty that she had not, but it is essentially impossible for many other cases.

FAULTY MEMORY BY INFORMANTS

Abby's mother might have remembered the conversation she had with Abby that night incorrectly. Arguing against this is the fact that as she waited to hear Abby's response to her question about the great-grandmother's name, her mother knew its significance. This was not something that occurred unexpectedly while she was under great duress, as is the case for witnesses at crime scenes, whose testimony we still use to convict people even if we recognize that eyewitness reports in those circumstances can be imperfect. Her mother waited with great anticipation to hear if Abby could give evidence that confirmed the past-life claim she had just made, increasing her chances of remembering it correctly.

This possibility of faulty memory by informants is the most likely normal explanation for many of our cases, since we often have not gotten to the Asian cases until well after the events in question. Numerous cases have been found in which the family made the following report: The child gave a number of specific details about a past life, including the name of the village in which the previous personality lived. The family then went to the village with the child, who recognized members of the previous family or items belonging to the previous personality. In some cases, the child was also able to give a detail about a person or the location of a particular item that only one or two people knew.

Critics have said that the families must have remembered the events incorrectly. The argument goes like this: A child in a culture with a belief in reincarnation fantasizes about having had a previous life and tells the family about it. The parents, in their eagerness to confirm the existence of the past life, find another family with a deceased individual whose life shared some general features with those reported by the child. The two families then meet and share information. They become convinced that the deceased individual has been reborn, and they tell others about it. When a researcher eventually comes to investigate the case, both families credit the child with giving far more details about the previous individual than he or she actually did.

This possibility exists because the villagers involved generally make no written records of what the child has said, and the investigators often get to a case only after the two families have met. A number of exceptions to this have been documented; for example, the case in India of Bishen Chand Kapoor. The initial investigator of that case made notes of what the boy had said before the case was solved, and his statements included the name of the previous personality's father (though the boy referred to him as his uncle), his caste, the city where he lived (thirty miles away from the boy's home), the facts that he was unmarried, had attended the

Government High School near a river up to the sixth class, and knew Urdu, Hindi, and English, a description of his house as a two-story building with a shrine room and separate apartments for men and women, his great fondness for wine, rohu fish, and dancing girls, and the name of a neighbor, Sunder Lal, who had a house with a green gate. All of those statements were correct, but the boy gave the wrong age for the previous personality at his death (he said twenty when the man died at age thirty-two) and the wrong name of the quarter of the city where the man had lived. When he was taken to that city, he identified the previous personality and his father in an old photograph and also recognized seven places there. He was even able to identify the room in which the previous personality's father had hidden some gold coins that were only found after the boy gave the location.

In all, written records have been made in more than thirty cases before the previous personality was identified, and we will discuss several of them in the upcoming chapters. This number is barely more than 1 percent of the 2,500 cases that have been collected. Does the faulty memory scenario mean that we should disregard the other 99 percent of the cases?

As I mentioned earlier, we know that human memory is not infallible, but that does not mean that it is worthless. To the contrary, we place great value on memory in many situations. Aspects of these cases argue for giving it value here. These children often do not tell their parents about a previous life just once, as Abby did, but repeat their claims again and again. The parents sometimes take the child to the previous place because the child has worn them down with repeated requests to go there. The parents have had numerous opportunities to learn exactly what the child is claiming before they ever meet the other family.

In many of the cases, multiple witnesses have heard what the children said about the previous life before the two families met, since they talked about their memories emphatically for several years. A number of people would have to have faulty memories about the children's statements for the scenario of faulty memory of informants to be accurate.

We should also note that in a case involving strangers, the child has to give enough details for the parents to identify a family with a deceased member whose life matched the statements. This often means names of people or places or a substantial number of details. Even if the families have imperfect memories about the child's statements before the families met, those statements would have to include a number of discriminating ones.

Other cases exist in which the faulty memory explanation is largely irrelevant: those with written records of the statements that were recorded before the two families met, for example. Also the birthmark and birth defect cases, in which autopsy reports confirm that the child was born with a mark or defect that corresponds to a wound suffered by the previous personality, clearly do not involve faulty memory.

Even without those features, the other components that many of our cases show are important to remember. Intense emotional longing for the previous family, long-standing phobias related to the mode of death of the previous personality, and unusual preferences can be part of these cases, and they are not dependent on the families' memories of particular statements. Since Abby's case does not have any of these characteristics, the faulty memory by informants possibility is more likely here than it is in many of the other cases. On the other hand, Abby's case, along with the dozens of others like it from the United States, shows that children can talk about previous lives even in cultures without a belief in reincarnation. This undercuts the premise of the faulty memory argument that the Asian cultures help create the cases there because of the predominant belief in reincarnation. Though we should keep in mind that her mother's belief in reincarnation could have affected Abby, we have the question of what would make children in America, many of whom have parents who do not believe in reincarnation, think that they have been reincarnated. And what do we make of the fact that not only did Abby think she had been reincarnated, but she also came up with information from a previous life?

If we think that Abby's mother had faulty memory, we have to assume that the families of other nearly identical American cases did as well. I recently corresponded with a mother whose two-and-a-half-year-old daughter told her one day, "I'm your mom. I'm your mom, Debbie." The mother did not think that she had ever mentioned her own mother, who had been dead for twenty-five years, to her toddler daughter, and certainly not by her first name. In another case, a girl, when she was between two and a half and three years old, said to her mother, "I was your grandma, and I couldn't walk." Her family said that the girl had never been told that her great-grandmother had been unable to walk on account of polio. In a fourth case, a three-year-old girl made a number of statements about being her great-grandmother, including telling her grandmother, who was adopted at the age of three, "You were just little like I am now, and you came to live with me at my house." Her grandmother was stunned, as were the witnesses in these other cases. Can we think that they all had faulty memory about these very distinctive statements?

GENETIC MEMORY

This explanation, included here only for the sake of complete-ness, bridges the two categories of explanations, those of normal means and those of paranormal means, because it involves a "nor-mal" process that is not accepted in mainstream medical thought. Genetic memory is the concept that knowledge people acquire can be transmitted through their genes to their offspring. How information could change the genetic structure in an individual's cells is unknown, and most people in medicine do not believe it is possible. Even if we grant that such a transmission could be possi-ble, the obvious problem with genetic memory as an explanation for these cases is that, in many of them, the child is not related to the previous personality. Some people might think that we are all distantly related in some way, but here the child would have to be not only related but a direct descendent of the previous personal-ity in order to have gotten any of the memories that existed in that person's genes. That is not the situation in many of our cases, so genetic memory does not provide an explanation for them. In Abby's case, of course, she is a direct descendent of her great-grandmother, but since her great-grandmother's memory of bathing her mother came after she had produced her offspring, those memories could not have been included in the genes that Abby eventually received.

Paranormal Explanations

Since paranormal means something that is beyond normal sci-entific explanation, some readers may view all such scenarios as absurd. Those readers are probably not aware of the volume of research that has been done in parapsychology, which I will not review here. If we are going to consider reincarnation as a possible explanation for these cases, we might as well consider other paranormal possibilities as well.

EXTRASENSORY PERCEPTION (ESP)

As the name states, ESP involves perception by means other than the physical senses, and several types have been described. With *telepathy,* one person gains knowledge from the mind of another person through paranormal means. In Abby's case, this would mean that she read her mother's mind when she came up with her great-grandmother's name. Another type is *clairvoyance,* in which a person gains knowledge in a paranormal way without learning it from another person's mind. For instance, a person who can give details about people after handling such objects as their car keys is a clairvoyant if those details could not have been deduced from the appearance of the objects.

The concept of *superpsi* holds that individuals, through ESP or psi, as it is also called, can essentially know anything that is possible to know. This means that Abby could have known her great-grandmother's name, even if her mother did not, as long as someone somewhere knew the name, whether they were thinking of it at the time or not. For that matter, she could have known it even if no one alive knew it as long as it was written down somewhere for her to learn through clairvoyance. This concept argues that ESP is powerful enough to explain all evidence that suggests survival after bodily death. If a medium tells someone that their deceased Aunt Suzy says there is a box of money buried underneath a particular tree in the backyard, and the person then digs up such a box, the superpsi hypothesis would say that the medium gained the knowledge through clairvoyance about the box and not by speaking with the spirit of Aunt Suzy. Any knowledge that can be later verified could have been available to an individual through superpsi.

One problem with the idea of superpsi is that it is so broad that it can be used to explain anything. Since superpsi could be responsible for anything that anyone might know, the hypothesis cannot be disproved in a test, meaning that it cannot be proved in a test either.

Even if one does accept the possibility of telepathy, clairvoyance, or superpsi, the ESP explanation, like many of those in the normal group, can only account for part of a case. It might explain how Abby was able to come up with her great-grandmother's name, but it would not explain why she thought she had been her great-grandmother. The sense of identification that is so strong in many of these cases is more than just paranormal knowledge; it represents a sense of having been another person. The knowledge that the children express about the previous lives comes from the vantage point of one individual, the previous personality.

The ESP explanation also does not explain the birthmark cases. When we consider the 225 cases in *Reincarnation and Biology* in which the subject of the case had a birthmark or birth defect that matched a wound on the deceased individual, we need another, separate explanation for the birthmarks if we decide that those children's statements were due to ESP.

Along with these problems is the fact that, with very rare exceptions, these children never demonstrate any other paranormal abilities. Abby certainly did not. These children are not young mystics waiting to grow up to be professional psychics; they are children who develop normally, just like their peers.

In Abby's case, she was a four-year-old child without any paranormal ability who gave her great-grandmother's name after describing a memory from her life. Her impression of having been her great-grandmother did not grow from her knowledge of the name. Instead, her ability to give the name came after she seemed to remember a part of that life. This makes ESP a weak and incomplete explanation for the case.

POSSESSION

This refers to the idea that a spirit has inhabited the body and mind of an individual. When many people hear the term possession, they think of evil spirits taking over someone's body, as in the movie *The Exorcist*. It can refer to more benign ideas as well, such as the spirit of a deceased individual, without a body of its own, coming to inhabit the body of someone else. As such, the main difference between possession and reincarnation would be when the spirit came to inhabit the body. If the spirit of the deceased individual entered the new body before birth, then that would be no different from reincarnation unless it forced another spirit out of the body. For all we know, spirits may fight over new bodies routinely.

Possession would be worth considering in situations in which a person underwent a major personality change, developed memories of the previous life, and lost memories of past events of the current life. That is not the case with these children and certainly not the case with Abby. She seemed briefly to have a glimmer of a distant memory, and this is far different from having her mind and body taken over by the spirit of her great-grandmother. In cases with more memories and statements, the families do not report that major changes in personality or skills occur when the statements begin. Instead, some features of the cases, for example, phobias related to the cause of death of the previous personality, often come well before the children start talking about a previous life.

REINCARNATION

We are now down to the last possibility: reincarnation, the concept of an individual dying and then being reborn into another body. In this scenario, when Abby's great-grandmother died, her consciousness did not cease to exist. Instead, it was reborn as part of Abby, who later had some memories of the previous life.

This idea fits with what Abby thought she remembered, giving her mother baths when her mother was a baby and being her mother's grandmother. There are, at most, two people who could have remembered doing both, and one of them was named Ruthie. This explanation does not reveal where she was in the intervening years or how she ended up as Abby, but it does seem to fit the facts of the case better than the ESP and possession explanations do.

The reincarnation idea does not explain why this memory was so fleeting for Abby. In other cases, some of the children only talk about the memories at certain times, while some seem to have access to them at all times during their early years. Perhaps we should not be surprised that memory varies. Some people remember virtually nothing about their childhoods, while others remember voluminous amounts. Sometimes, things happen that trigger a memory that we had not thought of for many years. We also have memories from the very distant past that can be hard to grasp fully at times. We have a vague sense of them that may become stronger if we focus on them. This situation can be similar to remembering dreams. We remember some dreams when we first wake up, but then they disappear, sometimes almost instantly. The memory was there, and then it was gone. So this memory appears to have been for Abby.

Of course, given how remarkable the idea seems that a child could remember a previous life at all, perhaps we should not gripe that the memory was so short-lived. When we look at the whole group of cases, we will see that many of the children had similar memories for at least several years.

One advantage of the idea of reincarnation is that it provides an explanation for the various parts of the cases. The identification with the previous personality is present because the children were, in fact, the previous personalities in the prior lifetime. The memories were simply carried over by the surviving consciousness into the new life. The birthmarks reflect wounds that were so profound to the previous individuals that they affected the consciousness as it went on to the next life, so the scars were carried over into the next body.

A disadvantage of this explanation is that the term reincarnation does not tell us everything that we would like to know. Where does the consciousness go between lives? When does it enter the new body? Why do these children have memories of past lives when most people do not? The cases offer some hints to these questions, as we will see in the upcoming chapters, but no definitive answers are available. And then the biggest question of them all is this: If these children had previous lives, does that mean that we all reincarnate? We can only speculate about this one, and we will do so later in the book.

If we accept for the moment the possibility that Abby's case is an example of reincarnation, then we need to think about what we can learn from it. Abby, like most of these children, did not talk about any experiences between lives, so she did not say how and why she came back. To consider why she might have been reborn to Abby's mother in particular, we should recognize that her mother and great-grandmother had a close connection. Since they had some conflict during her mother's teen years, the great-grandmother may have returned to work out their differences. Her mother said that they had already reconciled while the great-grandmother was still alive, so what seems more likely is that she would have been drawn to Abby's mother because of the positive aspects of their relationship.

Abby's case sheds almost no light on how that occurred, if it did. We do not know if her great-grandmother chose to be born to Abby's mother or chose to be born at all. Perhaps she did not make a conscious decision to return but was drawn to Abby's mother in an emotional way analogous to a magnetic attraction. We can only speculate. We will examine cases in which the children have described memories of events between lives, and we can see if those cases provide any clues as to what happens to lead an individual to return to one particular set of parents. For now, we must be content with the awareness that cases like Abby's suggest that the relationships that we have in one lifetime may be capable of continuing to the next.

Let us look back at Abby's case now with the entire list of explanations in mind. The most likely *normal* explanation is probably that of faulty memory by the informant, in this case the mother.

The other explanations do not seem as reasonable. Though Abby's mother could have made up the story, there is no evidence of fraud and no apparent motivation for it. Abby seems unlikely to have come up with her great-grandmother's name simply by coincidence. Even if Abby knew her great-grandmother's name because she had heard it, this would not explain why she thought that she had been her great-grandmother and why she could not tell her mother the name a few days later. That leaves Abby's mother recalling their conversation incorrectly as the best explanation that uses normal processes, despite the fact that she was fully aware of the significance of Abby's answer before Abby gave it, meaning that she focused on it, improving her chances of recalling it correctly.

Part of the attraction of this explanation is the feeling, "That couldn't have happened; her mother must be mistaken." In other words, if her mother has remembered that conversation correctly, then we have trouble explaining the case by normal means. This means that we need to consider paranormal means. Among those possibilities, reincarnation is more plausible for this case than either ESP or possession.

The choice seems to boil down to reincarnation or a case in which Abby's mother embellished the story, either intentionally in the case of fraud or accidentally in the case of faulty memory. Which one do we think is the best explanation? The answer at this point must be that we do not yet have enough information. Critics would surely say that one curious conversation does not prove anything, and it is certainly not enough to alter our view of the world radically. We should remember though that this topic involves more than just one conversation. Along with Abby's case, dozens of other American cases exist, many of which involve parents who had never given reincarnation a second thought before their children started talking. We must also consider the hundreds of cases of children from other cultures, some with birthmarks matching wounds on the deceased, some with detailed knowledge about strangers from distant places, and some with desperate longings to return to the previous family or dramatic behaviors matching the previous life. Abby's case is not even one of the stronger ones.

Let us not dismiss the whole matter until we have reviewed it fully. Perhaps we are being premature at this point even to ask what explains this phenomenon, but this question lurks behind every aspect of the cases that we will explore. We will therefore return to it as we look at each type of case.

CHAPTER 4

Marked for Life

Patrick Christenson is a boy who was born by cesarean section in Michigan in 1991. When the nurses brought him to his mother, she immediately felt that he was connected to her first son, who had died of cancer at the age of two in 1979, twelve years earlier. She soon noticed that Patrick displayed three defects that matched those her other son had when he died.

Her first son, Kevin, began to limp when he was one and a half years old. One day, he fell and broke his left leg. This led to a medical workup that included a biopsy of a nodule on his scalp above his right ear. Doctors diagnosed him with metastatic cancer. A bone scan showed many abnormal sites. His left eye was protruding and bruised due to a tumor. He received chemotherapy through a central line, a large IV line, in the right side of his neck. Though the site on his neck where the chemotherapy agents were entering his body became flushed and slightly swollen several times, he had no major problems with the treatment and was eventually discharged home. He received outpatient treatment but returned to the hospital five months later. At that point, he appeared blind in his left eye. He was admitted with a fever, treated with antibiotics, and discharged from the hospital. He died two days later, three weeks after his second birthday.

Kevin's parents had separated before his death, and his mother eventually remarried. She gave birth to a daughter and son before Patrick was born. At birth, he had a slanting birthmark with the appearance of a small cut on the right side of his neck—the same location of Kevin's central line—a nodule on his scalp above his right ear as Kevin's biopsied tumor had been, and an opacity in his left eye, diagnosed as a corneal leukoma, that caused him, like Kevin, to have very little vision in that eye. When he began walking, he limped, favoring his left leg.

When Patrick was almost four and a half years old, he began telling his mother things that she felt were related to the life of Kevin. He talked for some time about wanting to go back to their previous home and told his mother that he had left her there. He said that the home was orange and brown, which was correct. He asked his mother if she remembered him having surgery, and when she replied that he had not had any surgery, he said that he had and pointed to the area above his right ear where Kevin had his nodule biopsied. He also said that he did not remember the actual surgery because he was asleep when it was done. At another time, Patrick saw a picture of Kevin, whose pictures were not normally displayed in the family's home, and said that the picture was of him.

After Patrick began making these statements, his mother contacted Carol Bowman, an author who has written two books about children who talk about previous lives—*Children's Past Lives* and *Return from Heaven*. They talked on the phone a number of times, with Carol offering guidance on how to deal with the past-life issues that seemed to be coming up. She eventually referred the case to us for investigation. Dr. Stevenson and I then visited the family when Patrick was five years old.

While we were there, we saw and photographed the birthmark on Patrick's neck, a 4-millimeter dark slanting line on the lower part of the right side of his neck that looked like a healed cut. The nodule on his head was very hard to see but easy to palpate, so we documented the small mass we felt there. We could see the opacity in Patrick's left eye and obtained copies of the eye exams he had received. We watched him walk and could easily determine that he had a slight limp, despite having no medical condition that would explain it. We obtained Kevin's medical records, and they documented the history described earlier, including the lesions that appeared to correspond to Patrick's subsequent birthmarks. We took Patrick to the home that Kevin had shared with his mother. Patrick, unfortunately, did not have great enunciation and could be difficult to understand at times, but he did not make any statements that definitely indicated that he recognized the home.

In summary, Patrick had three unusual lesions at birth that appeared to correspond to lesions that his half-brother Kevin had suffered. In addition, he limped when he began walking and also alluded to events in Kevin's life when talking to his mother.

Patrick's case is an example of the birthmark and birth defect cases that Dr. Stevenson wrote about in *Reincarnation and Biology: A Contribution to the Etiology of Birthmarks and Birth Defects,* in which he presents numerous cases of children who have not only reported past-life memories but also have birthmarks or birth defects that appear to match wounds on the body of the previous personality. They come from various parts of the world, and they have many different types of birthmarks and birth defects. Though

I will not attempt to summarize all 225 cases in the book, some cases are especially worth highlighting.

The Case of Chanai Choomalaiwong

Chanai Choomalaiwong was born in central Thailand in 1967 with two birthmarks, one on the back of his head and one above his left eye. When he was born, his family did not think that his birthmarks were particularly significant, but when he was three years old, he began talking about a previous life. He said that he had been a schoolteacher named Bua Kai and that he had been shot and killed while on the way to school. He gave the names of his parents, his wife, and two of his children from that life, and he persistently begged his grandmother, with whom he lived, to take him to his previous parents' home in a place called Khao Phra.

Eventually, when he was still three years old, his grandmother did just that. She and Chanai took a bus to a town near Khao Phra, which was fifteen miles from their home village. After the two of them got off the bus, Chanai led the way to a house where he said his parents lived. The house belonged to an elderly couple whose son, Bua Kai Lawnak, had been a teacher who was murdered five years before Chanai was born. Chanai's grandmother, it turned out, had previously lived three miles away. Since she had a stall where she sold goods to many people in the surrounding area, she vaguely knew Bua Kai and his wife. She had never been to their home and had no idea to whose home Chanai was leading her. Once there, Chanai identified Bua Kai's parents, who were there with a number of other family members, as his own. They were impressed enough by his statements and his birthmarks to invite him to return a short time later. When he did, they tested him by asking him to pick out Bua Kai's belongings from others, and he was able to do that. He recognized one of Bua Kai's daughters and asked for the other one by name. Bua Kai's family accepted that Chanai was Bua Kai reborn, and he visited them a number of times. He insisted that Bua Kai's daughters call him "Father," and if they did not, he refused to talk to them.

As for Bua Kai's wounds, no autopsy report was available, but Dr. Stevenson talked with a number of family members about his injuries, and they said that he had two wounds on his head from being shot. His wife remembered that the doctor who examined Bua Kai's body said that the entrance wound was the one on the back of his head because it was much smaller than the wound on his forehead that would have been the exit wound. These matched Chanai's birthmarks: a small, circular one on the back of his head and a larger, more irregular one on the front. They were both hairless and puckered. No one photographed them until Chanai was eleven and a half years old, so determining exactly where they were on his head at birth is difficult. In the photographs, the larger one is on the left toward the top of his head in front, but witnesses said that it had been lower on his forehead when he was younger.

In this case, a number of witnesses stated that a young child with birthmarks that matched the entrance and exit wounds on a deceased man had knowledge about that man's life that he seemingly could not have obtained through normal means, and he was able to pass tests that the man's family constructed for him.

The Case of Necip Ünlütaşkiran

Another case from *Reincarnation and Biology* is that of Necip Ünlütaşkiran from Turkey. At the time of his birth, he was noted to
have a number of birthmarks on his head, face, and trunk. His
parents initially named him Malik, but three days after his birth,
his mother had a dream in which her baby told her that he was
called Necip. The parents then chose to change his name to
Necati instead of Necip, since the names were similar and another child in the family was already named Necip. When the
boy became old enough to speak, he insisted that his name was
really Necip and refused to answer to anything else, so his parents
eventually agreed to call him Necip.

Necip was slow in speaking and late in speaking about a previous life, but when he was six years old, he began saying that he
had children. He gradually gave other details, including the fact
that he had been stabbed repeatedly. He said he had lived in the
city of Mersin, fifty miles from the family's home. The family
did not immediately take him there, because of their lack of
means as well as their lack of interest in what he was saying.

When Necip was twelve years old, his mother took him to a
town near Mersin to visit her father and his wife, whom neither
Necip nor his mother had met before. When Necip did meet her,
he said that she was now his real grandmother after being only
like a grandmother to him in the past. He told her about his
memories of a previous life, and she confirmed that they were
true. She had previously lived in Mersin, where she was known as
"Grandmother." A neighbor of hers there named Necip Budak
had been stabbed and killed shortly before the child Necip was

born. Necip's grandfather then took him to Mersin, where he recognized a number of Necip Budak's family members. He identified two items that had belonged to Necip Budak, and he correctly said that Necip Budak had once cut his wife on her leg with a knife during an argument. The boy had not seen the widow's legs, of course, but a woman in Dr. Stevenson's group examined them and confirmed that she had a scar on her thigh that she said her husband had given her.

Dr. Stevenson was able to obtain a copy of Necip Budak's autopsy report, and he found that Necip the boy had three birthmarks, ones that his family had noted at his birth that were still visible when Dr. Stevenson examined him at age thirteen, that matched wounds described in the autopsy report. In addition, Necip had previously had three birthmarks that his family noted at birth that were no longer visible at age thirteen that matched wounds in the report. Dr. Stevenson also found two marks on Necip that corresponded to wounds in the report, but his parents had not noticed these marks before. Lastly, the autopsy described a number of wounds on the left arm of Necip Budak that did not match any birthmarks on Necip the boy.

In summary, Necip had up to eight birthmarks that matched documented wounds on Necip Budak, who was killed fifty miles away, and he also gave correct details about Necip Budak's life and recognized his family members.

In the two cases I have just described, the subject had a very slight connection to the previous personality. Chanai's grandmother had known the previous personality somewhat, and Necip's stepgrandmother had known his previous personality well. In most of the cases in *Reincarnation and Biology,* the connection is even stronger than these are. Many of them are either same-family cases or ones in which the child and the previous personality lived in the same village or at least in villages close to each other.

We can look at these connections in different ways. One explanation in many of the cases is that the child's birthmark pointed to a likely previous personality since someone had died in the area with a similar wound. Relatively few statements were then required from the child to confirm the match. For example, in one case, a man died from a shotgun blast to the lower chest, and a child was later born in the same village with a birthmark that looked exactly like a shotgun blast on his lower chest. Consequently, his family suspected that he was the deceased man returned. He then only had to make a few statements about the previous life—including that he was the previous personality and that he had been shot in the chest—before he was accepted as the reincarnation of the deceased man.

On the other hand, if a child is born with a similar birthmark, but no one nearby has died from such an injury, then he must give more details in order for the case to be solved. In particular, he must give the location of the previous personality, and he must get his parents interested enough in the case to go to the other location to try to solve it. Obviously, a nearby birthmark case develops much more easily than a long-distance one.

The cases of Chanai and Necip, despite their slight connections to the previous personalities, do not particularly fit this pattern, because their birthmarks did not lead their parents to think of one particular previous personality. In Chanai's case, his grandmother did not associate him with the previous personality until Chanai took her to the home of that man's parents. In Necip's case, the previous personality would not have been identified except for the fact that the boy recognized his grandfather's wife as someone he had known from his previous life.

A skeptical reader might conclude that the connections in these cases led people to identify the children as rebirth cases erroneously. The idea would be that the families must have known enough about the previous personalities either to share the information with the boys or to infer that the boys were talking about particular deceased individuals when they were not. The next two cases are not open to that criticism, since no connection existed between the two families at all.

The Case of Indika Ishwara

Indika Ishwara, an identical twin, was born in Sri Lanka in 1972. His brother talked about a previous life at an early age, as I will discuss in Chapter 6. When Indika was three years old, he also began talking about one. He said that he was from Balapitiya, a town nearly thirty miles from his hometown. He talked about his previous parents. He did not give their names but referred to them as his Ambalangoda mother and Ambalangoda father. He said that he attended a big school in Ambalangoda, a larger town near to Balapitiya, and that he traveled there by train. He said that he was called "Baby Mahattaya." *Mahattaya* means "master" or "boss" in Sinhalese, and Baby Mahattaya is a fairly common nickname in Sri Lanka. He claimed he had an older sister named Malkanthie, with whom he had bicycled. He described an uncle named Premasiri as well as a "Mudalali Bappa." *Mudalali* means an individual with a substantial business, and *bappa* means a paternal uncle. He mentioned that the family had a calf and a dog and said that a car and a truck were at the home.

In addition, he talked of going with his sister to the temple, where he said a red curtain hung in front of the Buddha image. He said that his previous father wore trousers; his own father wore a sarong. His previous home, where a wedding had taken place, had electricity. His family's home did not. He described his previous mother as being darker, taller, and fatter than his present one. He said that he had gone to school through the fourth grade and had a classmate named Sepali.

Indika's family did not know anyone who lived in Ambalangoda. His father had a friend who worked there, and he asked the friend to try to locate the previous personality's family based on what Indika had said. The friend quickly located a family in Balapitiya who seemed to fit Indika's statements. Their oldest son, Dharshana, had died at ten of viral encephalitis four years before Indika was born.

The friend spoke with Dharshana's mother about Indika, since Dharshana's father was away at the time. When the father learned what Indika had been saying, he was quite interested, and he soon made an unannounced trip to Indika's hometown. He went to the shop of Indika's father. While he was waiting there for someone to take him to the family's home, an employee asked him if he had a daughter named Malkanthie and a son called Mahatmaya, since Indika had been reporting these things. He did, and he then went to the family's home and met Indika, who was not yet four years old. People thought that Indika recognized him, because even though he did not call him by name directly, he said to his mother, "Father has come."

Shortly after that, various members of Dharshana's family

made two trips to see Indika. Indika was thought to recognize several of them, but their interactions occurred in uncontrolled conditions with a lot of people around. Dr. Stevenson's longtime associate in Sri Lanka, Godwin Samararatne, later accompanied Indika to Balapitiya and Ambalangoda, but Indika did not say anything that suggested that he recognized anything he saw. At that point, most of Dharshana's family members had already met Indika, but Mr. Samararatne was able to set up controlled tests to see if Indika could recognize an additional uncle and cousin. He did not. On his second visit to Dharshana's family, he appeared to be looking for something outside a house in the family's compound. He discovered what he had been looking for and pointed out Dharshana's name and the date 1965 that had been scratched, presumably by Dharshana, in the wall of a concrete drain when the concrete was still wet. No one in Dharshana's family knew about this or had ever noticed the writing until Indika pointed it out to them.

Mr. Samararatne, Dr. Stevenson's associate, had learned of the case soon after it developed, and he conducted interviews with Indika's parents three weeks after the initial meeting between Indika and Dharshana's father, and with Dharshana's father a week after that. All of Indika's statements about the previous life in these pages come from those initial interviews that occurred very soon after the families first met. The memory that Dharshana's father had of hearing the two names at the shop of Indika's father seems particularly striking, and I think we must conclude that Indika gave those names before the families ever met.

Almost all of the statements that Indika made proved to be correct for the life of Dharshana. Dharshana's family did live in Balapitiya, and he attended school in Ambalangoda. Dharshana was called "Baby Mahattaya" as a nickname. His older sister was named Malkanthie, and they did bicycle together. One of his uncles was named Premasiri (his full name was Sangama Premasiri de Silva), and a paternal uncle was a contractor and a timber merchant, thus a *mudalali*. Dharshana's family had a car and a dog. Though they did not own a truck, one was parked in the family's compound. Likewise, the family did not own a calf, but other people brought their calves to graze on the grass at the family's compound.

The temple that Indika's family attended had a white curtain in front of its image of Buddha, while the one that Dharshana's family attended had a red one. Dharshana's father did wear trousers, and the family's home did have electricity. Though Dharshana may not have witnessed a wedding directly in the family's home, several had taken place nearby, including one in a neighbor's house a few weeks before Dharshana died. Dharshana had fallen from a wall during the wedding, and his doctors later thought he might have sustained a head injury then that was related to his subsequent encephalitis. Indika's description of Dharshana's mother was accurate. Dharshana attended school through grade 4. He was just starting grade 5 when he became ill. As far as Dharshana's family and one of his classmates could recall, he did not have a classmate named Sepali.

How Indika could possibly have known all these details about an ordinary boy who died in another village almost thirty miles away is certainly worth wondering about. In addition, he had a nasal polyp his parents noticed when he was a year old. Though nasal polyps are not unusual in later ages, they are quite rare in infancy, and Indika's identical twin did not have one. So why did Indika have one? If we accept the possibility that some birthmarks and defects may arise through the process of reincarnation, one possibility to consider is that since Dharshana, the previous personality, had received both nasal oxygen and a nasal feeding tube during his illness, an irritation from one of those could have produced the subsequent polyp in Indika. The nasal polyp, though not as dramatic as some of the unusual deformities in *Reincarnation and Biology,* is rare and has no known cause, and the explanation that it somehow mirrored irritation from the nasal tubes that Dharshana had is consistent with the numerous statements that Indika made that were correct for Dharshana's life.

The Case of Purnima Ekanayake

The last case of this type that I want to present does not come from *Reincarnation and Biology.* Instead, our colleague Erlendur Haraldsson investigated and published this case. Purnima Ekanayake, a girl in Sri Lanka, was born with a group of light-colored birthmarks over the left side of her chest and her lower ribs. She began talking about a previous life when she was between two and a half and three years old, but her parents did not initially pay much attention to her statements. When she was four years old, she saw a television program about the Kelaniya temple, a well-known temple that was 145 miles away, and said that she recognized it. Later, her father, a school principal, and her mother, a teacher, took a group of students to the Kelaniya temple. Purnima went with the group on the visit. While there, she said that she had lived on the other side of the river that flowed beside the temple grounds.

By the time she was six, Purnima had made some twenty statements about the previous life, describing a male incense maker who was killed in a traffic accident. She had mentioned the names of two incense brands, Ambiga and Geta Pichcha. Her parents had never heard of these, and when Dr. Haraldsson later checked the shops in their town, none of them sold those brands of incense.

A new teacher began working in Purnima's town. He spent his weekends in Kelaniya where his wife lived. Purnima's father told him what Purnima had said, and the teacher decided to check in Kelaniya to see if anyone had died there who matched her statements. The teacher said that Purnima's father gave him the following items to check:

- She had lived on the other side of the river from the Kelaniya temple.
- She had made Ambiga and Geta Pichcha incense sticks.
- She was selling incense sticks on a bicycle.
- She was killed in an accident with a big vehicle.

He then went with his brother-in-law, who did not believe in reincarnation, to see if a person matching those statements could be located. They went to the Kelaniya temple and took a ferry across the river. There, they asked about incense makers and found that three small family incense businesses were in the area. The owner of one of them called his brands Ambiga and Geta Pichcha. His brother-in-law and associate, Jinadasa Perera, had been killed by a bus when he was taking incense sticks to the market on his bicycle two years before Purnima was born.

Purnima's family visited the owner's home soon after. There, Purnima made various comments about family members and their business that were correct, and the family accepted her as being Jinadasa reborn. Dr. Haraldsson began investigating the case when Purnima was nine years old. He recorded the twenty statements that her parents said Purnima had made before the two families met. In addition to the ones already mentioned, they included the names of Jinadasa's mother and wife and the name of the school that Jinadasa had attended. Dr. Haraldsson verified that fourteen of the statements were accurate for the life of Jinadasa. Three were incorrect, and the accuracy of three of them could not be determined. He also obtained Jinadasa's autopsy report, which documented fractured ribs on the left, a ruptured spleen, and abrasions running diagonally from the right shoulder across the chest to the left lower abdomen. These corresponded to the birthmarks that Purnima had over her chest and ribs.

This case challenges attempts to write off this work with a quick, normal explanation. The two families, living 145 miles apart, were, by all accounts, complete strangers to each other, and Purnima had no way of learning about Jinadasa's death before they met. Coincidence seems very unlikely, given the specificity of Purnima's statements, including the names of the incense brands. The various informants could all have faulty memories perhaps, but this case is strengthened by the presence of the intermediary, the teacher, who was independent of the two families and searched for the previous personality before they met. The birthmark is also large and prominent, and it fits nicely with the injuries of the previous personality.

A Way to Understand the Birthmark Cases

We may well wonder, even if we believe in reincarnation, how an injury to one body could then show up on the next one. We can understand how this might be possible by looking at research that has examined the interaction between psychological and physical issues. To start with, studies have shown that mental factors can produce general changes in the body. For instance, stress can contribute to illness, because it produces changes in hormones and nerve pathways that cause the immune system to be less able to fight off infections. Likewise, hopelessness has been shown to increase the risk of a heart attack or cancer. What is far less accepted, and understood not at all, is the idea that individual mental images can produce very specific changes in the body, and this is what we need to consider in order to make sense of the birthmark cases.

Dr. Stevenson presents evidence at the start of *Reincarnation and Biology*. He begins with stigmata. These are skin wounds that some usually very devout individuals develop that match the crucifixion wounds of Jesus as described in the Bible. St. Francis of Assisi may well have been the first stigmatic, and since his time, more than 350 others have been reported. These cases were first thought to represent miracles, but they were observed to occur in individuals who could not be described as saintly. They have often occurred when the individual has engaged in a particularly intense religious practice, and they have come to be regarded as psychosomatic in origin. While some cases of fraud have been exposed—individuals who intentionally created the wounds by using chemical irritants or even paint—many cases have been documented in which we can reasonably eliminate artificially induced wounds as a possibility. Thus, the mental image of Jesus' wounds in the mind of a particularly susceptible person can produce very specific changes on the skin that match the mental images.

Another example of changes in the body that the mind can produce occurs with certain individuals under hypnosis. As Dr. Stevenson notes, suggestion under hypnosis has been shown capable of producing various changes in the body; for example, not just the sensation of thirst but also changes in the kidneys that occur during dehydration, changes in heart rate, control of bleeding, changes in the timing of a woman's menstrual cycle, even enlargement of the breasts.

In addition to these, a number of cases have been published in which hypnotists produced blisters on subjects by saying that they were being burned and then touching the subjects with a cool object, such as the tip of a finger. In some cases, the hypnotists used an object in the shape of a letter or other recognizable symbol, and the subsequent wounds that were produced were in that shape. One case involved both stigmata and hypnosis, as a subject was induced under hypnosis to produce bleeding wounds on her feet and palms along with a number of triangular wounds on her forehead that looked as if a crown of thorns might have made them.

In another type of case, subjects have "relived" traumatic experiences with the help of either hypnosis or drugs and then developed skin manifestations that matched those they experienced during the original experiences. In one notable case, a man reexperienced an event that included having his arms tied behind his back with rope. He developed deep indentations on his forearms that looked like rope marks. Mainstream science has had difficulty determining a mechanism that would explain such cases, so it has largely ignored them.

We can all agree that hypnosis can use mental images to produce at least some physiological changes in certain individuals. For instance, if a person is reliving a frightening event under hypnosis, she may develop an increased heart rate. In fact, many individuals may develop an increased heart rate by simply recalling a frightening event, even without undergoing hypnosis. In that case, we can, without too much trouble, map out the mechanism similar to the "fight or flight" response that a person develops when faced with an actual experience that is frightening or dangerous. We cannot yet map out the mechanism to explain how a person can develop blisters while thinking that he is being burned or rope marks while reliving an incident of being tied up, but we can see that such cases vary only by degree from ones in which physiological changes that we can readily explain are produced by similar mental image stimuli.

The point of all this is that the mind can produce changes in the body that, given our current state of knowledge, we are unable to explain. When I say the mind, I do not necessarily mean the brain. I am referring to the world of thoughts, or the consciousness, that exists in the brain, and I will discuss this more when I address materialism in Chapter 9. If this consciousness or mind can exist after the brain dies—if some part of us survives when our bodies die—and can enter a fetus to be reborn, then it follows that it can produce changes in the development of that fetus, just as it can produce changes during a life. Since we may assume that the period of development in the womb would be a particularly vulnerable time for the body to be affected, we can easily see that if a mind occupied a fetus while carrying traumatic memories, which previous studies have shown can produce specific lesions on the skin of certain individuals, those memories could produce birthmarks or even birth defects that matched wounds that the mind had experienced in its previous life. If the mind does survive one life and moves on to another, the birthmark cases could logically involve the same process as the previously documented hypnosis cases.

Our birthmark cases often seem to fit this model. In Patrick's case, he had marks and defects that seemed to correspond to lesions that his half-brother Kevin had experienced. Accepting for a moment that Patrick is the rebirth of Kevin, his having those lesions might seem unfair after he already had to suffer through the original traumas as Kevin, but the natural process of the mind affecting the body could produce those defects, even if we wish that such were not the case. Patrick's birthmarks are different from many of the birthmark cases in that his birthmarks do not match fatal wounds on his half-brother Kevin, who of course did not die violently, but instead match scars or deficits that would have been particularly troubling to Kevin—the scalp scar where a tumor was biopsied, the neck scar where the toddler had a central line inserted, the opacity in the left eye where he could not see, and eventually the limp matching Kevin's difficulty in walking. All of these must have been hard for young Kevin to handle, and such traumatic memories may have produced scars on Patrick's developing fetus even though they were not fatal wounds.

The same logic could apply in Indika's case of the nasal polyp corresponding to the nasal tubes that his previous personality experienced at the end of his life. In the case of Chanai, being shot and killed would clearly be a traumatic experience to a surviving mind, and similarly, Purnima's birthmarks correspond to the physically and emotionally traumatic injuries that her previous personality suffered when he was hit by a bus.

Necip's case is a little more complicated. If we accept for a moment that he might have been the reincarnation of Necip Budak, then we may wonder why he had birthmarks that matched some of Necip Budak's wounds but not others. Dr. Stevenson has suggested that in an attack, earlier wounds would be more likely to carry over to the next life because the victim would be more fully conscious when he or she received them. In this case, Necip's most prominent birthmarks were on his head, and he also had birthmarks on his chest and abdomen. Necip Budak had head wounds, but the chest and abdomen ones were the fatal ones. Dr. Stevenson suggests that if Necip Budak received his head wounds before the fatal chest and abdomen wounds, then they would have been in his mind longer before he lost consciousness.

The difficulty comes, as Dr. Stevenson likes to point out, because the people who perform autopsies do not work for us, and they often make no attempt to determine the order of wounds. In this case, Necip Budak may have been groggy after being hit on the head, so the other wounds had less impact on his mind and subsequently on his new body. We have no way of knowing. One likely scenario is that the cuts on his left arm came when he was trying to defend himself, so he would have had at least some conscious awareness. Nonetheless, Necip the boy, as noted above, did not have any birthmarks on his arm.

Another possibility to consider is that the wounds that are the most traumatic emotionally have the greatest likelihood of carrying over to the next life. These would often be the ones received when the person was first attacked and fully conscious, but this might not always be the case. Necip Budak was presumably as conscious when he received the cuts on his arm as when he received the ones on his body, but Necip the boy had no birthmarks on his arm. We can conjecture that after Necip Budak received blows to his head when he was fully conscious, the cuts he received on his body were more emotionally traumatic to him than the cuts on his arm, because they were more life-threatening. Therefore, the most prominent birthmarks occurred on Necip's head, and he also had less prominent marks on his body.

Still another possibility, of course, is that the wounds on his body led to birthmarks because the body wounds were more serious injuries than the cuts on his arm. Dr. Stevenson has noted though that the fatal wound does not always produce the most significant birthmark, so a factor other than just the severity of a wound must be involved. Presumably, it involves some factor related to consciousness, perhaps either the level of consciousness at the time of the injury or the emotional impact on the individual's consciousness.

Questions About Birthmark Cases

In surveying the cases, a question that arises is if trauma at the end of a life can produce birthmarks and birth defects in the next one, why are more babies not born with marks or defects? An explanation for this involves an idea I alluded to earlier. In the discussion on hypnosis, I said that it could produce changes in certain individuals. Some people respond to hypnosis much more strongly than others. In fact, some cannot be hypnotized at all. In the case of rebirth, we might also expect that some individuals would be more susceptible than others to having lesions on the new body produced by past-life trauma. Hypnosis is unable to produce marks on the skin of most people, but some subjects are particularly susceptible to it. Likewise, injuries at death may be unlikely to affect the next life's fetus for most individuals, but some may be particularly susceptible to it.

We do not have any clear sense of what factors might determine how susceptible a particular individual would be to trauma transfer, but one may be cultural beliefs. If a general belief in the culture supports the possibility that past-life trauma can affect a developing fetus, then individuals in that culture might be more susceptible to developing lesions than individuals in other cultures. In hypnosis, the subject's expectations for what can happen under hypnosis can have an effect on what does happen. Likewise, an individual's beliefs about life and death may affect such subsequent occurrences as birthmarks. This could explain, at least in part, why the birthmarks occur more frequently in some places than in others. Patrick's case notwithstanding, we have very few birthmark cases from the United States. The lack of acceptance of the phenomenon here may cause Americans to be less prone to developing past-life trauma birthmarks than people in other places.

Having said that, I should point out that the birthmark cases do not necessarily correspond to the religious beliefs held in many of the communities where the cases are found. The concept of *karma,* which is so central to Hindu and Buddhist beliefs, holds that the conditions into which a person is born are determined by his or her conduct in previous lives. Based on that, we might think that following a murder, the killer and not the victim would bear the birthmarks or birth defects in the next life as a result of karmic debt, but that is not what we see. We have only three cases in which the children thought that their birth defects were retribution for acts they remembered in a prior life. One subject, a boy in Sri Lanka named Wijeratne, remembered the life of his uncle, who had been hanged eighteen years before Wijeratne's birth for stabbing a woman after she called off their marriage. Wijeratne was born with a deformed right arm and hand, both being much shorter than normal, and an absent pectoral muscle on the right side of his chest. Wijeratne said that he had a defective hand because he had killed the woman with his hand in his previous life.

In all the other cases, the children described getting wounds in the previous life that carried over to their new bodies, so the patterns in the cases seem more consistent with the idea of mental images or memories producing bodily changes. Nonetheless, individuals in these cultures seem more open generally to spiritual effects on health or on the body, so such openness may make them more susceptible to having past-life birthmarks even if the marks do not conform to their notions of karma.

Beyond the cultural differences, we also need to consider differences in individuals. Even though a past-life cause for birthmarks and birth defects is accepted much more easily in many countries than it is in ours, expectations among individuals may vary a great deal. People in the cultures where most of the cases are found have varying degrees of belief in reincarnation, just as religious beliefs in the United States vary from individual to individual, and the degree of belief and expectation in an individual mind may affect the likelihood of subsequent birthmarks. Similarly, the general cultural beliefs in the U.S. do not include a belief in reincarnation, but some individuals do expect to be reborn. An example is William, the boy I presented in Chapter 1 who was born with the heart defect that matched the fatal wounds that his grandfather received in a shooting. His grandfather was a practicing Roman Catholic, but he also had a belief in reincarnation. That belief conceivably could have made him more susceptible to having a birth defect related to his fatal wounds in his next life.

Another question that comes up is why so many of the cases involve the skin. Some involve such deformities as missing digits or limbs, but only a few involve internal diseases. We can only speculate about the reasons for this, but it may also relate to being a phenomenon of consciousness. We are much more conscious of lesions of the skin than we are of lesions of internal organs, so we might then be more likely to carry the memory of those lesions to the next life. Likewise, if a man has his fingers cut off while being killed, he is surely aware of that happening, but he may not be aware, for instance, of his liver being lacerated by a bullet. Deformities may arise due to the previous personality's awareness of the injuries, and internal organs may be spared because the victim is not aware of the specific injuries.

William's case is an exception to this. If his heart defect is a manifestation of his grandfather's injuries, we may wonder why he did not at least have a birthmark on his chest to go along with the heart defect. I do not have a definitive answer to that question, but I wonder if the grandfather thought that the chest pain he was feeling meant that he had been hit in the heart. He would have focused more on his heart than on his skin. To complicate matters, even though William did not have a birthmark on his chest to coincide with his heart defect, he did have a birthmark on his neck that may relate to his grandfather's death. Carol Bowman referred me to William and his mother. When I first met with them, his mother did not report that he had any birthmarks. In our subsequent correspondence, she noted that he did have one on his neck below his left ear, and she sent me a picture of it. This birthmark is in the same location as an area of bruising on the neck of William's grandfather that his autopsy documented. That bruise must have been severe, because it was included in the autopsy's one-paragraph description of the external examination of the body. William's mother, in fact, thought that her father had been shot there, but since the autopsy does not indicate an entrance or exit wound there, the bruising likely came from a bullet grazing that area of his neck. Along with a heart defect that matches trauma that his grandfather suffered, William has a birthmark corresponding to a bruise but not any birthmarks that match the various entrance and exit wounds that bullets created on his grandfather's body. To speculate on this, perhaps William's grandfather was conscious of the injury to his neck before focusing on the fatal heart trauma, and he did not focus particularly on the impact of the other bullets.

William's case also indicates a practical factor that may be involved in producing few cases of internal organ defects. A baby born in an Asian village with the heart defect that William had would surely have died within a few days after birth, if not sooner. He would never have had the opportunity to talk about the previous life, and we would never have learned about the case. Perhaps cases with internal organ defects occur, but they do not become known as rebirth cases, because the children die at such an early age.

Experimental Birthmarks

As I described earlier, experimental birthmarks are practiced in several Asian countries. Someone, usually a family member or close family friend, makes a mark on the body of a dying or deceased person, often with soot or paste, in the belief that when the individual is reborn, the baby will bear a birthmark that corresponds to the mark made on the body. The marker often says a prayer while making the mark, asking that the dying person take the mark with him or her to the new body. A child is later born with a birthmark that is said to match the marking made on the body.

Dr. Stevenson was the first person in the West to fully document this practice, but other authors have mentioned it. For instance, the Dalai Lama wrote in his autobiography about a case that occurred in his family. His younger brother died at two years of age. A small mark was made on the boy's body with a smear of butter after he died, and his mother subsequently gave birth to another son who had a pale mark on his body in the same place where the first body had been marked.

That case is fairly typical of the cases that we have found. Dr. Stevenson describes twenty such cases in *Reincarnation and Biology,* and Jürgen Keil and I found eighteen more during trips to Thailand and Myanmar. In these cases, the mark is usually made with the expectation that the reincarnated individual carrying the mark will be born into the same family as the deceased individual, and fifteen of our eighteen cases were same-family. This would seem to lessen the chances that the marking and the birthmark matched simply out of coincidence, compared to a situation where any baby in the area could be considered the re-birth of the deceased individual.

In addition, in six of our eighteen cases, the children had also made statements that related to the previous life, and some of the other children were so young when we saw them that they may have later made statements. Some of the cases feature behaviors as well as statements that suggest a connection between the subject and the previous personality, while in others, the birthmark is the only sign of a connection.

One case that Dr. Keil and I investigated can serve as a good example. Kloy Matwiset is a boy who was born in Thailand in 1990. Eleven months before he was born, his maternal grand-mother died of diabetes. Before she died, she told her daughter-in-law that she would like to be reborn as a male so that she could have a mistress as her husband did. The day after she died, her daughter-in-law used white paste to make a mark down the back of her neck so that she could recognize her mother-in-law when she was reborn.

Kloy's mother had an announcing dream when she was three months pregnant in which the grandmother said that she wanted to be reborn to her. His mother had seen the mark made on the grandmother's body. When Kloy was born, she noticed that he had a birthmark on the back of his neck in the same place where the mark had been made. We met him and saw a very noticeable vertical pale discoloration on the back of his neck that had a shape that matched a finger making a mark down his neck. The marker confirmed that this unusual birthmark was in the same place that she had marked his grandmother's body.

When Kloy was quite young, he made several statements about the previous life. He said that he was his grandmother and told his mother that he was her mother. He also said that his grandmother's rice field belonged to him. In addition, he showed a number of feminine behaviors. He said that he wanted to be a girl, and as a young child, he generally sat down to urinate. He also enjoyed wearing women's clothing and wore his mother's lipstick, earrings, and dresses many times. At school, he enjoyed playing and studying with the girls rather than the boys, and he did not engage in typical male behaviors for boys in that area such as climbing trees. Both of his parents complained about his feminine behaviors, and they said that they never talked to him about being the rebirth of his grandmother.

His feminine behaviors suggest that he has what is known as a gender identity disorder, and I will talk more about such behaviors in Chapter 6. I want to focus now on the birthmark and how it may have come about. One possibility, of course, is coincidence. That would not explain the other features of the case. In addition, for us to say that this unusual birthmark just happened to occur after the previous personality's daughter-in-law asked for exactly such a mark, we have to stretch the coincidence explanation beyond what may be reasonable.

Another possibility worth considering is that though the child is not the rebirth of the previous personality, the mother's wish or expectation somehow produced the mark. Since most of the experimental birthmark cases are same-family ones, the mother of the subject has often either seen the marking on the body or at least known about it. The question becomes whether her wishing or expecting to have the deceased family member reborn as her child could lead her to give birth to a child with the predicted birthmark. In considering this possibility, we need again to recall the hypnosis cases. If an image in the mind can produce a mark on a person's skin, then could an image in a mother's mind produce a mark on the skin of a developing fetus? This would be similar to cases of maternal impression, a concept popular at the end of the nineteenth century that was used to describe cases in which a pregnant mother who was troubled by the sight of a person with a physical deformity then gave birth to a child with the same defect. People eventually decided that the concept was absurd, because they could not imagine a mechanism that would explain it, though we now know that the placental barrier is a lot more porous than people previously thought. Dr. Stevenson lists various published cases of maternal impression in *Reincarnation and Biology,* and they include what would certainly be some remarkable coincidences, the most remarkable perhaps being the case of a pregnant woman who, after being quite troubled upon seeing her brother's wounds from the amputation of his cancerous penis, gave birth to a boy with a congenital absence of the penis, a condition fortunately so rare as to be almost unheard of.

In any event, the experimental birthmark cases differ from the hypnosis and maternal impression cases in at least one important way. Hypnosis is obviously an unusual state of mind, and similarly, most of the maternal impression mothers were strongly affected emotionally by the deformities they saw. In the experimental birthmark cases, the mother, though presumably upset about the death of a family member, often noted the marking but was not particularly moved by it emotionally. In addition, the mother usually saw the marking some time before she became pregnant, and while we can well imagine that pregnancy would be a particularly susceptible time for a traumatized consciousness to affect the development of a fetus, the idea that an image that the mother saw months or years before she became pregnant could produce a mark on her baby's body seems less logical. Perhaps we could consider that her expectation or wish that her child would be the rebirth of the previous personality might be strong enough to lead her to give birth to a baby with a birthmark matching the mark made on that person's body. Such an explanation of the birthmark would not, of course, explain the children's statements and behaviors in some of the cases.

As for the reincarnation possibility, we have the issue of when the bodies are marked. The markings are sometimes made when the individual is still dying, but the person has often died first. At times, the bodies may be marked a couple of days after the person has died or at the beginning of the cremation service. That being the case, more would have to be involved in producing the birthmark than simply the physical mark on the body, since a cremation immediately following it might be expected to produce results as much as a marking could, and a baby does not later show any effects from it.

At least two possibilities are worth considering. One is that the surviving consciousness can stay near the body for some time after death, which would be consistent with the occasional reports that we get from children describing the funerals of the previous personality as I will discuss in Chapter 8. A mark made on the body might produce an emotional impact that would cause the subsequent birthmark, just as wounds in the other cases can match later birthmarks on the subjects. Another possibility is that the prayer that the marker says may be more important than the marking itself. When that person asks the individual to carry the mark to the next life, the consciousness of the marker may connect with the consciousness of the deceased individual to produce the subsequent birthmark. We might speculate that the time around death would be a particularly susceptible time, and the prayer would act almost like a posthypnotic suggestion in causing the mark to appear on the future child.

In any event, these experimental birthmark cases can certainly be challenging, and they may give us clues about the phenomenon in general. They show that cases can occur that involve blemishes that are made following death as well as before. If these are cases of reincarnation, this would seem to indicate that a consciousness can be affected by events that occur for at least some period of time after death. They also suggest, to me at least, that the birthmark cases are due to more than just the physical wound on a body. This is logical in a way, since we would have trouble imagining how the consciousness might be able to carry a physical wound without the actual physical body. If we conceptualize that the physical wound produces a mental image, the idea that the mental image could affect the development of an embryo when the consciousness enters it is consistent with the effects of mental images in other special situations.

Considering the Explanations

In looking for an explanation for the birthmark cases in general, we see that in many of the cases, the family of the subject knows about the death of the previous personality before the child is born, because that person was a family member, friend, or at least an acquaintance. In such a situation, we cannot assume that the parents' knowledge about the death causes the birthmark or birth defect if we are restricting ourselves to normal explanations, but we can speculate that the mark or defect leads the parents to decide that the child is the rebirth of the deceased individual. We can then try to explain the child's past-life statements with either a scenario of knowledge acquired through normal means or one of faulty memory by informants, as follows. After deciding that the child is a rebirth case, the parents may plant the idea in the head of the young child, who comes to believe the past-life story. The child can then start to claim to be the previous personality and can also pick up tidbits about that person's life that he says are memories of the past life. In addition, in their enthusiasm, the parents may misinterpret statements by the child as showing more knowledge about the previous life than the child actually has. In either case, the parents' initial beliefs will come to be confirmed by the child's statements, and all involved will believe that the child is the previous personality reborn.

All of this goes against the frequent testimony of the families that the child possessed knowledge about the previous life that the parents feel he or she could not have learned about in this life, even though the family knew the previous personality. Regardless of that issue, we still have the birthmark or birth defect to explain, and we should remember that some of them are very unusual. In Patrick Christenson's case, he had three unusual ones, and he also developed a limp when he learned to walk. Such a combination would be unusual in any situation, but the fact that all of his defects matched ones on his deceased half-brother makes the situation rather extraordinary. Similarly, Chanai Choomalaiwong had a small, round birthmark on the back of his head that looked like a bullet entrance wound and a larger, irregular mark toward the front of his head that looked like an exit wound. Unusual by themselves, but when they are considered along with his statements about the life of a schoolteacher who was shot from behind, they become extraordinary. In these situations, the only normal explanation available to explain the birthmarks is that of coincidence, and given the unlikelihood of the matches occurring simply by chance, this explanation seems unsatisfactory.

And these are the easy cases to explain. When we look at the ones in which the subject's family had never heard of the previous personality, a normal explanation gets even tougher. Indika Ishwara and Purnima Ekanayake not only had birthmarks, but they made numerous statements about strangers who died a long distance away. The statements proved to be accurate for a specific deceased individual who had a lesion that corresponded to the child's birthmark.

We can again fall back on coincidence as a way to explain the birthmarks, but then we have to explain the statements as well. Coincidence can only go so far, and in a case like Purnima's, in which she made twenty statements about the previous personality that included details about an incense maker being killed on a bicycle and in which she even named the correct brands of incense, ones that were not available locally, coincidence is really not a realistic explanation. In such a case, we might try to use coincidence to explain the birthmark while using another explanation for the accuracy of the statements.

Knowledge acquired through normal means can be an explanation if the previous personality lived in the same community as the child, but it seems quite inadequate to explain the statements in a case such as Purnima's where the previous personality lived 145 miles from the subject's home. Another way to explain the statements is to blame faulty memory by the informants. In this explanation, Purnima and children like her did not really make the statements that they are credited with making. We do not have to say that their accuracy is an incredible coincidence because we do not give the children credit for the statements in the first place.

Thus, for the cases that have birthmarks and previous personalities who lived a significant distance away, we can say that the birthmarks occur by a strange coincidence and that the statements are remembered incorrectly. No other normal explanation really makes sense. We will come back to this question of faulty memory by informants after looking at the other types of cases.

As for the paranormal explanations, ESP cannot easily explain the birthmark cases since they obviously involve more than just the paranormal transfer of information. Similarly, possession cannot explain the birthmarks as long as we think of it as something that takes place after birth. Reincarnation, on the other hand, can explain them, as we have already discussed, by using the idea that the consciousness is so affected by the trauma that led to the injuries on the body of the previous personality that it affects the development of the fetus and produces a similar mark. Given the fact that the children also report memories of the previous life of a person who had matching injuries, reincarnation is certainly the most obvious paranormal explanation and perhaps the only viable one for this type of case.

To summarize our exploration of the birthmark cases, we can say that though most of the cases take place among family members or friends, some occur among complete strangers as well. If these are cases of reincarnation, the likely mechanism involves mental images imprinted on the surviving consciousness by trauma, and the experimental birthmark cases suggest that this imprinting can even occur for a short time after the death of the previous personality.

CHAPTER 5

Remembering the Past

Sujith Jayaratne, a boy from a suburb of the Sri Lankan capital, Colombo, began showing an intense fear of trucks and even the word *lorry*, a British word for truck that has become part of the Sinhalese language, when he was only eight months old. When he became old enough to talk, he said that he had lived in Gorakana, a village seven miles away, and that he had died after being hit by a truck.

He made numerous statements about that life. His great-uncle, a monk at a nearby temple, heard some of them and mentioned Sujith to a younger monk at the temple. The story interested this monk, so he talked with Sujith, who was a little more than two and a half years old at the time, about his memories, and then wrote up notes of the conversations before he attempted to verify any of the statements. His notes document that Sujith said that he was from Gorakana and lived in the section of Gorakawatte, that his father was named Jamis and had a bad right eye, that he had attended the *kabal iskole*, which means "dilapidated school," and had a teacher named Francis there, and that he gave money to a woman named Kusuma, who prepared string hoppers, a type of food, for him. He implied that he gave money to the Kale Pansala, or Forest Temple, and said two monks were there, one of whom was named Amitha. He said that his house was whitewashed, that its lavatory was beside a fence, and that he bathed in cool water.

Sujith had also told his mother and grandmother a number of other things about the previous life that no one wrote down until after the previous personality had been identified. He said his name was Sammy, and he sometimes called himself "Gorakana Sammy." Kusuma, the woman he had mentioned to the monk, was his younger sister's daughter, and she lived in Gorakana and had long, thick hair. He said that his wife's name was Maggie and their daughter's was Nandanie. He had worked for the railways and had once climbed Adam's Peak, a high mountain in central Sri Lanka. He had transported arrack, a liquor that was illegally traded, in a boat that had once capsized, causing him to lose his entire shipment of arrack. He said that on the day he died, he and Maggie had quarreled. She left the house, and he then went out to the store. While he was crossing the road, a truck ran over him, and he died.

The young monk went to Gorakana to look for a family who had a deceased member whose life matched Sujith's statements. After some effort, he discovered that a fifty-year-old man named Sammy Fernando, or "Gorakana Sammy" as he was sometimes called, had died after being hit by a truck six months before Sujith was born. All of Sujith's statements proved to be correct for Sammy Fernando, except for his statement that he had died immediately when the truck hit him. Sammy Fernando died one to two hours after being admitted to a hospital following the accident.

Once Sammy Fernando was identified as the previous personality, Sujith was able to recognize several people from Sammy's life and to comment on changes that had been made in the Fernando property. He made many of the recognitions when no witnesses outside of the two families were present, but the monk heard him give the name of Sammy Fernando's nephew.

Dr. Stevenson interviewed witnesses a year after Sammy Fernando had first been identified as the previous personality. He interviewed thirty-five people as part of his investigation of the case, including Sujith, who was still talking about the previous life at the age of three and a half. Dr. Stevenson discovered that though Sujith's and Sammy's families had not known each other before the case developed, two people in Sujith's neighborhood had connections to Sammy Fernando. Sujith's family knew one of them, a former drinking buddy of Sammy's, slightly, and the other one, Sammy's younger sister, not at all. The family had no idea who Sujith was talking about until the monk went to Gorakana. In fact, neither Sujith's mother nor the monk had heard of Gorakana before the case developed, as it was a fairly small village some distance away from the Colombo area.

Sujith displayed other behaviors along with the phobia of trucks that were consistent with Sammy Fernando's life. He would pretend to drink arrack and then would act drunk. He also attempted to get arrack from neighbors, including one who obliged him until his grandmother intervened. In addition, he tried to smoke cigarettes. No one in his family drank arrack or smoked cigarettes, but Sammy Fernando consumed plenty of both. Sujith also asked for spicy foods Sammy Fernando frequently enjoyed, ones his family, who only ate them occasionally, would not normally have considered giving to a small child. In addition, he had a tendency as a toddler to be physically aggressive and to use obscenities, two habits that Sammy Fernando demonstrated when he was intoxicated. By the time Sujith was six years old, he had stopped talking about Sammy Fernando's life and displayed less of the unusual behavior that he had shown earlier. He still continued to ask for arrack if he saw others drinking it.

What are we to make of this? Though we might like to have a simple, normal explanation for the case, do we really think that all these people worked out an elaborate ruse to fool Dr. Stevenson? Or that the details Sujith gave just happened to match the life of Sammy Fernando? Or that Sammy's sister or former drinking buddy, who had no connection to Sujith's family, secretly told him these meaningless details about Sammy's life, leading him to think that he had been Sammy? We must also keep in mind that Sujith's case is just one of many, and we will review more of them shortly.

Features of Past-life Statements

Sujith's case has many of the typical features of these cases: a young child repeatedly claims to have memories of a previous life and gives enough details to identify a deceased individual whose life matched the child's statements. Let us look at the features of the statements in more detail.

AGE WHEN TALKING ABOUT A PREVIOUS LIFE
Sujith first communicated about the previous life when he was two and a half years old, and the average age is thirty-five

months. In some cases, some of the communication is nonverbal, as the children make gestures related to the previous life before they have developed the language skills necessary to convey the information. Kumkum Verma, whose case I will describe shortly, did not know the word for blacksmith, so she said that her previous son worked with a hammer, and used gestures to show how a blacksmith hammered and how his bellows worked. The early age of communication seems logical, since we would expect memories of a past life, if they are present, to be there from the beginning. Nevertheless, exceptions do exist. When older children report past-life memories, they often have seen things that seemed to remind them of past events. Dr. James Matlock analyzed ninety-five cases and found that the older a subject was when first speaking of a previous life, the more likely that a reminder in the environment stimulated the initial memories.

Sujith's case is also typical in that he stopped talking about the previous life by the time he was six years old. Most of the children stop by the age of six or seven, and not only do they stop talking about the previous life, they often deny any memories of it when asked. We might wonder why this would be so. One possibility is that since this is the age when children generally start school, they may get more fully involved in this life and let the other memories go. More importantly, perhaps, this is the age when all children lose most of their early childhood memories. A toddler can know a family friend, but if that friend moves away, the child will often have no memory of the person by the age of six or seven. This has been called "early childhood amnesia," and though the reasons for it may be debatable, the phenomenon unquestionably occurs.

We would logically expect children with apparent past-life

memories to lose those memories at the same age; otherwise, we would wonder how children could keep memories older than the ones they had lost. The children vary, and some subjects report that they still have past-life memories even into adulthood just as some individuals report having a fair number of early childhood memories when they are adults. Nonetheless, the vast majority of subjects seem to have forgotten all about the past life after a few years. Among 300 cases across different cultures, the median age at which the subjects stopped talking about the previous life was seventy-two months (or six years), but that age varied quite a bit among different subjects. In particular, the subjects of solved cases tend to keep the memories longer than those of unsolved ones, presumably because visits between the families reinforce them.

DETAILS OF THE STATEMENTS

What Sujith said about the previous life is fairly typical of our cases. Since he described the life of someone who died as an adult, he mostly talked about people and places from the previous personality's adulthood. Subjects occasionally talk about older items, as Sujith did when he described the school that Sammy attended, but for the most part, they stick to items from near the end of the previous personality's life. This includes, of course, talk about the previous personality's death. Sujith described the events of the day that led up to the fatal accident and talked about the way in which the previous personality died, as 75 percent of the subjects do. This pattern is consistent with the idea of memory carrying over from one life to the next. Just as our memories in this life are sharper for more recent events than for older ones, these children focus on items from the end of the previous life as if the memories simply carried over from the time that the previous personality died.

That does not mean that the children report no memories from earlier in the previous life. Sujith's talk about Sammy's school and a teacher there involved issues that were presumably not a major concern of Sammy Fernando's at the end of his life, but this demonstrates how the children's recall of past-life events is similar to our memories as adults: Even though we usually recall the most important events from the past, we can also possess other fairly random memories from our childhoods.

Sujith's description of a violent death is typical of many of our cases. In cases in which the mode of death of the previous personality is known, 70 percent died by unnatural means. This includes drownings as well as violent deaths, either intentional as with murder or suicide or unintentional deaths from accidents. This figure is much higher than the actual proportion of deaths due to unnatural means in any of the areas where we find cases.

A skeptic might argue that people tend to talk about violent deaths more than natural ones, so children would be more likely to learn about them and thus claim to remember them. Sujith's case demonstrates the weaknesses in that argument. Sammy Fernando's death, which occurred when he stepped in front of a truck, was not so unusual that it would have been a likely topic for conversation three years after it happened. Moreover, Sujith described many details about Sammy Fernando that had nothing to do with his death and could hardly have been discussed at that point by anyone anywhere.

Though most of the children talk about dying, those statements are more common in cases in which the previous personalities died violently compared to ones where they died naturally. While

75 percent of the children overall describe the way that the previous personality died, only 57 percent do in the case of a natural death, suggesting that a death from an illness may not affect a consciousness in the same way that a sudden or violent death might. I will talk more about what the violent deaths might say about the process of reincarnation, if we accept it as a possibility, when we get to the final chapter.

MANNER OF SPEAKING

The manner in which the children talk about the previous life can vary. Some of the children speak about the past-life memories in a detached way, but many of them show great emotion as they recount events or talk about people from the previous life. Some cry on an almost daily basis to go back to their old family. On the other hand, an American girl named Olivia only talked about a past life once, when she was not yet three years old. During that one instance, her mother reported that she became completely distraught as she talked about needing to get back to her family. Olivia described her son being killed and a man grabbing her arm and refusing to let her go. She cried intensely about this for thirty minutes but then recovered, never to speak about those events again. Her case was unsolved and a mystery in more ways than one. Though there is no evidence of a link to a particular past life, it seems unusual that a child would become that upset in a game of make-believe or because of something she had heard on a television or radio.

Children do not express their apparent knowledge of the previous life as a list of objective facts but as specifics from the viewpoint of one deceased individual. Sujith did not give the facts of Sammy Fernando's life as simply details about a fifty-year-old man but as details about having been this man. He said "my wife" and "my house," showing that he identified himself as the deceased individual.

In doing so, some children use the past tense while others use the present. Sujith frequently talked about people from Sammy's life in the present tense. He was so young when he began talking about that life that we cannot be sure whether this was due to his confusing the past with the present or whether his language skills were simply too primitive to convey his thoughts clearly. Some children do confuse past and present, as they tell their parents, "You are not my parents. My parents live somewhere else." In such situations, the children understandably clamor to be taken to their "real parents." If they have not given enough information to identify the previous parents, their parents can sometimes mollify them by saying, "Yes, you had that life before, but now you are our child in this life." This helps the child distinguish the past from the present.

Some children become preoccupied with the previous life, but others show a tendency to speak with great emotion about the previous life one minute and then to go off and play the next. Some parents say that their children tend to speak about their past life at particular times. In Myanmar, this is often on "gloomy days," during overcast weather. American parents often say that their children usually speak about the previous life during such relaxed times as long car rides or after baths. For reasons that we do not understand, this material seems to be available only at certain times for some children, whereas other children seem able to talk about their memories at any time.

One thing that Sujith's case does not include—as most cases do not—is enlightened words of wisdom. Some of the children who claim to remember events between lives do occasionally make philosophical statements. When Kenny, a boy I mentioned in Chapter 1, was nine years old, he learned that a playmate had died, and told his mother, "I know that it's not good that Greg died, but it's not so bad either. I just wish that his mother knew that it's only Greg's body that is gone. Besides, God expects everyone to go to heaven sooner or later." Even in this case, it is unclear if he said this because of his memories or because of his Catholic religion.

In general, these children tend to focus on people and events from the end of the previous life, and their opinions about them are no different from the ones that we might assume the previous personality had. Some parents say that their children seem more mature or serious-minded than other children their age, but in many ways, the children are indistinguishable from their peers. If we thought that enlightenment came with the memories, we might have to assume that the children would stop being enlightened when they lost the memories. While some children have shown a tendency to be unusually religious or devout, the previous personalities in those cases have often been very devout, and this is not a general pattern for the children overall.

WRITTEN RECORDS

One way that Sujith's case is different from most of the others is that a written record of his statements was made before his previous personality was identified. The cases with written records make up only a small percentage, but this is hardly surprising. In the same-family cases, making a written record before the previous personality has been identified is hardly possible. Many of the others originate in areas where people tend to write down very little. These cases are usually ones in which the families are trying to satisfy themselves that a child is the rebirth of a specific previous personality, but they are not particularly interested in establishing proof for others to see. They might remember what the child said and may discuss it with others, but they usually do not write down the statements.

The number of cases in our research with written records, thirty-three at last count, seems minute compared to the number of cases overall. Collecting thirty-three cases in which written records document accurate statements that a child made about a past life is noteworthy, however, regardless of how many other cases without written records have been found, and we can review a couple more of them.

The Case of Kumkum Verma

Kumkum Verma, a girl in India, began talking about a previous life at the age of three and a half. She said that she had lived in Darbhanga, a city of 200,000 people that was twenty-five miles away from her village, and that Urdu Bazar was the name of the section of the city where she had been. Her father, an educated man who was a landowner, homeopathic physician, and author, did not know anyone in Urdu Bazar, a commercial district where artisans, craftsmen, and owners of small businesses lived.

Kumkum asked her family to call her Sunnary, which means beautiful, and made many statements about the previous life. Her aunt made notes of some of them six months before anyone tried to identify the previous personality. Dr. Stevenson, who met Kumkum's family when she was nine years old, obtained an

English translation of extracts of the notes, but he was unable to get the complete notebook, because it had been lost after being loaned to someone. The extracts listed eighteen statements that Kumkum made that all proved to be correct for the previous personality, including the name of Urdu Bazar, her son's name and the fact that he worked with a hammer, her grandson's name, the name of the town where her father lived, the location of his home near mango orchards, and the presence of a pond at her house. She had correctly stated that she had an iron safe at her house, a sword hanging near her cot, and a snake near the safe to which she fed milk.

Kumkum's father eventually talked about her statements to a friend who lived in Darbhanga. That friend had an employee from the Urdu Bazar section of the city, who was able to identify the previous personality, Sunnary or Sundari Mistry, whom Kumkum seemed to be describing. The previous personality's family belonged to a relatively low artisan class and would have been quite unlikely to have social contact with a family with the education and social status of Dr. Verma's family. In fact, they had little contact even after the case developed. The previous personality's grandson visited Kumkum's family twice. Dr. Verma went to Urdu Bazar once to meet the previous personality's family, but he never allowed Kumkum to go. Apparently he was not proud of his daughter's claim to have been a blacksmith's wife in her previous life.

One interesting note is that Kumkum said that she died during an altercation and that her stepson's wife had poisoned her. Sundari, who died quite unexpectedly five years before Kumkum was born, was preparing to be a witness for her son in his suit against her second husband, involving the son's belief that his stepfather had misappropriated his deceased father's money, when she died. No autopsy was performed, and Kumkum's statement that she was poisoned remained unverified.

Also of note is that Kumkum spoke with an accent different from that of her family. The family associated it with the lower classes of Darbhanga and reported that in addition, Kumkum used some unusual expressions that seemed related to the lower classes as well.

The Case of Jagdish Chandra

The case of Jagdish Chandra in India was quite old when Dr. Stevenson arrived on the scene. The subject was then in his late thirties. The subject's father, a prominent lawyer, had made a written record of the boy's statements and their verifications at the time that the case developed. Jagdish was born in a large city in northern India. When he was three and a half years old, he began saying that he had lived in Benares, a city approximately 300 miles away. He gave a number of details, and his father had several friends and colleagues talk with Jagdish so that they could confirm that he was making those statements. His father then sent a letter to the chairman of the municipal board in Benares. The chairman wrote back that he could tell whom Jagdish was referring to as soon as he read the letter and that he had made inquiries and found that most of the boy's statements were quite accurate.

Jagdish's father then sent a letter to a national newspaper asking for help in verifying the child's statements. In the letter, he said that Jagdish stated that his father was named Babuji Pandey and had a house in Benares with a big gate, a sitting room, and an underground room with an iron safe fixed in one of the walls. *Ji* added to the end of a name means *respected,* so Jagdish was saying that his father was called Babu. He added that Jagdish described a courtyard in which Babuji sat in the evenings and people gathered to drink bhang, an Indian drink. He said that Babuji received massages and put powder or clay on his face after washing it. He described two cars—which were very unusual in India in those days—and a horse-drawn carriage and said that Babuji had two deceased sons and a deceased wife. The father added that his son "described many private and family matters."

The day after this was published, Jagdish's father went to a magistrate to have Jagdish's statements officially recorded before they traveled to Benares, where the previous personality had lived. The recorded statements, in addition to those listed in the paper, included that his name had been Jai Gopal, and that his brother, who was bigger than he was, had been named Jai Mangal and had died of poisoning. The Ganges River was near the house, and the Dash Ashwamadh Ghat was there. (Ghats are piers where people go to bathe, and Babu Pandey was the supervisor of one.) A prostitute named Bhagwati had sung for Babu.

Jagdish was then taken to Benares, where all of the above statements were verified, with the exception that Babu Pandey had used automobiles but not actually owned them. Jagdish appeared to recognize people and places there.

As we look for ways to explain such cases as these, the fact that the child's statements were recorded before anyone attempted to verify them means that we can eliminate one possibility: that the families mistakenly credited the child later with more knowledge about the previous personality than he or she in fact had before the families met. That still leaves several possibilities. One is that the correct statements are coincidental. When we consider how specific some of the children's statements are—for example, Sujith's statement that his father Jamis had a bad right eye, Kumkum's statement that the previous personality kept a snake that she fed milk to, and Jagdish's descriptions of the habits of the previous personality's father—along with the proper names that they gave, coincidence seems extremely unlikely. Fraud is a possibility, but we do not see any motive for one, especially in Kumkum's case, because her father seemed embarrassed about her claim to have been a blacksmith's wife. Jagdish's father appeared interested in documenting an apparent case of reincarnation, but whether this wish could motivate a prominent lawyer to fake a case is certainly open to question. The other normal explanation left is that the children acquired the knowledge about the previous lives through normal means by hearing about the previous personalities. Though this may have been more likely for Sujith than for the other two, since his previous personality had lived closer, the idea that these children somehow learned these minute details about deceased strangers in other places without their parents' knowledge and then decided that they had been those strangers in a past life seems close to absurd.

When we remove the possibility that the children were credited with more information about the previous personality than they in fact had demonstrated, as we can do in cases in which a written record of the statements existed before they were verified, we are left with few palatable options that do not include a paranormal process. If we then find that numerous other cases exist that are similar to these cases in every way except that no written record was made before verification of the statements, can we reasonably discount the others as being situations in which the families mistakenly credited the children with more knowledge than they actually demonstrated?

The Case of Ratana Wongsombat

Ratana Wongsombat was born in Bangkok in 1964. Her adoptive father meditated once a week at the Wat Mahathat, a large temple with more than 300 monks on the other side of Bangkok from the family's home. Ratana began asking to go there. When she was fourteen months old, her father took her for the first time. While they were there, she seemed to show knowledge of the buildings. After they returned home, her father asked her where she had been before this life. She began talking about a previous life at that point and eventually told the following story. She had been a Chinese woman named Kim Lan and had stayed at the temple, where she lived in a green hut with a nun named Mae Chan. After eventually being driven from there, she moved to a district of Bangkok named Banglampoo. She said that she had had only one daughter, who lived in Kim Lan's old hometown, which she named, and Kim Lan had returned there at the end of her life, where she died after surgery. Ratana expressed displeasure that after she died as Kim Lan, her ashes had been scattered rather than buried.

Ratana's father was not familiar with a woman named Kim Lan, and he apparently made no immediate attempts to verify Ratana's statements. When Ratana was two years old, he again took her to the temple. When they passed a large group of nuns there, Ratana appeared to recognize one and called out "Mae Chan" to her. The nun did not respond to her, but Ratana told her father that she had lived with that nun in her previous life. Ratana's father returned to the temple a few days later and spoke with the nun. Her name was Mae Chee Chan Suthipat (*Mae Chee* is an honorific for nuns in Thailand meaning "mother nun"), but some people, including the previous personality, called her Mae Chan. She confirmed that almost all of the statements that Ratana had made, including all the ones listed in this summary, were correct for the life of Kim Lan Prayoon Supamitr, who died one and a half years before Ratana was born.

Kim Lan's daughter also confirmed Ratana's statements, including even the matter of her remains. Kim Lan had wanted her ashes to be buried under the bo tree at the temple complex, but when her daughter tried to honor her wish, the roots of the tree were so extensive that she ended up spreading the ashes rather than burying them.

The Case of Gamini Jayasena

Gamini Jayasena was born in Colombo, Sri Lanka, in 1962, and he began talking about a previous life before he was two years old. Over time, he gave details that included the following: He had another mother who was bigger than his present one. Someone named Nimal had bitten him. He had a schoolbag that was still sitting on a chair. He had a toy elephant that he bathed in a well. He had once fallen into a well. Someone named Charlie

Uncle had a car that he used to drive the subject to school, and Charlie Uncle's family also had a red motorcycle.

Since Gamini did not name a place or give a last name, the case might well have remained unsolved if his family had not taken a bus trip when he was two and a half years old. When the bus stopped briefly at a place called Nittambuwe, Gamini told the person next to him, a family friend, that this had been his home. That person relayed the information to Gamini's parents, who in turn told his mother's cousin, a well-known monk.

The monk decided to look into the matter, and he took the family back to Nittambuwe. They got out of the car at the place where Gamini had made his comment and began walking toward the four houses that were down the road. Gamini said that his mother lived there, but the monk decided not to proceed further. He apparently was unsure if this was the correct place and was concerned that he would likely be entering the home of a Christian family. Gamini's family thought he was probably remembering the life of a Christian because he knelt during prayer with his trunk erect rather than with his buttocks resting on his heels in the typical Buddhist position, and because he had once asked his mother to hang up a wooden cross he had found. The family returned to Colombo, but some Nittambuwe villagers had recognized the monk during the family's stop and told a family living at the place indicated by Gamini. This family, which was in fact a Christian family, had lost a son two years before Gamini was born. The boy, named Palitha, had died after a short illness. Just before getting sick, he had returned from school on vacation and left his schoolbag on a chair instead of putting it in the cupboard as he usually did, while announcing that he would not be going to school again.

He had a younger brother named Nimal, who had once bitten him.

Palitha's parents visited the monk. They gave the monk a picture of Palitha that Gamini subsequently appeared to recognize. Following that, Gamini's family returned to Nittambuwe to meet Palitha's parents. There, Gamini was judged to recognize a number of people and places. When he was taken to Palitha's school and the boardinghouse where Palitha stayed while attending school, he made additional recognitions and statements about Palitha's life.

All of Gamini's statements listed here proved to be correct for Palitha, except that Charles Senewiratne, Palitha's uncle, owned a car but did not drive Palitha to school. No possible connection could be found between Gamini's family in Colombo and Palitha's family in Nittambuwe, some twenty miles away.

In both of these cases, no written record of the children's statements was made before the previous personality was identified, but if we are going to decide that the families credited the children with more knowledge than they initially possessed—for instance, that they did not really give the proper names they were said to have given—then we have to explain why these cases would be different from the ones in which written records document that the children did in fact make very specific statements. They show that some children can make specific statements about past lives that are later found to be accurate for a particular deceased individual, and since the cases are so similar in all other ways, the ones with the written records have to make us question the explanation of falsely credited information for many of the other cases.

Making a Strong Case

In looking at cases without written records, some types are stronger than others. For instance, cases in which the children repeated their claims over and over again are stronger than ones in which they did not, because the parents had a better chance to recall accurately what the children had said even though they did not have the benefit of notes.

Another feature that strengthens a case is an intermediary being present between the families. Purnima's case from Chapter 4 is a good example of this. Her father told a teacher about her statements of having been an incense maker, and the teacher and his brother-in-law located the previous personality's family. In such a situation, the intermediaries serve as additional witnesses to the child's statements, of course, but more importantly, they also serve as third parties who are more disinterested. Although the teacher and his brother-in-law were curious about whether Purnima's statements would match anyone's life in Kelaniya, they did not have the emotional investment in confirming the statements that a parent might.

Another feature that makes a case stronger is multiple witnesses. When written records are not available to show exactly what the child said, having ten witnesses who recall a child making a statement is obviously better than only having one. We always attempt to interview as many informants as possible. That is not to say that the memories of several individuals cannot mold together to form an inaccurate story, but the chances of inaccurate memory clearly decrease as more witnesses are available.

Occasionally, inaccurate statements by the child can even strengthen a case. In this situation, the child's version of events is different from the "official version," showing that his or her statements were not reconstructed after the fact. An example is the case of a boy named Ekkaphong that Dr. Keil and I investigated in Thailand. In that case, the previous personality was a young man in Ekkaphong's village who was accidentally killed while on a hunting outing with three friends. One of them dropped his rifle, which discharged and shot the young man. People in the village all identified a friend named Aet as the one whose rifle discharged, but Ekkaphong was so convinced that it was another friend named Phon that as a toddler, he tried to strangle Phon. He could not have obtained that belief from others in the village, since they thought that Aet was the one who dropped his rifle. It also makes no sense that the villagers would have falsely claimed to us that Ekkaphong had accused Phon incorrectly.

A case like this in which the subject and the previous personality were from the same village is not as impressive as when children report memories of the life of an individual who was completely unknown to their family. We see many cases of both types. In 971 cases from various cultures, 195 were same-family cases. In another sixty, the two families had a close association before the cases developed. In 115, they had a slight association. In ninety-three cases, the subject's family knew of the previous personality but had no association with him or her. Of the 971 cases, 508 were stranger cases. Of those, 239 were solved cases, 232 were unsolved, and a tentative identification had been made in the rest. Thus, we see a wide range of connections in the cases.

Considering the Explanations

Many of these cases are very similar to the cases of Indika and Purnima from the last chapter, only without the birthmarks. In some of them, fantasy along with coincidence might be used as an explanation if the child's statements are not too specific. When the child gives very specific details, however—for example, when Ratana Wongsombat stated the name of the previous personality, the places where she had lived, and even the fact that the previous personality's remains were scattered rather than buried—I think we can remove coincidence as a reasonable explanation.

One possibility is that the children learned about the previous life in normal ways. This can apply in the same-family cases and in ones where the child and the previous personality are from the same village. It gets less believable when we are talking about strangers who lived some distance away. The previous personality in Ratana's case lived for some time at a temple that Ratana's father attended, but since it was a very large temple on the other side of Bangkok from where Ratana lived, it is hard to see how Ratana could have learned about her. Many of the cases do not even have that kind of slight connection, so we cannot reasonably assume that the children somehow learned various personal details about their previous personalities by overhearing people talk about them.

In the case of Sujith Jayaratne, the previous personality lived in a village that was only seven miles from the child's home, so we might think that he had heard of the previous personality. When we consider, however, that the previous personality's village was a very different environment from the Colombo suburb where Sujith lived and that no one else in Sujith's family had ever heard of the previous personality, much less his father with a bad right eye, knowledge acquired through normal means does not seem a reasonable explanation either. When we add cases such as Kumkum Verma, whose previous personality lived twenty-five miles away, and Kemal Atasoy, the Turkish boy in the Introduction whose previous personality lived 500 miles away, it becomes quite unreasonable.

In such a situation, that problem is then compounded by the question of how, for instance, overhearing someone talk about a person in a market could lead children to identify with a deceased person who had led an ordinary life. On the whole, this explanation makes little sense for cases in which the families did not know the previous personalities and where we have no reason to think that the children would have even heard of them.

This brings us back to the possibility of faulty memory by informants. If we are going to use a normal explanation, we almost have to use this one for these cases. We can decide, for example, that Ratana did not actually say that the ashes of the previous personality were scattered rather than buried but that her father later recalled incorrectly that she did. Problems certainly exist with this explanation—the children have often made their claims repeatedly and multiple witnesses often recall the same specific claims—but without written documentation as evidence, we can try to place the blame on imperfect human memory.

This explanation fails when we consider cases in which a written record was made of the children's statements before the previous personality was identified. We cannot blame faulty memory in those cases, and as we have just seen, the other options for explaining the statements are limited. When Sujith Jayaratne said that the father of the previous personality was named Jamis and had a bad right eye, we can hardly think that all of his statements were due to coincidence. In fact, given the specificity of the statements in many of the cases, I would not have thought that any reasonable person would say that coincidence could be used to explain them, but Richard Wiseman, a psychologist at the University of Hertfordshire in Great Britain, has made that argument. He did an experiment in which he asked a few young children to make up stories about past lives, and he then tried to find a report of a death that matched the details that the child gave. His argument is that our cases could be like his, in which young children simply make up stories that in some ways match facts for a particular deceased person.

Dr. Wiseman has not published the results of his work, but he discussed it on two television documentaries in which we both participated. In his best case, a little girl named Molly told a story of a three-year-old girl named Katie, who was bitten by a monster and died. He then searched through newspaper archives and found a report of a three-year-old girl named Rosie who was kidnapped and killed. Molly's story had a number of features that were true for Rosie, including red hair, blue eyes, and a pink dress with flowers on it. Molly did not give a specific location but said that Katie had lived near the sea, which Rosie in fact did.

This case has obvious critical differences from ours. Along with the fact that Molly's story had the fantastic element of the monster, her description did not include a correct name of the child or a specific location, factors that are often crucial in our cases. While Dr. Wiseman's work may show that with a large enough archive, people can find some interesting things, it does not relate to cases of families going to specific places looking for specific people. In some ways, his study demonstrates that coincidence fails to explain important parts of the cases, even though his intention was to show the opposite.

This leaves us with out-and-out fraud as an explanation for the cases with written records. Of course, fraud could be used for the other cases we have talked about as well. Several problems exist with this option. First of all, we have no reason to question the integrity of the informants, who give us their time and attention while getting no benefit whatsoever from the investigations, and I think talking with these families about their experiences would convince any fair person that the people are being as straightforward and honest as they can be.

Second, in many of the cases, the families involved have no motive at all to perpetrate a fraud. Why would Sujith Jayaratne's mother convince him to pretend to have been a bootlegger? In Kumkum Verma's case, her father was not proud of her claim to have been in a lower class, and he never even allowed her to visit the previous family. Therefore, we have no reason to think that he coerced her into making her claims. Kemal Atasoy belonged to a prosperous family, and his parents would have absolutely no reason to encourage him to claim to have been a man who died fifty years before.

Third, in addition to the motive problems, engineering a fraud would not be feasible in many of the cases. The star of the show is usually a very young child, hardly the most reliable kind of person to use if you are trying to fool someone. Also, in many cases several people state that they have heard the children talk about the previous life over time, so we might have to decide that all of them would be involved in the fraud. The children are often said to recognize people or things from the previous life as well, and we can wonder how the parents would be able to help them do this.

In summary, the idea that a large number of these cases arise out of fraud does not really make sense, and were it not for the lack of alternative explanations, we would hardly even consider the possibility. In some ways, when people make an accusation of fraud without any evidence for it, they are admitting that they do not have a way of explaining a phenomenon. Labeling these cases as fraud means that we do not have an adequate normal explanation for them, but since we do not, we have to resort to fraud if we do not want to consider the paranormal explanations.

Regarding the paranormal explanations, ESP certainly seems worth considering, since the children appear to have knowledge about the previous life that they could not have obtained through normal means. As I discussed in Chapter 3, such an explanation presents several problems. Individuals who appear capable of extrasensory perception generally show abilities in more than one circumstance, except for cases in which two close family members appear at times to show a telepathic connection to each other. This situation is quite different, in that children who show no other paranormal abilities are able to give very specific details of the life of a deceased individual. The ESP explanation would also be in complete contrast to the subjective impression of the children, who believe they are recalling memories from the perspective of the deceased individual whose life they previously led.

Possession might also be able to explain the statements, but several factors argue against it. Although the children are often said to share some traits with the previous personality, no one says that they suddenly become the previous person. In addition, the statements are often intermittent. In many cases, the memories do not appear to be accessible to the children all the time, as they would if the previous personality had taken over the body. This might make us consider some type of temporary possession, except that the children do not lose the memories or personalities of their current life when they have the memories of the previous one. Lastly, the statements almost always start at a very early age. If these were examples of possession, then we might expect them to occur at various ages rather than only when the children are beginning to talk.

Reincarnation clearly explains the statements, as the children say that they remember previous lives. Several factors about the statements are odd, however, if reincarnation is the explanation. One, again, is that the memories do not appear to be accessible at all times to many of the children. If a child is a rebirth and is able to recall memories of the previous life, then we might think that he or she would be able to recall them all the time. While many of the children do not have access to the memories at all times, the other aspects of the cases show that the memories are more than just intermittent knowledge of paranormal material, as the ESP scenario would say. These "memories" are very meaningful to many of the children, and they certainly feel ownership of them, as if they are of prior events that the children experienced.

The statements often seem to represent a very incomplete description of the previous life. Some of the children, of course, appear to remember seemingly countless details of the previous life, but others report only a few. This might seem odd with respect to reincarnation until we compare it to memories from early in our lives. Early memories are often quite fuzzy, and at times, insignificant details can stand out as much as important events. Just as Kumkum Verma remembered that her father in the previous life lived near mango orchards, we might recall a particular feature about a place or perhaps a person we knew. The children talk about people and events from near the end of the previous life, because those memories are less distant than earlier ones.

The statements the children make remain the core of the cases. As we have seen, the children are often said to possess knowledge about a deceased individual that their parents feel they could not have obtained by normal means. Though this knowledge provides the strongest evidence in the cases, the other features we study are important in showing that this phenomenon is about more than just the statements. Behaviors like Sujith's phobia of trucks that began in infancy and his desire for alcohol and tobacco clearly demand an explanation. We will look more at such behaviors in the next chapter.

CHAPTER 6

Unusual Behaviors

Kendra Carter, a girl who lives in Florida, was four and a half years old when she went to her first swimming lesson with a coach named Ginger. She immediately jumped into Ginger's lap and acted very lovingly toward her. When Ginger had to cancel a lesson three weeks later, Kendra sobbed uncontrollably. When she was able to have a lesson soon after, she was very happy and began talking about Ginger all the time.

A few weeks later, Kendra began saying that Ginger's baby had died and that Ginger had been sick and had pushed her baby out. When her mother asked her how she knew these things, Kendra replied, "I'm the baby that was in her tummy." At that point, Kendra had only seen Ginger at their lessons, and her mother knew that the two of them had never been alone. Kendra described an abortion, saying that Ginger had allowed a bad man to pull her out and that she had tried to hang on but could not. She described being scared in a dark and cold place afterwards. Kendra's mother eventually found out from Ginger that she had in fact had an abortion nine years before Kendra was born when she was unmarried, sick, and dealing with anorexia nervosa.

Kendra began saying that she would die, because Ginger had been unable to deliver her. She said, "I have to die, and I won't come back this time." This fear of dying became so severe that Kendra's mother took her to a therapist, who suggested a ceremony in which Kendra would be "born" to Ginger. Following this, her fear of dying seemed to resolve.

Even though Ginger was often cool toward her, Kendra began being very bubbly and happy when she was with Ginger but quiet and withdrawn otherwise. Her mother allowed her to spend more and more time with Ginger. Eventually, Ginger set up a room for Kendra in her home, and Kendra spent three nights a week there. Kendra's absences were hard for her mother, but she permitted them, because Kendra's wish to be with Ginger was so intense.

Unfortunately, Ginger and Kendra's mother eventually had a falling-out, and Ginger said that she did not want to see Kendra anymore. Following this, Kendra did not speak for four and a half months. She showed no interest in activities, ate little, and slept a lot. At the end of that time, Ginger met with Kendra for two hours. During this meeting, Kendra talked again for the first time when she told Ginger that she loved her. Ginger began calling Kendra again, but Kendra did not feel comfortable going to her home. Kendra slowly began talking more, and she began participating more in activities.

Kendra's mother found all of this very troubling. Her daughter's struggle with the situation upset her, and the possibility of reincarnation troubled her as well. She attended a conservative Christian church, and she felt that she was committing a sin by merely buying a book on reincarnation during Kendra's troubles. She decided that perhaps Kendra's spirit had been looking for another body after Ginger's abortion, but she did not accept the idea that reincarnation is a process that normally occurs.

This case presents us with a number of perplexing questions. Why would a four-year-old girl think that she had been involved in an abortion? What caused her to develop the idea of reincarnation when she was being raised by a mother who could not even consider the possibility? And why did she become so emotionally attached to a woman who was often not very warm toward her?

Surviving Emotions

The depression that Kendra suffered is an example of the emotional component that is present in many of these cases. To hear of children crying for years for their family to take them to their previous parents until the family finally relents is not unusual. Other children can show emotional outbursts for a very short time, just as Olivia in the last chapter became distraught during the one time that she talked about losing her family. In addition to the longing for the previous family that many of the children demonstrate, some show emotions toward individual members of that family that would be appropriate for the relationship that the previous personality had with that person. For instance, the children are often deferential toward a husband or parents of the previous personality, but they may be bossy toward younger siblings, even if the siblings are adults at the time that the young subjects meet them.

Sukla Gupta in India is another subject who showed great emotion. She was less than two years old when she began the habit of cradling a block of wood or a pillow and calling it "Minu." She said that Minu was her daughter, and during the next three years, she gradually spoke more about a previous life. She gave a number of details, including the name and section of a village eleven miles away. A woman there who had an infant daughter named Minu had died six years before Sukla was born and was identified as the previous personality. When Sukla was five years old, her family went to meet the family of the previous personality. She cried when she met Minu, then eleven years old, and she appeared affectionate and maternal toward her. At one point, one of the previous personality's cousins tested Sukla by telling her falsely that Minu was sick with a high fever. Sukla began to weep, and she could not be comforted for some time. In another instance, Minu actually was sick, and when Sukla learned the news, she began crying and demanded to be taken to her. She remained agitated until the next day when her family took her to see Minu, who had improved by then.

Sukla also appeared deferential toward the previous personality's husband. After they met, she longed for him to visit her. He did so weekly for about a year, until his second wife complained about the visits, and he began to visit less frequently. Sukla talked less about the previous life after the age of seven, and she also gradually lost her feelings of attachment toward the previous personality's husband and Minu. By the time she was an early teen, she complained that they were pestering her when they came to visit.

The feelings of the subjects do not always diminish over time, and at least one subject, Maung Aye Kyaw in Myanmar, grew up to marry the widow of the previous personality. The longevity of the feelings often depends on how much contact the families have after they initially meet. Many of the families become quite friendly, with frequent visits at least initially, but some are resistant. This resistance may relate to the previous family's occasional concern that the subject's family is looking for gifts from them or the feeling of the subject's family that the child may become too attached to the previous one. Significant socioeconomic distance between the families can also produce awkwardness at times.

Subjects can also show very negative feelings toward figures in the life of the previous personality. I have already mentioned the case of Ekkaphong, who tried to strangle the man he thought was responsible for the death of the previous personality. Other subjects have shown either similar anger or fear toward the individuals that they said killed the previous personality. Bongkuch Promsin, a case I will discuss in more detail in Chapter 8, said that he would kill the previous personality's murderers when he grew up, but his threats fortunately lessened as he became older. Maung Aye Kyaw, the subject who married the widow of his previous personality, threw stones at one of the men he said had killed him in his previous life, and other subjects have done the same with the killers or alleged killers of their previous personalities.

Fear-death Experiences

Many of the subjects show a phobia that relates to the mode of death of the previous personality. In cases in which the previous personality died by unnatural means, more than 35 percent of the subjects show phobias related to the previous life. They seem particularly common in drowning cases, appearing in thirty-one out of fifty-three cases. We might speculate that this increased frequency could be because drowning victims spend more time in the process of dying than individuals who are killed in an automobile accident or shot to death.

These phobias can appear when the children are very young. Shamlinie Prema, whom I mentioned in Chapter 1, showed an intense fear of being immersed in water from the time she was an infant. Three people had to hold her down for her baths. Beginning at the age of six months, she also showed a great fear of buses. When she became old enough to talk, she reported memories of the life of a girl in the nearby village of Galtudawa, and, in fact, her first words were "Galtudawa mother." The girl in Galtudawa was eleven years old when she died one and a half years before Shamlinie was born. She had been walking along a narrow road when a bus came by. When she tried to step out of its way, she fell into a flooded patty field next to the road and drowned.

Shamlinie began getting over her fear of being bathed when she was three years old, and the fear had completely resolved by the time she was four. Her fear of buses lasted longer, until she was at least five and a half years old, which was about the time that she stopped talking spontaneously about the previous life. Shamlinie's behavior was similar to that of Sujith Jayaratne, the boy in the previous chapter who showed a fear of trucks, and even of the word *lorry*, before he was a year old and before he related details of the life of a man who died when a truck ran over him.

In general, as the children grow older, the phobias tend to diminish along with the statements about the previous life. Exceptions do exist in which older children still show a fear even though they apparently no longer have memories of the events from the previous life that seemed to be connected to it.

Unacquired Tastes

Sujith Jayaratne's case demonstrates another unusual behavior we have found in some of these cases—interest in addictive substances that the previous personality used. Sujith displayed a desire to indulge in alcohol and cigarettes, and a number of the other subjects have as well. Though not common, thirty-four of the children out of 1,100 cases showed an unusual desire for alcohol or tobacco that was consistent with the previous personality's tastes.

Some of the children show unusual food habits and preferences, which can be problematic for some of the Indian children who report memories of lives in higher castes than their own. Jasbir Singh, an Indian boy, reported memories of the life of a Brahmin, a higher caste than that of his family. He refused to eat his family's food, and a kind Brahmin neighbor agreed to prepare food for him in the Brahmin manner. This went on for more than a year and a half until the boy finally relented to eating his family's food.

In some cases, the subject may be the only person in the family to enjoy a food for which the previous personality had a particular fondness. This is especially noticeable in the international cases. Dr. Stevenson, with some recent additions by Dr. Keil, has collected two dozen cases of Burmese children who reported being Japanese soldiers killed in Burma during World War II. None of the children has given enough specific details to identify a previous personality in Japan, but the children's behavior has often been quite distinctive, including food preferences. A number of these children complain about the spicy Burmese food and prefer sweet foods and raw or partially cooked fish.

The case of Ma Tin Aung Myo, born in 1953, is a good example. During her pregnancy, her mother dreamed three times that a Japanese army cook whom she had known during the Japanese army's occupation of Burma followed her and said that he wanted to come and stay with her family. When Ma Tin Aung Myo was four years old, she was walking with her father one day when she became very upset as an airplane flew overhead. After that, she cried every time a plane flew over, a behavior she showed for a number of years. She said that she was afraid that the planes would shoot her. Around that time, she began saying that she longed for Japan, and she gradually told the story of being a Japanese soldier who was killed by machine-gun fire from a low-flying plane while he was stationed in her family's village.

In addition to her phobia of planes and her longing for Japan, Ma Tin Aung Myo complained of the hot Burmese climate. She also did not like spicy Burmese food and preferred to eat sweet foods, and she liked fish, particularly half-cooked fish, as a young child. She used words that her family could not understand, but since no one around her knew Japanese, we have no way of determining if these might have been Japanese words.

Ma Tin Aung Myo did not show one feature that the children in a number of these Burmese-Japanese cases have shown, which is a great reluctance to wear traditional Burmese attire. Burmese men and women generally wear *longyis,* a garment similar to an ankle-length skirt, with shirts or blouses, but a number of the children have insisted on wearing trousers instead, as Japanese men would do.

These cases of Burmese children who claim to remember lives as Japanese soldiers are similar to the unsolved case of Carl Edon, a British boy who seemed to remember the life of a German pilot in World War II. Born in 1972, he began saying, "I crashed a plane through a window" when he was two years old. He gradually added details about having been on a bombing mission over England when he crashed. When he became able to draw, he drew swastikas and eagles and, later, the panel of a cockpit. He also demonstrated the Nazi salute and the goose-step march of German soldiers. He said that he wanted to live in Germany. He, unlike the other members of his family, liked to eat sausages and thick soups.

In addition to behaviors indicating a difference in nationality, some cases show behaviors indicative of a class or caste difference. I have already mentioned Jasbir Singh, who refused to eat non-Brahmin food. He also used terms for some objects that those in higher classes generally used. He continued to think of himself as a Brahmin as he grew older. As an adult, he had trouble getting a job that he did not consider beneath him. Some children have also shown unusual behaviors in the opposite direction. Swaran Lata, a girl who was born into a Brahmin family, reported memories of being a sweepress, a woman who sweeps streets and cleans latrines. She tended to be quite dirty and cleaned up the stools of younger children. She also resisted going to school when she was young by saying, "We are sweepers. Nobody studies in our family, and I never sent my children to school."

The Play's the Thing

A prominent area of behavior in these cases is that of the children's play. In Chapter 1, I mentioned Parmod Sharma, a boy who played at being a biscuit shopkeeper with such persistence that his schooling suffered. Such play is common, with at least a quarter of the subjects showing themes in their play that seem connected to the previous life. This often involves play mimicking the occupation of the previous personality as in Parmod's case, but other forms occur as well. I have described the case of Sukla Gupta, who would cradle a piece of wood or a pillow in her arms and call it "Minu," the name of the previous personality's daughter.

Some children act out the way the previous personality died. Maung Myint Soe, a boy in Myanmar who reported memories of a man who drowned on a ferryboat, would from time to time act out a scene in which he pretended to attempt an escape from a sinking boat. Ramez Shams of Lebanon reenacted the suicide of the previous personality by repeatedly putting a stick under his chin while pretending that it was a rifle. Such play is rare in our cases but when present is very similar to the play of children who have survived a major traumatic event in this lifetime. Those children may show behavior known as post-traumatic play in which they reenact the scene with dolls or other objects.

If our subjects are in fact cases of reincarnation, then this play, along with the phobias that some of the subjects show toward the mode of death of the previous personality, demonstrates that the emotional trauma of a violent death can carry over from one life to the next. Though this is not surprising in some ways and is consistent with birthmarks arising from fatal injuries in the previous life, the idea that those who experience difficult deaths have trouble putting the trauma immediately behind them is a sobering one.

Changing Sexes

In the sex-change cases, cases in which the child claims to remember the life of a member of the opposite sex, we have observed cross-gender behavior. In one series of sex-change cases, twenty-one out of thirty-four cases (62 percent), showed behavior that was appropriate for the opposite sex. Examples include Kloy Matwiset, the boy in Chapter 4 born with a birthmark on the back of his neck that matched an experimental mark made on his grandmother's body. He showed a number of cross-gender behaviors, including saying that he wanted to be a girl, sitting down to urinate, and repeatedly wearing his mother's lipstick, earrings, and dresses.

The other sex-change case I have described is Ma Tin Aung Myo, the Burmese girl who reported memories of the life of a Japanese soldier killed in Burma during World War II. She also showed a strong identification as a male. When she was young, she played with boys, and, in particular, she liked to pretend to be a soldier. She said that she wanted to be a soldier and asked her parents to buy toy guns for her. She also insisted on wearing boys' clothes, and this produced a crisis when school authorities demanded that she come to school dressed as a girl. She refused and dropped out of school at the age of eleven. As a young adult, she continued to identify herself as a male, and she preferred that people address her using a male honorific instead of a female one. Dr. Stevenson last saw her family when she was twenty-seven years old. At that point, she was living with her steady girlfriend in another town. Her family reported that she still talked about wanting to join the army and continued to dress as a male.

Before we consider what could lead to this cross-gender behavior, we need to look at current thinking about gender identity
disorder in general. It is a disorder in which children show an
identification with the opposite sex and discomfort with their
own sex. Though quite a bit of research has been done, its cause
is still largely unknown. A number of biological and psychological factors are thought to be required to interact during a critical
time period to produce the disorder. Some have speculated that
sex hormones during pregnancy could be involved, but little direct evidence is available to support that.

Most of the research that has been done on gender identity
disorder has been with boys. Though rare among all children, it
is much more common in boys than in girls. In that research,
no clear evidence exists that mothers of boys with the disorder
want to have a girl more than other mothers, but in some cases,
their disappointment about not having had a girl may affect
how they relate to their sons. Other factors that may be associated include psychological disturbance in the parents, anxiety in
many of the children about separating from their parents, and
such psychological issues as a distant father-son relationship and
a mother's perception that females are more nurturing than
males.

In Kloy's case, his parents thought that he was his grandmother reborn because of the birthmark on his neck, and we
might wonder if they unconsciously steered his behavior to be
feminine because of that, even though they said that they did not
talk to him about the previous life and that they discouraged his
cross-gender behaviors. The same scenario occurred in the case of
Ma Tin Aung Myo. Her mother's dreams about the Japanese soldier may have at least raised the possibility in her mind that he

would be reborn as her child, but she did not intentionally encourage Ma Tin Aung Myo to want to be a boy.

Whether a mother's wishes or expectations could exert a significant influence over a child's subsequent gender identity is not clear. Cases have recently been reported in which boys were raised as girls after they had accidents as infants in which they lost their penises. In one case, the patient did develop a female gender identity but also had a childhood history of being a "tomboy" and developed a bisexual orientation while being mainly attracted to women. In the others, the patients developed male gender identities despite their parents' best efforts to raise them as girls, so we have little reason to think that the parents in our cases, because of their past-life beliefs, could have unconsciously interacted with their children in ways that produced the gender identity disorder.

The case of Erin Jackson, an American whose Protestant parents did not believe in reincarnation before the case developed, is a strong example. When she was three years old, she talked about having been a boy and described a life with a stepmother and a brother, James, who only liked to wear black. She did not give any direct details of when that life took place, but she appeared to be remembering a life in the distant past, because she would say things like, "It was lots better when there were horses. These cars are awful. They've just ruined everything."

Erin sometimes said that she wished she were a boy, and she insisted on dressing as one when she was little. This extended to bathing suits. When Erin would only wear the bottom of a two-piece suit, her mother learned to buy one-piece suits. As Erin grew older, she would wear a dress perhaps three times a year, and then only if it did not have lace or ruffles.

We can consider several possibilities to explain cross-gender behavior in our cases. One is that the cross-gender behavior and the past-life claims only occur together by coincidence. Arguing against that are the dozens of cases we have that involve the combination of a gender identity disorder, which is a rare disorder, with claims of having been a member of the opposite sex. With so many cases, we must conclude that the two are connected.

We might like to suppose that the cross-gender behavior displayed by Kloy Matwiset and Ma Tin Aung Myo came because their parents thought they were the rebirths of members of the opposite sex, but we cannot do so in Erin's case. Her parents did not expect her to be the rebirth of anyone, and her talk of having been a boy, which occurred in combination with her boyish behavior, obviously came as a complete surprise. We might decide that her wish to be a boy happened first and that she then added a fantasy of having been a boy in a previous life. Such an explanation for these cases—that the gender identity disorder leads to the past-life claims—does not apply to Kloy's case because his parents thought that he might be his grandmother reborn before he ever had a gender identity. These cases put us in a bind when we look for a normal explanation. In Erin's case, we might like to blame the cross-gender wishes for producing the past-life beliefs, while in Kloy's case, we would be more inclined to blame the past-life beliefs for producing cross-gender behavior.

Since the connection between the cross-gender behavior and the belief that the child had a previous life as a member of the opposite sex can occur in either order, one of them does not always cause the other. How, then, do we explain the behavior? The final normal explanation would be that the families have exaggerated the extent of the cross-gender behaviors because of their belief that the child had a previous life as a member of the opposite sex. This seems quite unlikely in cases as extreme as that of Ma Tin Aung Myo, who once told Dr. Stevenson and his interpreter that they could kill her by any means they wanted if they could guarantee that she would be reborn as a male. Dr. Stevenson noted that they had no wish to carry out the former and no power to implement the latter.

Twins Who Remember

Subjects who are identical twins offer a unique contribution to our understanding of the behavior of these children. In Chapter 4, I discussed Indika Ishwara, an identical twin in Sri Lanka who described the life of a boy who had died of encephalitis at the age of ten. Indika's twin brother, Kakshappa, also claimed to remember a previous life. He spoke of it before Indika did, claiming that the police had shot him. Judging from other statements he made, his family decided he was talking about the life of an insurgent who died during an uprising in Sri Lanka in 1971. The family laughed at his claims, and he soon stopped making them.

The twins showed some differences in temperament and behavior. Indika, who remembered the life of a schoolboy, tended to be gentle and calm, while Kakshappa, who recalled the life of an insurgent, presented himself as being tough and tended to be hostile and aggressive. Indika was religious as a young child, as his previous personality was, but Kakshappa was not. Indika was more intelligent and was interested and successful in his schoolwork, while Kakshappa did poorly in school. Indika's features even matched those of the boy whose life he appeared to remember. The twins' parents noted that the differences in their personalities lessened as they grew older.

How do we explain the differences that they showed initially? Their statements about the previous lives seem to have come too late to cause their parents to interact with them in a manner that would produce the differences. As some twins develop, they show contrasting interests that emphasize each child's uniqueness. In this case, the way that the differences began early and lessened over time is more consistent with an inborn factor than with an environmental one, but we cannot use this normal explanation of inborn differences since the boys are identical twins. If the differences that were present initially were due to carryover from the previous lives, then the fact that they lessened suggests either that the effect from the previous lives naturally dissipated over time or that experiences in the current life gradually had a larger and larger effect on the boys.

The Case of the Pollock Twins

Gillian and Jennifer Pollock, born in Hexham, Northumberland, England, in 1958, form another interesting case involving identical twins. Their older sisters, Joanna and Jacqueline, had been killed a year and a half before the twins were born when a car struck them as they walked to church. When their mother became pregnant with Gillian and Jennifer, their father, who, unlike their mother, believed in reincarnation, stated confidently that the two deceased girls were going to be reborn as twins, despite the obstetrician's statement that only one fetus was present.

When the twins were born, their parents noticed two birthmarks on Jennifer, the younger twin, that matched two marks that had been present on Jacqueline, the younger of the deceased girls. One matched a birthmark that Jacqueline had on her hip, and the other matched a scar that Jacqueline had received when she fell on a bucket and cut her forehead. Gillian, the older of the twins, had no birthmarks.

The family moved from Hexham when the twins were nine months old. When they were three years old, they began talking about their older sisters, and in particular, their mother overheard them several times discussing details of the accident in which their sisters were killed. In addition, their parents had packed the toys of the older girls away when they were killed, but later got two dolls out. When the twins saw them, Gillian claimed the doll that had belonged to Joanna, the oldest sister, while Jennifer claimed Jacqueline's. They said that Santa Claus had given them the dolls, and their older sisters, in fact, had received them as Christmas presents. In addition, when Gillian saw a toy clothes wringer that had been a Christmas gift of Joanna's, she said, "Look! There is my toy wringer," and stated that Santa Claus had given it to her.

One day, Gillian pointed to the birthmark on Jennifer's forehead and said, "That is the mark Jennifer got when she fell on a bucket." While Jennifer had not had an accident producing the mark, Jacqueline had indeed fallen on a bucket, receiving an injury that required stitches and produced a permanent scar. At another time, when their father was painting, he wore a smock their mother had previously used when the older girls were alive. Jennifer saw it and asked, "Why are you wearing Mummy's coat?" When her father asked her how she knew that it was her mother's, she correctly responded that her mother had worn the smock when delivering milk.

When the twins were four years old, the family returned to Hexham for the first time to visit for the day. As the family walked along a road near a park where the older girls had frequently played, the twins said that they wanted to go across the road to the swings in the park. Neither the swings nor even the park was visible when they said this.

In addition to Jennifer's birthmarks and the twins' statements, the girls also demonstrated behaviors consistent with the lives of their older sisters. Gillian tended to "mother" Jennifer, who accepted her leadership, just as Joanna had tended to mother Jacqueline, who was five years younger. In addition, when the twins learned to write at around the age of four and a half, Gillian immediately held a pencil between her thumb and fingers, but Jennifer held a pencil upright in her fist. Jacqueline, who was six years old when she was killed, had persisted in holding her pencil this way despite her teacher's best efforts to get her to hold it properly. Jennifer eventually learned the correct grip when she was seven years old, but she lapsed into using the previous one at times even as an adult. Since she and Gillian were identical twins in the same environment, this difference is puzzling.

The obvious weakness of this case is the father's conviction before the twins were even born that they were the reincarnation of their sisters. It may have increased the connections he thought he observed and even the twins' propensity to talk about the sisters, though it clearly did not cause Jennifer's birthmarks. The twins stopped making any statements about their sisters at the age of seven. Their mother, who had not believed in reincarnation initially, by then was convinced by their statements, birthmarks, and behaviors that they were their deceased sisters reborn, sharing the belief that their father had voiced while they were still in the womb.

Explaining the behavioral differences in our identical twin subjects is a significant challenge. The two cases I have presented show that not only do the identical twin subjects show these differences, but the differences are quite consistent with the previous lives the children describe. These cases of twins bring up the issue of what contributes to personality. In general, scientists have assumed that individual differences of any kind are due to genetic or environmental factors. In child development, the degree of influence of genetics versus environment is controversial, but temperament is one useful concept of the biological factors that contribute to personality differences. Temperament refers to how individuals perform behaviors, as opposed to why they perform them, which is motivation, or what they perform, which is ability. Biological factors like temperament interact with environmental factors to produce the various personality differences in individuals. The temperament shown in early childhood tends to be stable, but as a child ages, temperament characteristics can change.

When we consider identical twins, we are dealing with two individuals who have the same genetic makeup. As expected, identical twins show a great deal of similarity in temperament, much more so than fraternal twins, but the similarity is not 100 percent. Since temperament is thought to be a biological dimension, the differences in identical twins become difficult to explain, because their genetic makeup is identical.

To explain personality differences in identical twins, we

must consider environmental factors. Most twins have the same general environment, but perhaps parents respond uniquely to each twin and produce differences that way. In addition, these cases suggest that, along with heredity and environment, we should consider the idea that differences may be caused by what the consciousness brings to a new life.

Emotional Consequences

The various behaviors in this chapter are evidence supporting the reincarnation explanation and indicate that more than just memories may be able to survive from one life to the next. Emotions, attachments, fears, addictions, likes and dislikes, and even identification with a particular country and with a gender may be able to carry over from one life to the next. If reincarnation does occur, emotions as well as memories survive.

The emotions do not necessarily continue throughout this life. The behaviors often persist past the point when the children stop talking about a previous life, but they generally fade away over time. Most of the subjects in sex-change cases eventually take on a gender identity consistent with their anatomical sex. Ma Tin Aung Myo, who showed a male gender identity as an adult, was an exception. We have plenty of cases where the emotions and behaviors did not fade away, but given the complications that can occur in such a situation, perhaps letting them go when they will is the best thing to do.

Along these lines, Kendra's case is a cautionary tale, as it shows the difficulty that can develop from apparent memories and demonstrates that talk about a previous life is not fun and games for the children involved. Kendra became extremely attached to her coach Ginger, and she was devastated when the attachment was ultimately disrupted. She would have been better off if she had not held the belief that she had been in Ginger's womb. Dr. Stevenson has written about the suffering in other cases as well. As he points out, many of the children suffer tremendously, because they feel separated from the families to which they feel such a strong attachment. Their parents, likewise, have to deal with a child who in many ways is rejecting them. On a more optimistic note, he also points out that later in life, benefits can occur from the apparent memories, as some subjects have talked of using their past mistakes as a guide to improving their behavior in the current life. He cites Bishen Chand Kapoor, whom I mentioned in Chapter 3, whose previous personality murdered a man when he saw him leaving the apartment of a prostitute whom the previous personality considered reserved for himself. Bishen Chand said that reflecting on the negative aspects of his previous life had helped make him a better person.

Others have shown a detachment from problems in the current life or a lack of any fear of death. Marta Lorenz, a girl in Brazil who made voluminous statements about the life of a friend of her mother's, experienced the death of a sister, Emilia. When another sister worried during a rainstorm that Emilia would get wet in her grave, Marta responded, "Emilia is not in the cemetery. She is in a safer and better place than this one where we are; her soul never can be wet." Similarly, when a family friend grieving the death of her father said that the dead never return, Marta replied, "Don't say that. I died also and look, I am living again."

Dr. Stevenson has also written about the relief that can occur after the children meet the previous personality's family for the first time. The children often seem better able to integrate the memories from the past life with the circumstances of their present life after the meeting, and the intensity of their emotions about the past life often lessens. Kendra's case points out that relationships individuals have in this life are different from those they may have had in a past life. Even if we accept that her consciousness was a part of Ginger's aborted fetus, that does not mean that they are mother and daughter in this life. They clearly are not, but Kendra seemed confused about this. She spoke of having two mothers and spent a good deal of time with Ginger. In such a situation, the child needs to understand that relationships from a past life are in the past and not the present, and the meeting with the previous family often seems to facilitate such an understanding.

In some ways, Asian parents may have an advantage in this situation compared to Western ones. In our cases in Asia, the parents usually accept a child's claims about a past life, even if they try to get the child to stop making them. They can address emotional issues directly and tell their children that though they had different parents in the past life, their current parents are the ones they have this time around. Western parents, on the other hand, may be puzzled by their child's statements and not know how to respond. They may ignore the statements, or they may say that the child is lying or pretending. None of these responses is satisfying to the child, and none sends the same message the Asian parents often convey. Kendra's mother eventually accepted that her spirit may have once inhabited Ginger's fetus, but unfortunately, Kendra showed little ability to place that relationship in the past.

Many of the Asian subjects have trouble letting go of the past as well, but they often seem to be able to do so more easily after they meet the previous family. Such a meeting validates their memories, yet the children understand that they will continue to live with their current family. A definite message that the past is in the past may be helpful, and this can be a hard message for Western parents to convey if they cannot accept the possibility, as Kendra's mother was able to do, that their children's claims about the past may be true.

Considering the Explanations

Developing a normal explanation for the behaviors can be difficult. In some cases, we may want to use the fantasy explanation and say that the children's behavior comes from their false identification with a previous personality. Where would such a fantasy come from in the first place? We might blame cultural factors for the cases in Asia, but we can hardly do so in the case of Kendra Carter, whose mother was appalled by the idea of reincarnation. Similarly, Erin Jackson, who showed cross-gender behavior, had Protestant parents who did not believe in reincarnation when her symptoms started. In addition, do we have a reasonable explanation for what would lead Burmese children to identify themselves as Japanese soldiers or a British boy to identify himself as a German pilot as Carl Edon did?

Regarding the emotions specifically, we might like to suppose that the ones that the children show when they interact with family members of the previous personality are the result of their fantasy that they were previously related. This idea gets less likely when we look at the longing that some of the children express before they ever meet the other family.

A case such as Sukla Gupta, who mothered objects she called "Minu" before other details she gave led to the identification of a previous personality who had an infant daughter named Minu, stretches this idea to the limit. How did she develop this intense longing for Minu before anyone located the previous family? We can conclude that this was a remarkable coincidence, that Sukla had somehow learned numerous details about the life of a woman who died in another village six years before she was born, or that the family falsely remembered her cradling "Minu." Regardless of which of these we choose, we also have to deal with the strong attachment that Sukla showed to the real Minu after they met. Can we really conclude that all of this emotion came from a child's fantasy?

The same question comes up when we look at Kendra's case. We can understand a young girl becoming attached to her swimming coach, but her attachment was so immediate and so intense that it would be highly unusual under any circumstances. To that, we then have to add that the girl, whose mother and church found the concept of reincarnation to be abhorrent, imagined that she had previously been the coach's aborted fetus. In her case, since the attachment seemed to come either simultaneously with or slightly prior to the reincarnation claim, we cannot realistically decide that it came from a reincarnation fantasy. Can we say the reverse—that the reincarnation fantasy came from the extreme attachment that she felt—when we know that no one in her environment had a belief in reincarnation? Even if we do, that means that in some cases we think that a fantasy produced the attachment, with Sukla being an example, while in others like Kendra's, the attachment led to the fantasy.

Complicating both of these scenarios is the intensity of the emotions that some of the children show. A child like Kendra, who did not speak for four months after her purported previous mother cut off contact, is not engaging in a childish game of make-believe. Similar examples abound, like Ekkaphong, who tried to strangle the man he thought had killed him in a previous life, and of course Sukla, who wept when she heard that Minu was sick. In addition, in some of the cases of gender confusion, the cross-gender behaviors persist into adulthood, so they hardly seem part of a child's fantasy play.

Let us look at phobias. Shamlinie Prema and Sujith Jayaratne both showed phobias as babies. Shamlinie's intense fear of being immersed in water from the time she was an infant obviously could not have grown out of a fantasy about a past life. We might want to use the faulty memory explanation here, so we would say that after the children talked about previous lives, their parents recalled their earlier behaviors as being more extreme than they really were. The same is true for the precocious interest in addictive substances and the unusual food habits that some of the parents report that their children show. Refuting this is Jasbir Singh's case, since we cannot say that his parents exaggerated his refusal to eat their food after they had to get a Brahmin neighbor to prepare food for him for a year and a half. Overall, we have enough witnesses and enough cases in which the behaviors persisted to say that some of the children definitely show behaviors that at least appear to be connected with the past-life memories they claim to have.

And so it goes with efforts to explain the behaviors the

children often show in these cases. We may be able to piece together a normal explanation for individual cases, even if, at times, it seems rather convoluted, but the explanations do not hold up when we look at the phenomena as a group. In some cases, the past-life claims come first, and in some, the behaviors come first. While the behaviors are often extreme enough to make a normal explanation difficult in either case, having a single explanation that encompasses both situations and provides an overall interpretation of the phenomena is essentially impossible, and the explanation for one group of cases is the opposite of the explanation for the other group.

As for the paranormal explanations, ESP does not do a good job of explaining these cases. It only works if we say that when the children acquire the knowledge through ESP, they think that they are experiencing memories. This mistaken impression then causes them to develop the emotions and behaviors. This is convoluted, obviously; but worse, some of the behaviors, such as the phobias, often exist well before the children make statements about the previous life. Perhaps we could argue that the children acquire the knowledge of the previous lives as infants, and while this seems odd, it is at least conceivable.

Possession seems to do a better job of explaining the emotions and behaviors than ESP does. If the previous consciousness has taken over the body of the child, then we might well expect that the child would show such traits. The weakness of this argument is that we would have to say the possession occurred almost at birth, since some of the behavioral traits start at such an early age. Therefore, it would be hard to justify this as a better explanation than reincarnation.

Reincarnation, again, does provide an explanation for the

emotions and behaviors. In fact, they show that if reincarnation is the explanation for the cases, then it involves more than just memories. It encompasses a more complete continuance from the previous life, as emotional connections, fears, and likes and dislikes are all part of the consciousness that moves on to the next life.

These behavioral features demonstrate that the children's past-life claims are very meaningful to them. Anyone who thinks that they are just a silly game of make-believe or something that children say to satisfy their parents' beliefs in reincarnation should remember Kendra, a small American child who was unable to speak for months after the woman that she remembered as her mother rejected her.

CHAPTER 7

Recognizing Familiar Faces

S am Taylor is a boy from Vermont who was born a year and a half after his paternal grandfather died. When Sam was one and a half years old, his father was changing his diaper one day when Sam told him, "When I was your age, I used to change your diapers." After his mother saw the puzzled look on his father's face as he brought Sam out of his room, they discussed the comment, which they both found odd. Neither had ever given reincarnation much thought. Though Sam's mother was the daughter of a Southern Baptist minister, his parents were not religious.

Following that incident, Sam gradually began saying that he had been his grandfather. He also said, "I used to be big, and now I'm small." While his father was initially skeptical about such a possibility, his mother was more open to the idea, and she began asking him questions about the life of his paternal grandfather. At one point, she and Sam were talking about the fact that his grandmother had taken care of his grandfather before he died. Sam's mother asked him what his grandmother made every day for his grandfather to drink, and Sam correctly said that she had made milkshakes and that she had made them in a machine in the kitchen. He got up to show her the food processor on the kitchen counter. When his mother showed him the blender in the pantry and asked if he meant that his grandmother had made the milkshakes with it, he said no and pointed out the food processor instead. In fact, his grandmother had made milkshakes for his grandfather in the food processor. She then had a series of strokes after the death of his grandfather, and Sam had never seen her make milkshakes for anyone.

At another time, Sam's mother asked him if he had had any brothers or sisters when he lived before. He answered, "Yeah, I had a sister. She turned into a fish." When she asked him who turned her into a fish, he said, "Some bad guys. She died. You know what, when we die, God lets us come back again. I used to be big, and now I'm a kid again." The sister of Sam's grandfather, in fact, had been killed some sixty years before. Her husband killed her while she was sleeping, rolled her body up in a blanket, and dumped it in the bay.

At other times, Sam correctly said that his grandfather's favorite place in the home was the garage where he worked on "inventions" and that Sam's father had a small steering wheel of his own when they rode in the car. When his father was a boy, he had a toy steering wheel that attached to the dashboard of a car by suction cups.

When Sam was four and a half years old, his grandmother died. His father flew out to her home to take care of her belongings and returned with a box of family photographs. Sam's parents had not had any pictures of his father's family before then. When his mother spread them out on the coffee table one night, Sam came over and began pointing to the pictures of his grandfather and saying, "That's me!" When he saw a snapshot that showed a car without any people, he said "Hey! That's my car!" This was a picture of the first new car that his grandfather ever purchased, a 1949 Pontiac that was very special to him.

His mother gave Sam a class picture from when his grandfather was in grammar school. The picture showed twenty-seven children, sixteen of them boys. Sam ran his finger over the faces, stopped it on his grandfather's face and said, "That's me."

His father says that Sam's grandfather did not communicate very well about emotional issues with his sons, particularly when they were adults. Sam's father let his own father know how he felt about him, but his father had great difficulty reciprocating. He feels that if his father has come back through Sam, then his deceased father is reaching out to return his love. Sam's father is very open with all of his children, and he and Sam seem to have a very good relationship.

Sam was thought to recognize someone or something from the previous life, identifying the previous personality, his grandfather, in pictures and also pointing out a picture of his grandfather's car. This is similar to the reports in many of our cases of children recognizing family members of the previous personality.

The recognitions in the cases fall into several categories. The first type involves uncontrolled recognitions. In these, the families attempt to test the child to see if he or she can recognize previous family members or belongings, but they do not conduct the tests under the controlled conditions that we would favor. Though the tests usually involve recognizing people, locations are sometimes involved. Witnesses in those cases say that the children led the way to the home of the previous personality or that they noted changes in buildings or landscapes that had occurred after the death of the previous personality.

Unfortunately, the conditions that the families frequently use to conduct recognition tests make us question their value. Before they perform a test, they make arrangements for the child to meet the previous family. Often, when word spreads that a child claiming to remember the life of a particular previous personality is coming to meet the family members of that person, a large crowd gathers before the child arrives. Someone then either asks the child, for example, "Do you see your wife?" or gives him a small item to take to the individual in question. As Dr. Stevenson has written, though those involved are not automatically assuming that the child is remembering the life of a particular individual and are trying to test the child, the crowd of people assembled to watch the testing may look expectantly at the wife of the previous personality when someone asks the child to identify her, and an observant child can hardly fail to point out the right person.

These apparent recognitions frequently impress those involved in the case. Though their hopes that the child will recognize the individuals from the previous life may well cloud their judgment, we should note in fairness that the manner of the child during the recognition—for instance, a look of recognition or of warm emotion—may make the event more impressive for those who experienced it. Witnesses do not always say that the child recognized the previous family members, or they may report that the child was able to recognize some but not all of the family members.

In some cases, informants have reported that the child recognized individuals from the previous life when few if any people were there who could have inadvertently identified the family members. This can occur if the previous family learns of the child's statements before the child's family has gone to verify them and goes unannounced to see the child at his home. Indika Ishwara in Chapter 4 told his mother, "Father has come," when the father of the previous personality visited his family.

In other situations, the families conduct additional tests requiring the child to have knowledge of the previous life in order to answer correctly. For instance, in the case of Chanai Choomalaiwong in Chapter 4, the previous family showed him five or six gunbelts and asked him to pick out his. He immediately picked the one that belonged to the previous personality. Just as with the uncontrolled recognition tests for family members, we do not know if family members unintentionally guided him in selecting the correct one.

In some cases, the parents of subjects have reported that the children led the way to the home of the previous personality. This occurred in Chanai's case, when he described the life of a schoolteacher and then led the way to the home of the parents of a murdered schoolteacher. In that instance, and in a number of others like it, no one who knew the way was with the child, so we do not have to consider the possibility that the child picked up unintentional cues from those nearby.

Some children also seem to recognize changes that have taken place since the death of the previous personality. For instance, when Sujith Jayaratne from Chapter 5 was taken to the property of the parents of the previous personality, Sammy Fernando, he commented correctly that the road had been moved and that some of the fencing was new since Sammy had died. In addition, he went to a place where a tree had been removed after Sammy's death and asked, "Where is the tree that was here?"

Similarly, Gamini Jayasena in Chapter 5 went to the home of the previous personality, Palitha Senewiratne. After Palitha's death, his family had replaced a thatched roof with one of corrugated iron, and Gamini commented to Palitha's parents that the roof had not been "shiny" in the past the way that it was then. When he visited the boardinghouse where Palitha had stayed while attending school, he told the owner that an olive tree had previously been there, and in fact one had been cut down after Palitha's death.

In other cases, families may have conducted recognition tests under conditions that we would not judge to be adequate, but the children have then made impressive statements afterwards. After identifying the widow of the previous personality, Necip Ünlütaşkiran in Chapter 4 said that he had cut her on the leg with a knife, and she confirmed that her husband had indeed done so during an argument.

In another example, when Jasbir Singh, the boy in Chapter 6 who refused to eat non-Brahmin food, saw a cousin of the previous personality, he said, "Come in, Gandhiji." Someone corrected him by saying, "This is Birbal," and Jasbir responded, "We call him Gandhiji." In fact, the man did have the nickname of Gandhiji, because people thought that his large ears made him look like Mahatma Gandhi.

These spontaneous observations undermine the idea that the subjects' parents have coached them to pretend to remember the previous lives. The knowledge the children have shown involved information that the parents would not have, and the children have demonstrated an ability to do more than recite facts about the previous life.

Some children also make spontaneous recognitions in which

they happen to recognize a person or place even though no one was intending to conduct a recognition test. In such circumstances, the environmental cues that may help the children succeed in the uncontrolled tests are generally not present. At times, they lead to a case being solved when otherwise it likely would not have been. An example of this is Gamini Jayasena in Chapter 5, who commented on a bus trip that his previous home had been at a particular stop, and this led his family to investigate the people in that area. Likewise, in Necip Ünlütaşkiran's case, his parents did not attempt to verify his statements about a past life until he met his grandfather's wife. At that point, he said that he recognized her from the past life that he had described being in a location, the city of Mersin, where she had previously lived. Similarly, Ratana Wongsombat in Chapter 5 recognized the nun Mae Chan, so her father went back to her temple to talk with her. He then learned that his daughter's statements about a past life were accurate for a woman who had died one and a half years before Ratana was born. In that case, Ratana had asked to go to the temple, so her recognition was not the coincidence that Gamini's appears to be.

The Case of Nazih Al-Danaf

One case that involved several recognitions is the case of Nazih Al-Danaf in Lebanon. At a very early age, Nazih described a past life to his parents and his seven siblings, all of whom were available for interviews. Nazih described the life of a man that his family did not know. He said that the man carried pistols and grenades, that he had a pretty wife and young children, that he had a two-story house with trees around it and a cave nearby, that he had a mute friend, and that he had been shot by a group of men.

His father reported that Nazih demanded that his parents take him to his previous house in a small town ten miles away. They took him to that town, along with two of his sisters and a brother, when he was six years old. About a half mile from the town, Nazih asked them to stop at a dirt road running off the main road. He told them that the road came to a dead end where there was a cave, but they drove on without confirming this. When they got to the center of town, six roads converged, and Nazih's father asked him which way to go. Nazih pointed to one of the roads and said to go on it until they came to a road that forked off upward, where they would see his house. When they got to the first fork that went up, the family got out and began asking about anyone who had died in the way that Nazih had described.

They quickly discovered that a man named Fuad, who had a house on that road before dying ten years prior to Nazih's birth, seemed to fit Nazih's statements. Fuad's widow asked Nazih, "Who built the foundation of this gate at the entrance of the house?" and Nazih correctly answered, "A man from the Faraj family." The group then went into the house, where Nazih correctly described how Fuad had kept his weapons in a cupboard. The widow asked him if she had had an accident at their previous home, and Nazih gave accurate details of her accident. She also asked if he remembered what had made their young daughter seriously ill, and Nazih correctly responded that she had accidentally taken some of her father's pills. He also accurately described a couple of other incidents from the previous personality's life.

The widow and her five children were all very impressed with the knowledge that Nazih demonstrated, and they were all convinced that he was the rebirth of Fuad.

Soon after that meeting, Nazih visited Fuad's brother, Sheikh Adeeb. When Nazih saw him, he ran up saying, "Here comes my brother Adeeb." Sheikh Adeeb asked Nazih for proof that he was his brother, and Nazih said, "I gave you a Checki 16." A Checki 16 is a type of pistol from Czechoslovakia that is not common in Lebanon, and Fuad had indeed given his brother one. Sheikh Adeeb then asked Nazih where his original house was, and Nazih led him down the road until he said correctly, "This is the house of my father and this [the next house] is my first house." They went in the latter house, where Fuad's first wife still lived, and when Sheikh Adeeb later asked who she was, Nazih correctly gave her name.

Sheikh Adeeb then showed Nazih a photograph of three men and asked him who they were. Nazih pointed to each and correctly gave the names of Adeeb, Fuad, and a deceased brother of theirs. Sheikh Adeeb showed Nazih another picture, and Nazih said correctly that the man in it was the father of those men. Later, Sheikh Adeeb visited Nazih's home, and he took a handgun with him. He asked Nazih if this was the gun that Fuad had given him, and Nazih correctly said that it was not.

Dr. Haraldsson investigated Nazih's case, and he was able to verify most of the statements that Nazih made, including the claim that the previous personality had a mute friend. He also found out that Nazih's description of Fuad's house matched another one in which Fuad lived for several years, including the time during which the house in town, which was not fully completed at the time of Fuad's death, was being built. The former house was by the dirt road that Nazih had pointed out during the family's first visit to the previous town, and a cave was also at the end of it as Nazih had said.

If the families in this case are remembering events correctly, then Nazih's statements are very difficult to explain by normal means. His spontaneous recognitions of the locations of two houses that the previous personality had owned are quite impressive by themselves. Adding his ability to correctly point out the previous personality's first house makes coincidence seem an unlikely explanation. On top of these, his statements to Fuad's family about various small details are also notable. His statement about the Checki 16 pistol is particularly impressive in a number of ways, one being that this knowledge could not have arisen from any environmental cues. His ability to state the names of the men in a picture is more impressive than cases in which a child simply points to a member of the previous personality's family, since environmental cues would not lead him to know the names that he gave. The informants stated that Nazih had not seen pictures of the previous personality before he identified him in the group photograph, and Sheikh Adeeb was certain that with the possible exception of his wife, no one knew that Fuad had given him a Checki 16 pistol.

In a limited number of cases, investigators have been able to conduct controlled recognition tests in which the child appeared able to recognize individuals from the life of the previous personality. Such tests occurred in the following two cases that Dr. Stevenson investigated.

The Case of Gnanatilleka
Baddewithana

Gnanatilleka Baddewithana was born in Sri Lanka in 1956, and when she was two years old, she began saying that she had a mother and father along with two brothers and many sisters in another place. After hearing about a town, Talawakelle, that was sixteen miles away, Gnanatilleka began saying that she had lived there, and she said that she wanted to visit her former parents there.

When Gnanatilleka was four and a half years old, a neighbor wrote about her to H.S.S. Nissanka, a journalist who had written several articles about reincarnation and who later obtained a Ph.D. in International Relations. He subsequently wrote a book about Gnanatilleka's case, and I have taken numerous details from it. Dr. Nissanka decided to go see the girl, and he asked a well-known Buddhist monk and a teacher at a nearby college to accompany him. They interviewed Gnanatilleka, and she described a number of incidents from a life in Talawakelle, including one in which she saw the Queen as she traveled by train.

She had not given any names other than Talawakelle and a sister named Lora—or sometimes Dora. Since Queen Elizabeth had traveled through Sri Lanka in 1954, Dr. Nissanka and his companions assumed that Gnanatilleka was describing someone from Talawakelle who had died between the time of that visit and Gnanatilleka's birth in 1956. Actually, they assumed that the previous personality must have died before Gnanatilleka's conception, but that is not an assumption that we would automatically share. Dr. Nissanka wrote two articles about the case for a

popular weekly newspaper, and the three men then went to Talawakelle to investigate.

While in Talawakelle, the group met a man who said that the
information in the articles matched the life of a family member,
a teenage boy named Tillekeratne, who had died in November
of 1954. Soon after that meeting, Tillekeratne's teacher went to
Gnanatilleka's home along with two men that Tillekeratne had
not known. Each of the men asked Gnanatilleka if she knew
him. She said no to two of them, but to her teacher, she said,
"Yes, you are from Talawakelle!" After a moment, she commented that he had taught her and had never punished her, and
she climbed into his lap.

The next day, the investigation team arranged for Gnanatilleka
to meet members of Tillekeratne's family at a rest house, or inn,
in Talawakelle, but they did not tell Gnanatilleka the reason for
her trip there. Gnanatilleka sat in a room with her mother, the
monk, and Dr. Nissanka, who recorded the events with a tape
recorder. Gnanatilleka's father and Tillekeratne's teacher stood
near the door, and other observers watched from the next room.
Tillekeratne's mother then entered the room. The monk asked
Gnanatilleka, "Do you know her?"

Gnanatilleka looked up and suddenly appeared excited, and
she stared at the woman. When asked again if she knew her, Gnanatilleka said, "Yes."

Tillekeratne's mother handed her a candy bar and then held
her arms out to Gnanatilleka, who quickly hugged her. Tillekeratne's mother said, "Tell me, where did I live?"

Gnanatilleka slowly answered, "Talawakelle."

Tillekeratne's mother said, "So tell me who I am."

Gnanatilleka, after making sure that her own mother could not hear her, whispered to Tillekeratne's mother (and to Dr. Nissanka's microphone), "Talawakelle mother."

After a minute, the observers asked Gnanatilleka again, "Who was that lady . . . tell us," and she replied, "She's my Talawakelle mother."

Next, Tillekeratne's father came in, and Gnanatilleka was asked, "Do you know him?"

She answered yes, and when she was asked who he was, she answered, "He's my Talawakelle father."

Following him, one of Tillekeratne's sisters, one who had accompanied him to school every day, came in, and when Gnanatilleka was asked who she was, she replied, "This is my sister from Talawakelle."

"Where did you go with this sister?"

"To school."

When asked how they had gone, she correctly answered that they had gone by train.

Coming in next was a man who had moved to Talawakelle after Tillekeratne died. He asked her, "Who am I?"

"No."

Dr. Nissanka asked her, "Do you know him? Look again carefully, who is he?"

She answered, "No, I don't know him."

Three women came in next. One asked, "Do you know me? Who am I?"

Gnanatilleka answered, "Yes, you're my fair sister."

Another asked, "Who am I?"

"The sister who lives in the house below ours."

Gnanatilleka's mother then asked her who the third woman was, and she answered, "The sister to whose house we go to sew clothes." These were all correct for Tillekeratne's sisters.

Two men from Talawakelle were sent in separately. One was a very close friend of Tillekeratne's family, while the other one had taught Tillekeratne at Sunday School. Gnanatilleka said that she knew each of them at Talawakelle but did not give other specifics.

Lastly, Tillekeratne's brother went in. He and Tillekeratne had constantly quarreled, and when Gnanatilleka was asked if she knew him, she angrily answered, "No!" She was asked again, and she answered, "No! No!" Dr. Nissanka then told her that she could tell just her mother if she knew him, so she whispered to her mother, "My brother from Talawakelle." Dr. Nissanka asked her to let everyone else hear, so she said, "My brother from Ta-lawakelle." When Dr. Nissanka told Gnanatilleka to let the brother hold her, she began crying and said that she would not.

Gnanatilleka made some very impressive recognitions, as she not only knew the relationship that the previous personality had with each individual but other facts that she could not have known from appearance alone. She stated correctly that she had not known individuals that the previous personality had not known—the two men who accompanied Tillekeratne's teacher to her home and the stranger whom the investigators brought in as a test for her.

Gnanatilleka also made a couple of spontaneous recognitions later. She developed a relationship with Tillekeratne's teacher, and one day when they were out together, Gnanatilleka pointed to a woman in a crowd of people and said, "I know her." She told the teacher, "She came to the Talawakelle temple with me," and he confirmed with the woman that she had been friendly with Tillekeratne when they worshipped at the temple. Another time, Gnanatilleka pointed out one woman who was in a group of others and said, "She is angry with my Talawakelle mother." The teacher checked with the woman and found out that she was a neighbor of Tillekeratne's family who had previously had disagreements with Tillekeratne's mother, but they had since patched up their differences.

Dr. Stevenson arrived on the scene a year after the controlled recognition tests and interviewed people from both families as well as Tillekeratne's teacher. Following the initial interviews, he continued to check on the family from time to time. One item that he discovered was that Tillekeratne did not have a sister named Lora or Dora. He had been classmates with a girl named Lora when he was younger, and they had had some contact before his death. Dr. Stevenson interviewed her in 1970. She had never met Gnanatilleka, so he took her and one of her friends, whom Tillekeratne had not known, unannounced to Gnanatilleka's home. He asked Gnanatilleka, who was almost fifteen years old by that time, if she could recognize the two women. She called Lora "Dora," confusing the names just as she had done as a young child, and said that she had known her in Talawakelle, but she could give no other details.

This was a remarkable accomplishment, even if we accept the possibility of reincarnation, since Lora had gone from being a teenager during Tillekeratne's life to being an approximately thirty-year-old woman, though we might suppose that this was not so different from being able to recognize an old classmate at a high school reunion. Gnanatilleka did accomplish the recognition. Though she might have guessed the location of Talawakelle, given the context of Dr. Stevenson's previous contact with the family, her ability to state the name, which she had not given for any of the other women that people had asked her to identify, demonstrated knowledge that is hard to dismiss.

Gnanatilleka's case was a sex-change case, but she did not show particularly masculine traits. When she was young, her parents noted that she was more boyish than her sister was, but not to a severe degree, and as a teenager, her appearance was that of a typical Sinhalese girl. The previous personality, however, tended to be rather feminine. He preferred to be with girls and at times painted his fingernails. He enjoyed sewing and liked silk shirts. In that area at that time, these characteristics made him different from most of the other boys.

The Case of Ma Choe Hnin Htet

The case of Ma Choe Hnin Htet in Myanmar involved not only a controlled recognition test but also an experimental birthmark. The previous personality in the case was a young woman, Ma Lai Lai Way, who was born with a heart defect. It limited her functioning significantly, and she was still attending high school at the age of twenty when she entered the Rangoon General Hospital for several months in 1975. She underwent open-heart surgery there and died during the surgery.

Following Ma Lai Lai Way's death, three of her friends offered to prepare her body for cremation. As they were doing this, they recalled the custom of marking a body, so they used red lipstick to make a mark on the left side of the back of her neck. They chose this spot as opposed to more visible ones, because they did not want a future child to be disfigured. Dr. Stevenson has pointed out that in choosing the back of the neck, the girls picked the worst possible site for producing an impressive experimental birthmark since "stork bite" birthmarks are quite common and occasionally persist into later childhood.

Thirteen months after Ma Lai Lai Way's death, her older sister gave birth to a baby girl she named Ma Choe Hnin Htet. After the birth, Ma Choe Hnin Htet's family noted that she had a red birthmark on the left side of the back of her neck. At the time, her family did not know that Ma Lai Lai Way's friends had marked her body, but they learned a few days later when a neighbor told them. Since Ma Choe Hnin Htet's mother did not learn about the body being marked until after she gave birth, we can be sure that maternal impression, the idea that the mother's wishes or expectations could have led to the birthmark on her baby, played no part in this case.

We can also be sure that the position of the birthmark did not lead witnesses to match it incorrectly with the site of the marking, because when Dr. Stevenson talked with one of the friends who had marked the body, Ma Myint Myint Oo, she gave the location without knowing that Ma Choe Hnin Htet had been born with a birthmark. He also interviewed the other two friends, who gave the same location for the marking.

Ma Choe Hnin Htet also had a mark on her chest that presumably was a birthmark, but her family did not notice it for several years, until someone suggested that she might have a birthmark to match Ma Lai Lai Way's surgical incision. It was a thin, pale line, lighter than the rest of her skin, and it ran down the middle of her lower chest and upper abdomen. It matched an incision scar for open-heart surgery, except that it was lower, at least by the time that Ma Choe Hnin Htet was four years old, than an incision for such a surgery would be.

Soon after Ma Choe Hnin Htet became old enough to talk, she spoke of the previous life with her grandparents, the previous personality's parents. She said that her grandmother had been her mother, and she talked of dying when the doctors operated on her. She also said that her name was Lai Lai, and she would cry if family members teased her by telling her that she was not Lai Lai. In addition, she called her mother the term for "older sister," her maternal uncle "brother," and her grandfather "papa."

Dr. Stevenson investigated the case when Ma Choe Hnin Htet was four years old. Three days before his interviews, two of Ma Lai Lai Way's friends, one of whom had marked her body, visited the family. The marker had not seen Ma Choe Hnin Htet since she was a baby, but Ma Choe Hnin Htet was very friendly with her. She walked out to the gate when she saw the women, rather than notifying the adults as she would normally do, and when she met them, she asked the woman to call her Lai Lai Way. She led her to meet her grandmother, who asked her, "Do you know her?" To which Ma Choe Hnin Htet responded, "Yes, of course. We were friends."

When Dr. Stevenson conducted his interviews, he discovered that Ma Myint Myint Oo, another of the women who had marked the body, had never met Ma Choe Hnin Htet. He and his interpreter, U Win Maung, decided to take her to Ma Choe Hnin Htet's home without letting the family know that they were coming. After they arrived at the house, they pointed to Ma Myint Myint Oo and asked Ma Choe Hnin Htet, "Who is she?" Ma Choe Hnin Htet quickly answered, "Myint Myint Oo."

We wish that we had more opportunities to conduct such tests. Unfortunately, the children in our cases have usually met the important figures in the life of the previous personality by the time that we arrive on the scene. During these meetings, the families have frequently judged them to recognize a number of persons from that life, but we have not been able to assess that for ourselves. In order to conduct more tests ourselves, we need to get to the cases sooner. Ideally, getting to a case before anyone has identified the previous personality would give us a wonderful opportunity to arrange such tests, but many such cases may never come to our attention. Some parents may not want others to know that their child is talking about a past life if the case is unsolved and the statements unverified. Even if the parents do not mind others knowing, people are naturally less likely to talk about a case that is unsolved, so our agents in the various countries are less likely to hear of them.

Along these lines, we need to hear about cases early enough so that the children still have the memories. Since most of the children seem to lose the memories by the time they are seven or eight years old, conducting a test when they are older may be fruitless. Exceptions certainly exist, as Dr. Stevenson's test of Gnanatilleka Baddewithana makes clear, but in general, conducting the test while the child is still young is essential. This means that we must hear about cases as early as possible in the subject's life. Unfortunately, our resources are limited, and we often have only one person looking for cases in a given country. If that person learns of a case from a newspaper report, the family has almost always solved it already. Learning of one through other connections offers a better chance of getting to a solvable case before the child has met the previous family, but significant obstacles can remain.

This leaves us with a handful of cases in which investigators have performed adequately controlled recognition tests. This limited number does not mean that these subjects are the only ones to have recognized members of the previous family, but since the conditions under which the other children made the recognitions were not adequately controlled, we cannot say with certainty that they actually did recognize family members.

We would expect that if the children are having real memories of previous lives, they should be able to recognize the people with whom they have described sharing a life, but the memories often seem to be murky and incomplete and only available at certain times for some of the children. If the previous personality has died some time ago, then the appearance of the individuals involved may also have changed substantially from when the previous personality lived. Both of these factors may explain why some of the children fail to recognize members of the previous family.

On the other hand, if we do not accept reincarnation as a possibility, we should be very surprised when a child does recognize individuals from the previous life under controlled conditions. In some ways, these few cases with controlled recognition tests confirm the results of the uncontrolled tests of many other cases, and they constitute an important type of evidence. Any explanation that seeks to dismiss the cases as the result of a normal, mundane process has to deal with these examples of children showing an ability to recognize people from the previous life and to give specific information about them.

Sam, the boy at the beginning of the chapter, appeared to recognize the previous personality, his grandfather, in pictures. When I first heard about those recognitions, I wondered if he could have picked out the previous personality in the class picture because he had just seen the pictures of his grandfather as an older person. When I looked at the pictures, I realized that I could not have picked the previous personality out in the class picture after seeing the others. Thinking a four-year-old child could do so is assuming a lot. In fact, many of the boys in the picture look similar—dark-haired boys wearing the same style clothes—but whether they look similar or not, we should keep in mind that we are talking about a four-year-old boy who picked his grandfather out of the picture. We need to include such recognitions in any overall assessment of this phenomenon. They show that some children not only claim memories of past lives but also seem to show the ability to recognize people or places from those lives.

Considering the Explanations

In trying to explain the recognitions using a normal process, we can easily dismiss the uncontrolled ones as having little scientific value because the children may be able to use environmental cues to figure out who they are being asked to recognize. The statements that the children frequently make during the meetings, such as a person's nickname or details of an event from the past, are more difficult to explain. For these, we must blame faulty memory by the informants about the statements.

We again have to rely on faulty memory by informants to

explain many of the spontaneous recognitions, since the children are said to make statements about the people that show knowledge they seemingly could not have acquired through normal means.

Finally, the controlled recognition tests offer the biggest challenge to explain by a normal process. In the case of Gnanatilleka Baddewithana, she recognized family members of the previous family as researchers brought them in one by one. We might suppose that Gnanatilleka guessed the relationship that each person had with the previous personality, except that she also correctly stated that she did not know a man who the previous personality had not known. In addition, we are giving a four-and-a-half-year-old child a lot of credit to think that her deductive abilities were good enough to enable her to guess all of the relationships correctly.

More problematic still is the fact that she also gave information about the previous personality's sisters that she could not have known from just their appearances. This, along with the recognitions, means that coincidence is not a reasonable explanation, and in addition, we cannot blame faulty memory as an explanation since the researchers made audio recordings of the tests. Fraud seems to be the only possible normal explanation left. We can suppose that Gnanatilleka's family tricked everyone else involved, that the two families conspired to fool the researchers, or that the researchers themselves did not accurately report the events that took place. None of these is likely, especially when we remember that Gnanatilleka was successful in recognizing the woman named Lora when Dr. Stevenson tested her eight years later.

Similarly, Ma Choe Hnin Htet was able to give the name of

one of the previous personality's friends, one who had marked the body, the first time that she met her. Since environmental cues could not have allowed her to know the name, we must suppose that family members lied to Dr. Stevenson when they told him that the girl had never heard the woman's name.

In the cases of controlled recognition tests, fraud is the only normal explanation that we can come up with, and it is not very reasonable. As for the paranormal explanations, any of the three can be used to explain the recognitions. Extrasensory perception could allow the children to be able to identify the previous individuals. If the previous consciousness has possessed the child, it could identify them. Lastly, if the child is the rebirth of the previous personality, then he or she could identify them as well.

CHAPTER 8

Divine Intermission

Bobby Hodges, a boy from North Carolina, frequently talked about wanting to live with his cousins. His cousins' family consisted of one boy, the oldest child, and three girls. In addition, Bobby's aunt had miscarried a set of twins after her son was born. Bobby said that the boy was his big brother and asked why his mother was keeping him from his real family. He repeatedly said that he belonged with his cousins. His parents, thinking that he liked his cousins' family because it had more children in it than his own, never gave his statements much thought until he began talking to his mother one night after his bath when he was four and a half years old.

He asked her if she remembered when he was in her tummy. She said yes and asked if he remembered when his two-and-a-half-year-old brother Donald was in her tummy. He then asked if she remembered when he and Donald were in her tummy at the same time. When she told him that they had not been in her tummy at the same time, he said they were in her tummy at the same time but did not get born. She told him that he did get born and later Donald was born. He responded that he and Donald had been in his Aunt Susan's tummy at the same time, rather than his mother's, and asked why Aunt Susan did not give birth to them.

Bobby then became very upset and began screaming at Donald. He said, "Donald, it is all your fault. I told you I wanted to get born real bad, and you didn't want to. How did you take me out of there, Donald? Why didn't you want to get born? Tell me how you did it. Tell me how you took me out of there."

At this point, Bobby's mother had to restrain him to keep him from going after Donald. She told him not to scream at Donald and that Donald did not know what he was talking about. Bobby screamed that Donald did know and asked him again why he had taken Bobby out of Aunt Susan's tummy.

Donald then took his pacifier out of his mouth and yelled, "No! I wanted Daddy!" before popping his pacifier back in. Bobby yelled back, "I didn't want Daddy, I wanted Uncle Ron!"

After Bobby calmed down somewhat, he told his mother that after the failed pregnancy, he had tried to get back in Aunt Susan's tummy, but Rebecca, his cousin, was there. He told his mother, "I wanted to be in there, and she wouldn't let me. I tried to kick her out, but it didn't work. She got to be born, and I didn't." He said that he then got in his mother's tummy and was born. He said, "I sure did have to work hard to get here, Mom."

To give some background, Bobby's Uncle Ron is his father's brother. Ron's wife Susan became pregnant with male twins seven years before Bobby was born. At thirty-three weeks' gestation, Susan did not feel any movement from the twins, and when she went to the hospital, the doctors found that both had died. The hospital records indicate that the attachment of one of the umbilical cords to the placenta did not have adequate coverings around the blood vessels and so was very susceptible to being compressed. The doctors told Susan that they suspected that one of the twins rolled over on the cord there. This stopped the blood flow, killing one twin, and because of shared circulation, the other one died soon thereafter.

Since the miscarriages were understandably upsetting to the parents, the family never spoke of them, and Bobby's parents feel sure that he had never heard about them. Susan and Ron became pregnant again a few months later, and they subsequently had three girls. The last one, Rebecca, was born eighteen months before Bobby was.

In addition to his talk of being one of Susan's twins, Bobby made a few comments about other lives that he said he remembered. He said that in one, he died from a gunshot wound, and in another, he was a teenager who died in a motor vehicle accident. One time, after recovering from the flu, Bobby told his mother, "Mom, people in the other world don't get sick." She responded, "The other world, Bobby?" and he said, "The world where I was waiting to get born. People don't get sick there. They are just happy and never get sick. I wish we didn't get sick in this world."

Another time, he talked about his parents' wedding, which occurred when his mother was pregnant with him. Since she was noticeably pregnant at the ceremony, she does not have any wedding pictures on display in their house. She and her husband got married in a gazebo on a hill, and they had to climb steps up to the hill and again into the gazebo. They do not believe that Bobby had ever seen a picture of the wedding or heard them discuss it, until one day Bobby saw his mother looking through a pile of pictures. She gave him a picture of his parents' wedding—a close-up shot of them standing in front of a railing. It is the railing of the gazebo, but that is not obvious from the picture. His mother is holding flowers, and his father is wearing a boutonniere. They are standing in profile, apparently facing the minister, but the back of a woman, presumably a member of the wedding party, blocks the viewer from seeing the person in front of them.

When Bobby's mother asked him if he knew what it was a picture of, he answered, "Yes, Mom. It's a picture of you and Dad getting married. I was there. I saw the whole thing." She asked, "You did?" and he answered, "Yes, Mom, you walked up the stairs, and then you gave each other rings, and then you ate cake."

I happened to call her immediately after this exchange, and she told me what Bobby had said. She did not see any way he could have known that she and her husband walked up stairs to start their wedding. At the one wedding he had attended, cake had not been served because of an air-conditioning problem. His mother does not normally even eat cake, but she did so at her own wedding, because she thought that not eating it might bring bad luck.

On his fourth birthday, Bobby had talked about being born. His mother reports that he was born by cesarean section after a prolonged labor. He had presented in a face-up position, called an occiput-posterior position, and nurses were unable to get him to turn. When Bobby talked about his birth, he said that he had been kicking in the womb because he was trying to get out. His mother responded that he had to wait to get born, and he said, "I know, and it was making me mad, and I was pushing to get out and then they were pushing on my head, Mom, trying to get me to go back in, and that was making me really mad, 'cause I wanted to get out, but I couldn't 'cause I was stuck."

His mother was shocked and said, "Yes, you were stuck, and they were pushing on your head to get you to turn over. All you had to do was turn over, and you could have gotten out."

He responded, "Oh, I didn't know that. I would have turned over, but I thought they were pushing me back in. Anyway, then I saw the light, and then the doctor took me out of your tummy, and then they cleaned all that slime off, and then they put me in a bed, and then I could get some sleep."

Bobby's case is an example of one in which the child talks about the interval between the death of the previous personality and his birth. In his case, he talked about events that took place when he was in his mother's womb and made one reference to being in another world before coming to his mother. Most of the subjects in our cases do not make such statements. In 1,100 cases, sixty-nine subjects reported memories of the previous personality's funeral or the handling of the remains; ninety-one described other events happening on Earth; 112 reported memories of being in another realm; and forty-five reported memories either of conception or of being reborn. Some of the children are counted in more than one category since they described more than one type of experience, and only 217 out of the 1,100 reported having at least one of these experiences.

Since we obviously cannot verify any claims that the children make about another realm and often cannot verify the other statements about experiences between lives, the intermission memories tend to be a more speculative area than the other parts of the cases. A couple of factors suggest that we should at least consider the statements. First, some children have made statements about events that occurred that were later verified as accurate. Limited evidence exists in those cases that supports the children's claims to remember events that took place between lives, and we will briefly look at several of those shortly.

Children in the stronger cases tend to make these statements more often than children do in the weaker ones, adding some support for their validity. I developed a scale that rates the strength of each case. When we look at the different types of intermission memories—ones of the previous personality's funeral, ones of other events, ones of being in another realm, and ones of conception or birth—either individually or as a group, we find that the likelihood that a child will report them has a positive correlation with the score that the child gets on the strength-of-case scale. Poonam Sharma, a medical student working with us, also ran statistics that showed that the children who report intermission memories are more likely to remember the name of the previous personality and the way that the person died than are the children who do not report them. They tend to remember more names from the previous life in general, and they make more statements about that life that are later verified to be accurate.

A number of the reports are fascinating in any event and seem worth noting.

Hanging Around

Twenty-five out of 1,100 subjects described details of the previous personality's funeral or the handling of the remains that were verified to be accurate. One example is Ratana Wongsombat from Chapter 5, who correctly described the previous personality's ashes being spread under the bo tree of the temple complex rather than being buried as she had wanted. Sometimes, the statements are not specific enough to be verifiable. For instance, Purnima Ekanayake from Chapter 4 said that after her fatal accident, she floated in the air in semi-darkness for several days. She saw people crying for her and saw her body at the funeral. She said that many people were floating around as she was. She then saw some light, went to it, and came to her new family.

The children who make comments about the funeral of the previous personality do not tend to make many of them, so they do not seem to focus on it. If we accept the statements that they do make, they imply that the consciousness of the previous personality stayed around the body or the family for a while after the death.

Some children have reported that they stayed for an extended amount of time after the funeral. In some instances, the previous family has confirmed some of the statements. A boy in India named Veer Singh claimed to remember the life of Som Dutt, a boy from a village five miles away who died eleven years before Veer Singh was born. He said that he stayed around Som Dutt's home and lived in a tree. He said that he went to the wedding of Som Dutt's brother during that time and gave details about the type of food served. Though he was correct, the food was typical for an Indian wedding. He also said that he went with family members when they left the house. This memory matched a dream that Som Dutt's mother had several months after Som Dutt's death in which he came to her and said that he was going with his brother as he sneaked out of the house at night to attend fairs. After the dream, the brother admitted to his mother that he had been leaving the house. Veer Singh also reported that he had become irritated by some women playing on a swing suspended from the tree where he was staying and had broken the plank of the swing. Som Dutt's father remembered that such an accident had taken place. Veer Singh talked with Som Dutt's mother about lawsuits that the family had become involved in after Som Dutt's death. He talked of siblings who had been born during the intermission, and he correctly told Som Dutt's father that a particular man had moved from the village after Som Dutt's death.

Other children talk of staying near the area where they died in the previous life. A good example of this is Bongkuch Promsin, a boy in Thailand who appeared to remember the life of an eighteen-year-old man who was murdered eight years before Bongkuch's birth in a town six miles from his village. He made twenty-nine statements about the previous life that were verified to be accurate, including descriptions of the actions of the killers immediately after they murdered the previous personality. He said that he stayed for seven years over a bamboo tree near where they left the previous personality's body. After seven years, he went to look for the previous personality's mother on a rainy day. He said that he got lost in the market, saw his future father, and decided to go with him on the bus to his future home. In fact, Bongkuch's father had attended a meeting in that area on a rainy day during the month when Bongkuch was conceived, so Bongkuch's memories were at least partially verified.

Reports of Another Realm

Subjects in other cases have described experiences in another realm during the interval between death and rebirth. A boy named Lee said that he remembered deciding to be reborn. He said that other beings helped him with his decision to come down to Earth. He also said that his previous mother was prettier than his current one, who accepted the comparison with good humor. William, the boy in Chapter 1, said that he floated up after dying, and he talked about being in heaven, where he saw God as well as animals.

Sam Taylor, the boy in Chapter 7 who picked his grandfather out of a grammar school class picture, also talked of seeing God. He said that God gave him a card to come back from heaven, and as he described it, it looked like a business card with green arrows on it. Along with this rather fanciful-sounding detail, he said that his body shot up to heaven when he died and that someone else died at the same time he had. In addition, Sam talked about seeing Uncle Phil in heaven. His grandfather's best friend was the husband of his wife's sister, and the grandfather called him Uncle Phil. Sam commented that in his previous life he had made Uncle Phil's feet hot. His grandfather and Uncle Phil enjoyed playing pranks on each other, and his grandfather would give Phil a "hot foot" by warming his shoes before Phil put them on.

Similarly, Patrick Christenson, the boy in Chapter 4 with three birthmarks that matched lesions on his deceased half-brother, spoke of talking in heaven with a relative named "Billy the Pirate," who he said told him about being shot at close range and dying while up in the mountains. Patrick's mother reported that she had never heard of such a relative, but when she called her mother to ask about Patrick's statements, she learned that a cousin with the nickname Billy the Pirate had in fact died that way.

Other particularly vivid descriptions of another realm include those of Disna Samarasinghe, a girl in Sri Lanka who made numerous statements about the life of an elderly woman who died in a village three miles away. She described being lifted up, even though her body was buried, and flying like a bird. She talked of meeting a king or governor whose reddish clothes and beautiful pointed shoes were never taken off, never dirty, and never washed. The same was true for her own clothes except that they were golden. She said that she played at the king's home, which was made of glass and had beautiful red beds. She said that when she got hungry there, she simply thought of food and it appeared. The sight of the food satisfied her appetite, so she did not need to eat it. She said that the king took her to the home of her new family after asking her to go there.

Another child who made similar statements is Sunita Khandelwal, a girl in India who talked about the life of a woman from a city 220 miles away. She reported that after a fatal fall from a balcony, "I went up. There was a *baba* (holy man) with a long beard. They checked my record and said, 'Send her back.' There are some rooms there. I have seen God's house. It is very nice. You do not know everything that is there."

Certainly, no one would disagree with that last remark.

Memories from Earth Versus Another Realm

One issue for us to consider is why some children describe an existence in this world after the previous death while others describe one in another world. If we take these reports seriously, we can consider what factors might lead an individual to have one type of experience after death compared to the other. Two we can examine are the way that the previous personality died and the suddenness of that death. In looking at the way that the previous personality died, we can compare natural deaths to unnatural ones to see if the two types could produce different types of experiences afterwards. Unnatural deaths include accidents, drownings, and any violent deaths, whether intentional or unintentional. When we compare the two types for 1,100 cases, we find that whether the previous personality died by natural versus unnatural means does not seem to affect whether the child in the case will later talk about earthly events that occurred after the death. On the other hand, cases in which the previous personality died by natural means are slightly but significantly more likely to include statements about an existence in another realm than ones involving unnatural means—19 percent of the natural means cases versus 13 percent of the unnatural means ones.

We can look at the issue of suddenness of death in two ways. First, when we consider how long the death was expected, we divide the cases into five categories—unexpected up until the time of death, up until the day of death, up until the week of death, up until the month of death, or expected for more than one month. When we look to see how that length of time correlates with the subsequent statements that the children make about each kind of experience during the time between lives, we find that the suddenness does not affect how likely the child will be to describe memories about events in this world, but the more unexpected the death, the less likely the subject will be to make statements about an existence in another realm.

The other way to look at the issue of suddenness of death is to compare deaths that were unexpected at the time of death with ones that were expected for at least some length of time, even if it is only part of a day. In other words, we are comparing cases in which the previous personality died instantly with ones in which he or she did not. Instant deaths would include many deaths by unnatural means but would also include deaths by natural means in cases in which the person died immediately from, for instance, a heart attack. When we make the comparison, again we see no difference in the frequency of statements about earthly events. On the other hand, cases in which the previous personality died suddenly are less likely to include statements by the children about an existence in another realm than ones are where the person did not die suddenly—12 percent versus 22 percent.

This analysis suggests that how the previous personality dies or how suddenly he or she dies does not change the likelihood that the child in the case will talk later about earthly events that took place between that death and the child's birth. On the other hand, cases in which the previous personality's death occurred by natural means or was expected are somewhat more likely to include subjects' statements about an existence in another realm between the time of the previous personality's death and the child's birth.

Though we might take from this that dying a violent or unexpected death somehow short-circuits the process and decreases a person's chances of going on to another world, these findings, though statistically significant, are not absolute. We should also realize that if individuals go to another realm when they die and then come back to earth to be reborn, this analysis suggests that the way that a person dies and the suddenness of that death may be two factors that can affect how likely *memories* of the other realm are—but not necessarily how likely the experiences themselves are.

While we are speculating, we can look at whether personality and behavioral characteristics of the previous personality affect the likelihood that the subject of a case will describe earthly events or ones from another realm. The features of the previous personality we register in our computer database include the following: Was PP (the previous personality) attached to wealth? Was PP a criminal? Was PP philanthropic or generous? Was PP active in religious observances? Was PP a meditator? And, was PP saintly? I should add that we do not have information on the items for most of our cases, so we are dealing with small numbers—not so small that we cannot do statistical analyses with them, but small enough that we need to be aware that any interpretations are preliminary.

When we look to see if any of these characteristics affect the chances that the child will later report intermission memories, we find that none of them affect the likelihood of memories of earthly events. In addition, none of them affect the likelihood of memories of another realm except for one—being a meditator. We only have information on whether the previous personality meditated in thirty-three of the 1,100 cases in the database, so these results are preliminary in the extreme, but nonetheless statistically significant. The more that the previous personality meditated, the more likely the child was to describe memories from another realm.

I obtained these results when I used the question of the child recalling an existence in another realm as a yes/no question—either the child recalled an existence or not. We actually do not code the item of recalling an existence in another realm as a yes/no question, but as a question of degree. We rate whether the child recalled an existence in another realm in great detail, in some detail, in little detail, or not at all. When we break the item down this way and compare it to the previous personality's tendency to meditate, we still get a positive correlation. This means that the more the previous personality meditated, the more detail the child subsequently used in describing events in another realm. Given this, if we are open to the possibility of reincarnation and if we are going to draw any conclusion from this at all, then it should be that meditating might increase the ability of individuals to recall an existence in another realm in their next life. This is quite different from saying that meditating might increase an individual's chances of being able to go to another realm after a life, but that is also a possibility. Any conclusion at all is preliminary. Another factor could be involved that creates the illusion of a correlation between meditating and recall of another realm.

I also looked at the other personality characteristics of the previous personality to see if they affect the degree of the child's recall of another realm, and none of them does. Our current, preliminary information indicates that the ability to have memories of earthly events or of another realm after dying is not affected by whether a person was attached to wealth, was a criminal, was philanthropic or generous, was active in religious observances, or was saintly. These statistical tests, of course, only look at the likelihood that the child will report memories, and they do not answer the question of whether any of these factors could influence the likelihood of continuing to exist after dying or of being reincarnated.

Memorable Pregnancies

The last type of intermission memory involves those of conception or of being reborn. This category can also include memories either of the baby's experiences in the womb or of the parents' actions during the pregnancy, as in Bobby's case at the beginning of the chapter. He reported memories of his parents' wedding as well as of his birth. Another example is William from Chapter 1. When he saw a picture of his mother when she was pregnant, he commented that when he was in her tummy, she always held it when she ran up the stairs of their previous house. She asked him how he knew that, and he said that he knew because he had been watching her. As for memories of being born, many scientists have thought that infants were incapable of retaining memories for longer than a few seconds or minutes at most. If that was true, then children's claims to remember their births would clearly be impossible.

Our understanding of infant memory has been undergoing change because of recent research. In the past, conventional wisdom held that infants possessed a primitive memory system, while a different, more mature system developed late in the first year of life. Scientists spoke of implicit or procedural memory in infants and explicit or declarative memory that developed later. This conventional wisdom was not based on solid research. As one researcher has noted, "Most scientists probably believe that there is empirical evidence for the conclusion that different systems mediate the retention of different types of acquired knowledge at different points in development, but there is none."

Designing studies of infants' memory has been challenging since they are not able to communicate, but researchers have used various procedures. In some studies, a ribbon is strung from an infant's ankle to a crib mobile so that the baby learns through training that the mobile moves with kicking. If infants see the same mobile in a subsequent session and remember it, they kick more than if they do not remember it. Other techniques have included deferred imitation, which involves having infants reproduce a behavior that an investigator modeled for them earlier. Such studies have indicated, contrary to previous beliefs, that the same fundamental mechanisms are involved in memory processing in infants as in older individuals. In both groups, memories are forgotten gradually; they are recovered by reminders; and they can be changed by new information that overlaps with the old. Studies have shown that the memories of young infants, particularly when they experience appropriate reminders, last longer and are more specific than previously thought. As one researcher has noted, "The growing consensus from the literature on very early memory development is that from the earliest days of life infants can encode, store, and retrieve a great deal of information about events in the world they experience and that they retain this information over considerable time periods."

Though the evidence is clear that infants are able to remember events over longer periods of time as they grow older, the studies indicate that the neural mechanisms associated with the improvement are probably not ones that involve encoding or storing the information. In other words, the fact that most of us cannot recall memories of birth or early infancy does not seem to be due to infants being unable to lay down the memory tracks in their brains in the first place. Instead, the inability to retain such memories is probably due to brain mechanisms that are involved in *retrieving* the memories.

The question becomes whether some children, perhaps through reminders or some other mechanism, are able to retrieve early memories to which most children do not have access. Researchers have documented occasional examples of unusual memory retrieval in children. For example, a child was able at an age of almost three years old to state correctly that a picture he had last seen in a laboratory at the age of nine months was that of a whale. In another study, researchers interviewed ten children under the age of three, and they were all able to recall at least one event that had occurred more than six months earlier. Although young children do not usually have memories of being born—though we might find that more children than we know have such memories if we were to ask—this research suggests that such a possibility is not the crazy idea that conventional wisdom has held it to be. When Bobby, the boy at the beginning of the chapter, appears to remember events from his birth, we may conclude that he is demonstrating an unusual or even extraordinary ability to retrieve early memories, but that is different from saying that he could not possibly remember them since infants are not able to encode memories in their brains.

Now let us move on to prenatal memories—ones of events that occur when a baby is developing in the womb. In one study, researchers asked pregnant women to read a passage from a children's story aloud every day for the last six weeks of their pregnancy. Two days after the babies were born, testing was done in which a recording of that passage was played to reward one pattern of sucking while a recording of a different passage was played to reward another pattern of sucking. The results demonstrated that the babies preferred hearing the original passage compared to the new one. When babies whose mothers had not read the passage were tested, they showed no preference. The study indicated that the babies could retain memories that were created before they were born for at least two days after birth.

Reports like Bobby's involve much more than showing a

preference for one story over another. What about more involved memories? Dr. David Cheek, an obstetrician, elicited fetal memories from subjects through hypnosis and ideomotor techniques, in which he taught hypnotized subjects to answer questions using finger signals that were out of their conscious control. As I will discuss in Chapter 10, hypnosis can be an unreliable tool for obtaining accurate memories, but Dr. Cheek got some accurate ones with the process. In one report, he described four cases in which hypnotized subjects reported memories from the womb that their mothers later verified were accurate. In the first case, a girl remembered a scene in which her father became upset when he saw that her mother, while pregnant, was knitting an item for a girl. The subject remembered her mother saying, "It has to be a girl!" along with the fact that she was wearing a dark green plaid dress. Her mother confirmed the details and added that she had given away the dress soon after her pregnancy, meaning that the girl could not have seen it later.

In another case, Dr. Cheek treated a woman in the early 1960s who remembered an incident under hypnosis that occurred when her mother was six months pregnant with her. Her mother began to attempt an abortion with a buttonhook after her husband, who was an alcoholic, threatened to kill her. The mother could not go through with the act, and she never spoke to the subject about it until after the daughter recalled it under hypnosis.

In the next case, a man recalled an incident in which his mother, while pregnant with him, learned that his grandfather had died suddenly of a heart attack, accurately describing the dress that his mother was wearing. He also described his mother's fear during labor that she would die as her father recently had.

His mother later confirmed his memories of her appearance as well as of her emotions.

In the last case, a German woman remembered that her mother felt scared when she learned that she was pregnant, as her father was in combat in World War II at the time. The woman also recalled that when she was born, the doctor told her mother in a flat voice, "The baby is very beautiful" while her mother was very happy. Her mother confirmed that these memories were accurate. Though the delivery room greeting seems somewhat distinctive, we may wonder if the woman could have deduced that her mother would have been initially anxious about the pregnancy given the events going on then.

Dr. Cheek thought that the subjects initially stored the memories as sensory impressions while in the womb and then organized them later after being capable of understanding language, much as a person might tape a lecture in a foreign language and then listen to it years later after learning the language. He concluded that the fetus's experience mirrors what the mother perceives and responds to in her environment throughout the pregnancy. The evidence suggested to him that telepathy, clairvoyance, and some form of hearing are available to the fetus once its mother knows that she is pregnant. Though such a conclusion seems premature, I cannot come up with a better explanation for some of the cases that he describes.

His cases differ from ours in that they involve memories that adult subjects are not consciously aware of until their hypnotic sessions, but if we conclude that subjects can access the memories through hypnosis as adults, then the idea that some young children would have conscious awareness of them does not seem so unlikely. Dr. Cheek's reports undermine the idea that infants at birth, or even before birth, are incapable of laying down memory tracks, since his subjects were later able to recall events from those times while they were under hypnosis.

The memories that Dr. Cheek documented are like the ones that some of our subjects claim about birth or their time in the womb, but they differ from memories of another realm or of events on Earth before the subject was conceived. Those types of memories naturally are less likely to be corroborated. Though the descriptions of another realm may well be fantasy, when we evaluate such claims, we should keep them in context with other statements that the child has made that have been verified.

We may also want to question why so few of the subjects in our cases talk about the time between lives. If the children are re-membering previous lives, then we might expect them all to have memories of the time between the lives as well. In some ways, the issue seems absurd, in that we are talking about fairly incred-ible statements and then wondering why we do not hear more of them, but we may logically ask how a child could remember a previous life but lose memories of events after that.

One possibility is that memories from the time between lives are less likely to make an imprint on a developing brain if they were not associated with a brain when they were originally ac-quired. Memories of events that take place between lives, other than ones from time in the womb, would obviously have to be stored in something other than a brain. That other something, that consciousness, might carry memories of the previous life to the next one. Though it might also store memories of events that occur between lives, those new memories would be unlikely to imprint on a developing brain since they did not come from a brain in the first place.

Regardless of the cause, we can say that only a minority of children who claim past-life memories also report remembering events that took place between the end of that life and their own births. Their reports are intriguing and in some cases have been verified, at least partially, to be accurate.

CHAPTER 9

Opposing Points of View

Critics have challenged the concept of reincarnation in various ways, and in this chapter, we will look at the main arguments they have made. If they are convincing enough, then we may have to question whether we should even consider the evidence of the cases. After all, if we know that the idea of reincarnation is impossible, then we do not need to devote a lot of energy into looking at work that suggests that it happens. I do not need to spend much time studying a mathematical proof that shows that $1=2$ if I know for a fact that $1 \neq 2$. On the other hand, I may feel very sure about something but, when I look carefully, find that I am mistaken. To quote an old line, "The trouble with people is not that they don't know but that they know so much that ain't so." The question for us is whether the certainty that some people feel in rejecting the concept of reincarnation is based on fact or on things that just ain't so.

In looking at the arguments, I will not focus on the criticisms of the various religious beliefs that are associated with reincarnation, since those beliefs are not the basis of the work in this book. The research does not assume that they are correct and, as we will discuss in Chapter 10, does not necessarily support them. It considers the possibility of reincarnation in its most basic form—that the consciousness of an individual can survive after the person dies and then continue in a future individual.

Before beginning this discussion, I want to quote a noted skeptic. Carl Sagan, the popular astronomer, was a founding member of a debunking organization, the Committee for the Scientific Investigation of Claims of the Paranormal (CSICOP). In 1996, he wrote a book called *The Demon-Haunted World* in which he was extremely critical of many New Age or paranormal ideas. In it, he also wrote, "At the time of writing there are three claims in the [parapsychology] field which, in my opinion, deserve serious study," with the third being "that young children sometimes report details of a previous life, which upon checking turn out to be accurate and which they could not have known about in any other way than reincarnation." He was not saying that he believed in reincarnation, because he did not, but he thought that we should take this work seriously.

Do we have reasons for ignoring that opinion? Let us find out.

The Materialist Worldview

In the scientific world, the primary criticism of reincarnation is that it cannot happen because the material world is all that exists. In such a view, consciousness is only the result of a functioning brain, and it cannot exist independently from one. Thus, consciousness ends when the brain dies. Scientists say that they know this, either because the idea of survival after death conflicts too much with what we know about the materialist nature of the world or because there is no evidence that it happens.

Recently, a number of respected scientists, mainly physicists, have put forth views in several areas that, taken together, challenge this materialist dismissal of consciousness as being merely an insignificant byproduct of a functioning brain. Different groups have argued that we should consider consciousness separate from the brain, that modern physics can incorporate paranormal phenomena, and even that consciousness is an essential part of the universe. Though none of these arguments deals directly with reincarnation, we will see how they could be part of a new overall understanding of the universe in which consciousness is a key player rather than just an insignificant byproduct of the brain. Such an understanding may eventually allow the idea of an independently functioning consciousness to become part of our scientific knowledge.

The idea that consciousness can be considered separately from the brain is in many ways at the crux of the question of reincarnation, and it has been present for centuries. Descartes developed the concept of dualism in the 1600s to separate mind—the world of thoughts—from matter, including the brain. With it, he argued that an immaterial world, the world of thoughts, existed along with the material world. If the immaterial mind is separate from the matter of the brain, then this raises the question of whether it can exist after the brain dies.

Many mainstream scientists would say that the idea that the immaterial substance of the mind could interact with the material of the brain is nonsensical, and some go so far as to say that the concept of dualism violates known laws of physics. If the mind is to affect the body, then it must change a physical entity, namely the brain cells, even though it has no physical energy or mass associated with it. Such a change requires an expenditure of energy. Since no source of energy is available, the process would violate the principle of the conservation of energy. As one critic has written, "this confrontation between quite standard physics and dualism has been endlessly discussed since Descartes's own day, and is widely regarded as the inescapable and fatal flaw of dualism."

In response to this, physicist Henry Stapp has written, "This argument depends on identifying 'standard physics' with nineteenth century physics. But the argument collapses when one goes over to contemporary physics, . . . in which conscious effort can influence brain activity without violating the laws of physics. Contemporary physical theory allows, and in its orthodox von Neumann form entails, an interactive dualism." In his model, consciousness can produce effects, "yet it is fully compatible with all known laws of physics, including the law of conservation of energy." When he says contemporary physics, he is referring to quantum mechanics, the understanding of the physical world at the microscopic level of molecules, atoms, and subatomic particles. Likewise, John C. Eccles, a Nobel Prize–winning neuroscientist, advanced a dualist solution to the problem. He and quantum physicist Friedrich Beck hypothesized a mechanism using quantum mechanics for how the mind could act on the brain without violating the laws of conservation, and this involved mental intention affecting the brain by increasing the probabilities for the release of chemicals, called neurotransmitters, into the junctions between nerve cells.

In the area of physics and paranormal phenomena, some physicists have challenged the idea that the two are incompatible. Elizabeth Rauscher and Russell Targ have argued that the usual four dimensions of time and space cannot incorporate the findings of parapsychological research, but that a geometrical model of space-time known as "complex Minkowski space" can be used successfully to describe the major findings of parapsychology. On the other hand, O. Costa de Beauregard has challenged the idea that the geometrical time-space idea is even necessary to explain psychic phenomena. He has written that the occurrence of the paranormal phenomena is clearly implied by theoretical physics and that precognition, telepathy, and psychokinesis are allowed by its laws. In fact, he has written that "far from being 'irrational,' *the paranormal is postulated by today's physics.*" Brian Josephson, a Nobel Prize–winning physicist, created controversy when he contributed a short piece for a booklet that accompanied a set of stamps that the Royal Mail issued in Great Britain to commemorate the 100th anniversary of the Nobel Prizes. In it, he wrote that quantum theory was now being combined with theories of information and computation and that "these developments may lead to an explanation of processes still not understood within conventional science, such as telepathy." He has written that he thinks that in the long run, such phenomena as telepathy and mind-matter interactions, which I will discuss shortly, will be accepted and confirmed by science.

In the area of the importance of consciousness in the universe, experiments have demonstrated that with subatomic particles, several potential realities can be present at the same time until observation forces them to be limited to one possibility. This can be a difficult concept to comprehend, so here is an example. In a classic experiment called a double slit experiment, light particles, or photons, act like waves, appearing to spread out and go through two slits at once, unless physicists set up detectors beside the slits that record the individual photons as they pass through. In that case, each photon goes through one slit or the other but not both, giving the impression that the observation forces the photons down one path or the other.

John Wheeler, an important physicist who, among many other achievements, gave black holes their name, has extended this concept to demonstrate how conscious observers in the present can affect events in the past. He developed a thought experiment that showed that measurements made now by astronomers on Earth could affect the path that a particle of light from a faraway quasar had taken for billions of years before the astronomers made their observations. The experiment later was demonstrated in principle in a laboratory. Wheeler thinks that on a quantum level the universe is a work in progress in which not only the future is still undetermined but the past is as well, and conscious observers are one factor that can help select one out of many possible quantum pasts for the universe. Andrei Linde, a Stanford University physicist, goes even further and says that conscious observers are an essential component of the universe. He says, "I cannot imagine a consistent theory of everything [the goal in physics to have a unified theory of the universe that explains both the large-scale universe of gravity and relativity and the small-scale universe of quantum mechanics] that ignores consciousness."

When we combine the ideas of these well-respected scientists—that we should consider consciousness separate from the brain, that modern physics can be used to explain paranormal phenomena, and that consciousness is an essential part of the universe—we get a view of consciousness that is very different from the materialist dismissal of it. Consciousness is an essential and independent force in the universe in this view, and the parapsychological effects that it might be expected to produce are consistent with current understandings in physics. If this view is correct, we should be able to find evidence beyond what our cases provide that supports the idea of consciousness functioning independently from a brain.

Other Pieces of Evidence

In fact, researchers in several areas have produced evidence that consciousness is not confined to an individual brain. Research indicates that a person's consciousness or mental effort can produce effects on objects or living things that are in a different location from the person, meaning that the consciousness has had an effect some distance away from the person's brain. One group of studies has looked at whether people can influence the functioning of physical systems using only their minds—this is called mind-matter interactions. In these studies, subjects use their minds to attempt to change the output of machines called random number generators so that the outputs are no longer random. This is like trying to influence the outcome of coin flips with your mind so that heads comes up more than half of the time. This research has produced a mountain of data showing a small but significant effect. One large review looked at more than 800 studies conducted by sixty-eight different researchers and determined that "it is difficult to avoid the conclusion that under certain circumstances, consciousness interacts with random physical systems."

Another group of studies has looked at the effect that mental intention can have on other living organisms. This area is known as Direct Mental Interaction with Living Systems or DMILS. Researchers have conducted dozens of studies looking at the ability of subjects to affect the rates of various processes, including, among others, plant growth, recovery of animals from anesthesia, growth of tumors in animals, wound healing in animals, and the growth of yeasts and bacteria. At last count, out of 191 controlled studies that had been done, eighty-three had produced results that were statistically significant to the point that the likelihood of their being due to chance was less than one in a hundred, and another forty-one had results that would occur by chance only two to five times out of a hundred. Where we might expect no more than a handful of studies to be positive by chance, 124 of them recorded positive results.

Some studies have looked specifically at whether one person's consciousness can produce health benefits in another person by having subjects try to improve the condition of patients either through prayer or, more generally, through what is known as distant healing. As the name suggests, distant healing is the practice of attempting to improve another person's health using only mental effort while being apart from that person. In these studies, the patients have not known whether subjects were attempting prayer or distant healing for them. The studies have shown positive results for such conditions as heart disease and AIDS. One review found that out of twenty-three studies, thirteen showed statistically significant treatment effects, which is far above what we would expect by chance.

All of these studies, whether with machines, living organisms, or patients, suggest that consciousness can have an effect at a distance from the brain. Though this is not the same as saying that consciousness survives after the brain dies, if consciousness can act in a way that is physically separate from the brain, we have to wonder if it can operate separated in time from a functioning brain as well.

Does other evidence exist to support the idea of consciousness continuing after a patient dies? One area of research into this question is the field of near death experiences. Many people who survive an incident in which they come very close to death or are clinically dead for a short period of time report experiences that they had during that time. These often involve an impression of leaving their bodies and witnessing events from above and then going to another realm where they meet deceased relatives or religious beings. Much of this is subjective, of course, and cannot be proven, but some people have reported hearing or seeing events take place below them during the near-death experience that were later verified to have happened.

One of these, Pam Reynolds, accurately described medical equipment that was not visible while she was awake and a conversation that took place in the operating room while she was unconscious during surgery for a brain aneurysm in which her body was cooled to 60 degrees, her heart was stopped, and the blood was drained from her body. In another example, Dr. Bruce Greyson here at the University of Virginia investigated the report by a man named Al Sullivan about his experiences during an emergency coronary bypass operation. He said that when he looked down on the scene during his near-death experience, he saw his surgeon flapping his elbows. The surgeon and Mr. Sullivan's cardiologist confirmed to Dr. Greyson that the surgeon does have the unusual habit of flapping his elbows after scrubbing in for surgery.

Another area of research focuses on reports of apparitions, which are accounts by people of being visited by individuals who are not physically present. Studies of these began in the late 1800s. They can involve individuals who are either living or deceased, and some have included visits by individuals at the time of their death, even though the person who witnessed the apparition had no reason to think that the individual was dying. In a number of the reports, people have described learning details about the nature of the death that they could not have known at the time. Collective cases have also occurred in which more than one person saw the apparition appear.

Research with mediums, individuals who claim to communicate with the dead, also began in the late 1800s. Though some mediums have either been exposed as frauds or have been found to give no information that they could not have inferred through normal means, some gifted individuals, who have been carefully studied, have been able to demonstrate specific and personal knowledge about sitters—those who come to them for readings—and their deceased loved ones. One such medium, Mrs. Leonora Piper, was first studied by William James, the early American psychologist, in the 1880s. She was also taken to England and studied by the Society for Psychical Research. Investigators went to great lengths to guard against fraud by using such measures as having detectives follow her for weeks to make sure that she was not trying to find out information about potential sitters. In that context, she produced intimate material in remarkable detail about the strangers who came for readings. Mrs. Osborne Leonard, a British medium in the early twentieth century, was similarly studied and proved to be similarly impressive. She demonstrated a particular ability to provide information that was unknown to sitters at the time and was later verified to be accurate.

In recent times, mediumship has practically become a cottage industry with a number of mediums becoming television personalities. While this new group has not been investigated with the intensity that Mrs. Piper and Mrs. Leonard were, some have participated in recent studies, and other studies are ongoing.

Each of these fields has weaknesses along with strengths, but when you consider them as a group, you may wonder why mainstream science has ignored all the evidence that this research has produced. Science is very conservative, and its stability rests on the idea that new understandings of the world must fit in with the previous knowledge about it. Biologist E. O. Wilson has used the term "consilience" to describe this, the "jumping together" of knowledge when facts and theories from different areas link and form a common foundation of knowledge. As he says, "the explanations of different phenomena most likely to survive are those that can be connected and proved consistent with one another."

Though such a view is undoubtedly true, it can lead mainstream science to favor strongly the status quo for as long as possible, unable at times to accept new knowledge that will later look completely obvious. The history of the field is filled with unfortunate examples in which mainstream science turned its back on large amounts of evidence that challenged conventional wisdom. These go back at least as far as Galileo, who had to go before the Inquisition in 1633 for advocating the idea that the earth revolved around the sun.

Other particularly infamous examples include the failure of scientists to recognize the existence of meteorites despite reports by farmers of rocks falling from the sky into their fields. Scientists considered such an idea to be ridiculous—how could stones fall from the sky when there are no stones in the sky? Then there was poor Ignaz Semmelweis, an obstetrician in the 1800s who died in a mental institution at the age of forty-seven after he was vilified for producing data that showed that death rates during childbirth dropped significantly if doctors washed their hands before examining patients.

In the twentieth century, Alfred Wegener's idea of continental drift was initially ridiculed, despite considerable evidence to support it, because as one geologist put it, "If we are to believe Wegener's hypothesis, we must forget everything which has been learned in the last seventy years and start all over again." His theory languished for decades before it became the premise for the currently accepted idea of plate tectonics.

Mainstream science, of course, has rightly rejected many kooky ideas. Determining which ideas should be considered and which should be rejected can be difficult. The conservative nature of science has been its biggest strength and its biggest weakness. The basic understanding of the world tends to change at a pace that is almost as slow as continental drift, but the reluctance to accept new ideas too readily keeps that understanding from bouncing back and forth haphazardly. The need for consilience—the ability of new knowledge to be woven into the fabric of current understanding—helps to filter out erroneous beliefs, but it can also keep new insights from being accepted.

The question for us is whether the idea of reincarnation could ever be consilient with what we know, or think we know, about the world in general. One problem is that we do not have an adequate theory to explain how reincarnation might work. We only have the outlines of a theory, based on the notion that consciousness is not confined to the brain. The consciousness in a particular individual continues to exist after that person dies and then can attach itself to a developing fetus, bringing memories, emotions, and even traumas with it.

Though such a concept conflicts with a materialistic view of the world, when we consider the evidence for a separate and surviving consciousness I have described along with the recent ideas put forth by physicists, we can see that a blanket statement that anything that conflicts with a materialist view of the universe must be false risks becoming considered one day as shortsighted as the past rejections by mainstream science of phenomena such as meteorites do now. The field of quantum mechanics may provide a model for how a world of consciousness could become consilient with our other knowledge. The world of the universe's smallest particles has rules that are very different from the larger world that is made up of those particles, leading scientists to speak of quantum weirdness, but the field of quantum mechanics has been accepted alongside our understandings of the larger universe. Similarly, the rules of the world of consciousness may be very different from the rules of the material universe, but this would not preclude its acceptance as part of the universe as a whole. We will need to understand more about consciousness before most mainstream scientists would accept reincarnation, but the positions of well-respected scientists suggest that consilience might one day be possible.

Unknown Mechanisms

An argument along lines similar to the materialist one is that we should not consider reincarnation as a possibility, because we do not know of a mechanism that could explain it—we do not know how a consciousness might survive without a body, how it could affect a developing fetus, and so on. The weakness of this argument is fairly obvious on the face of it, but even more so when we consider it in other contexts. We are fortunate that the field of medicine has not waited for mechanisms to be uncovered before taking advantage of effective treatments, since physicians have successfully used numerous medications before knowing their mechanisms of action.

The mechanism of gravity was a complete mystery at the time that Isaac Newton proposed the concept, but people accepted its existence nonetheless. We did not have a mechanism to explain it until Albert Einstein proposed in his general theory of relativity that gravity is the warping of space and time. This case demonstrates that even arguing that no mechanism is conceivable is not enough to reject an idea since the warping of space and time was certainly an inconceivable idea when Newton proposed the concept of gravity. Unless we are willing to say that we know that no mechanism is even possible, we should not dismiss a concept simply because we do not know its mechanism.

The Population Explosion

Some have argued that population growth rules out reincarnation as a possibility. Their reasoning goes that the increase in the numbers of humans in modern times means that all the individuals currently alive could not have been reincarnating through multiple past lives, because the modern population is so much larger than populations in the past. A number of objections undercut this argument. In the first place, reincarnation does not have to happen to everyone. Some might get reborn because of "unfinished business" from their previous lives or because of the manner of their deaths or some other factor, but others might not get reborn. Some modern individuals would possess previous lives even if most would not. We also have no reason to think that new individuals could not be created, so again, even if all individuals have multiple lifetimes, some people who are currently alive could have had past lives while others would be here for the first time. In either of these situations, the number of individuals living at a given time would be irrelevant.

David Bishai of the Johns Hopkins School of Public Health has shown that we do not even need these scenarios to explain reincarnation in the presence of population growth. He looked at the question of how many humans have ever lived on Earth. Estimates are required, of course, since we do not know a lot about the size of the human population in ancient times, and a judgment has to made about which of our early ancestors we should consider human. Dr. Bishai quotes a calculation using a start date for human existence of 50,000 B.C.E. that estimated that 105 billion human beings have lived on Earth. Since population growth is predicted to max out at around ten billion people later this century, the number of humans in the past is certainly big enough to allow for reincarnation. Dr. Bishai does point out that the average amount of time between lives would have to shorten to accommodate the increase in population. We have no reason, of course, to think that the average amount of time between lives would have to remain constant, so population growth does not rule out reincarnation.

Alzheimer's Disease

Another argument is that the loss of memory and personality that comes with the brain deterioration of Alzheimer's disease shows that an intact brain is necessary for consciousness to occur. If memories and personality features cannot survive the partial destruction of the brain, they surely cannot survive death. In considering this, we can acknowledge that a person certainly needs an intact brain to express memories and personality, but that does not necessarily mean that the brain is producing those things. William James looked at this question in the late 1800s in relation to the overall question of life after death. He suggested that the brain, rather than producing thoughts, might permit or transmit them. In this transmission theory, he likened the brain to a colored glass that sifts and limits the color of light that passes through it, even though it does not produce the light itself. He pointed out that though consciousness depends on the brain to transmit it in the natural world, this dependence could be quite compatible with the possibility of its continuing supernaturally after the end of a life. He said that when the brain decays or stops altogether, the stream of consciousness associated with it vanishes from this natural world, but the "sphere of being" that supplied that consciousness could still be intact.

I do not know if James would have approved of the following analogy, but we can consider the modern example of the television. If your television breaks, the stream of images it supplied is no longer present for you to enjoy, but since it simply transmitted those images instead of creating them, the television programs continue to exist until you find another television to bring those images to life in your home. Similarly, the consciousness that found expression in the natural world through a particular brain may continue after that brain decays or dies, and it may then associate with a new brain, a new transmitter, at a later date.

Though this line of reasoning does not prove that such a phenomenon actually happens, James pointed out that the idea that the brain produces consciousness out of nothing is no more simple or credible in itself than any other theory, such as the proposal that it is an organ that transmits consciousness. Indeed, science has made little more progress today in pinpointing a source of consciousness in the brain than it had in James's day 100 years ago.

Another "argument" that some people make against reincarnation is simply that the idea is absurd. Well, ridicule is a poor substitute for reasoned discussion. The important issue is to determine what it is about reincarnation that would make it absurd. I believe that I have addressed the strongest scientific and logical criticisms of reincarnation, and I do not see any reason to reject it out of hand.

Religious Objections

At the other end of the spectrum, some people object to the idea of reincarnation because it conflicts with their religious beliefs. Addressing this objection in a scientific way is not possible since it is not a scientific objection, but it is still an issue that warrants consideration. Those making the objection tend to have Judeo-Christian beliefs, so we will look at those religions.

Although reincarnation is not a part of mainstream Judeo-Christian doctrine, some members of those religions have believed in it. Many in the West today believe in reincarnation as individuals, and some Judeo-Christian groups have included reincarnation in their beliefs. In Judaism, the Kabbalah includes reincarnation, which is also a part of the Hasidic Jewish belief system. Some groups of early Christians, particularly the Gnostic Christians, believed in reincarnation, and some Christians in southern Europe believed in it until the Second Council of Constantinople in 553 C.E. Exactly what happened at that meeting has been a source of controversy, but church leaders there were believed to have condemned the idea of souls existing before conception.

The Bible contains passages in the New Testament that seem to refer to reincarnation. In Matthew 11:10–14 and 17:10–13, Jesus says that John the Baptist is the prophet Elijah who had lived centuries before, and he does not appear to be speaking metaphorically. Some point out in response to this that Elijah did not die according to the Old Testament, but ascended to heaven in a whirlwind, so he would have been returning to Earth rather than being reborn. The Gospel of Luke contradicts this line of reasoning in describing John the Baptist's birth, beginning life as a baby and not as a mature prophet returned to Earth.

Another possible allusion to reincarnation takes place when the disciples ask Jesus in John 9:2 whether a particular man was born blind because of his sins or those of his parents. This obviously implies that they thought the man had an opportunity to sin before he was born, suggesting a previous existence. In response, Jesus does not reject that possibility but says that the man was born blind so that the works of God could be manifest in him, and proceeds to cure the blindness.

Beyond these specific passages, we should consider whether reincarnation conflicts with Judeo-Christian doctrines in general. The existence of reincarnation would mean that we have not had a full understanding of life after death. Many other religious issues are not clear-cut either. The Bible is open to multiple interpretations, as the different views of the various denominations make clear. The Bible does not spell out the concept of reincarnation to be sure, but that does not mean that reincarnation necessarily conflicts with what is in the Bible. In fact, it does not even necessarily conflict with the concepts of heaven and hell, since some people with a belief in reincarnation, including some Shiite Muslim groups, believe that an ultimate Judgment Day comes after a series of lives, when God sends souls to heaven or hell based on the moral quality of their actions during all their various lives.

In addition, the doctrine of reincarnation would certainly not conflict with the value given to love and kindness by the Judeo-Christian religions as well as the other major world religions. It does nothing to change the idea that living a loving, ethical life is important, whether it is a single life or one in a series.

In summary, we have looked at various criticisms of reincarnation, and we have seen that any certainty that people feel about the impossibility of reincarnation is not justified. We have looked at some objections—for example, the claims that there is no evidence of survival after death, and that population growth rules out reincarnation—and seen that they just ain't so. We have also seen that none of the other criticisms justifies ignoring evidence that supports it. None of them makes believing in the possibility of reincarnation resemble believing that $1 = 2$. We do not have an adequate reason to reject the concept and this body of work out of hand. As Carl Sagan wrote, we need to study seriously the evidence that this work has produced.

CHAPTER 10

Conclusions and Speculations

To review the possible explanations for this phenomenon, the best normal explanation in the cases with birthmarks and birth defects involves coincidence for the birthmarks and faulty memory by informants for the statements that the children make. In the cases that primarily involve statements by the child, knowledge acquired through normal means can be used for cases in which the previous personality either was a family member of the subject or lived in the same village, and faulty memory by informants is the best normal explanation for most of the others. It is clearly not sufficient, however, for the cases with written records that were made of the child's statements before the previous personality was identified, so we have to resort to fraud as a way to explain those. The best normal explanations for the past-life behaviors of the children are fantasy combined with coincidence and faulty memory by informants, but they both have weaknesses. Finally, in the cases with recognitions by the children, we can use faulty memory by informants to explain many of them, but we are again left with fraud as the only normal explanation possible for the controlled recognition tests.

Since faulty memory by informants provides the best normal explanation for many of the cases, I want to present a couple of studies that have looked at that possibility. In the first one, Dr. Stevenson and Dr. Keil compared reports that the families made about cases at different times. The study began when Dr. Keil unintentionally restudied several cases that Dr. Stevenson had studied twenty years before. He then intentionally reinvestigated more of Dr. Stevenson's earlier ones until he had studied fifteen of them. He did this to see if the reports by the families had become exaggerated over time. After all, the whole idea behind the faulty memory by informants possibility is that the families are crediting the children with more specific knowledge about the previous lives than they actually demonstrated before the two families met, so Dr. Keil wanted to see if the claims had grown following the original reports that the families gave to Dr. Stevenson.

When Dr. Keil interviewed the families, he did not know what information they had originally given to Dr. Stevenson. Even after he began intentionally restudying cases, he only had the names and addresses of the subjects whose cases Dr. Stevenson had investigated years before. He then went to the families and made notes of the new interviews that he had with them. Once he completed his investigation, he and Dr. Stevenson compared the information that he got with what Dr. Stevenson had obtained years before. Given the time that had elapsed, the investigations were not identical, and in some cases, the people that Dr. Keil interviewed differed somewhat from the ones available to Dr. Stevenson twenty years before.

When Dr. Keil and Dr. Stevenson reviewed the information that each of them had collected, they found that only one of the cases had become stronger based on what the witnesses said. In that case, the subject's family described an incident to Dr. Keil that they had not mentioned to Dr. Stevenson that involved the subject finding a special spoon that the previous personality, the subject's deceased brother, had kept on a high shelf in a fairly inaccessible place.

In three other cases, the strength of the reports basically remained the same. Some of the details were different in one report compared to the other, but overall, the cases had not grown stronger or weaker over time. The reports of the other eleven cases had actually become weaker by the time that Dr. Keil talked with the families. This was often because the informants gave fewer details than they had given to Dr. Stevenson years before. This is logical, of course, since we generally remember fewer details about events as time goes on, but in this situation, it is also important. It shows that the cases do not grow stronger in people's minds over time, and in fact, these had become weaker over time. As we have seen, a number of the cases include features that tempt us to conclude that witnesses must be remembering statements or events incorrectly. This study does not provide any support for such a conclusion.

Dr. Sybo Schouten and Dr. Stevenson conducted the other study that looked at this question. They compared cases in which written records were made of the children's statements before the families met with cases that did not include such records. They were testing the idea that the parents exaggerate the statements that the child made about the previous personality before the families met. They expected that if this were true, the cases in which written records document what the children actually said before the families met would include fewer statements and fewer correct ones than the cases without such records.

Since the cases with written records have come mainly from

India and Sri Lanka, Drs. Schouten and Stevenson looked at all thoroughly investigated cases from those two countries in which the number of correct and incorrect statements had been determined and recorded. This produced twenty-one cases with written records made before the families met and eighty-two cases without, and they then compared the two groups. What they found was surprising. The average number of statements in the cases with the written records was twenty-five and a half, while the average in the cases without the records was significantly lower, at eighteen and a half. The percentage of correct statements was essentially the same in both groups—76.7 percent in the written record cases and 78.4 percent in the cases without records.

Thus, the findings of the study are the opposite of what we would expect if because of faulty memory the informants were crediting the children with more (and more correct) statements than they had actually made before the families met. In the cases without written records, they were crediting the children with fewer statements, presumably because they had forgotten some of the statements since no one had written them down. As Drs. Schouten and Stevenson point out, the findings show that if the families do credit the children with more knowledge about the previous life than they actually demonstrated before the families met, they do not do so enough to affect the data in a measurable way.

This study meshes well with the results of the previous one in that it indicates that the reports in the cases grow less detailed over time rather than more, since informants in the cases without written records remembered fewer statements by the children than the number documented in the cases with written records.

This is consistent with the finding of Drs. Stevenson and Keil that many cases become weaker over time. Taken together, these two studies really cast doubt on the proposition that the main cause of the cases is that witnesses incorrectly remember the children's statements about the previous life as being more impressive than they really were. If this were the case, we would expect the reports to become stronger over the years as the memories of the witnesses become less accurate, when in fact the reports frequently become weaker, and we would expect the cases that include written documentation of what the children actually said to have fewer statements and fewer correct ones, when they actually have more statements and the same percentage of correct ones.

Given that faulty memory by informants is the primary normal explanation for many of the cases, this leaves us without a solid way of explaining them through normal means. Of course, as we have already seen, no single normal explanation can explain all the different types of cases, but having grave doubt cast over the most common explanation is especially challenging.

Since no single explanation can explain all the cases, the only feasible way at this point to explain them through normal means is to say that a normal process produces each case through some imperfection in the case, and different processes are responsible for different cases. In considering this, we should first note that no perfect case exists. Perfection is rarely found in science—for any medical study that is done, someone can always find a way to criticize it or to doubt its findings. This is particularly true in the study of spontaneous phenomena. These cases do not take place in a laboratory where we can control all of the conditions to produce the cleanest cases possible. Instead, they take place in the real world of uncontrolled conditions. Some phenomena occur in nature and cannot be reproduced in a lab, and if we think that they are important enough to study, then we have to accept the limitations that come with that.

Therefore, none of these cases is perfect, and we recognize that. With the imperfections, we can argue that a dishonest set of parents here or a coincidence there or a conversation about the previous life in front of a young child or else bad memory can explain each case, so perhaps together they can explain all the cases.

Is such an explanation satisfactory? In a particular case, we may think, for example, that coincidence is quite unlikely but nonetheless possible. If we use such reasoning to explain all 2,500 cases, then we are taking the unlikely and raising it to extremes. After a while, looking for any conceivable defect in each individual case begins to feel like missing the forest for the trees. If we stand back and look at this worldwide phenomenon as a whole, then we see a pattern of remarkable events. Even though the cases are only evidence and not "proof" of a paranormal process, when we consider the weaknesses of the normal explanations, I do not think that they can adequately explain the strongest cases as a group. I think they fail, and therefore, we must turn to the paranormal possibilities to see if they can provide a better explanation.

When we look at the different types of cases all together, reincarnation provides a much more straightforward explanation overall than either ESP or possession. It easily explains all of the cases, which the others do not do, and it certainly is a more obvious explanation than the other two. The big question becomes whether the cases provide enough evidence of a paranormal process so that we should favor reincarnation over the normal explanations.

Dr. Stevenson has written that he has become persuaded that "reincarnation is the best—even though not the only—explanation for the stronger cases we have investigated." To be slightly more conservative, I would say that the best explanation for the strongest cases is that memories, emotions, and even physical injuries can sometimes carry over from one life to the next. If this is what we mean by reincarnation, then my conclusion is the same as Dr. Stevenson's, but since, as he has also written, we know almost nothing about reincarnation, I prefer to use the more specific terminology.

While this may seem to be an astounding statement—that memories, emotions, and physical injuries can sometimes carry over from one life to the next—the evidence, I think, leads us to that conclusion. It is no more astounding than many currently accepted ideas in physics seemed to be when they were originally proposed, and since the evidence has led us to it, we need to consider it. I fully acknowledge that I may be wrong—as Dr. Stevenson wrote, this is the best explanation of the cases but not the only one—but the skeptics may be wrong as well, whether they admit it or not. Though such skeptics would obviously make a different determination, the idea of reincarnation or carry-over from one life to the next appears to be the best conclusion based on the evidence that this research has produced over the last forty years. If this means that we need to question some of our materialistic assumptions about how the world works, then so be it.

In attempting to understand this, we should keep in mind that some physicists now consider consciousness to be an entity separate from the brain and one with important functions in the universe.

Conscious observation, at least, appears capable of affecting the future and even the past on the level of the microscopic quantum world, and if consciousness is indeed a fundamental part of the universe—if Stanford physicist Andrei Linde is correct when he says that a consistent theory of everything that ignores consciousness is unimaginable—then the world is a far more complex and wondrous place than what the physical world shows us in everyday life.

In physics, concepts in relativity and quantum mechanics have already shown us that the universe as we currently understand it is far different from what our everyday experience tells us about it. Similarly, most of us are only aware of our own consciousness, and we process that awareness with our individual brains. This may cause us to have trouble fully accepting evidence that consciousness is a factor in the universe beyond what seems to be occurring in our individual brains. If consciousness is a fundamental part of the universe, then we have to consider whether we can logically decide that it is simply a byproduct of functioning brains. If conscious observation can determine the path that a particle of light took billions of years ago, as John Wheeler has proposed, then does it make sense that consciousness just happened to develop as a temporary state of a functioning human brain? I think not. We may assume that a fundamental component of the universe, if that is what consciousness is, exists separately from our little brains here on Earth. Even though our everyday experience may tell us that our consciousness begins with our birth and ends with our death, a reasonable alternative is that our brains serve as vehicles for consciousness during our lifetimes, and that consciousness existed before our births and can continue after our deaths until it finds another vehicle in a new body.

The evidence in our cases supports this idea, and for the re mainder of this chapter, we will operate from the perspective that if this is true, we can consider what the cases may tell us about the process of reincarnation. We will have to speculate a fair amount as we do so, and we should remember that the world of consciousness may operate very differently from the physical universe. Therefore, any conclusions that we make about reincarnation are tentative at this point, but we have some fascinating questions to explore.

Does Everybody Reincarnate?

When we see evidence for reincarnation, one reaction is to think about how it could affect us individually. Clearly, we would all love the opportunity to see our deceased loved ones again. We can think about the emotions that Patrick Christenson's mother must have felt when she determined that her first son, who had died as a toddler, had returned to her. A loss of that kind is obviously devastating, and we would all be comforted to know that such a loss might not be permanent.

Unfortunately, we must remember that what is true about the children who report past-life memories may not be true for the rest of us. They may be a unique group, and even if they have reincarnated, no one else may have. For instance, they may have had issues that kept them connected to their earthly experiences so that they came back while others do not. The situation could be like stories of haunted houses in which people say that a ghost is stuck there because of a grisly death or a similar reason. As I discussed earlier, 70 percent of the previous personalities died by unnatural means in cases where the mode of death is known, and of course a number of those dying by natural means died suddenly as well. This suggests that a violent or sudden death is much more likely to produce a future case of a child with past-life memories than other types of deaths. Such a death may be one factor that can cause our subjects to have connections to the Earth that lead them to be exceptions to the normal state of affairs. After death, the consciousness may typically blend into a larger universal consciousness or go off to another realm of existence— heaven, for example. For all we know, the traditional Judeo-Christian views of life after death may be correct in general even if our cases are legitimate examples of reincarnation.

On the other hand, reincarnation may normally occur but without memories continuing from the previous life. In that case, we may all have had previous lives even though most of us do not remember them. If this is true, then the usual process may get disrupted either by a factor in the previous life like an unexpected death or by some factor in the next life. This may lead some memories to be present in the next life, and therefore, even though everyone may reincarnate, our cases are unusual because of the presence of the memories.

The cases do not answer which possibility is more likely, past lives being unusual or just the memories of past lives being unusual, even though they indicate that reincarnation occurs in some circumstances. Although we would all like either to see our deceased loved ones return to us, or to return ourselves to our children or grandchildren after our deaths, these cases do not answer the question of whether reincarnation is universal. They provide evidence that we *can* reincarnate, at least under certain circumstances—which is certainly a significant finding—but they do not indicate if all of us actually do.

Even if we all do reincarnate, the patterns we see in the cases with memories may not apply to the rest of us. The type of death or some other factor might change the normal process to produce patterns that could go along with the enduring memories. For instance, the children who have past-life memories may be more connected to a certain location than others would be. These children tend to reincarnate close to where the previous personality lived, yet others who reincarnate without memories may not be similarly constrained. Likewise, the children who describe staying in one particular location for years between lives may not be typical of all who reincarnate. We should remember that other differences could occur as well between the cases of children who have past-life memories and any others who reincarnate without such memories.

In Cases of Reincarnation, What Reincarnates?

Despite these reservations, we should still examine these cases closely to see what they say about life after death. One question is this: If these cases are examples of reincarnation, then exactly what reincarnates? The cases show that memories, emotions, and physical traumas can carry over to a future life. I have referred to a consciousness continuing, but this is not a very specific term. Other terms that can be used, such as "soul" or "astral body," have connotations we may not feel are accurate. For that reason,

Dr. Stevenson coined the term "psychophore," which he derived from the Greek meaning "soul bearing," to describe the vehicle that would carry the memories after a death.

This entity, the psychophore or consciousness, appears to be able to obtain new information, based on cases in which the children describe events that occurred after the previous personality died. We might wonder how it could do so, since the consciousness obviously does not have sense organs like eyes and ears. The answer must be that it can get information through paranormal means. This is similar to the reports of patients who have near-death experiences, as they often describe watching events from above their bodies. It also fits with other studies in parapsychology that show some people are able to gain knowledge that they do not obtain through their normal sense organs. Rather, they gain it through paranormal means, and though we do not know what those means are, if a person can do so during a life, then we can logically assume that their consciousness could do so if it survives death.

While we tend to think that reincarnation means that some entity has continued from one life to the next, many Buddhists, particularly Theravada Buddhists, say that this is not the case. Their doctrine of *anatta,* or "no soul," emphasizes that there is no "self" and thus no entity that continues from one life to the next. At the death of one personality, a new one comes into being, much as the flame of a dying candle can serve to light the flame of another. Continuity between personalities occurs, because the karmic forces that the previous person sets in motion lead to the subsequent rebirth, but no identity persists. Since I am far from a Buddhist scholar, I confess that I have trouble embracing or even fully understanding this concept, but I can at least note that despite this doctrine, most practicing Buddhists do, in fact, believe that an actual entity gets reborn.

As Dr. Stevenson notes, our cases certainly suggest that some vehicle has carried the enduring memories with it to the next life. Something more seems to have survived than just the memories and emotions. We have talked about how the birthmarks might arise when the consciousness is so traumatized by the injuries in one life that it then affects the developing fetus to produce similar marks on the new body. I have trouble imagining that such a process could take place without *something,* whether we call it a consciousness or a psychophore or some other term, carrying the effects of the injury on to the next life. Though some Buddhists would no doubt disagree, our cases imply that some entity, which I have called a consciousness, can continue from one life to the next.

The fact that physical trauma can affect the consciousness to such a degree that it produces marks on the developing fetus implies that this consciousness can affect the physical body. This goes back to our discussion of dualism in Chapter 9 and the question of whether immaterial thoughts can affect the material world, in this case the developing fetus. These cases suggest that they can. In addition, the cases show that the mind itself can be affected by traumatic events. We discussed cases in Chapter 4 in which patients developed physical marks when they re-experienced traumas under hypnosis. Reincarnation cases indicate that such effects can even persist into the next life. The traumas can "scar" the consciousness to such an extent that the scars affect the next body that it occupies.

The long-lasting effects of the trauma may seem odd at first, until we remember the way that traumatic events can affect the mind in this life. People who experience significant emotional or physical trauma can develop post-traumatic stress disorder in which they experience physical and emotional symptoms years after the original event occurred. We should not be surprised then to learn that such traumas can travel with the consciousness into the next life, whether as scars or as phobias. We might hope that all our past difficulties would disappear when one life ended, but these cases indicate that they do not.

The When and Where of Reincarnation

Now let us consider whether the surviving consciousness has any control over when and where it is reborn. In a number of cases, the children have reported that they chose their next parents. In the Asian cases, they sometimes describe an episode in which they see one of their future parents and decide to follow that person home to join the family. In the American cases, the children may talk about being in heaven and picking their next parents. Although those stories are obviously unverifiable, some of the Asian ones have been at least partially verified in that the parent had been in the area described by the child around the time of conception.

In other cases, when we think of how bitterly the children complain about the family that they are in, we may conclude that they show no sign of having chosen their parents. Since most of the children do not report any memories of the time between lives, we get no indication from them if they were involved in any decision-making or not. It is possible that they were but do not have access to the memory of being so. We have no way of knowing for sure, but given the variety of cases, it is possible that some individuals choose their parents or their place of rebirth while others do not.

This brings up the larger question of whether anybody at all makes decisions in the process of reincarnation. If the individual consciousness does not decide when to be reborn, do guides, angels, or gods decide? Or does it occur naturally without any conscious decision-making? Various belief systems have different scenarios for how the individual goes on to the next life. Though a few of our subjects talk about guides directing them to their current family, most of them do not say anything about the time between lives, so our cases really shed very little light on this important question.

Along these lines, we can look specifically at the location of rebirths. One conclusion we can draw from these cases is that the place where the rebirth occurs, at least in situations in which the child retains memories of the previous life, is not random. The vast majority of the children report past lives in the same country of their current life, and many of them say that they lived in the same village or even in the same family. What are we to make of this? One possibility is that geographical constraints affect where the consciousness can go to be reborn. Though the idea that consciousness would be limited to a small area seems odd, it fits with the stories by some children of staying in a particular location, the place where the previous personality died for instance, until they saw one of their future parents.

I am more inclined to believe that consciousness is drawn to particular areas because of emotional connections with them. Many of us identify strongly with being from a particular country, so we might naturally be more likely to be reborn in the same country. In addition, people may have emotional attachments to particular places and would be drawn to return to them. Most importantly, an individual's connections to other people may play a big role in where the rebirth occurs. In the same-family cases, the children may be reborn in the family because a strong emotional connection has continued. Particularly in cases in which the previous personality was a child who died young, the individual consciousness may still be closely tied to the family, so it is drawn to be reborn in it. The mechanism of how it is drawn is of course a mystery, but I can imagine an emotional force in the world of consciousness that would draw individuals to particular places or families with an almost magnetic pull.

The cases in which the children report past lives from other countries offer possible insight into this. In these cases, the children usually say that they died in their past life in the country where they currently live, an example being Burmese children who say they were Japanese soldiers killed in Burma during World War II. Many of those Burmese children express a longing to return to Japan, as if they were trapped in Burma after dying there. We do not know if they were trapped there by geographical limitations or by emotional ties. Their actions as soldiers, many of whom were very harsh with the Burmese people, may have created an unresolved emotional connection that caused them to stay in Burma for their next life.

Whether the explanation is geographical or emotional, we can say that these cases show that individuals often keep some links with a life after the end of it. We do not know if this is true in general or just in the cases with preserved memories, but these cases demonstrate that in some situations links do continue into the next life. In the cases of Burmese children who report memories as Japanese soldiers, a link is maintained with both Burma and Japan, as the children are born in Burma but still long for Japan.

The Question of Karma

Karma is a concept that is part of many religions that have a belief in reincarnation, notably Hinduism and Buddhism. It includes many subtleties in the various religious systems that we are not able to discuss here, but in general, it is the belief that an individual's actions determine his or her future circumstances. This includes the idea that actions in previous lives affect an individual's circumstances in the current one. One interpretation of the Burmese-Japanese cases I just mentioned is that their past actions against Burmese people caused them to be reborn as Burmese individuals.

Do our cases in general provide any evidence for the existence of karma? Before answering that question, I should point out that with karma, an individual's circumstances in the current life are thought to be due not just to actions in the last life but also to actions in any of the previous lives, so assessing the effects of those in only the last life is difficult.

I looked at our computer database to see if any characteristics of the previous personality would correlate with the circumstances that the subject was born into. Specifically, I looked at the following items about the previous personality—Was PP saintly? Was PP a criminal? Did PP commit moral transgressions? Was PP philanthropic or generous? And was PP active in religious observances?—to see if any of them correlated with the economic status of the subject, the social status of the subject, or the caste of the subject for Indian cases. In doing so, I am aware that we would consider a child with loving, supportive, but poor parents to be born into positive circumstances, but we might at least think that positive circumstances would be more likely to include higher economic settings than lower ones.

When I ran the correlation tests, only one of the characteristics of the previous personality correlated with the circumstances of the subject. Saintliness in the previous personality showed a very strong correlation with the economic status of the subject and a significant correlation with the social status of the subject. This means that the more saintly the previous personality was considered to have been, the higher the economic status and social status that the child is likely to have. Saintliness did not correlate with the caste of the subject in the cases in India, and none of the other characteristics of the previous personality correlated with the circumstances of the subject. We have to consider then that the correlations that the saintliness item shows may just be a statistical fluke, and we have little evidence that karma from the previous life affects the circumstances of the rebirth.

Another factor that argues against karmic effects is one that I mentioned in Chapter 4. The birthmark and birth defect cases involve lesions that match wounds that the children remember suffering in the previous life. If we thought that karma was responsible for them, then we might expect them to match wounds that the previous personalities inflicted on someone else rather than ones that they suffered themselves. Since this is not the case, we have to say that the marks and defects do not support the idea of karmic effects.

To repeat, the doctrine of karma is a complex one, and though it may be able to explain the findings covered in this book, we have to conclude that our cases offer very little evidence to support it.

Enduring Emotions

To consider further the possible emotional links, we might like to think that the love and positive emotions we give to others can last more than one lifetime, and the cases give us hope that they may. Not only do birthmarks and phobias occur in these cases, but the children also continue to express love for the previous family. Love endures.

This seems particularly evident in the same-family cases. William, the boy in Chapter 1, told his mother that he would always take care of her, just as his grandfather had told her. Patrick Christenson, the boy in Chapter 4 with multiple birthmarks, talked about when he left his mother at the end of the short life of her first son, and he has a very close relationship with her now. Such examples indicate that love can survive death and continue into the next life.

Abby Swanson in Chapter 3 said that she had been her great-grandmother. If she was correct, then she came back in a very different relationship with her mother than in the previous time as her grandmother. To go from being grandmother to daughter is quite a change, yet it mirrors what can often happen in a single lifetime when elderly parents eventually come to depend on the children who previously depended on them. Perhaps the question of who is taking care of whom is not as important as the

224 LIFE BEFORE LIFE

connection that the individuals share. That connection is one that may continue across lifetimes.

Such an idea is not only comforting but may well be true, based on the evidence from many of our cases. The idea of the emotional connection, but not the roles, enduring across lifetimes can affect the way that parents look at their children, because it suggests that parents need to provide discipline for their children, not in a domineering or harsh way, but as guidance for fellow travelers. Children can be seen as equal partners sharing life's journey instead of inferior beings, even though they are partners that need direction and need to feel a sense of security that their parents are in control.

In Abby's case, perhaps her great-grandmother chose to return to Abby's mother so that they could continue their journey together. The roles are different this time, and Abby's mother will need to teach her many things. In the end, she may learn as much from the relationship with Abby as Abby learns from her.

When the rebirth does not occur in the same family, this enduring connection, or at least the longing that it creates, can be a problem in the new life. Many of the children show great emotional upset, because they feel that they are being kept from their real parents. This generally resolves as the children grow older, but it can be very intense when it is present. As I noted in Chapter 6, many of the Asian parents respect what their children say about their past lives since they usually believe them, but they also make clear to the children that the current life is different from the past one. Unfortunately, they sometimes make this point with great emphasis, and some of them use very harsh methods to get their children to stop talking about the previous life.

Even this might be better in the long run than emphasizing

the link to the past life. Relationships from the past life are in the past, and we do not benefit from focusing on past lives to the detriment of the current life. Some of the children certainly experience great distress in wanting to continue the relationships they recall from previous lives, and this can affect their interactions with their current parents. Similarly, some adults get so caught up in the possibility of their past lives that they neglect to experience the current one. Surely, this is not the best course to take. While being aware of the possibility of reincarnation may make people more appreciative of the spiritual aspects of life and of the spiritual component of others, people should not focus too much on possible past lives.

Along these lines, some people undergo hypnotic past-life regression to try to uncover their past lives. Even if people could gain from exploring their past lives, little evidence exists to support using hypnotic regression to do so. Many hypnotists can place subjects under hypnosis and get them to recall apparent memories from the past, often with great detail and emotion. The hard part comes in trying to verify that these "memories" are of events that actually happened. In many cases, the subject has appeared to remember a life from ancient times, so determining whether it actually occurred is impossible. In others, the subject's report has included historical absurdities. Additionally, in some cases, subjects have recalled details that were then discovered to have come from another source, such as a book they had read years before and forgotten about.

I discussed cases in Chapter 8 in which hypnosis produced some dramatic results, but unfortunately, it is a very unreliable tool, whether being used to uncover memories from the present life or from past ones. Hypnosis can lead to some remarkable memories from the present life, but it can also produce fantasy material. Under hypnosis, the mind tends to fill in the blanks. If a person is being asked to give details that he or she does not remember, the mind will usually come up with some. Once this has happened, the person may then have great difficulty distinguishing actual memories from fantasy ones.

This is not to say that all hypnotic past-life regression cases are worthless. After all, if some young children can have memories of previous lives, then logic would dictate that some adults may be able to discover such memories through the use of hypnosis just as they can pull up early childhood memories. Even so, the vast majority of cases contain no evidence supporting the idea that the images people see under hypnosis are ones from actual past lives that they led. As Alan Gauld has written, though a few strong cases may be found, "they will be so small a solid residue from so great a flood of entertaining but inconclusive eyewash, that one would be ill-advised to waste one's lifetime in attempting to induce them."

Advice for Parents

Parents frequently ask us for advice on how to handle their children's statements about past lives. Though each case has individual differences, I can offer some general guidance that I hope will be helpful. First, parents should know that these statements do not indicate mental illness. We have talked with many families in which a child claimed to remember another set of parents, another home, or a previous death, and the children rarely show any mental health problems.

Several studies have looked at this question. I recently completed a study with a colleague, Dr. Don Nidiffer, in which we looked at psychological testing results of fifteen young American subjects. They were between the ages of three and six years old at the time of the testing, and we found that they were generally quite intelligent. When we looked at scales measuring problem behaviors, their averages were all in the normal range, and they did not show any evidence of psychological problems.

These results are similar to ones that Erlendur Haraldsson and his colleagues have found when they tested subjects in other countries. In Sri Lanka, the subjects also did very well in school but showed some mild behavioral problems at home. Most significantly, they were not more suggestible than other children, arguing against the idea that they claimed memories of a past life because other people had suggested that they had one. In Lebanon, the children also showed no clinically relevant symptoms, though they tended to daydream a lot. The testing again showed that the subjects were not unusually suggestible. Overall, the children appear to be functioning quite well.

When children talk about a past life, parents are sometimes unsure how to respond. We recommend that parents be open to what their children are reporting. Some of the children show emotional intensity regarding these issues, and parents should be respectful in listening just as they are with other topics that their children bring up.

When a child talks about a past life, parents should avoid asking a lot of pointed questions. This could be upsetting to the child and, more importantly from our standpoint, could lead the child to make up answers to the questions. Separating memories from fantasy would then be difficult or impossible. Asking general, open-ended questions such as, "Do you remember anything else?" is fine, and empathizing with a child's statements—"That must have been scary," for instance, when a child describes a fatal accident—certainly is as well.

We encourage parents to write down any statements about a past life that their children make. This is particularly important in cases in which the children give enough information so that identifying a particular deceased individual might be possible. In such a situation, having the statements recorded ahead of time would be critical in providing the best evidence that the child actually recalled events from a previous life.

At the same time, parents should not become so focused on the statements that they and their children lose sight of the fact that the current life is what is most important now. If children persist in saying they want their old family or old home, explaining that their current family is the one they have for this life may be helpful. Parents should acknowledge and value what their children have told them while making clear that the past life is truly in the past.

Parents are sometimes more upset by the statements than their child is. Hearing a child describe the experience of dying in a painful or difficult way can be hard, but both parent and child can know that the child is safe now in this life. Some parents may be comforted to know that the vast majority of these children stop talking about a previous life by the time they are five to seven years old. As I have mentioned, the memories will persist into adolescence or adulthood on rare occasions, but they are usually much less intense then than they were during the younger years. In many cases, as children get older, they do not even remember that they ever talked about a past life.

Overall, parents often find children's claims to remember previous lives more remarkable than do the children, for whom the apparent memories are simply part of their experience of life. The children then move on from the memories to lead typical childhoods.

Spiritual Speculations

Our cases contribute to the evidence that consciousness can survive death in at least some situations, and this is surely a more important finding than any specific ones that we may discern. This means that each of us is more than just a physical body. We have a consciousness as well that is capable of surviving the death of that body. If we change the terminology from consciousness to spirit, then we can say that we all have a spiritual component along with our physical bodies.

If we conclude that every person we meet is a spiritual being as well as a physical one, can we use this knowledge to change the way we treat each other? We might think that we could, but as a monk, Swami Muklyananda, once told Dr. Stevenson, "We in India know that reincarnation occurs, but it makes no difference. Here in India we have just as many rogues and villains as you have in the West." Dr. Stevenson points out that though this is probably correct on the whole, the belief in reincarnation can certainly make a difference for an individual who accepts all that the doctrine involves.

I do hope that having awareness that we each have a spiritual component that may need attention and care just as the physical part of us does could make a difference. An exclusive focus on

the physical may keep us from seeing what we need to do to fos-
ter our spiritual side, and it may also tend to make us more com-
petitive and selfish in our interactions with others. Surely, we can
learn to be less materialistic if we understand that a larger spiritual world is available to us. Fully accepting that we are all spiritual
beings will clearly take more than just knowing about reincarnation research, but having that knowledge may enable people to
explore ways of living a more spiritual life.

To consider another issue: If those of us who do not remember previous lives do reincarnate, then some emotional issues may
come with us even if specific memories do not. Babies are born
with different temperaments and different emotional reactions to
things. This leads biologists to focus on how our genes may affect
our emotions, but we can wonder if a consciousness or spiritual
component that brings emotions with it from previous lives is
involved as well. If so, this implies that we may have multiple
lifetimes to work through difficult emotional issues. Though the
idea of carrying emotional baggage from one life to the next may
seem unpleasant, the prospect of having more than one lifetime to
deal with it also suggests that we may be able eventually to resolve
more issues than we know. The concept of reincarnation is compelling to many people because of the idea that an individual can
live multiple lives and accumulate wisdom, becoming more loving and peaceful in successive lives. Though we should not expect perfection even after multiple lives, we can surely get closer
if we have more than one life in which to make progress.

At the risk of sounding philosophical, we can speculate further
that such reasoning also suggests that our purpose in life can
change from one lifetime to the next. We may not find one single

"meaning of life" but rather different purposes in each life. One individual may be working on very different emotional issues from another person, and thus we see some people content to invest all their energy in connecting with their loved ones. Other people are content to be alone while focusing on asserting themselves in the work world. Perhaps we all take turns working on different aspects of ourselves until we get closer to getting it right. The idea that we get more than one crack at life and that we do not have to get everything sorted through in one lifetime is certainly appealing, but the hard part for some people comes in developing a sense of purpose of any kind in their lives. This is a task for us whether we live one life or more than one, but it may seem less daunting if we decide that developing a sense of purpose in one aspect of life is enough for this time around. We do not have to participate in every type of experience or success in one lifetime in order for it to have value.

Future Research

Even after forty years of research, our work here is still very much unfinished. I am planning to continue to focus primarily on American cases of past-life memories. Along with doing studies in which we look at particular facets of the cases, I hope that as more people hear about our work, we will be able to conduct investigations of more American cases and stronger American cases. If we could study cases in the United States as strong as the best of Asia, then the work would be very hard for people to dismiss. Cases have been harder to find here, but I remain optimistic that at some point, we will have a collection of cases that are so well documented that we can confidently answer the question of whether some children are able to remember previous lives.

We may also have another tool at our disposal in the future to help answer that question. A number of researchers have looked at how the brain functions in recalling actual memories compared to false ones—things that people think they remember happening that actually did not. The work is preliminary at this point. It has involved showing people lists of words. They are then shown a word and asked whether it was on the previous list. Sometimes, the people think they remember seeing the word on the list when they actually did not. Thus, they have a false memory. The researchers have done brain imaging studies in which they measure brain activity when the people are recalling the false memories compared to when they are recalling actual memories, and they have found that different parts of the brain are active during the different recalls. If this research progresses enough so that such testing could determine whether particular individuals have accurate memories of events from earlier in their lives, then we might be able to use it to evaluate memories of previous lives as well. This would be years off, if ever, but it is an intriguing possibility.

If we do eventually establish, to our own satisfaction at least, that some children are able to recall events from previous lives, then we can move on to explore further the questions in this chapter. We would love to learn more about the process of reincarnation, if it occurs, and I hope that this knowledge would then enable people to make positive changes in how they live their lives.

Other work is going on at the Division of Personality Studies at the University of Virginia. Dr. Bruce Greyson, who is now the director of the division, focuses primarily on near-death experiences. One of his current studies involves placing a laptop computer high in a hospital treatment room in which patients have heart defibrillators implanted. Since heart arrhythmias that could normally be fatal are induced in these patients during the procedure, Dr. Greyson is looking to see if any of them will have a near-death experience and be able to describe the particular screensaver displayed on the laptop computer during their procedure.

Dr. Emily Kelly conducts research looking at a variety of unusual experiences, including apparitions and death-bed visions. She is currently doing a study with mediums in which they describe messages that they say deceased individuals want to convey to particular volunteers who have deceased loved ones, and the mediums must give this report without getting any feedback from the volunteers at all. In fact, they never even meet or talk to the volunteers. If they produce accurate information, we will know that they did not infer it from anything that the volunteers did or said.

These studies are exciting, and we hope to continue to make advances in considering the possibility of survival after death. The Division of Perceptual Studies is still dependent on donations to fund much of its day-to-day operation. When money has been plentiful, the division has been able to perform more research projects, and during lean times, activities and personnel have had to be cut back. The state of Virginia does not contribute to the work at the division, and the generosity of people like Chester Carlson, along with other individuals and private foundations that have made substantial donations, is what has made this research possible. We hope to be fortunate enough to continue and even expand the work that we are doing to look at this most interesting question of life after death.

Final Thoughts

If we are able one day to answer definitively the question of whether we can survive death, I hope that this work with young children will be an important part of that answer. If it is, then that will demonstrate that the smallest and youngest among us have wisdom to share with everyone else—they may be "old souls" in new bodies. If we are all spiritual beings, we should aspire to treat others with all the respect that this implies, and treating children with such respect must include listening to them. Just as the children in this book may have important knowledge to impart to us, so may others if we are ready to listen to these small fellow travelers on this most remarkable road of life.

Out of the mouth of babes . . .

I would like to hear from parents of children who have reported memories of a previous life, if they are willing to be interviewed about their experiences. Our email address is DOPS@virginia.edu and our postal address is:

Division of Perceptual Studies
University of Virginia Health System
P.O. Box 800152
Charlottesville, VA 22908-0152.

All cases will be handled confidentially, as we always conceal the identities of families in any reports that we publish.

ACKNOWLEDGMENTS

First and foremost, I want to thank Ian Stevenson, whose work provided the foundation for much of this book. He has been an inspiring pioneer and a wonderful mentor. He gave me the opportunity to participate in this field despite my lack of research experience, and he has continued to provide much support and encouragement for my efforts. His books were also important resources for this one. In particular, I found his overview of the work, *Children Who Remember Previous Lives,* to be very helpful.

Many thanks go to the families who have cooperated with our research. Not only have they demonstrated tolerance for our many questions, but they have even shown great hospitality as we intruded on their time. Similarly, our interpreters in the various countries have been indispensable, and they have always maintained positive attitudes despite long work days on the road. I want to thank the other researchers in this field, whose cases are included both in the overall statistics I cite and, at times, in the individual case write-ups. They are Erlendur Haraldsson, Jürgen Keil, Antonia Mills, and Satwant Pasricha. Thanks as well to Carol Bowman, who referred several of the cases in this book to us, and to the Bial Foundation, which provided a grant that funded several of the American investigations.

I am grateful to my literary agent, Patricia Van der Leun, who found a publisher for me in a remarkably short period of time, and to my editor, Diane Reverand, who helped me make countless improvements in the text. In addition, Martha Stockhausen, my former research assistant, offered many helpful suggestions about several of the chapters. I owe thanks also to Raymond Moody, whose classic work on near-death experiences, *Life After Life,* inspired the title of this book.

Finally, I want to thank my wife, Chris, who acts as my unofficial editor, my colleague, my support, my soul mate. While I would love to spend multiple lifetimes with her, I feel so very fortunate to share even one.

NOTES

Introduction

p. xi: The case of Kemal Atasoy: Keil & Tucker, 2005.

1: Children Who Report Memories of Previous Lives

p. 4: between 20 and 27 percent: see Gallup, with Proctor, 1982; Inglehart, Basañez, and Moreno, 1998; and the Taylor references.

p. 4: a similar percentage of Europeans: Walter & Waterhouse, 1999.

p. 4: a Harris poll in 2003: Taylor, 2003.

p. 7: making a prediction: Stevenson, 2001, pp. 98–99.

p. 8: the current Dalai Lama: Dalai Lama, 1962, pp. 23–24.

p. 8: Of forty-six cases: Stevenson, 1966.

p. 8: Victor Vincent: Stevenson, 1974, pp. 259–69.

p. 9: Süleyman Çaper: Stevenson, 1997a, pp. 1429–42.

p. 11: Suzanne Ghanem: Dr. Stevenson, who investigated Suzanne Ghanem's case, has not published a case report on it, but she is featured in Chapters 6 and 8 of Shroder, 1999.

p. 14: Parmod Sharma: Stevenson, 1974, pp. 109–27.

p. 15: Shamlinie Prema: Stevenson, 1977a, pp. 15–42.

2: Investigating the Cases

p. 17: Dr. Ian Stevenson: For more information on Dr. Stevenson's career, see Stevenson, 1989 and Shroder, 1999.

p. 17: "The Evidence for Survival": Stevenson, 1960.

p. 18: "These forty-four cases": Shroder, 1999, p. 103.

p. 20: "in regard to reincarnation": King, 1975, p. 978.

p. 20: "He has placed on record": ibid.

p. 20: "a methodical, careful": Lief, 1977, p. 171.

p. 20: "Either he is making": ibid.

p. 27: Dr. Keil eventually: Keil & Tucker, 2000.

3: Explanations to Consider

p. 33: The following list: For another discussion of the possible explanations, see Chapter 7 in Stevenson, 2001.

p. 39: The argument goes: This so-called socio-psychological hypothesis is described in Stevenson & Samararatne, 1988. For another discussion of it, see Brody, 1979.

p. 39: Bishen Chand Kapoor: Stevenson, 1975, pp. 176–205.

p. 44: research that has been done in parapsychology: A number of good reviews are available, including Radin, 1997.

4: Marked for Life

p. 55: The case of Chanai Choomalaiwong: Stevenson, 1997a, pp. 300–23.

p. 57: The case of Necip Ünlütaşkiran: Stevenson, 1997a, pp. 430–55.

p. 59: a shotgun blast: Hanumant Saxena in Stevenson, 1997a, pp. 455–67.

p. 60: The case of Indika Ishwara: Stevenson, 1997a, pp. 1970–2000.

p. 64: The case of Purnima Ekanayake: Haraldsson, 2000.

p. 67: stress can contribute: See Sternberg, 2000, for a detailed overview of this area.

p. 68: one notable case: Moody, 1946.

p. 74: a boy in Sri Lanka named Wijeratne: Stevenson, 1997a, pp. 1366–73.

p. 77: the Dalai Lama wrote: The Dalai Lama, 1962.

p. 77: Dr. Stevenson describes twenty: Stevenson, 1997a, pp. 803–79.

p. 77: Jürgen Keil and I found: Tucker & Keil, in press.

p. 78: Kloy Matwiset: Tucker & Keil, 2001.

5: Remembering the Past

p. 86: Sujith Jayaratne: Stevenson, 1977a, pp. 235–80.

p. 90: Dr. James Matlock: Matlock, 1989.

p. 96: The case of Kumkum Verma: Stevenson, 1975, pp. 206–40.

p. 98: The case of Jagdish Chandra: Stevenson, 1975, pp. 144–75.

p. 101: The case of Ratana Wongsombat: Stevenson, 1983, pp. 12–48.

p. 102: The case of Gamini Jayasena: Stevenson, 1977a, pp. 43–76.

6: Unusual Behaviors

p. 116: Sukla Gupta: Stevenson, 1974. pp. 52–67.

p. 117: Maung Aye Kyaw: Stevenson, 1997a, pp. 212–26.

p. 118: Bongkuch Promsin: Stevenson, 1983, pp. 109–39.

p. 118: Fear-death Experiences: Dr. Stevenson and colleagues (Stevenson, Cook, & McClean-Rice, 1989–90) coined this term to refer to near-death experiences that occur when people fear they are going to die but do not actually approach physiological death. I am using it differently here to highlight the fears that our subjects show about the mode of the previous death.

p. 118: a phobia that relates: for more details, see Stevenson, 1990.

p. 119: Shamlinie Prema: Stevenson, 1977a, pp. 15–42.

p. 120: Jasbir Singh: Stevenson, 1974, pp. 34–52.

p. 121: Ma Tin Aung Myo: Stevenson, 1983, pp. 229–41.

p. 121: Carl Edon: Stevenson, 2003, pp. 67–74. Dr. Nicholas McLean-Rice investigated the case along with Dr. Stevenson.

p. 122: Swaran Lata: Pasricha & Stevenson, 1977.

p. 122: children's play: For more on subjects' play, see Stevenson, 2000.

p. 123: Maung Myint Soe: Stevenson, 1997a, pp. 1403–10.

p. 123: Ramez Shams: Stevenson, 1997a, p. 1406.

p. 124: one series of sex-change cases: Stevenson, 1997a.

p. 125: current thinking about gender identity disorder: References are included in the case report on Kloy Matwiset: Tucker & Keil, 2001.

p. 126: Erin Jackson: Stevenson, 2001, pp. 87–89.

p. 129: The case of the Pollock twins: Stevenson, 1997a, pp. 2041–58 and Stevenson, 2003, pp. 89–93.

p. 132: temperament: Thomas & Chess, 1984.

p. 134: suffering in other cases: Stevenson, 2001, p. 217.

p. 134: Bishen Chand Kapoor: Stevenson, 1974, pp. 176–205 and Stevenson, 2001, p. 303.

p. 134: Marta Lorenz: Stevenson, 1974, 183–203.

p. 134: "Emilia is not in the cemetery": Stevenson, 1974: pp. 187, 196.

p. 134: "Don't say that": Stevenson, 1974: p. 187.

p. 134: relief that can occur: Stevenson, 2001, p. 281.

7: Recognizing Familiar Faces

p. 144: As Dr. Stevenson has written: Stevenson, 2001.

p. 147: The case of Nazih Al-Danaf: Haraldsson & Abu-Izzeddin, 2002.

p. 151: The case of Gnanatilleka Baddewithana: Stevenson, 1974, pp. 131–49 and Nissanka, 2001.

p. 156: The case of Ma Choe Hnin Htet: Stevenson, 1997a, pp. 839–52.

8: Divine Intermission

p. 169: a scale that rates: Tucker, 2000.

p. 169: Poonam Sharma: Sharma & Tucker, 2005.

p. 170: Veer Singh: Stevenson, 1975, pp. 312–36.

p. 171: Bongkuch Promsin: Stevenson, 1983, pp. 102–39.

p. 172: Disna Samarasinghe: Stevenson, 1977a, pp. 77–116.

p. 173: Sunita Khandelwal: Stevenson, 1997a, pp. 468–91.

p. 178: "Most scientists probably": Rovee-Collier, 1997, p. 468.

p. 179: last longer and are more specific: Rovee-Collier & Hayne, 2000.

p. 179: "The growing consensus": Howe, 2000, p. 19.

p. 179: the inability to retain: Rovee-Collier, Hartshorn & DiRubbo, 1999.

p. 180: a child was able: Myers, Clifton & Clarkson, 1987.

p. 180: researchers interviewed ten children: Fivush, Gray & Fromhoff, 1987.

p. 180: researchers asked pregnant women: DeCasper & Spence, 1986.

p. 181: In one report: Cheek, 1992.

p. 182: Dr. Cheek thought that: Cheek, 1996.

9: Opposing Points of View

p. 185: "The trouble with people": People have attributed various versions of this line to a number of individuals, notably Will Rogers, as Walter Mondale did in a 1984 debate with Ronald Reagan. *Respectfully Quoted* from the Library of Congress (Platt, 1989) credits Josh Billings as the most likely author.

p. 185: various religious beliefs: Almeder makes this distinction in Almeder, 1997.

p. 186: "At the time of writing": Sagan, 1996, p. 302.

p. 188: "this confrontation between": Dennett, 1991, p. 35.

p. 188: "This argument depends": Stapp, 2005, p. 45.

p. 188: "yet it is fully": Stapp, 1993, p. 23.

p. 188: quantum mechanics: For an overview of quantum mechanics, see Greene, 1999.

p. 188: He and quantum physicist Friedrich Beck: Eccles, 1994, Chapter 9.

p. 188: Elizabeth Rauscher and Russell Targ: Rauscher & Targ, 2001, and Rauscher & Targ, 2002.

p. 189: clearly implied by theoretical physics: Costa de Beauregard, 1987, p. 569.

p. 189: precognition, telepathy, and psychokinesis: Costa de Beauregard, 1998.

p. 189: "far from being": Costa de Beauregard, 2002, p. 653.

p. 189: "these developments may": Klarreich, 2001, p. 339.

p. 189: in the long run: Josephson & Pallikari-Viras, 1991, p. 199.

p. 189: the importance of consciousness: The material in these two paragraphs is from Folger, 2002.

p. 190: "I cannot imagine": ibid, p. 48.

p. 191: "it is difficult": Radin & Nelson, 1989, p. 1512.

p. 192: At last count: Benor, 2001.

p. 192: heart disease: Byrd, 1988 and Harris, et al., 1999.

p. 192: AIDS: Sicher, et al., 1998.

p. 192: One review found: Astin, Harkness, & Ernst, 2000.

p. 193: Does other evidence: For a brief review, see Stevenson, 1977b.

p. 193: near-death experiences: See Greyson & Flynn, 1984 and Moody, 1975/2001 for more on near-death experiences.

p. 193: Pam Reynolds: Sabom, 1998. Also, Broome, 2003.

p. 193: Al Sullivan: Cook, et al., 1998.

p. 193: reports of apparitions: Stevenson, 1982.

p. 194: Research with mediums: The information on Mrs. Piper and Mrs. Leonard comes from Gauld, 1982.

p. 195: recent studies: Schwartz (with Simon), 2002.

p. 195: "consilience": Wilson, 1998, p. 8.

p. 195: "the explanations": Wilson, 1998, p. 53.

p. 195: how could stones: The quote "Stones cannot fall from the sky, because there are no stones in the sky" is often attributed to the great chemist Antoine Lavoisier, but I could not find solid documentation that he actually said it.

p. 195: Ignaz Semmelweis: Lyons & Petrucelli, 1987 and Bender, 1966.

p. 196: "If we are": Plate tectonics, 2002.

p. 199: David Bishai: Bishai, 2000.

p. 199: 105 billion human beings: The calculation is in Haub, 1995.

p. 200: William James looked: James, 1898/1956.

p. 202: Second Council of Constantinople: Head & Cranston, 1977, pp. 156–60.

10: Conclusions and Speculations

p. 206: In the first one: Stevenson & Keil, 2000.

p. 207: Dr. Sybo Schouten: Schouten & Stevenson, 1998.

p. 211: "reincarnation is the best": Stevenson, 2001, p. 254.

p. 211: we know almost nothing: ibid.

p. 216: "psychophore": Stevenson, 2001, p. 234.

p. 216: Their doctrine of *anatta*: This description summarizes Dr. Stevenson's discussion of *anatta* in Stevenson, 1977a, pp. 3–5.

p. 217: most practicing Buddhists: Head & Cranston, 1977, pp. 63–66.

p. 225: the subject has appeared: Gauld, 1982, pp. 166–71.

p. 226: "they will be": Gauld, 1982, p. 171.

p. 227: In Sri Lanka: Haraldsson, 1995; Haraldsson, 1997; Haraldsson, Fowler & Periyannanpillai, 2000.

p. 227: In Lebanon: Haraldsson, 2003.

p. 229: "We in India": Stevenson, 2001, p. 232.

p. 234: "Out of the mouth of babes": *The Holy Bible: King James Version,* Psalms 8:2.

REFERENCES

Almeder, R. 1997. A critique of arguments offered against reincarnation. *Journal of Scientific Exploration* 11(4): 499–526.

Astin, J. A., E. Harkness, and E. Ernst, 2000. The efficacy of "distant healing": A systematic review of randomized trials. *Annals of Internal Medicine* 132(11):903–10.

Bender, G. A. 1966. *Great moments in medicine.* Detroit: Northwood Institute Press.

Benor, D. J. 2001. *Spiritual healing: Scientific validation of a healing revolution.* Southfield, Mich.: Vision Publications.

Bishai, D. 2000. Can population growth rule out reincarnation? A model of circular migration. *Journal of Scientific Exploration* 14(3):411–20.

Bowman, C. 1997. *Children's past lives: How past life memories affect your child.* New York: Bantam Books.

Bowman, C. 2001. *Return from heaven: Beloved relatives reincarnated within your family.* New York: HarperCollins.

Brody, E. B. 1979. Review of *Cases of the reincarnation type. Vol. II: Ten cases in Sri Lanka* by Ian Stevenson. *Journal of Nervous and Mental Disease* 167:769–74.

Broome, K. (producer). 2003, February 5. *The day I died* [Television broadcast]. London: BBC Two.

Byrd, R. 1988. Positive therapeutic effects of intercessory prayer in a coronary care unit population. *Southern Medical Journal* 81(7):826–29.

Cheek, D. B. 1992. Are telepathy, clairvoyance and "hearing" possible in utero? Suggestive evidence as revealed during hypnotic age-regression studies of prenatal memory. *Pre- and Perinatal Psychology Journal* 7(2):125–37.

Cheek, D. B. 1996. An interview with David Cheek, M.D. Interview by Michael D. Yapko. *American Journal of Clinical Hypnosis* 39(1):2–17.

Cook, E. W., B. Greyson, and I. Stevenson. 1998. Do any near-death experiences provide evidence for the survival of human personality after death? Relevant features and illustrative case reports. *Journal of Scientific Exploration* 12(3):377–406.

Costa de Beauregard, O. 1987. According to "physical irreversibility," the "paranormal" is not de jure suppressed, but is de facto repressed. *Behavioral and Brain Sciences* 10(4):569–70.

Costa de Beauregard, O. 1998. The paranormal is not excluded from physics. *Journal of Scientific Exploration* 12(2):315–20.

Costa de Beauregard, O. 2002. Wavelike coherence and CPT invariance: Sesames of the Paranormal. *Journal of Scientific Exploration* 16(4):651–54.

Dalai Lama. 1962. *My land and my people: Autobiography of the Dalai Lama.* New York: McGraw-Hill.

DeCasper, A. J. and M. J. Spence. 1986. Prenatal maternal speech influences newborns' perception of speech sounds. *Infant Behavior & Development* 9(2):133–50.

Dennett, D. C. 1991. *Consciousness explained.* Boston: Little, Brown.

Eccles, J. C. 1994. *How the self controls its brain.* Berlin: Springer-Verlag.

Fivush, R., J. T. Gray, and F. A. Fromhoff. 1987. Two-year-olds talk about the past. *Cognitive Development* 2:393–409.

Folger, T. 2002. Does the universe exist if we're not looking? *Discover* June:44–48.

Gallup, G., with W. Proctor. 1982. *Adventures in immortality.* New York: McGraw-Hill.

Gauld, A. 1982. *Mediumship and survival: A century of investigations.* London: William Heinemann.

Greene, B. 1999. *The elegant universe: Superstrings, hidden dimensions, and the quest for the ultimate theory.* New York: W. W. Norton.

Greyson, B. and C. P. Flynn, eds. 1984. *The near-death experience: Problems, prospects, perspectives.* Springfield, Ill.: Charles C. Thomas.

Haraldsson, E. 1995. Personality and abilities of children claiming previous-life memories. *Journal of Nervous and Mental Disease* 183(7):445–51.

Haraldsson, E. 1997. A psychological comparison between ordinary children and those who claim previous-life memories. *Journal of Scientific Exploration* 11(3):323–35.

Haraldsson, E. 2000. Birthmarks and claims of previous-life memories: I. The case of Purnima Ekanayake. *Journal of the Society for Psychical Research* 64(858):16–25.

Haraldsson, E. 2003. Children who speak of past-life experiences: Is there a psychological explanation? *Psychology and Psychotherapy: Theory, Research and Practice* 76:55–67.

Haraldsson, E. and M. Abu-Izzeddin. 2002. Development of certainty about the correct deceased person in a case of the reincarnation type in Lebanon: The case of Nazih Al-Danaf. *Journal of Scientific Exploration* 16:363–80.

Haraldsson, E., P. C. Fowler, and V. Periyannanpillai. 2000. Psychological characteristics of children who speak of a previous life: A further field study in Sri Lanka. *Transcultural Psychiatry* 37(4):525–44.

Harris, W. S., M. Gowda, J. W. Kolb, C. P. Strychacz, J. L. Vacek, P. G. Jones, A. Forker, J. H. O'Keefe, and B. D. McCallister. 1999. A randomized, controlled trial of the effects of remote, intercessory prayer on outcomes in patients admitted to the coronary care unit. *Archives of Internal Medicine* 159(19):2273–78.

Haub, C. 1995. How many people have ever lived on earth? *Population Today* 23(2):4–5.

Head, J. and S. L. Cranston. 1977. *Reincarnation: The phoenix fire mystery.* New York: Julian Press/Crown Publishers.

Howe, M. L. 2000. *The fate of early memories: Developmental science and the retention of childhood experiences.* Washington, D.C.: American Psychological Association.

Inglehart, R., M. Basañez, and A. Moreno. 1998. *Human values and beliefs: A cross-cultural sourcebook.* Ann Arbor, Mich.: University of Michigan Press.

James, W. 1898/1956. *Human immortality: Two supposed objections to the doctrine.* 2nd ed. Originally published 1898 Boston: Houghton, Mifflin. Republished in 1956 as *The will to believe and other essays in popular philosophy and human immortality: Two supposed objections to the doctrine.* New York: Dover Publications.

Josephson, B. D. and F. Pallikari-Viras. 1991. Biological utilization of quantum nonlocality. *Foundations of Physics* 21(2):197–207.

Keil, H. H. J. and J. B. Tucker. 2000. An unusual birthmark case thought to be linked to a person who had previously died. *Psychological Reports* 87:1067–74.

Keil, H. H. J. and J. B. Tucker. 2005. Children who claim to remember previous lives: Cases with written records made before the previous personality was identified. *Journal of Scientific Exploration* 19:91–101.

King, L. S. 1975. Reincarnation. *JAMA* 234:978.

Klarreich, E. 2001. Stamp booklet has physicists licked. *Nature* 413:339.

Lief, H. I. 1977. Commentary on Dr. Ian Stevenson's "The evidence of man's survival after death." *Journal of Nervous and Mental Disease* 165:171–73.

Lyons, A. S. and R. J. Petrucelli. 1987. *Medicine: An illustrated history*. New York: Harry N. Abrams.

Matlock, J. G. 1989. Age and stimulus in past life memory cases: A study of published cases. *Journal of the American Society for Psychical Research* 83:303–16.

Moody, R. A. 1975/2001. *Life after life: The investigation of a phenomenon—survival of bodily death*. 2nd ed. New York: HarperSanFrancisco.

Moody, R. L. 1946. Bodily changes during abreaction. *Lancet* 2:934–35.

Myers, N. A., R. K. Clifton, and M. G. Clarkson. 1987. When they were very young: Almost-threes remember two years ago. *Infant Behavior and Development* 10:123–32.

Nissanka, H. S. S. 2001. *The girl who was reborn: A case-study suggestive of reincarnation*. Colombo, Sri Lanka: S. Godage Brothers.

Pasricha, S. and I. Stevenson. 1977. Three cases of the reincarnation type in India. *Indian Journal of Psychiatry* 19:36–42.

Plate tectonics. 2002. In *The new encyclopædia Britannica* (Vol. 25, p. 886). Chicago: Encyclopædia Britannica.

Platt, S. ed. 1989. *Respectfully quoted: A dictionary of quotations requested from the congressional research service*. Washington, D.C.: Library of Congress.

Radin, D. 1997. *The conscious universe: The scientific truth of psychic phenomena*. New York: HarperCollins.

Radin, D. I. and R. D. Nelson. 1989. Evidence for consciousness-related anomalies in random physical systems. *Foundations of Physics* 19(12):1499–1514.

Rauscher, E. A. and R. Targ. 2001. The speed of thought: Investigation of a complex space-time metric to describe psychic phenomena. *Journal of Scientific Exploration* 15(3):331–54.

Rauscher, E. A. and R. Targ. 2002. Why only four dimensions will not explain the relationship of the perceived and perceiver in precognition. *Journal of Scientific Exploration* 16(4):655–58.

Rovee-Collier, C. 1997. Dissociations in infant memory: Rethinking the development of implicit and explicit memory. *Psychological Review* 104:467–98.

Rovee-Collier, C., K. Hartshorn, and M. DiRubbo. 1999. Long-term maintenance of infant memory. *Developmental Psychobiology* 35:91–102.

Rovee-Collier, C. and H. Hayne. 2000. Memory in infancy and early childhood. In *The Oxford handbook of memory,* ed. E. Tulving and F. I. M. Craik, 267–82. New York: Oxford University Press.

Sabom, M. 1998. *Light and death: One doctor's fascinating account of near-death experiences.* Grand Rapids, Mich.: Zondervan Publishing House.

Sagan, C. 1996. *The demon-haunted world: Science as a candle in the dark.* New York: Random House.

Schouten, S. A. and I. Stevenson. 1998. Does the socio-psychological hypothesis explain cases of the reincarnation type? *Journal of Nervous and Mental Disease* 186(8):504–6.

Schwartz, G. E., with W. L. Simon. 2002. *The afterlife experiments: Breakthrough scientific evidence of life after death.* New York: Pocket Books.

Sharma, P. and J. B. Tucker. 2005. Cases of the reincarnation type with memories from the intermission between lives. *Journal of Near-Death Studies* 23(2):101–18.

Shroder, T. 1999. *Old souls: The scientific evidence for past lives.* New York: Simon & Schuster.

Sicher, F., E. Targ, D. Moore, and H. S. Smith. 1998. A randomized double-blind study of the effect of distant healing in a population with advanced AIDS. Report of a small scale study. *Western Journal of Medicine* 169(6):356–63.

Stapp, H. P. 1993. *Mind, matter, and quantum mechanics.* Berlin: Springer-Verlag.

Stapp, H. P. 2005. *The mindful universe.* http://www-physics.lbl.gov/~stapp/MUA.pdf (accessed March 14, 2005).

Sternberg, E. M. 2000. *The balance within: The science connecting health and emotions.* New York: W. H. Freeman.

Stevenson, I. 1960. The evidence for survival from claimed memories of former incarnations. *Journal of the American Society for Psychical Research* 54:51–71 and 95–117.

Stevenson, I. 1966. Cultural patterns in cases suggestive of reincarnation among the Tlingit Indians of Southeastern Alaska. *Journal of the American Society for Psychical Research* 60:229–43.

Stevenson, I. 1974. *Twenty cases suggestive of reincarnation.* (rev. ed.) Charlottesville: University Press of Virginia.

Stevenson, I. 1975. *Cases of the reincarnation type, Vol. I: Ten cases in India.* Charlottesville: University Press of Virginia.

Stevenson, I. 1977a. *Cases of the reincarnation type, Vol. II: Ten cases in Sri Lanka.* Charlottesville: University Press of Virginia.

Stevenson, I. 1977b. Research into the evidence of man's survival after death. *Journal of Nervous and Mental Disease* 165(3):152–70.

Stevenson, I. 1980. *Cases of the reincarnation type, Vol. III: Twelve cases in Lebanon and Turkey*. Charlottesville: University Press of Virginia.

Stevenson, I. 1982. The contribution of apparitions to the evidence for survival. *Journal of the American Society for Psychical Research* 76:341–58.

Stevenson, I. 1983. *Cases of the reincarnation type, Vol. IV: Twelve cases in Thailand and Burma*. Charlottesville: University Press of Virginia.

Stevenson, I. 1989. Some of my journeys in medicine. *The Flora Levy lecture in the humanities 1989*. Lafayette, La.: University of Southwestern Louisiana. Also available online at http://www.healthsystem.virginia.edu/personalitystudies/Some-of-My-Journeys-in-Medicine.pdf.

Stevenson, I. 1990. Phobias in children who claim to remember previous lives. *Journal of Scientific Exploration* 4:243–54.

Stevenson, I. 1997a. *Reincarnation and biology: A contribution to the etiology of birthmarks and birth defects*. Westport, Conn.: Praeger.

Stevenson, I. 1997b. *Where reincarnation and biology intersect*. Westport, Conn.: Praeger.

Stevenson, I. 2000. Unusual play in young children who claim to remember previous lives. *Journal of Scientific Exploration* 14:557–70.

Stevenson, I. 2001. *Children who remember previous lives: A question of reincarnation*. (rev. ed.) Jefferson, N.C.: McFarland.

Stevenson, I. 2003. *European cases of the reincarnation type*. Jefferson, N.C.: McFarland.

Stevenson, I., E. W. Cook, and N. McClean-Rice. 1989–90. Are persons reporting "near-death experiences" really near death? A study of medical records. *Omega* 20(1):45–54.

Stevenson, I. and J. Keil. 2000. The stability of assessments of paranormal connections in reincarnation-type cases. *Journal of Scientific Exploration* 14(3):365–82.

Stevenson, I. and G. Samararatne. 1988. Three new cases of the reincarnation type in Sri Lanka with written records made before verification. *Journal of Scientific Exploration* 2:217–38.

Taylor, H. 1998. Large majority of people believe they will go to heaven; only one in fifty thinks they will go to hell. http://www.harrisinteractive.com/harris_poll/index.asp?PID=167 (accessed February 1, 2005).

Taylor, H. 2000. No significant changes in the large majorities who believe in God, heaven, the resurrection, survival of soul, miracles and virgin birth.

http://www.harrisinteractive.com/harris_poll/index.asp?PID=112 (accessed February 1, 2005).

Taylor, H. 2003. The religious and other beliefs of Americans 2003. http://www.harrisinteractive.com/harris_poll/index.asp?PID=359 (accessed February 1, 2005).

Thomas, A. and S. Chess. 1984. Genesis and evolution of behavioral disorders: from infancy to early adult life. *American Journal of Psychiatry* 141:1–9.

Tucker, J. B. 2000. A scale to measure the strength of children's claims of previous lives: Methodology and initial findings. *Journal of Scientific Exploration* 14(4):571–81.

Tucker, J. B. and H. H. J. Keil. 2001. Can cultural beliefs cause a gender identity disorder? *Journal of Psychology & Human Sexuality* 13(2):21–30.

Tucker, J. B. and H. H. J. Keil. in press. Experimental birthmarks: New cases of an Asian practice. *International Journal of Parapsychology*.

Walter, T. and H. Waterhouse. 1999. A very private belief: Reincarnation in contemporary England. *Sociology of Religion* 60(2):187–97.

Wilson, E. O. 1998. *Consilience: The unity of knowledge*. New York: Alfred A. Knopf.

Return to
Life

Extraordinary Cases of Children

Who Remember Past Lives

JIM B. TUCKER, M.D.

For Ian, in memoriam

Contents

It is not more surprising to be born twice than once; everything in nature is resurrection.

—VOLTAIRE

Return to
Life

Chapter 1

A COMEBACK KID?

Patrick, a cute little boy with long dark hair and an impish smile, was my first case. He had just turned five when I met him and his family in their home, a compact house in a small Midwestern suburb. I was there accompanying Dr. Ian Stevenson. Once "a young man in a hurry," becoming the head of a psychiatry department in his late thirties, Ian had walked away from the ladder of academic success for an interest he would doggedly pursue for forty years—children who report memories of previous lives. Nearly eighty but with curiosity still unabated, Ian was meeting the family because Patrick's mother had become convinced her son was his deceased half brother returned to life.

Ian viewed Patrick's case as potentially important. Though he had published many articles and books about children who had made numerous statements that matched details of someone who had died, Ian's best cases were all from other countries, mostly in Asia, where a general belief in reincarnation existed. His American cases tended to be weaker. They included two basic types: children who seemed to remember being a deceased family member, and children who talked about a past life but did not give enough details for a previous person to be identified. The same-family cases had the inherent weakness that the child might have overheard others discussing the deceased. While Patrick's case was a same-family one, it had another critical feature: he had three birthmarks that appeared to match lesions on his deceased half brother, marks that had nothing to do with what he might have heard people say.

Ian arranged a three-day trip with a plan to be thorough. We would have a long interview with the family on the first day, a second one the next day to cover items we had overlooked or that we needed to clarify, and interviews on the second and third days with other people involved in Patrick's life. We hoped the extended time with Patrick would help him become comfortable enough to talk to us about any memories he had.

We arrived at the home and sat down in the living room with Patrick's mother, Lisa. Ian took a clipboard and a tape recorder out of his satchel, well-worn from his trips around the world. He tested the recorder and placed it on the coffee table. He began by asking Lisa about her deceased son, the one whose life Patrick seemed to be remembering. Ian asked, "That's not troublesome to you, is it, to talk about that?" Lisa said, "No. I mean it is, but no. Where do you want me to start?" Ian asked her to begin when her son first became ill, and with an even voice, she began the story.

Kevin had been born twenty years before. Lisa, a young mother, and Kevin, her first child, were doing well despite her split from his father, until Kevin began limping at sixteen months of age. This was intermittent at first, but after about three weeks he was limping all the time, and Lisa took him to his doctor. He was admitted to the hospital for three days and underwent various tests. A bone scan appeared to be normal, but x-rays showed extra fluid in his left hip joint. The doctor thought it might be infected.

Kevin was still limping when he was discharged. He fell two days later, and doctors at another hospital found he had a broken leg. They put his leg in a cast, but it caused the little boy so much pain they took it off after three days. At that point, he couldn't bear weight on the leg and refused to walk. Lisa took him to another doctor, an orthopedic surgeon. He ordered more x-rays, and these showed some destruction in two of the bones in his left leg. Kevin was again hospitalized. The doctor told Lisa he had a tumor in his leg. This difficult time was made even worse by the uncertainty of the situation. As Lisa said, they went through "probably a two-week period of being told he had leukemia, that he didn't have leukemia, it went back and forth." But the upcoming news would only be worse.

Kevin was transferred to a tertiary children's hospital to continue the workup. Along with his swollen leg, the doctors noted his left eye was bulging and bruised and he had a nodule above his right ear that might be a tumor. They suspected a neuroblastoma, a cancer that begins in nerve tissue somewhere in the body, often in the adrenal gland above one of the kidneys, and then spreads to other places. An x-ray of Kevin's kidneys showed a mass at the top of his left one. A skeletal survey found various lesions and an opaque area over his bulging left eye. On his fourth day in the hospital, Kevin was taken to the operating room. The doctors took a biopsy of the nodule above his right ear and inserted a central line, a large IV, in the right side of his neck.

The biopsy confirmed the diagnosis of metastatic neuroblastoma. At least a definite diagnosis had finally been made, but it was not a good one. Kevin began treatment, getting chemotherapy through the central line. The site where the chemotherapy entered his neck became inflamed at times, but overall, he tolerated the treatment well. He also started radiation therapy that would continue after he left the hospital, including to his left eye and his left leg. After ten days, he got to go home.

Kevin seemed okay for a while. Lisa showed us pictures of him. The first one was taken before he got sick, and he is laughing, a plump baby with lots of light, curly hair. The other two are from later. They reveal a thinner, bald little boy with bruising around his left eye, which looks displaced. Too young to understand he was dying, he appears happy in both pictures, beaming in one and exploring a toy fire station in the other. They are heartbreaking.

Kevin returned to the hospital six months after his first admission. He was bleeding from his gums because the cancer had infiltrated his bone marrow and it couldn't make enough platelets. He had also developed bruising around his right eye along with the faded bruising around his left. Lisa said he was blind in the left eye at that point. His disease was considered end stage by then, meaning the little boy would die soon, but along with a platelet transfusion, he did receive one day of chemotherapy and one day of radiation to his right eye socket. He was discharged and died two days later.

Lisa talked about all of this in a calm, unemotional manner. This may have been because Ian and I focused more on the facts than any emotions. Ian did comment that she must have been very affected by Kevin's death, but when she gave little response, we moved on to other matters. We were not expecting her to pour out her heart to us, and we were asking a lot just to have her recount the events of his illness and death.

Lisa carried on after Kevin died. Long separated from his father, she had started dating a new man before Kevin got sick. They married following Kevin's death, and Lisa soon gave birth to a daughter, Sarah. The couple divorced after four years, and Lisa later remarried again. She had a second son, Jason, and then, twelve years after Kevin died, gave birth to Patrick by C-section. She said that as soon as the nurses handed Patrick to her, she knew that he was connected to Kevin in some way. She didn't have that feeling when her other children were born, but this birth was different somehow. Lisa said she felt empty after Kevin died, wanting him back every day. When Patrick, her new son, was brought to her, she imagined a weight being lifted as her grief for Kevin was released. While Lisa saw a physical resemblance between the two boys, there was a link that went beyond that.

She soon noticed a white opacity covering Patrick's left eye. The doctors diagnosed it as a corneal leukoma. Patrick was seen by an ophthalmologist and examined periodically. The opacity shrunk after several weeks but did not completely disappear. While his vision was hard to assess with any precision when he was very young, he was essentially blind in his left eye just as Kevin had been blind in that eye at the end of his life.

Lisa also felt a lump on Patrick's head above his right ear at the same location where Kevin's tumor had been biopsied. When we examined Patrick, we felt the nodule above his ear. It had migrated slightly behind his ear by the time he was five, but Lisa said it was directly above the ear when he was born. It was hard, elevated, and more or less round. We measured it at about one centimeter in diameter. It was not tender at all, and Patrick let us press on it as much as we wanted.

Patrick was also born with an unusual mark on his neck. A dark slanted line that was about four millimeters long when we met him, it looked like a small cut. It was on the front of his neck on the right. This was the area where Kevin's central line had been inserted, though we had trouble confirming which side of his neck had been used for it. When we reviewed Kevin's medical records, we searched to find documentation of the central line's location. We finally found one mention in an operative note that was fortunately one of the more legible handwritten notes. It listed the procedures, including "Insertion of central line (Ext. Jugular), tip in SVC or Rt. Subcl." Translated into English, that meant the IV had been placed in the external jugular vein, which is a vein on each side of the front of the neck. As it was snaked in, the tip of the IV had ended up either in the right subclavian vein running below the collarbone, which the external jugular feeds into, or all the way to the superior vena cava, which carries the blood from those other veins into the heart. The keys for us were that it was the external jugular, meaning the IV was inserted into the neck, and that it was the right subclavian, meaning it was on the right side of his neck, where Patrick's birthmark was.

One of the most inexplicable features of the case was that Patrick limped once he got old enough to walk. He had an unusual gait in which he would swing out his left leg. This matched the way Kevin had walked, since he had to wear a brace after breaking his leg. We asked Patrick to walk across the room several times, and he was still limping slightly at age five, even though he seemed to have no medical reason to do so.

When Patrick was four years old, he began talking about Kevin's life. The first thing he said was that he wanted to go to the other house. Patrick talked about it for a while and seemed desperate at times to go there. Lisa asked him why he needed to return; was there a certain toy or clothes he wanted? He answered, "Don't you remember, I left you there." She answered,

"Yeah, but you have me here now." Lisa asked Patrick what their home looked like, and he said it was "chocolate and orange." Lisa and Kevin's home, actually an apartment rather than a house, was indeed a brown and orange building.

Patrick began talking about events from Kevin's life, coming out with statements at unpredictable times. If Lisa tried to get him to talk about Kevin, he usually wanted no part of it. Later he might mention him out of the blue. Lisa was getting ready for work one day when Patrick asked if she remembered when he had surgery. After she told him he had never had surgery, he said, "Sure I did, right here on my ear" and pointed to the spot above his right ear where Kevin's tumor was biopsied. Lisa asked him to describe the surgery, but he said he didn't remember it because he had been asleep.

Another time, Patrick became excited when he saw a picture of Kevin. He had never seen it before because Lisa didn't keep pictures of Kevin up in the house. His hands shaking, Patrick said, "Here is my picture. I've been looking for that." He was definite as he said, "That's me." He also talked once about the small, brown puppy that stayed with the family. Lisa and Kevin had indeed kept a dog like that, one belonging to Lisa's mother when she moved into an apartment complex that didn't allow pets.

The week before we visited, Patrick was sitting back on the couch and asked, "Do you remember when we went swimming?" Patrick had never actually been swimming but described a day when Kevin swam in the pool at his grandmother's apartment complex. He said his grandmother was there along with his sister's father. He recalled how they had dunked the man's head underwater and mimicked the sound he had made as he came up for air.

Lisa also told us that Patrick had talked with his brother

Jason about heaven. When we asked Jason, he told us about a couple of instances, with Patrick once saying he wanted to take the family to heaven, especially his mother. The next morning, we visited Lisa's sister. She also spoke about comments Patrick made about heaven. She described similarities between Kevin and Patrick, their tendencies to be soft-spoken, timid, even tremulous at times.

After that, what we hoped would be a great opportunity ended up falling flat. We took Patrick and Lisa to the apartment building where Lisa had lived with Kevin. Patrick had stopped talking about that home a while before, but we hoped that seeing it would spur his memory. We weren't able to go inside their actual apartment, and Patrick didn't show any signs of recognizing the building. He did say something about a race car track, which Lisa thought referred to one Kevin had there, but since he described playing with it with Jason, I didn't know what to make of it. We did at least confirm that the building was brown and orange.

We then met Patrick's father at his work. He said Patrick's lesions—the opacity over his eye, the nodule on his head, and the scar on his neck—were definitely present when Patrick was born. He said Patrick hadn't talked to him about Kevin's life, but he had overheard Patrick talking to Lisa about it. He thought the situation was bizarre but had accepted that Patrick was remembering Kevin's life.

We also met with Lisa's ex-husband, the father of Patrick's sister. He recalled all the time he and Lisa spent taking Kevin to and from medical centers. He didn't remember going swimming with Kevin as Patrick had described. Since that would have been at least seventeen years before, that wasn't surprising, though he did recall taking Kevin to the park one day. He had seen little of Patrick and was noncommittal about the possibility of previous lives, but he thought the situation with Patrick had helped ease Lisa's grief. He said Lisa had been extremely close to Kevin and suffered tremendously when he died. He told us he came to the interview because he hoped our study of the possible past-life memories might help her.

By the following day, Patrick became comfortable enough to talk with us. He often spoke softly, and that tendency, combined with poor enunciation, made him difficult to understand at times. Adding to the confusion, he sometimes talked about Kevin in the third person and about things they did together. I wondered if this was because Patrick, a five-year-old boy, had memories of Kevin's life but couldn't make sense of being another person.

He told us about going to the zoo with Kevin and their cousin. Patrick had been to a zoo once two years before but not with the cousin, while Kevin had gone a number of times. Patrick talked about Kevin's bedroom and its two closets. While Kevin's bedroom actually had only one closet, it had two sliding doors that opened on both ends. Patrick described an apple-shaped "water ball," and Lisa said Kevin had a bathtub toy like that. He also talked about going with Kevin to a ranch that had bulls. Patrick had never been to one, but Kevin had indeed visited a cattle ranch that his aunt owned.

Our trip was a success. We had learned all the history from Lisa, studied documentation of Kevin's lesions, and even gotten Patrick to describe some memories to us. Having enjoyed meeting Lisa and her family, I had a greater appreciation for the people involved in these situations. They were not just characters in the pages of Ian's reports. They were flesh and blood, and some had experienced the human tragedies that led to the end of a life a child later seemed to remember.

After we returned home, we wanted to calculate the likelihood that Patrick's defects matched Kevin's just by coincidence. Not even taking the limp into account, how likely was it
that a child would be born with three lesions that matched
ones on a sibling? Ian had previously determined that the
odds of two birthmarks matching wounds on another body by
chance were about 1 in 25,000. He began with the surface area
of the skin of the average adult male being 1.6 square meters. He
then imagined that if this area were square and laid on a flat
surface, it would be approximately 127 centimeters by 127 centimeters. Since he considered a correspondence between a birthmark and a wound to be satisfactory if they were both within
an area of 10 square centimeters at the same location, he calcu-
lated how many 10 centimeter squares would fit into this body
surface area and found that 160 would. The probability that a
single birthmark would correspond to a wound was therefore
1/160. The probability that two birthmarks would correspond
to two wounds was $(1/160)^2$ or 1 in 25,600.

Critics challenged that figure. For Patrick's case, we decided to get some help. I met with two statisticians from the
medical school and explained the situation to them. Though
they seemed interested, one of them eventually sent me a report declining to estimate the likelihood. He said any calcula-
tions would oversimplify a complex system. He added, "Phrases
like 'highly improbable' and 'extremely rare' come to mind as
descriptive of the situation."

Ian had been intrigued by birthmark cases for a long time.
They drew on his interest in the interaction between mind and
body that dated back to his mainstream days in psychosomatic medicine. The year before we met Patrick, he published
Reincarnation and Biology, a two-thousand-page work, many
years in the making, that covered over two hundred cases of

children born with birthmarks or birth defects that matched wounds, usually fatal ones, on the body of a previous person.

While Ian was intrigued by these cases, I was initially uncomfortable with them. I didn't see how a wound on one body could show up as a birthmark on another, even if you accepted the idea of past-life connections. A student asked about this at a talk Ian gave. Ian responded with a quote from Charles Richet, a Nobel Prize–winning physiologist who also studied séances and ectoplasm: "I never said it was possible. I only said it was true."

That explanation did little for me. But Ian also wrote in *Reincarnation and Biology* about work that in various ways showed that mental images can produce specific effects on the body. An example was the case of a man who vividly recalled a traumatic event from nine years before in which his arms were tied behind him. During his recall, he developed what certainly looked like rope marks on his forearms. If images in a mind can produce specific effects like that on the body, and if the mind continues after death and inhabits a developing fetus, then I could see how the images could affect the fetus. It would not be the wounds on the previous body per se that produced the birthmark or birth defect, but rather the images of the wound in the individual's mind that did it. In Patrick's case, his marks seemed to match lesions that would have made a strong impression on Kevin: the blindness in his left eye, the scalp nodule that had been biopsied, and the IV site used for his chemotherapy.

Two years later, we visited Patrick and Lisa again. Patrick had continued to say unusual things. He had talked about a life prior to the one as Kevin, this one in Hawaii. He talked about his family there and a son who died. He mentioned a statue that melted due to a volcano and how the townspeople rebuilt it. From his descriptions, his parents believed he was recalling events from the 1940s.

Several months before we met this second time, Patrick began talking one night as his mother fixed dinner. He asked, "Do you know that you have a relative that no one talks about?" He said he had met this relative in heaven before being born. He was tall and thin with brown hair and brown eyes. He told Patrick that his name was Billy and he was called "Billy the Pirate." He had been killed by his stepfather, shot point-blank up in the mountains. He said he was upset that no one talked about him after his death.

Lisa knew nothing about any relative named Billy. When she called to ask her mother, she discovered that her mother's oldest sister had a son named Billy. The details Patrick gave were correct. Billy had been killed by his stepfather three years before Lisa was born. The murder was never talked about in the family. When Lisa asked about the nickname "Billy the Pirate," her mother laughed. His wildness had led to the nickname, and Lisa's mother said she hadn't heard it since Billy's death. There seemed to be no way that Patrick could have ever heard about Billy or his nickname before.

SCIENTIST WITH A VERY OPEN MIND

Patrick's story may sound familiar. I included a brief summary of it in my first book, and Carol Bowman, an author of two books on children's past-life memories who referred the case to us for Ian's unique type of investigation, wrote about it in one of hers. Ian had been hearing such stories for a long time. He was a singular figure. He could be the most prototypic, staid academician—formal at times and precise in his language—while exploring the strangest things. Exploring them did not automatically mean accepting them, and he never lost his analytic approach to every case he encountered. Patrick's mother said Ian reminded her of Jimmy Stewart, a comparison that, minus Stewart's folksiness, was pretty apt. Both were tall, lanky, distinguished older men with kindly smiles. Ian was also pleasant and supportive—unfailingly so as I took my first baby steps in the field—with a wry sense of humor he could on rare occasion use to devastating effect. His comment about a book whose author claimed was channeled from the spirit of William James, the great American psychologist and philosopher: "If the vapid writings . . . did indeed emanate from him, I can only say that this implies a terrible post-mortem reduction of personal capacities. (Survival of death with such an appalling decay of personality makes it, at least to me, a rather unattractive prospect.)"

Before focusing on this research, Ian had an accomplished academic career with dozens of publications to his credit when he arrived at the University of Virginia in 1957 to be chairman of the Department of Psychiatry. He also had longstanding interests in parapsychology and the question of whether any part of our minds survives after death. He started devoting more time to those interests and stepped down as chairman after ten years to focus on them full-time, mostly on children's reports of past-life memories. When he first began writing about the cases, journal editors knew him by his reputation from his mainstream successes. This led prominent publications to at least take note, offering respectful reviews of his various books. In a review of one of his books in 1975, *JAMA, The Journal of the American Medical Association,* said that "in regard to reincarnation he has painstakingly and unemotionally collected a detailed series of cases from India, cases in which the evidence is difficult to explain on any other grounds. . . .

He has placed on record a large amount of data that cannot be ignored." Two years later, *The Journal of Nervous and Mental Disease* devoted most of an entire issue to Ian's work.

He was far removed from those years by the time we met Patrick. Ian had always aimed for a scientific audience, writing densely detailed reports of cases for academic readers rather than the general public. The number of such readers open to considering his work had dwindled over the years, but Ian was still trying. At the end of our first trip to Patrick's family, we were eating dinner when Ian began discussing plans for a paper about Patrick's case. He imagined a title of "Unexpected Correspondence of 4 Physical Abnormalities between a Boy and his Deceased Brother," and he thought we should submit it to *The Lancet*, a British journal that is one of the leading medical journals in the world.

That proved to be too optimistic. Nine days after we sent the manuscript to the journal, we received a reply stating "after discussion among several editors here, we decided that it might be better placed elsewhere." We then sent it to another journal. And another, and another. In all, we submitted the paper to six mainstream journals over the course of a year, and none of them accepted it.

We eventually included Patrick's story in an article about several birthmark and birth defect cases that we published in the *Journal of Scientific Exploration*. It is produced by the Society for Scientific Exploration, an organization started by a group of academic scientists, including Ian, who had interests that the journals in their various fields were not friendly to, such as astronomers who studied UFO reports. The articles in it are thus scholarly efforts to address controversial topics. While our paper fit right in, Patrick's case did not reach the broader academic audience Ian had hoped for.

Nonetheless, his optimism was not entirely misplaced. The year after *The Lancet* rejected our paper, it published a letter from Ian about the forty-two cases of twins he and colleagues had studied in which at least one of the pair claimed to remember a previous life. The letter was more than a column long, and the journal gave it a title of "Past lives of twins" without even a question mark at the end.

When Ian died in 2007, the *Journal of Scientific Exploration* devoted an issue to reviews of his work and to people's remembrances of him. One was from Tom Shroder, an editor at *The Washington Post* who accompanied Ian on two research trips and then wrote a book about them. Shroder finished his piece by saying, "Whatever the truth turns out to be, Ian's work, those countless files filled to overflowing with the passionate precision of his research . . . well, they are something. They are really something."

The issue also included an article of Ian's from 1958 that may have portended his future. Called "Scientists with Half-closed Minds," it was an essay Ian wrote for *Harper's Magazine* that reviewed various examples of initial failure by the scientific community to recognize breakthrough insights. He warned of our tendency, especially dangerous in scientists, to reject new ideas that conflict with our previous understandings.

Ian's awareness of this pattern did not keep him from pursuing the work he thought was important. He once told me—with a smile—that he would die a failure because he had not achieved his primary goal of getting mainstream science as a whole to seriously consider reincarnation as a possibility. That objective may have been quixotic, but Ian expressed no regrets about the course he had chosen. To the contrary, he had enjoyed the journey, having been fortunate and resourceful enough to be able to devote many years of his life to studying matters that interested him. And though he may not have convinced the whole of mainstream science, he did open a lot of eyes, including those of numerous scientists.

Throughout his life, Ian kept the attitude of open-minded inquiry he encouraged in 1958. His final paper was a wonderful summary of his last forty years called "Half a Career with the Paranormal." He finished it by writing, "Let no one think that I know the answer. I am still seeking."

I hope you will approach the cases in this book with such an attitude. You may be tempted to think the idea of past-life memories is just too fantastic. I can understand that way of thinking. I'm not in this field because I'm a big believer in past lives, and I'm not here to promote the idea. I got involved in this work because I wanted to figure out for myself whether life after death might be possible. Even though I have become persuaded that something is indeed going on in some of the cases, I continue to consider the various possibilities for each one. I won't bore you with those considerations as I relate the cases, but I would encourage you to be open to all of them, both the ordinary and the extraordinary.

In my first book, I gave an overview of what is now fifty years of research. With this one, I'm focusing on some remarkable cases I've studied in recent years, ones I didn't include in the first book (except for Patrick's). But I want not only to show you the phenomenon but also to make sense of it. If you're having trouble taking this kind of work seriously, it may be because the cases can seem so outside of science, so outside of the real world. The *JAMA* book review notwithstanding, I suspect that's why many people have ignored this large amount of data for so long. At the end of the book, I'll address this concern, showing you how past-life memories can be consistent with current scientific understandings. If you are skeptical, I would challenge you to make a final determination only after you have heard all the facts. I will also explore how this phenomenon, beyond being consistent with scientific knowledge, can even lead to new insights about the true nature of reality, both about our existence in this world and about the possibility of life after death.

I hope all of us can try to emulate Ian's attitude of maintaining a critical eye but also an open mind. In this way, you can appreciate the astonishing experiences some of these families have had, and you can consider any meaning to take from stories of children like Patrick, a little boy who may have come to this life bearing marks and memories from his dear, deceased half brother.

Chapter 2

WANDERING THROUGH ASIA

While Ian wrote after decades of research that he was still seeking, my seeking was just beginning with Patrick's case. Nothing in the trajectory of most of my life had hinted that I would one day investigate reports of past-life memories. Growing up in North Carolina, I went with my family to a Southern Baptist church every week, and being the ever dutiful son, I believed what I heard on Sundays. I largely stopped attending church when I was in college at the University of North Carolina and stopped entirely when I left Chapel Hill and moved to Charlottesville to begin my psychiatry training at the University of Virginia. I left behind much of the dogma I had learned growing up. Though I did not reach a firm conclusion against spirituality, the leanings I had in that direction became quiescent.

I first heard about Ian during my training. I was intrigued that someone would do what he had done—walk away from a prestigious academic position to focus on a topic such as past lives—but not intrigued enough to contact him, and I never met him during my five years at the medical center.

After completing my training, I stayed in Charlottesville

and set up a private practice in a nearby community. I became interested again in spiritual matters when I remarried, as my wife, Chris, though not religious, was open to topics I had given little thought to, such as psychics, spirits, even past lives. I began reading a variety of books on such matters, including one by Ian Stevenson, *Children Who Remember Previous Lives*, that described his work with young children who reported past-life memories. Though I was not particularly drawn to the possibility of previous lives at the time, I was impressed that he had studied hundreds of cases over the years, using a careful, analytic approach I found appealing.

While I was reading the book, we saw in the local newspaper that his research division (then known as the Division of Personality Studies, or DOPS) had gotten a grant to study the effects that near-death experiences produce in the lives of the people who have them. In near-death experiences, people often report leaving their bodies and observing them from above, reviewing all the events of their lives, and going through a tunnel-like space to another world that may include deceased relatives and a bright light or a being of light. Since I was feeling unfulfilled with my private practice work, Chris suggested I call the division's office to see if the researchers needed any help interviewing patients for the study. When I called, I was invited to their next weekly research lunch.

As I prepared to attend the meeting, I wondered how people who did this kind of work dressed. For instance, did the men wear ties? I decided to go with the most casual work outfit I had, wearing a shirt and tie but not a dressy one. Ian then walked in wearing a three-piece suit.

I began going to DOPS every week for the meeting. After a while, I started working on a study to review the medical records of people who reported having near-death experiences, to assess how close they had actually been to death. It quickly became clear that we were also assessing the quality of the medical record documentation, as some of the records, particularly in the older cases, contained surprisingly few details. In any event, I enjoyed working with the others on the project, and even if it was only for a short amount of time each week, the project felt like a worthwhile, unpaid hobby.

After I had been coming to the division for almost two years, Ian asked if I would be interested in traveling to Thailand and Burma to study past-life cases with one of our colleagues, Jürgen Keil. I jumped at the chance and began making plans. Three weeks after our first trip to see Patrick, I set off to Asia for a month. In Bangkok, I met up with Jürgen, who had studied cases in Thailand before. German by birth, he had immigrated to Australia as a young man during the postwar years, originally as a fitter and turner for machinery. He then became a psychologist and held an emeritus position at the University of Tasmania by the time I met him. We connected with our translator and headed off to see cases.

CHASING AFTER A DEAD BODY

One of the first cases we saw involved a girl named Ampan. The case was old by the time we got to it—Ampan was nineteen years old at that point—but the details still seemed fresh in the minds of the people we talked to. Her parents said she started talking about a past life when she was five years old, older than many of the other children when they begin. She was crying one day and said she wanted to go home. Her mom said, "Your home is here. Where is the home that you're talking about?"

Ampan answered, "Buhom village." Buhom was three miles from the family's village. A paved road connected them when we were there, but witnesses said only a dirt road existed at the time, with buses rarely going between the two. Though Ampan's father had a distant relative in Buhom, her parents had never been there, and they didn't know of anyone from Buhom coming to their village to do business.

Ampan then told the story of a previous life. She said she had developed dengue fever and died at the district hospital. Dengue fever is a viral illness spread by mosquitoes in tropical and subtropical climates. It's usually not deadly, but a variant, dengue hemorrhagic fever, definitely can be.

Her parents asked Ampan what her name had been and she said "Wong" or "Somwong." They reported that she also gave a family name, but they didn't remember what it was. When her mother asked how she had come to them, Ampan said that after she died at the district hospital, a van took her body away. She ran after it but couldn't catch it. She then began walking, and after five miles she passed by the road in front of her parents' house. She said she was looking for drinking water. She saw her future mother, and there was a cool breeze. Rather than continue on her journey, she lay down to rest there, and she was subsequently born to her mother.

On that first day when Ampan told the story, she cried to go home. She continued to cry frequently, sometimes on a daily basis, for three years. Finally, when she was eight years old, thirty people from Ampan's village rented a bus to attend a merit-making festival, a Buddhist religious event, that was being held in Buhom. Ampan went with her mother and a family friend. When the bus reached Buhom, Ampan led her mother and their friend to a home where she ran to hug a woman there, calling her Mommy.

This woman had had a daughter named Somwong who had indeed died the way Ampan had described. We talked to

Somwong's parents, her sister, and her brothers. Ampan's mother had let them take Ampan in their home for some private time on that first visit. Ampan told them she wanted Somwong's Buddha amulet, a religious piece often worn as a pendant and thought to protect the owner from dangers. Somwong's family reported that Ampan told them where the amulet was and then found it. She also looked for some of Somwong's clothes, but they were no longer in the house.

After about an hour, Ampan's mother said they needed to leave, though Ampan didn't want to. She continued to visit after that, often two or three times a month, sometimes staying as long as ten days. Her parents, glad she was finally happy, did not object. They reported she still had the memories at age nineteen, which is much longer than these children usually report them, but we didn't get to meet her because she was away visiting friends. We tried again on a later trip, but she was away that time as well.

Though we didn't get a chance to talk to her, I was struck by her story. It offers interesting evidence for past-life memories, both in the way her statements corresponded to the other girl's life and with her apparent ability to find the girl's amulet. What impressed me most, however, was the image of a deceased spirit chasing after a van taking her body away from the hospital. She then tried to find her way back home after the van was gone. That longing to be with her family seemed to continue into another life, as Ampan cried so frequently to see them.

Her report of events between lives may seem surprisingly concrete; it's certainly not very ethereal. As I explained in my first book, only about twenty percent of these children talk about events between lives. For the ones that do, the reports can vary tremendously, some describing terrestrial events as

Ampan did, others saying they went to another realm like heaven. Some of this may be due to cultural influence, of course, but as I will argue later, there is good reason to think that the *afterlife*, if we want to use that term, is not homogeneous. It can vary from individual to individual, there being not just one place (or two) where people go and not just one kind of experience that they have after they die.

In this case, if Ampan was indeed Somwong in a previous life, Somwong's consciousness (or soul or spirit if you like) seems to have remained tightly connected to this realm and to her family. This led to some anguish on her part during Ampan's early life but also to an eventual reunion. Somwong's attachment to her parents may have affected her experiences after she died and may have contributed to memories of that life carrying over to her life as Ampan. This would not mean necessarily that we will all have similar experiences after we die or that we all come back to live another life near our last one. I'll explore this further at the end of the book, but for now just consider that our attitudes in this life may affect what we experience after we die and perhaps even whether we come back here for another life at all.

ANOMALOUS DATES

Another case involved a boy named Juta, who was a little over four years old when we first met him. We visited his family in their home, a nice house in a small town in northeast Thailand where Juta lived with his mother and his grandparents. Four months after he was born, his maternal uncle, his mother's older brother, was killed in a motorcycle accident near Bangkok. He was hit by a truck, and his head struck the guardrail of a bridge.

Three or four months later, Juta developed respiratory

symptoms and a high fever for several days, his body shaking and teeth chattering with chills. After he recovered, his family noticed he had developed two dark spots on his left upper arm, which were still clearly visible when we met him. They were irregularly shaped, almost triangular, and about a quarter inch in diameter. They matched spots on his deceased uncle's left arm. His uncle had planned to get a tattoo there. The procedure was so painful, however, that he stopped it after receiving three spots as the start of the image, two of which now seemed to be reproduced on Juta's arm. Juta also developed a protruding navel at that time, an "outie," as his uncle had had.

Even though Juta's mother was his primary caretaker, when he got old enough to talk, he called his grandparents Mother and Father. His deceased uncle had been the only one of their children to call them by the more formal expression for Mother and Father, rather than Mom and Dad. And for his own mother, whose name was Noey, he called her an expression that meant "Little Noey" or "Silly Noey." His uncle had called his little sister this nickname to tease her, but no one else used it. Juta's grandparents told us about this first, and when we asked his mother about it later, she laughed and said she had to threaten to spank Juta to get him to stop calling her that.

Juta showed other behaviors that reminded his family of his uncle, especially when the uncle's friends came to visit. He joked with them in the impolite way that buddies can do with each other. He would put ice in several glasses, then pour beer or whiskey into them and stir them with his finger, just as his uncle had done. He would distribute the drinks to his friends and then drink one himself(!). One friend noted that he used the same gesture pouring beer as his uncle had, pouring the beer and then hitting the bottom of the bottle to get the last bit out.

When Juta was two, he said he had worked for a company in Bangkok building condominiums, which his uncle had done. He also showed a lot of interest in construction equipment. He would point to his uncle's motorcycle and say it was his.

We visited the family again eight months after our initial meeting. At that point, Juta was turning five, and he was no longer talking about his uncle's life. He had stopped calling his grandparents Mother and Father. Instead, he called his own mother "Mother" or "Mother Noey" (which was unusual). He no longer drank alcohol, refusing beer if given a glass, in contrast to his behavior at age two when he would drink a small amount of whiskey. The spots on his arm were becoming more faint. He seemed to be a typical little boy at that point.

This is an example of what Ian innocuously called an anomalous dates case. The dates were anomalous in that the child's date of birth was before the previous person died. The implication of a child developing memories of a person who died after the child had already been born is that a soul came into a young child and pushed out the soul that had been there before. Or perhaps the souls had an ongoing tug of war. Juta's family said his behavior had gone back and forth when he was younger, wanting alcohol on some days and not others. Perhaps two souls were battling for supremacy.

As odd as this may seem, it receives support from two of the most remarkable and perplexing cases that Ian ever studied. He investigated them with Satwant Pasricha, a clinical psychologist in India who, until her recent retirement, was a Professor of Clinical Psychology at NIMHANS, the National Institute of Mental Health and Neurosciences. The subject of the first case was a woman named Uttara, who at the age of thirty-two suddenly displayed a new personality. Uttara had been hospitalized due to several health issues when a yogi came to the hospital and gave instructions on meditation, including breathing exercises that induced a somewhat altered state of consciousness. Though Uttara had meditated in the past without incident, her behavior changed drastically this time, as she alternated between times of excitement and periods of silence. She would wander away from the hospital. Oddest of all, she began speaking in another language that her doctor thought was Bengali, the language from the Bengal area of India, which Uttara did not know. The doctor said his hospital could not take care of a patient behaving so strangely, and he instructed Uttara's parents to take her home.

This meant that they had to manage their daughter, who not only was acting very strangely but was no longer able to converse with them. She spoke a language they didn't know, and she could no longer understand Marathi, their native language. They initially had to communicate with her using gestures. They found Bengali-speaking people to talk with her and eventually picked up some Bengali words themselves. She said her name was Sharada. She gave many details of what she said was her life in Bengal. Though she apparently thought that life was ongoing, she seemed to come from another time, as she appeared completely unfamiliar with any tools, appliances, or vehicles developed after the industrial revolution. She did not recognize Uttara's family or friends. Sharada stayed "in control" for several weeks before Uttara returned to her normal personality. But her family was not done with Sharada. She continued to emerge intermittently for years. Ian and Satwant found out that Sharada appeared twenty-three times during the first three years. Most of the Sharada phases only lasted a day or two, but some were much longer, including one that went on for seven weeks.

In addition to discussing various locations in Bengal, including five obscure villages, Sharada gave the names of a number of people she said were her family members. The names were traced to a family that lived in West Bengal in the early nineteenth century. The names and relationships she gave for her father and six other male members of the family all matched a male genealogy of a family that was discovered. This genealogy had been published sixty-five years before in a Bengali magazine with a local circulation, but as Uttara had never visited that state, Ian and Satwant were confident she had never seen it. Since it only included the names of the men, they did not find conclusive proof that Sharada had existed as a real person, but her statements about her family were confirmed. It appeared that Uttara's body had been taken over by this personality named Sharada, a woman who had lived in another part of the country 150 years before.

Regarding Sharada's ability to speak Bengali, Uttara and her family said she had never learned it, other than taking a few high school lessons in reading Bengali script from a teacher who himself could not speak the language. One of the researchers' associates, Professor Pal, had four long talks with Sharada in Bengali, and he and five other native Bengali speakers all agreed that despite some imperfections in her speech, she had a solid command of the language. Ian and Satwant published a paper on the case, and four years later, Ian also wrote it up for a book. In the latter report, he noted that Uttara had been accused of having learned to speak Bengali in school, though the evidence for that was meager. He had also asked a linguist to listen to two recordings made of Sharada speaking and singing. The linguist said that based on the recordings, he did not hear indications of archaic speech that others had heard in conversation with her. He also said her accent was not native Bengali.

I'm willing to overlook the imperfections in her speech and accent. It's like Samuel Johnson's line about a dog walking on its hind legs: "It is not done well; but you are surprised to find it done at all." If the woman actually started speaking a language she did not know, that calls for an explanation.

Was this a case of possession by a Bengali spirit using the imperfect instrument of a woman who had never spoken Bengali? Or was it a bizarre case of dissociation, in which a woman, like patients with multiple personality disorder (now called dissociative identity disorder), suddenly took on the identification and behaviors of a different person? In this situation, however, she somehow displayed knowledge she seemingly could not have acquired in this life.

Ian corresponded sporadically with Uttara for thirty years after her adventures with Sharada began. Sharada was still coming even at the end, but only once a year for a brief appearance, and she did not affect Uttara's life at that point.

The second case involved a young woman named Sumitra. Ian and Satwant studied this one along with another psychiatrist, Nicholas McClean-Rice. Sumitra began experiencing episodes, lasting from a few minutes to an entire day, in which she would appear to go into a trance with her eyes rolled upward and her teeth clenched. During a couple of these, she seemed to be taken over by different personalities, one who said she had ended her life by drowning herself in a well and another who said he had been a man in another part of India. These culminated in a time when she lost consciousness and then, by all appearances, died. She stopped breathing and had no pulse for at least five minutes.

As Sumitra's family began grieving around her, she somehow revived. She initially appeared confused and said little for the next day. After that, she didn't recognize the family and friends around her. She said her name was Shiva and that she had been murdered by her in-laws in a place called Dibiyapur, some sixty miles away. She gave many details that were found to correspond to the life of one Shiva Divedi, who was unknown to Sumitra's family and who had died violently in Dibiyapur two months before Sumitra's transformation. On the day of her death, Shiva had been quarreling with her in-laws and told her uncle that her mother-in-law and one of her sisters-in-law had beaten her. The next morning, her body was found on the train tracks. Her in-laws said she had killed herself by jumping in front of a train, but when her uncle saw her body, he thought it was suspicious that her head appeared to be the only part of her that was injured. He asked Shiva's in-laws to hold off cremating her for four hours until he could bring her father there. They ignored his request, and Shiva's body was ashes by the time her father arrived. When Sumitra was later shown a picture of Rama Kanti, Shiva's sister-in-law, she said, "This is Rama Kanti, who hit me with a brick."

Sumitra, still calling herself Shiva, rejected her husband (and his amorous advances) and her son for some time and asked to be taken to Shiva's two children. Her family initially thought she had gone crazy and later that she had become possessed. They made no efforts to verify what she was saying. Eventually, Shiva's father heard a rumor that his daughter had taken possession of a young woman in a distant village. Three months after Sumitra's revival, he visited her. Sumitra recognized him and said she was his daughter. She ultimately recognized twenty-three people from Shiva's life, either in person or in photographs.

Sumitra's transformation also included changes in her behavior, as the researchers put it, "from that of a simple village girl to that of a moderately well-educated woman of higher caste and more urban manners, who could now read and write Hindi fluently." She wrote letters to Shiva's father, demonstrating writing ability somewhere between Sumitra's previously limited abilities and Shiva's educated ones. A letter found during a follow-up investigation (by Antonia Mills and Kuldip Dhiman) included lines like, "Papa I do not like it here . . . God is bad as he has dumped me here." A year after her revival, Sumitra once seemed to resume her original personality for a few hours. Otherwise, she had remained Shiva constantly for two years when the initial investigation was completed. Indeed, as the follow-up study determined, she remained Shiva all the way until the time of her death, thirteen years after her revival. Everyone, including Sumitra, seemed to gradually adjust to the new reality after her transformation. She warmed up to her family and presumably her husband, as she had two more children. Shiva's family stopped visiting after a while and let Sumitra live her life.

Satwant began investigating the case a month after Sumitra first met Shiva's father. She and Ian ultimately interviewed twenty-four members of the two families, along with twenty-nine other individuals for background information. Unless the case is an elaborate fraud perpetrated by a large number of people for no apparent purpose, the researchers seem to have documented a case of possession. In discussing this possibility, they wrote: "Although we do not dogmatically assert that this is the correct interpretation of this case, we believe much of the evidence makes it the most plausible one."

These cases are unusual, even by our standards. I present them to point out that while we normally think there is a one-to-one correspondence between a brain and a mind, that may not always be true. A basic assumption of modern neuroscience is that the brain creates the mind or consciousness we experience. So how could a consciousness, originally associated with a brain that is long since dead, take over the body of a living person? An alternative is that consciousness goes through the brain but exists outside of it. It would be a separate entity from the brain, normally linked to it quite closely for the duration of a life, but separate nonetheless. These cases in which a brain seems to have contained two consciousnesses that developed independently are much more consistent with this alternative theory than with the modern idea that the mind is what the brain does, end of story.

The normal course is for a brain to house only one mind during a lifetime, to be sure. But the rarity of these cases doesn't lessen their potential importance. As William James said, "If you wish to upset the law that all crows are black, you mustn't seek to show that no crows are; it is enough if you prove one single crow to be white." Cases in which the consciousness of a deceased individual appears to take over the body of a living person challenge the belief that a consciousness or mind is confined to one brain, which is wholly responsible for creating it.

AN UNFORTUNATE HUNTING ACCIDENT

Another case Jürgen and I studied in Thailand had some interesting twists to it. The child and the previous person lived in the same village and were in fact related, the child's grandfather being the older brother of the previous person's mother. The previous person was a young man named Boon who went hunting one day with three friends. One of them accidentally dropped his gun. It discharged, shooting Boon in the chest. The friend apparently panicked and ran off, but one of the other young men, a fellow named Phon, carried Boon's body out of the forest back to the village. Villagers tried to help, but Boon was dead at that point.

We talked with the man who dressed the body after the death. He reported that Boon had a wound on his chest under his left nipple that had bled profusely. The bullet had not passed all the way through the body, and Boon had a bulge on his back where the bullet was thought to be. It was a large area, blue with bruising, on the right side of his back below his shoulder blade.

Two months later, a boy named Somsak was born. His family reported he was born with a birthmark on his left chest and one on his back. Somsak was nine years old when we met him, and at that point, though the marks were hard to see and even harder to photograph, the one on his chest was still visible. Boon's mother, who saw her son's body after he died, told us Somsak's birthmark was in the same place where Boon had been shot.

Somsak's mother died of cancer when he was five, so we interviewed his grandmother and his aunt to learn about his previous behavior. They said that when he was first old enough to talk, Somsak woke up early one morning and asked his mother why Phon had shot him. He continued to ask this for the next couple of years. By all accounts, he was confused in thinking that Phon had killed Boon, since it was actually another friend's gun that had discharged, but he was upset at Phon anyway.

At the age of two, he approached Phon and said, "You are a murderer. You are the person who killed me." We talked with Phon, who said Somsak was so mad he tried to strangle him. After talking with us a bit, Phon said he didn't remember the events surrounding Boon's death and abruptly walked away. That death must have been quite painful to him, but I wondered if being called a killer, even if by a toddler, contributed to his discomfort.

We talked with Boon's parents, who told us that when Somsak was little, he was able to point out Boon's room in the house, and he correctly identified the pillow that belonged to each family member. He remembered items that had been Boon's, such as a saw and a locket. He took things that belonged to Boon but nothing that did not. Boon's parents felt Somsak still remembered them from his life as their son, calling them by the familiar names that Boon had. He was said to have recognized Boon's girlfriend as well, but she was away working in the fields and wasn't available to talk to us.

Somsak had also named four people who he said had walked past Boon's body after Phon brought it back from the woods. He refused to visit one of them when he was in the hospital because he said the man had ignored him back then. We talked with another one he named. The man explained his actions on the day Boon was shot. He had initially started out to help, he said, but he needed to go to a field to chase one of his cows that was in trouble due to flooding during the rainy season. When he saw Boon's parents behind him, he assumed they would take care of Boon, so he went to attend to the cow. He said he came back afterward, but it was too late to help at that point.

The man said no one else had ever said anything to him about ignoring the body. Yet somehow Somsak had known about it. As the man was rationalizing his behavior to us, I was struck by his need to explain himself because of a young boy's accusation about events from a previous life.

The following day, we spoke with Somsak himself. Even though he was nine years old by then and had stopped talking about Boon long before, we still wanted to see what he might say to us. He gave numerous details regarding Boon's death, some of which were incorrect as far as we could tell, but then acknowledged that though he still remembered being shot, he was mixing in details he had heard from others with his own memories.

I actually found this more credible than if, after several years of not talking about Boon, he would claim to still have perfect memory of his death. In general, we don't put much stock into what the child says years after the previous person has been identified. By that time, he or she may well have had an opportunity to hear all kinds of things about that person. What we focus on are the things the child says when the case first starts. Those are most impressive—when the child begins to talk about the life of a complete stranger. Here, even though Somsak was describing someone known to his family, the statements he made and the behaviors he showed made the case intriguing.

After Thailand, we headed to Burma. The country's name was changed to Myanmar in 1989 by the military regime running the country. That change has received varying degrees of acceptance, and most of its citizens seem to prefer the name Burma. The contrast with Thailand was striking. Thailand showed many signs of development, particularly in Bangkok. In fact, it was a scene of massive construction during my first trip there, as giant expressways were being built above its clogged roads, so that in some areas Bangkok looked like a futuristic city gone horribly wrong.

There was nothing futuristic about Yangon (or Rangoon), the largest city of Burma. The buildings were run-down, and modern skyscraper office buildings were absent. The people were very pleasant, however, and we saw cases in Yangon before traveling north to places such as Meiktila and Mandalay.

DISTINCTIVE MARKINGS

One of the cases we saw in Burma was an example of what Ian called experimental birthmarks, a practice I discussed in my first book. People in certain areas of Southeast Asia sometimes make a mark on a body after someone dies, with the hope that the deceased individual will take the mark to the next life. In that way, when a baby is born with a birthmark that matches it, people can identify the infant as the previous person come back. Ian studied twenty such cases, and Jürgen and I found eighteen more.

Yin Yin was a little girl who was seven years old when we met her. Her maternal grandmother had died of kidney disease nine years before Yin Yin was born. An hour or two after she died, her daughter (Yin Yin's aunt) used soot to make two marks on her body. One was on the outside part of her left leg just above her ankle, and the other was on the inside part of her right leg on and below her ankle. Several people saw her make the marks, including a neighbor we talked to. Yin Yin's mother did not see the marks but knew her sister had made them.

Before Yin Yin's mother became pregnant with her, she had three dreams in which Yin Yin's grandmother said she wanted to come live with her. In the dreams, Yin Yin's mother initially said no, but her grandmother became more insistent with each successive dream until her mother relented, telling her, "As you wish." A month later, she became pregnant. During the pregnancy, she had cravings for tea and cake, Indian spiced food, and milk. While she didn't normally like these, Yin Yin's grandmother, whose father was Indian, did.

When Yin Yin was born, she had birthmarks that matched both of the marks her aunt had made on her grandmother's body. We confirmed this with her family and with the neighbor. She had no other birthmarks, and her two brothers didn't have any either. Her two had faded away by the time she was six years old, so they weren't present for us to see a year later.

Yin Yin began talking at around eighteen months of age, and she made a number of statements related to the life of her grandmother. She asked about a mortar that the grandmother had owned, and when her uncle hurt his knee, she said that medicine should be pounded in the mortar and put on his knee. The grandmother also had a shell that she had used during ceremonies. Others in the family did not use shells, but during a ceremony Yin Yin asked about hers. Both of these questions came before she turned two, and as a youngster, she began talking about the previous life frequently. For example, she asked about her money and jewelry. Her grandmother had apparently been quite well off. The family developed financial problems after her death, and Yin Yin once asked why the family had spent her money. When she was being spanked, she would ask, "Why do you not respect your mother?"

The neighbor we talked to was known to Yin Yin's family as "Ma Win Kyi." Yin Yin's grandmother, however, had called her "Daw Win Kyi," and so did Yin Yin, even though no one around her did. She also called her parents and her aunt and uncle by their given names.

During World War II, Yin Yin's grandmother had lived with a cousin in Tavoy, a city in a different part of Burma. She called the cousin "Baby" and was the only person to do so. That cousin later lived with Yin Yin's family for a while, beginning when Yin Yin was five years old. Yin Yin also called her "Baby" and once said to her, "Please shut your ears because

the English bombers will drop the bombs." Her family interpreted this as a reference to the bombing of Japanese soldiers
in Burma by the English during World War II.

Feeling sad when they heard Yin Yin talk about the life of
her grandmother, her family tried to discourage her from saying such things. They fed her eggs for a while in the belief,
common in Burma, that this would make her forget about her
previous life. That didn't seem to work, but her statements did
become less frequent as she got older. By the time we met her,
she generally talked about her grandmother's life only when
she was angry or sad. Two days before we met her, however, she
did say to her female first cousin, who was visiting, "You look
like my son." The family said the cousin does, in fact, closely
resemble the grandmother's son (the cousin's father), but he
wasn't with her on the visit.

Along with her statements, Yin Yin had a habit that reminded her family of her grandmother: she would eat with
one leg hiked up in her chair. She and her grandmother were
the only two in the family to do that. This is similar to the behavior of a child Ian studied, a boy in Sri Lanka named Sujith.
When he drank, he drew his legs up, just as the man whose
life he seemed to remember had.

We talked to Yin Yin, but she didn't say much to us. She
did report a memory of a group photograph being taken. Her
family produced a photo that included her grandmother. Yin
Yin didn't identify anyone in the shot, but she then said she
remembered another photograph that had been taken in a particular room of the house, which she pointed to. Her family reported that a group photograph that included Yin Yin's
grandmother had, in fact, been taken in that room twenty-five
years before. The photograph had been given to other family
members in Tavoy more than twenty years before, and Yin

Yin's immediate family members hadn't thought of it for many years.

ANIMAL BEHAVIOR

For the sake of completeness, I will mention that Yin Yin's aunt, the one who marked her grandmother's body, told us that she had also marked a dog one time. A boy was subsequently born in that family with birthmarks on his leg that matched the ones she had made on the dog.

This brings up the uncomfortable topic of past lives as animals. Ian wrote that he had to overcome his initial prejudice against such cases. (In fact, he once wrote in a letter that when he first went to Asia, he was inclined to ridicule such claims.) Once he managed to overcome that prejudice, he kept records on any claims about animal past lives and found them to be extremely rare. He pointed out that if cases were created purely by religious beliefs, we should expect to find more in South Asia than we do, since Hindus and Buddhists there believe that animals can reincarnate as humans and vice versa.

Most of the claims of past lives as animals are of course unverifiable. One strange case in Thailand seems to be an exception. Ian was traveling there with an associate named Francis Story when someone gave them a booklet about the case of a boy who claimed to have been a python in a previous life. Story wanted to study it, but as it was on the other side of the country, Ian thought it would be a waste of time and money. Nonetheless, after Ian left, Story did go to the site of the case and thought it seemed quite authentic. He talked with the boy, his parents, and his older sister. He was unable to talk to a key figure in the case, a Mr. Hiew, because the way to his village was under water and impassable, but Hiew had been interviewed for an article in a newspaper, the *Bangkok Times*.

The boy, named Dalawong, claimed he had been a deer in a past life. He said that after he was killed by a hunter, he was reborn as a snake. Just before Dalawong was conceived, his father had eaten snake meat when it was served to him by an acquaintance who had killed a python after an extended struggle. When Dalawong was three, that acquaintance, Mr. Hiew, came to a party at the house next to Dalawong's family. Neither Dalawong nor his mother had met him before. When Dalawong saw him, he became infuriated and tried to find a hammer or stick to use to attack him. He said Mr. Hiew had killed him when he was a snake and gave details of how the killing occurred. These were ones that Dalawong seemingly had no way of knowing, involving a particular cave and a fight between a snake and two dogs, followed by a confrontation with the owner of the dogs, who killed the snake. Hiew confirmed that all the details were correct. Dalawong said that after he was killed, his spirit saw his future father and thought he was kinder than the other men who ate the snake meat. He followed him home and soon entered his mother's body.

His father reported that when Dalawong met Hiew, he touched him on his left shoulder and said he had been bitten by a snake there. His father said that Hiew did indeed have a scar at that spot from a snake bite. The others didn't mention that aspect of the story. Dalawong got over his initial anger toward Hiew and said it was better to be a human than a snake. In fact, he began killing snakes as he got older, doing this out of pity because he said being a snake is very difficult.

Jürgen Keil visited Dalawong some twenty years after Francis Story met him. Dalawong still believed he had been a snake in his last life. He continued to visit the cave where the snake had been killed. He would go there every couple of months and meditate. During his meditation, he obtained information about using herbs to help the sick, and he was recognized in his village at that point as a local doctor.

I should also add that Dalawong was born with ichthyosis, a skin condition that caused his body, particularly the lower half, to be covered in scales. You might say they made his skin appear snakelike.

I may be well past your boggle threshold now, the point at which a story becomes too mind-boggling to accept. I confess this case approaches my own boggle threshold. But it is not entirely unique. I recently received an e-mail from an American mother writing about her son, Peter. One day when he was six, she gave him a candy necklace. He told her, "When I was a chimpanzee a boy threw one in my cage. I didn't know what to do with it." She asked him how he got in the cage, and he described falling into a trap and being taken to a zoo. She also asked what happened after he died as a chimp but before he got into "Mommy's stomach," but he only answered, "Nothing." Her husband then came home with their other children, and things got busy. When she later tried to ask Peter more about what he had said, he didn't even remember their conversation. If the candy necklace stirred a memory, nothing else ever did, because Peter never talked about being a chimp again.

I bring up the animal cases to make a point. Though I might be able to believe that a chimpanzee could have some conscious memory of a candy necklace, I certainly don't believe a snake would remember details about a particular location and a series of events, and years later be able to recognize a man who was its final nemesis. It's true I don't know what goes on in the mind of a snake, but that does cross my boggle threshold. What I can consider, however, is that a consciousness was associated with the snake while also being apart from it. Though the brain's activities would supply information to it, the consciousness would involve more than what was being recorded in the brain. It would transcend the physical. And this transcendental, nonphysical aspect could continue on after the death of the brain and the body.

This concept receives some support from cases of near-death experiences in which an individual's brain is not functioning. People often report memories of events that happened around them, ones whose specifics are sometimes later verified to be extremely accurate. The consciousness that was associated with the dying body is taking in new information (through some mechanism outside the five normal senses) even though the brain is not working. Many people in that situation report then leaving the physical and having out-of-this-world experiences.

This consciousness that these near-death cases suggest, which functions when the brain is no longer working, may function separately from the brain during life as well. Dalawong seemed to have an awareness of events in the snake's life in a way that the snake would not have had. This awareness belonged to the consciousness that he said continued on in spirit form after the snake died, before becoming attached to his present life.

All in all, Asia proved to be fertile ground for finding new cases. This was not surprising. The places I visited were ones where most people believe in reincarnation or are at least quite open to it. Word gets around when a child claims memories of a previous life. If the claims are compelling enough, reports of the cases may appear in newspapers. If our associates in those places are looking for cases for us to study, people can usually point them in the right direction.

The situation tends to be quite different here in the West. Many of the American families who contact us have told no one else about their children's statements. The grandparents and extended family may not know and may not be receptive to hearing about them. Cases only get into the media very rarely, and while I will describe one of those later, we are usually dependent on parents to send us their stories, as we have no other way of discovering them.

After three trips to Asia, I decided to focus on Western cases anyway. I enjoyed my travels with Jürgen, and we saw a lot of interesting cases. But it seemed to me that just collecting more Asian ones wouldn't accomplish a great deal; if Ian's two thousand Asian cases hadn't convinced people to take a look at the research, studying more was unlikely to do so. I hoped that Western examples might get people's attention in a way that the Asian ones had not. Though they are harder to find, some of them have proved well worth the effort.

Chapter 3

THE BOY FROM BARRA

Ian received an e-mail one day from a producer in London who wanted to discuss the possibility of a documentary about our work. We get contacted from time to time by television producers. Sometimes they just want an interview; other times they want our work to be the primary focus of a program. Ian was always extremely careful with media of any kind. He would usually say no to TV folks immediately. If not, with only a couple of exceptions, he would say no to them eventually.

I have been more open. Once I decided to focus on Western cases, I needed people to know about our work so they would contact us if their children started talking about past lives. Ian was always concerned about the work being sensationalized in the media, and the unfailing habit of producers to say they intended to make a serious film did little to alleviate that concern. Sensationalism, to some extent, can be in the eye of the beholder. I understand the coverage a program gives the work will be superficial to some extent—it's television after all—but I think such a show can have value despite its inherent limitations. I even did an interview for *Unsolved Mysteries* at one point. I knew it wouldn't challenge Edward R. Murrow for journalistic prestige, but at the time I was looking for American cases for a psychological testing study we were conducting. One mother, in quite a bit of distress, contacted me about her daughter after seeing the show, and I highlighted her case in my first book.

Even though Ian generally declined to participate in television productions or newspaper articles, he never objected to my involvement. At times, he would even help, supplying information or pictures from his old cases. When the e-mail came from the London producer, Ian, who had retired at that point, had our research assistant write back to decline. She added, however, that I was continuing his research and that, while I was open to the project, I wanted more details before deciding whether to participate.

The producer responded four months later. This is often a pattern with television producers. They approach us with great interest, disappear for a while, then contact us again, sometimes with a different person now leading the production. This tends to involve independent production companies who want to check out our interest before trying to sell a concept to a network. We understand this, so I never get too excited about any idea a producer is pitching. This producer explained that her production company had gotten swept up in another big project, which had required her to put potential future programs to the side.

A month later she wrote to say that Channel 5 in the UK had provided the production company she worked for, October Films, with some development money for a documentary about our work. It would air as part of a series on Channel 5 called *Extraordinary People*. We began discussing possible cases to be presented on such a program. This can be quite challenging. Production companies don't usually have the money to fly to Asia, where most of Ian's strongest cases are. Those cases are generally decades old by now anyway. A colleague of ours, a psychologist from Iceland named Erlendur Haraldsson, has investigated cases there more recently. I put the producer in touch with Erlendur, but the cost of a trip to Sri Lanka was more than Channel 5 wanted to pay.

Families in the West are often reluctant to go on television because they don't want people to know their child is talking about a past life. I discussed this program with several of the families of previous cases, so we had some potential leads. I then heard from Brenda Goldblatt, another producer at October Films. The first producer was now off the project due to maternity leave, so I started corresponding with Brenda about possible cases.

Time moved on, and eleven months after the initial contact, I had a phone conversation with Brenda. She said the network was committing a third of the project budget for a trip to film me investigating a new case. They wanted to be certain, however, that the outcome of the investigation would be positive. They were essentially asking for the impossible: for me to know that I would be able to confirm a child's claim about a past life *before* I confirmed it. As it turned out, the results from the case I eventually investigated were mixed, but it made for an interesting hour of television anyway.

The channel's wish for a guarantee of success wasn't the worst part. They also suggested that the program include a man who was "about to become famous" in England. He was a "baby whisperer." He would sit with babies and supposedly read their minds. The folks at Channel 5 wanted to see what he could glean about children's past lives. That didn't interest me in the least. The last thing I needed was for them to link another weird idea onto the topic of past lives, and I told Brenda that wouldn't work for me.

I think Channel 5 must have been talking about Derek Ogilvie, a professional psychic from Scotland who claims to read babies' minds. He was eventually the subject of an *Extraordinary People* episode. On that show, he failed two controlled tests, but he seems to have stayed plenty busy with his career since then.

I didn't hear from Brenda for a while, but in the meantime, October Films advertised in one part of Scotland for a family with a child reporting past-life memories. I learned later that though they got several responses, only one fit what they were looking for. Brenda e-mailed one day to say she had just had a fantastic call with the mother of a five-year-old boy named Cameron. He had been telling a consistent story for a couple of years. The family lived in Glasgow, but Cameron claimed he had another mother on Barra. Part of the Outer Hebrides off the west coast of Scotland, Barra is a remote island with little more than a thousand inhabitants. The family had never been there and had no connections with it. Brenda was preparing to meet Cameron and his mother the next day and wanted guidance about how to handle the situation. I emphasized that the key was to document as carefully as possible every statement Cameron had made. Only after that was done should he be taken to Barra. She said she would want me there for any trip to Barra, which certainly suited me.

Another three months went by because Cameron's mother pulled out of the project. The producers were ultimately able to get her back on board and were ready to proceed. In the hurry-up-and-wait fashion that seems to be the norm in television, they contacted me to plan a trip to Scotland as soon as possible. I would meet Cameron and his family in Glasgow, and we would then go together to Barra. The producers wanted to get the trip done in time for the end of that year's *Extraordinary People* series, but it ultimately didn't air until the next year. Their urgency meant we would need to go in February, a time, I soon discovered, when the Outer Hebrides tend to have inhospitable weather.

MEETING THE FAMILY

I took a red-eye flight from Washington to London and then a short flight on to Glasgow. I can never sleep much on planes and arrived a bit worse for wear, but after a short rest at my hotel, I received a call from Leslie, the director of the program, asking about a visit to Cameron's family. And so we went.

Cameron lived with his mother and his six-year-old brother, Martin, in a well-kept house. We sat down in their living room, and I started by talking with his mother, Norma. She said Cameron began talking about his Barra family when he was two and a half, and even more after he turned three. He would say, "I want to go to Barra to my other family," and he was quite adamant about it. He talked about Barra hundreds of times and daily when he was in nursery school.

He had given various details about his Barra family. He said his Barra father's name was Shane Robertson. In retrospect, I wish I had asked more about how Cameron had come to use that name because in the end, I wasn't sure we had the correct one. Leslie the director had told me in an e-mail a month before that she had just talked to Cameron's uncle, who remembered that when Cameron was about two and a half years old, he referred to his Barra father as Sean or Shane. By the time I met Norma, we also knew the Robertson part, but I didn't ask how long or how often Cameron had been saying it.

Regardless, he had been quite clear that his Barra father had stepped off the curb onto a road, didn't look both ways, and was hit by a car and killed. Cameron had talked about the car being either green and silver or greenish silver.

Cameron also talked a lot about his Barra mother. He said she had long brown hair but then got it cut short. He was crying one day and said his Barra family would miss him. He wanted his Barra mom to pick him up from preschool and said she would come and see him. He reported having three brothers and three sisters and said they played tag together. He once said one of his sisters was named Lindsay but at other times said he couldn't remember. He said the family lived in a white house that was much larger than the one he lived in with Norma and Martin. It had multiple toilets. Big stacks of boxes sat outside of it.

He talked a lot about things he did on Barra. He said he swam in rock pools and went down to the beach and played with friends. The family had a black dog with white on its chest, and he would take the dog out where there was lots of space. He said he used to go on holiday with his Barra family. At various times, he would say, "I used to do that in Barra." He once said he had used a black phone and described it as a dial phone.

Cameron never talked about being an adult and seemed to describe being a child who was a little older than he was himself. He never exactly said that he died. Instead, he said he "fell through" and came to Norma's tummy. The falling through seemed to involve a hole and the house he talked about. He said, "I was in Barra, and now I'm here."

Cameron talked about watching planes land on the beach at Barra. His mother hadn't known anything about that, but as we would soon find out, planes do in fact do that. Cameron talked about Barra so much that his brother, Martin, grew sick of it. Cameron would say, "Barra is real," but once when Martin was upset about it, told him, "If you want me to say Barra's not real, I'll say it's not real." He now wanted people to see that it was indeed real and was excited about our upcoming trip.

I then talked with Cameron. He was surprisingly forthcoming. We often have great difficulty getting the children to say anything to us about a past life. Not only are they uncomfortable talking to us as strangers, but many of the children have to be in the right frame of mind to discuss these things with anyone, even their parents. They usually do so during quiet, relaxed times. Cameron wasn't limited in that way, as he had talked about Barra in nursery school numerous times, and he talked to me as well, even with a camera rolling.

He said he used to run down and pick apples. He would play with friends in the family's front garden. He talked about crabs at the beach, saying he stayed away from them so they wouldn't nip him. He said his father's name was Shane Robertson and he had black, spiky hair. He had seen his father cross the road and then get knocked down by a car. He said it was a long car that was blue and green, this detail differing from his previous claims that the car had been silver and green.

Cameron told me his family lived in a white one-story house, but his mother said he had previously talked about stairs. The house was near the beach, and he had watched from it as planes landed. He said he had a sporty dog that was black and white and that it had a sore leg. He also described an orange cat. He said the boxes outside of his house had water and fish in them, though he had previously said he didn't remember what was in them. He also said he had been four years old when he fell out of bed and fell down a hole, leading him to come to his mother.

I was unsure what to make of that interview. Cameron seemed clear enough about the details, but some of them differed from ones he had given before. His mother had also said that his talk about Barra had calmed down for a while but now was back up. Being five and a half years old, Cameron was at the age when statements about past lives are typically tailing off. The resurgence in his might have been due to the increased focus on them from the television project; I was concerned it included new inaccuracies. Whenever a child's statements about a past life change over time, I'm inclined to put more stock in the earlier ones. Just as the accuracy of our memories for events in this life tends to decline with time, it may for past-life events as well, particularly since children seem to have less access to them as they get older. It was also possible that Cameron felt pressure to talk due to the cameras filming him and the doctor who had come so far to see him; perhaps this led him to give answers even if he wasn't sure he really remembered the details at that moment.

The TV folks had also talked with Cameron's uncle and the mother of one of his friends. I would have preferred to interview them myself, but in this situation it wasn't critical. When we get to a case only after the previous person has been identified, it's important to talk to as many people as possible who can confirm the statements the child made about that person before the identification. In Cameron's case, I was documenting his claims before anyone else attempted to verify them, and if we found someone whose life matched what he had said, we had a written record made beforehand.

Cameron's uncle remarked that Cameron had been consistent in his claims over the three years he had been making them. The friend's mother said Cameron had been adamant about his Barra family, talking about them over and over. She said her son told her one time that it's okay if you die because Cameron said you come back again as someone else.

At this point, we had established that Cameron had made claims about a life in Barra from a very early age. This seemed to go well beyond any kind of game. His Barra memories were clearly real in Cameron's mind. He talked with great emotion about a family and gave numerous details about life there. They included ones his mother didn't know. Even if Cameron had been exposed to information about Barra, latching onto it as the scene of a past life would have been peculiar, but he hadn't been exposed to any as far as Norma knew.

A TRIP TO BARRA

The next day, we headed to Barra. We took a commercial flight on a very small British Airways plane, and sure enough we landed on the beach, which served as the runway for the airport. The airport claims to be the only one in the world where scheduled flights use the beach as a runway. Cameron got off the plane telling his brother, "I told ya it was true." After we had walked from the beach into the airport building, he was beaming, saying he was happy to be back. The airport itself was so small that at the time, which was years after 9/11, it had no metal detectors. When we were boarding for our return flight, the airport staff simply checked our belongings by hand.

The TV folks then wanted us all to ride around for a while in the bus they had rented. Though Cameron said he recognized what he saw, there was no way to tell for sure, and the ride wasn't really productive.

More interesting were our activities the next day. Norma and I went to the island's heritage center to meet with the local historian, Calum MacNeil. I began by asking him about any accident in which a pedestrian had been killed as Cameron described. Calum said that he would know of any unusual deaths that had occurred, as drownings on the island back to the 1800s were still remembered. One man named Donald Mac-Lean had been killed by a bus in the early 1950s, but no one had been killed the way Cameron described his father dying.

I tried initially to withhold the name Robertson to see if Calum would give it spontaneously. I quickly discovered that the TV people had talked with him previously when they scouted the island, and he already knew we were looking for a Shane Robertson. What he had to say about one was not encouraging. He said that Robertson was a name that was only occasionally present on the island. There had been one man there in the 1930s. There was a Robertson family on the island at the current time, but the husband had moved there from elsewhere. And there were no Shane Robertsons at all.

Regarding other details, Calum said that for a person to watch planes land on the beach as Cameron had described, he would have to be on the northern end of the island, which Calum did not know as well as the southern part. He also said that toilets in houses only became common in the 1950s and '60s and only routine in the '60s and later. A house with multiple toilets as Cameron had claimed would have to be quite recent. He also said phones in houses were unusual when he was growing up but became more common in the 1960s. The phones available then would have been dial phones as Cameron described. Calum said that swimming in rock pools, as Cameron had reported, was very common. Cameron's story about Barra seemed plausible, except no family had been there that matched his description. Calum did mention that males named John were sometimes called Shawnie, especially if there was more than one John in the family. Shawnie was close enough to

Shane that it was a possibility, but the other details of the family still didn't fit for anyone.

At that point, it appeared we might be reaching a dead end. But then Calum called us later that afternoon—he had new information. When we went back to the heritage center, he told us he had done some more checking and learned that in fact there had been a family named Robertson who had lived on the north end of the island. They hadn't shown up in the records because they were from the mainland and had only holidayed on Barra. They were a shipping family who had a house on Barra in the 1960s and '70s, the time frame we were interested in. Their house, called the Sanderling, was a large white house very near the shore.

That was certainly a promising lead. The next morning, I went to the Council Records Department to look for any Robertsons I could find. Four marriages were listed, but there was little information that could be helpful. We went back to the heritage center yet again. Calum had continued to investigate. He had talked with one witness who said there were always children around the Sanderling. He had found the names of various members of the Robertson family there, though there wasn't a Shane.

The family had apparently spent quite a bit of time on Barra but didn't mix much with the locals. I did talk on the phone with a woman who said Mrs. Robertson had been a great friend of hers. Her memory seemed hazy, however, and she didn't even remember Mrs. Robertson's first name.

Calum had the name of a man who had supposedly known the Robertsons. We were able to get his address, and I went with Brenda the producer to talk with him. After a long ride, we got to his house and knocked on the front door. No answer. Brenda began looking for another way in. Being the intrepid journalist, she was preparing to climb a fence to get to the back door when the man came out on his porch proclaiming, "I don't know anything! I don't know anything!" And he didn't. The biting wind was whipping up as we stood outside cold and miserable and, worse, unsuccessful. As we climbed back into the van, Brenda's comment about the weather was a succinct "Bloody hell!"

While we were off on our wild goose chase, Leslie the director took Norma and Cameron to the Sanderling. They couldn't get inside, but they walked around the outside. As the video showed, Cameron seemed dumbstruck as he looked at the house. Though he eventually loosened up some, he was initially silent and downcast.

By the next day, the TV folks had talked with the current caretaker of the house. She agreed to open it for us and fortunately built a fire in the fireplace. As we walked through the house, Cameron acted as if it was familiar to him, commenting on parts of it. As we then sat around the fire, Cameron looked very sad. Norma asked if he missed his Barra mother. He nodded and leaned his head into her chest for a hug and comfort.

This kind of emotional reaction is something we often see in our cases. A five-year-old boy may not be able to express why he is feeling the way he is or even to know why, but Cameron was plainly experiencing feelings that were very real to him, ones of sadness and loss. Although these kinds of reactions may not carry the same objective weight as verified statements, such as his claim that planes used the Barra beach as a runway, that does not mean they are not important. They can be quite persuasive in their own way.

We have found that the emotions tend to travel with the more objective components of the cases. I developed a scale that measures the strength of each case. We code all of our cases on two hundred variables and enter them into a database. I picked out the items that would make one case stronger than another: the presence of birthmarks or birth defects that match wounds on the previous person's body, the number of statements the child has made that were verified to match the previous person's life, the behaviors the child shows that appear connected to the previous life, and the distance between the child's family and the previous person. The computer could then calculate a strength-of-case score for each case. I found that the amount of emotion the child showed when recalling the past life was strongly correlated with that score, meaning that children who showed more emotion were more likely to have the other features that make for a strong case. One aspect of greater carryover from a past life seems to be a continued emotional connection.

After the visit to the house, it was time for me to go home and for Cameron's family to return to Glasgow. We had found that a Robertson family had a house in the right location and with the right appearance. But the case still needed more investigation.

The TV folks continued the research. They contacted a genealogist who was able to trace the Robertson family. They were from Glasgow and owned the house on Barra for twenty-some years. She found contact information for one family member, a woman named Gillian who had spent holidays on Barra as a child.

Norma and Cameron visited Gillian. She confirmed the summers on Barra and said the couple who normally lived in the house did have a black-and-white sheepdog, as Cameron seemed to remember. There was no Shane Robertson. Though two men in the family had been named James (which can be referred to as Shamus), neither had been hit by a car. Indeed, no one in the family had died in any sort of car accident. Likewise, no children had died young, as Cameron's statements seemed to suggest he remembered doing.

Nonetheless, Norma said the family's trip to Barra had been therapeutic for Cameron. He was calmer about his memories after we took him to Barra, which she said was the best thing we could have done for him. Cameron said it was sad that his family wasn't there, but he was glad he got to see where he used to live. He seemed to have seen enough to validate in his own mind that the memories he had experienced were real. At the same time, he saw that the world had moved on. There was no family in Barra anxiously waiting for his return.

The trip was not as therapeutic for me as it was for Cameron. He had given accurate details of life on Barra, an island far away from his home, but some of the particulars he gave for his family appeared to be incorrect. This raised several possibilities.

A critic might conclude that perhaps Cameron saw something on TV about Barra and then imagined a life there. That, however, overlooks the emotional part. The memories that Cameron reported had great meaning for him. He didn't imagine these things on a lark; they were clearly very real to him. What could lead a child to create such things in his mind? And more to the point, was Cameron a child who would be likely to imagine a fantasy and then become convinced it was true?

One instrument that might be helpful in answering that question is called the Child Dissociative Checklist. It is a scale that was developed to measure dissociative behaviors in childhood. It includes simple behaviors such as daydreaming along with more worrisome items such as hearing voices and having two or more separate personalities that take control over the child's behavior. A parent or caretaker completes the checklist. Younger children tend to score higher than older ones, and a score of 12 or above indicates significant dissociative behavior, particularly in older children. Cameron scored a 1.

Studies of children who report past-life memories have found that most of them score quite low on the Child Dissociative Checklist, meaning they do not show significant signs of dissociating. When our colleague Erlendur Haraldsson studied children in Asia, he also included a scale measuring how suggestible individuals are. He found the children who had reported past-life memories were not more suggestible than other children. While skeptics might discount Cameron's claims as pure imagination, these children don't appear to be particularly fantasy prone.

For Cameron, there are a couple of other possibilities to consider. Several people contacted me about the name *Shane* after the documentary aired. Sean apparently means "old" in Gaelic, and the term for grandfather is *seanair* or *seanathair*. One woman wrote from the UK to say that her husband was from the Outer Hebrides, and his family referred to his father as Sean even though his actual name was something completely different. I'm not sure Sean would be pronounced there exactly like Shane, but it is evidently quite close.

The first name hardly matters, though, if the last name doesn't match. In this case, the only Robertson family we could find, though their life on Barra matched Cameron's statements in a general way, did not experience the specific events he had described. I was concerned we had latched onto the name too quickly. Cameron began by describing people and events he said he remembered, and it was only later that he gave the name Shane Robertson. He may have mistakenly put that name into his memories. In retrospect, perhaps we should have searched more intensely for a family whose father had been hit by a car and who had lost a child at an early age. Calum the historian had not heard of such a family, but he knew the southern part of the island better than the north, which is where Cameron's memories of watching planes landing on the beach would have taken place. We went with the name because it offered the potential of a definite verification, but that may have been a mistake. If Cameron was in fact remembering another family, that would mean his reaction at the Robertson house was perhaps from seeing a house similar enough to the one from his past life that he mistook it for that one.

Another possibility is that Cameron had memories from two past lives and mixed them together. His descriptions of Barra were accurate, but perhaps the particulars of his father being hit by a car came from another life. Though certainly not common, some children do indeed report memories from multiple past lives. This is easy to discern when the children clearly say they remember two distinct lives, but we don't know how many others may be unaware that the events they remember are actually from more than one.

SINGING AND DANCING

An example of a child with apparent memories from two separate lives is Ian's case in India of Swarnlata Mishra. Swarnlata first spoke of a previous life when she was on a trip with her family at age three. Passing through Katni, a city she had never seen before, she asked the driver of the truck they were riding in to turn down a road toward "my house." When the traveling group was having tea later, Swarnlata said they could get much better tea at her house nearby. After the trip, she began giving more details of a past life in Katni, saying her name had been Biya and that she was from the Pathak family. She gave details about her family's house, saying there had been four stuccoed rooms and the doors were black and fitted with iron bars. She said lime furnaces and a railway line could be seen from the house, and a girls' school was behind it.

Though Swarnlata's family moved around some, they never lived within a hundred miles of Katni. When Swarnlata was ten, she met a woman from Katni and said she recognized her from her previous life there. The following year, an investigator learned about her case. After gathering information from Swarnlata's family, he went to Katni and found that many of her statements (including all the ones I've given above) matched the life of a woman named Biya. She was from the Pathak family and had died nine years before Swarnlata was born.

When members of the Pathak family and Biya's marital family visited Swarnlata several months later, she appeared to recognize them, even though they arrived with a group of people and concealed their identities. Soon thereafter, Swarnlata and her family visited Katni and the places where Biya had lived after she married. Swarnlata recognized people and places Biya had known, commenting on various changes that had occurred after Biya died. Swarnlata continued to visit Biya's brothers as well as Biya's children, showing great affection for them.

Beginning at the age of five, Swarnlata also performed songs and dances, always one with the other, first for her mother and then in front of others as well. They were different from anything her parents had seen before. Swarnlata said they were from a different past life she remembered, a short one between the time of Biya's death and her own birth. She said she had been a girl named Kamlesh and she had lived in a place called Sylhet. (Sylhet was in East Pakistan, now Bangladesh, which limited Ian's ability to investigate Swarnlata's reports of her life there, and they remain unverified.) The songs were in a language other than Hindi, her native tongue. Her parents, not knowing what language it was, thought it might be Assamese, since Sylhet had been in Assam.

Ian's associate, Professor Pal, observed Swarnlata perform the songs and determined they were in fact Bengali, the predominant language spoken in Sylhet. He had her perform them three times so he could transcribe the words. He determined two of them were derived from poems by Rabindranath Tagore. The third was also in Bengali, but Professor Pal was unable to identify the source.

Professor Pal visited an institution founded by Rabindranath Tagore and watched a performance of one of the songs Swarnlata had shown him. He said the music was the same as Swarnlata presented it. The words she sang were very close to the original but with some changes. She said she had learned them from a friend named Madhu during her life as Kamlesh. Her performances suggested that Madhu had seen the songs performed and that Kamlesh then learned them from her imperfectly.

The name Kamlesh and the ones Swarnlata gave for other family members would be unusual for a Bengali family. She was unable to converse in Bengali and in fact had trouble recalling the words of the Bengali songs without performing the dances simultaneously. All of this suggested a life in Sylhet of a girl who, though from a non-Bengali family, had Bengali friends and learned the song and dance routines from one of them. Ian explored whether Swarnlata could have learned them in this life and thought it was improbable, if not impossible. He felt they were a paranormal part of her case.

Ian corresponded occasionally with Swarnlata and her family for the next forty years. At their last contact, Swarnlata, then married and a professor of botany, was writing to invite Ian to her son's wedding.

Swarnlata's family said she sometimes seemed to mix up the two past lives, though some of this may have been their own confusion about which life she was referring to. If Cameron's memories were perhaps fuzzier than Swarnlata's, it's plausible to consider that he was mixing up events from two different lives without realizing it. This would explain how he was so accurate about some aspects and so off on others.

The memories don't necessarily follow multiple past lives in a linear fashion. Ian noted that when children report memories of two lives, they usually talk more about the first one. The second one tends to be an unverified intermediate life that the child gives few details about. Thus, the memories are stronger for an earlier life. In contrast, in four of Ian's cases, the previous families said the deceased individuals had also remembered a past life themselves. The children in those cases, however, did not have memories of the earlier one.

Though memory is variable even in one life, the idea of a consciousness separate from our ordinary one again needs to be considered. The cases involving memories from multiple past lives seem more consistent with a separate consciousness carrying memories from different lives rather than one continuous stream of consciousness. Mind might be thought to have two parts, another one existing beyond the everyday one.

I am thinking of something along the lines of F. W. H. Myers's subliminal self. Myers was one of the founders of the Society for Psychical Research and a significant influence on William James, among others. He called the ordinary consciousness, the one above the surface, the supraliminal self. He imagined some sort of barrier or psychic membrane between it and the subliminal self. That membrane allowed information to move from the supraliminal ordinary self to the subliminal, but the reverse flow was much more limited. This was by necessity, so that the ordinary self could function in the physical world without being flooded by all the activities of the subliminal self. There could be uprushes, however, when material moved from the subliminal up into the supraliminal. These could cause problems but could also be positive, as Myers regarded genius and inspiration as arising out of the subliminal. Past-life memories might be thought of as subliminal uprushes, as material from the subliminal self that seeps into ordinary consciousness.

This subliminal self is more than what Freud called the Unconscious. Myers thought one part of each person was a soul that originated in a spiritual environment. It existed there even while embodied in a life in the physical world, and it continued there after the body's decay.

More about such things later, when I sketch out my view of what we can take from this research. As for Cameron, though he had some specific knowledge about Barra, his case is not completely fulfilling, largely because we were unable to find an individual whose life matched some of the details he gave. This limitation was not present in some American cases I would soon investigate, as the identity of the previous person in those was determined with certainty—to quite an interesting effect.

Chapter 4

THE THIRD JAMES

There has only been one case that I hounded the parents for years to study.

I first learned of James Leininger from a failed television program. I had agreed, against my better judgment, to be interviewed for a show about paranormal phenomena that ABC News was producing in collaboration with the ABC entertainment division. I initially declined, but one of their producers convinced me the segment on past-life memories would be "a serious look at this unusual occurrence." The producers had been in contact with past-life author Carol Bowman, who introduced them to two families with little boys who were talking about a past life. They decided to show one named James; his parents felt he was remembering the life of a World War II pilot shot down in the Pacific. The correspondent for the segment was Shari Belafonte. She and the crew were very pleasant when they came to our office to interview me about our research.

The show never aired. After viewing a tape that ABC eventually sent me, I was glad it didn't. It turned out to be a pilot for a show called *Strange Mysteries* that, as the introduction proclaimed, would explore "the supernatural, the mystical, the haunted." Along with "hair-raising memories" of past lives, it looked at topics such as animal psychics, séances, and psychic surgeries. The segment on past lives began with Shari Belafonte standing on a set in front of a spooky-looking house at night, complete with outdoor sounds such as a howl in the background. A haunted house intro was not exactly the "serious" approach I was hoping for.

The segment itself was okay as far as it went, and it included a look at James and his parents. He was a four-year-old boy with a fascination for airplanes. His parents reported that he began having terrible nightmares about a plane crash when he was two years old. By the time he was three, he had told them that before he was born, he was a pilot who flew from a boat. His plane got shot in the engine by the Japanese, he crashed in the water, and that's how he died.

Odd things for a little boy in Lafayette, Louisiana, to be saying. At that point, no one knew if what he was saying was true, if he was really remembering the life of an actual pilot. Though that uncertainty made the case less impressive at the time, the segment now exists as a record—made *before* a previous person was identified—of some of James's statements. This removes the possibility that his parents' memories of those statements later conformed erroneously to details of a deceased pilot's death.

Nearly two years after that interview was filmed, ABC's *Primetime* aired a different segment about James. This time the correspondent was Chris Cuomo, and he had conducted new interviews with James and his parents. The tone of the segment was more matter-of-fact, even as James's story had become more extraordinary. James's parents had now been able to verify much of what he had said. He said he had been a pilot named James on the boat *Natoma*, he had been shot down at Iwo Jima, and he had a friend named Jack Larsen. His father had discovered that a James Huston from the USS *Natoma Bay* had been shot down in the Iwo Jima operation. Another pilot on the *Natoma Bay* was named Jack Larsen.

That sounded like quite a case. I e-mailed Carol Bowman the next day and asked if she could find out if James's parents would be open to a visit from me. She responded a couple of days later to say that the parents were a little overwhelmed by the response to the *Primetime* piece, and at that point, they weren't interested in being interviewed. Not wanting to take no for an answer, I wrote to the Leiningers, explaining the potential importance of their story, since an American case in which a complete stranger, one who had been killed nearly sixty years before, was positively identified as the previous person was unprecedented in our studies.

Andrea, James's mother, called a week later. She was friendly and open in sharing details of events the family had experienced, and she agreed to have me study the case. After I e-mailed to thank her for talking with me, Bruce, James's father, e-mailed to say they would be happy to share what they had found. After a little back and forth, we figured out a date for me to head down to Louisiana to meet them.

I then received a call back. The *Primetime* piece had created quite a stir, and Bruce and Andrea were being advised to put off any interviews until they decided what they wanted to do with their story. Bruce felt their documentation of the facts of the case would hold up over time, so a meeting could wait. I had to accept that, not realizing it would be six years before we would sit down to discuss their experiences.

I sent periodic e-mails and letters to James's parents, with Bruce responding positively but never committing to a meeting.

In 2009, Bruce and Andrea published a book about James's case called *Soul Survivor*. I provided a blurb and sent a letter congratulating them on the book. Bruce responded, and at long last, we set up a time to meet. Bruce and Andrea hadn't wanted to get scooped on their own story, which I certainly understood, and since their book was out, they were open to sharing everything they had.

A MEETING AT LAST

By the time I flew down to Louisiana, James was about to turn twelve. Since these children usually stop talking about their memories by the time they are six or seven, speaking with James was unlikely to be fruitful. But that didn't concern me. I was most interested in what he had said before anyone identified James Huston as the pilot whose life he was remembering. Even if he were still talking about a past life, he might now have heard all kinds of things about this James Huston, and unless he showed knowledge about specific items he had not had the opportunity to acquire normally, his statements would provide little evidence that he was really remembering a past life.

I went to the Leiningers' house on a Saturday morning. Bruce and Andrea seemed like a typical American couple. Bruce worked as a human resources director, and Andrea, formerly a professional ballet dancer, worked both as a ballet teacher and as a résumé writer. Bruce came across as a no-nonsense kind of guy, completely cooperative and forthcoming but someone with definite opinions. He said that before everything started with James, he thought the idea of past lives was "pure baloney." To his credit, he was flexible enough for subsequent events to eventually change his mind. Even after all that had happened, his Christian faith clearly remained extremely important to him.

He made Biblical references at times, and he had worked to incorporate his experiences with James into his worldview of steadfast religious beliefs. Andrea was more open to nontraditional ways of thinking from the beginning, though she had no strong feelings about past lives.

I began with Bruce while Andrea and James were busy with other activities. We sat down at their dining room table. At one end of the room was a small bookcase filled with the research material Bruce had collected in trying to make sense of what James had said. The first noticeable incident in their story occurred when James was twenty-two months old. The family was living in Texas at the time, and Bruce took him to the Cavanaugh Flight Museum outside of Dallas. Before that, James would point at planes that flew overhead, but at the museum, he became transfixed. He kept wanting to return to the World War II exhibit. He and Bruce ended up spending three hours at the museum because James was so fascinated by those planes, and they left with a few toy planes and a video on the Blue Angels, the Navy's flight exhibition team.

The video became James's favorite object in the world, as he would watch it for hours at a time. I tried to find a copy, but it apparently never made its way onto DVD. Regardless, since the Blue Angels weren't formed until after World War II, the video could not be the source of the detailed knowledge James later displayed.

When James played with his toy airplanes, he repeatedly crashed them into the family's coffee table, saying "Airplane crash on fire." His parents are evidently tolerant, because Bruce has a picture that shows dozens of scratches and dents on the table. As if this weren't bad enough, whenever Andrea and James would see Bruce off at the airport as he was leaving on a business trip, James would tell him, "Daddy, airplane crash on fire." When he said that to his aunt before her flight, his dad gave him a stern reprimand.

A couple of months after the visit to the museum, the nightmares began. Andrea would find James thrashing around and kicking his legs up in the air, screaming "Airplane crash on fire! Little Man can't get out!" This was not just a one-time nightmare. James did the same thing night after night, multiple times a week. I talked with his aunt, Andrea's sister, after my trip to Louisiana. She emphasized several times just how disturbing these nightmares were to witness. Visiting James's family frequently, she saw a lot of them and said they were like watching someone in terror fighting for his life. They included blood-curdling shrieks from James as he kicked his legs up toward the ceiling, screaming about an airplane crash and a big fire and proclaiming, "Little Man can't get out!"

Several months into the nightmares, Andrea was reading James a bedtime story one night when he said, "Little Man's going like this" and reenacted his dreams, kicking his legs up in the air and saying, "Can't get out." She went and got Bruce to join them. This was a crucial event for Bruce. He had been dismissing James's nightmares as typical childhood events, but here was James talking about these things when he was wide awake. Bruce asked him what happened to his plane. James said it crashed on fire. Bruce asked him why, and James said it got shot. Bruce asked him who shot his plane. James, a little over two at the time, appeared exasperated and exclaimed, "The Japanese!"

A couple of weeks later, Andrea and Bruce had another bedtime talk with James. He said his plane was a Corsair, a fighter plane that was developed during World War II. He talked a number of times about flying a Corsair. Skeptics have pointed out that the Cavanaugh Flight Museum has a Corsair on display, arguing that James saw the plane there and the name stuck in his mind. Bruce told me that there wasn't one at the museum when he and James visited. There had been one, but it had crashed at an air show and was only replaced later. I looked into this and found out he was right. A Corsair on loan from the museum crashed at an air show in Wisconsin on July 29, 1999, six months before Bruce took James to the museum for the first time. I called the Cavanaugh Flight Museum and asked about the Corsair they have now. The woman there told me the current one was the replacement for the one that crashed in 1999, and that the museum obtained it around 2003. James did not see one on his trip to the museum and at twenty-eight months of age, knew the name from elsewhere.

Along with saying that night that he flew a Corsair, James also said he had flown off a boat. When Bruce asked if he remembered the name of the boat, James said, "*Natoma*." Bruce replied, understandably, that *Natoma* sounded Japanese. James, looking perturbed, said no, it was American.

Afterward, Bruce searched online for the word *Natoma*. After some effort, he found a description of USS *Natoma Bay*, an escort carrier stationed in the Pacific during World War II. Fortunately, he printed out the information and kept it, so we have a record of it. Each page of the printout has the name of the Web site as the footer, along with the date the pages were printed, 08/27/2000. Thus, we know that Bruce was searching for *Natoma* when James was twenty-eight months old. Some of the specifics of this case are dependent on the accuracy of Bruce and Andrea's memories, but not this. Unless you think this is an elaborate fraud, with this Christian couple in Louisiana faking a case of past-life memories despite potential derision by friends and neighbors, you have to conclude that little James did give the name *Natoma*. It's an unusual word, certainly not one people would typically give if they were trying to guess the name of a U.S. naval ship.

When Bruce and Andrea would ask James who the little man in the plane was, he would say "me" or "James," which at the time they took to be insignificant. A month or so later, he came up with another name. When his parents asked if anyone else was there in the dream with James, he gave the name Jack. They asked if he had another name, and he said Larsen. It was Jack Larsen.

In their book, the Leiningers write that Andrea then asked, "Was Jack James's friend?" and James replied, "He was a pilot, too." It seems obvious in retrospect that James was saying he was a pilot named James who knew another pilot named Jack Larsen. But at the time, Bruce wasn't seeing it that way. James was having nightmares. Beyond that, Bruce didn't know what he was dealing with, but he did know that James had given the name Jack Larsen. So he began looking for one. This search proved much harder than the *Natoma* one had been. He searched the World War II database on the American Battle Monuments Commission Web site on 10/16/2000. I have a copy of his search from that date, and I've since repeated it myself. It shows one Jack Larsen, one John Larsen, one Jack Larson spelled with an *o*, and four John Larsons. That site only includes those who are buried in the commission's cemeteries or listed on the Walls of the Missing. More important in this situation, it only lists casualties. The Jack Larsen from *Natoma Bay*, it turned out, had survived the war.

In my own online search, I went to the registry on the National World War II Memorial site. It combines four databases, though the one with survivors is unofficial and incomplete.

Searching for John or Jack combined with Larson or Larsen, I found nine listings for men who served in the Navy during World War II. Though that's an incomplete list, it at least gives some sense of how common the name was. Ships did not typically have a Jack Larsen on board. But *Natoma*, the one James had named, did.

Bruce wasn't searching for a living person because he assumed that James's dream, if it was a memory, was about being Jack Larsen. This was even though James kept saying he was "James" in the dream. I tried to sort this out with Bruce. He said he wasn't thinking James's dreams were memories of a past life. When Andrea's mother eventually suggested that, Bruce's initial response was, "That's bullshit." James said "me" or "James" was in the dreams with Jack Larsen, so Bruce apparently thought James was reporting a dream about a guy named Jack Larsen. Andrea, on the other hand, wasn't so focused on Larsen. She said she asked James thirty times what his name was in the dream, and he always said James. He said Jack Larsen was a friend he flew with. Given Bruce's confusion, it's possible that James's statement about their relationship may not have been as clear as Andrea now remembers it, but I do see how James referring to himself in the dream as "James" would be confusing.

Bruce's strong natural tendency to discount the possibility of past lives may also have contributed to his failure to understand what now appears to be the clear message of James's statements. Andrea's sister confirmed that for years, Bruce resisted past lives as an explanation for James's behaviors, because the idea conflicted with his Christian faith. Andrea grew frustrated with him about it, leading to disagreements at times.

THE SEARCH CONTINUES

About a month after mentioning Jack Larsen, James was just over two and a half when he gave another piece of information. Bruce had ordered a book, *The Battle for Iwo Jima 1945*, to give his father for Christmas. He was looking through it one Saturday morning when James climbed into his lap. They got to a place that showed a map of Iwo Jima on one page. On the other page is a photograph showing an aerial view of the base of the island, where Mount Suribachi, a dormant volcano, sits. James pointed at the picture and said, "That's where my plane was shot down." Bruce said, "What?" and James responded, "My airplane got shot down there, Daddy."

A week later, Bruce had his first talk with a *Natoma Bay* veteran. He found a reference to the *Natoma Bay* Association online and called one of the contact numbers. The man he talked to had served on *Natoma Bay* during the Iwo Jima operation. He remembered a pilot from the ship named Jack Larsen, but he didn't know what had happened to him. He said Larsen flew off one day and they never saw him again. Bruce assumed that meant Larsen did not return from a flight and became missing. At that point, he had confirmation that there was a ship named *Natoma Bay*, that it was at Iwo Jima, and that Jack Larsen had been a pilot on it. But he still had a long way to go to get all the puzzle pieces to fit together.

Andrea's mother sent her one of Carol Bowman's books. Despite his initial rejection of the possibility of past lives, Bruce read the book, and his resistance began to soften. Andrea contacted Carol. On Carol's advice, Andrea began talking to James about his nightmares right after he had them, and they quickly reduced in both frequency and intensity.

James also began talking more about his nightmares/memories when he was awake. This did not happen at predictable times and would often only consist of brief openings that didn't allow much follow-up from his parents. Soon after his third birthday, James began drawing pictures. He drew battle scenes with ships and planes over and over again—his parents report he drew hundreds of them. This kind of compulsive repetition is a phenomenon often seen in children who have survived or witnessed a major trauma; post-traumatic play, it's called. In this situation, how to distinguish post-traumatic play from the normal drawings of a boy who likes planes is not entirely obvious, but since the drawings occurred along with repeated nightmares about the same kind of scene, they suggest a child trying to work through a traumatic event. In James's case, this seemed to be an event from a past life.

James began signing the pictures, James 3. You might think this was because James was then three years old, but Bruce and Andrea say that wasn't why. When they asked him about it, he said, "I'm the third James. I'm James 3." I checked with each of them about this, and they were both definite that he said "I'm the third James." They have drawings he made after he turned four that still say James 3, so the 3 presumably does not refer to his age. What it may refer to is that James Huston was a junior. That would make James Leininger the third James.

Andrea's sister told me one story I had not heard from Bruce and Andrea. At one point when Bruce was frustrated with all the talk about a plane crash, he slapped a world map from an atlas down on a table and said to James, "Okay, where is Little Man's plane?" James pointed in the Pacific Ocean, and the adults all leaned down and saw that his finger was on a group of islands called the Ogasawara Archipelago. There in microscopic writing was the name Iwo Jima. Bruce confirmed the story and sent me a picture of the map. Spread across two pages and measuring twenty-two inches by seventeen inches altogether, it shows much of the globe. It's remarkable that a three- or four-year-old could identify any specific place on it, much less the location where events he was describing from a past life took place.

When James was three and a half, he talked one day about his plane getting shot. Bruce asked him where it had been hit. James immediately pointed to the front of the engine and said the plane had been hit right in the propeller. James was describing a plane with only one propeller, which was on the nose of the plane, so saying a plane had been hit in the propeller meant it had been hit in the front. Shari Belafonte pointed out on *Strange Mysteries* that none of James's toy planes still had their propellers on the nose, as James had apparently crashed them all until the propellers broke off.

Shari Belafonte and the *Strange Mysteries* crew arrived in Louisiana a couple of months after James turned four. Bruce talked with a producer about his search for Jack Larsen. After the filming, she sent him an e-mail (that I have a copy of) telling him to keep following the Jack Larsen lead. She said she had spoken with a contact at the Center for Naval History and asked about a Jack Larsen. That man found a John M. Larson, but there was no record of him dying in combat. That ultimately turned out to be the wrong person, but the e-mail does document that Bruce was looking for him long before he had everything figured out.

In September 2002, as James was nearing four and a half years old, Bruce attended his first *Natoma Bay* reunion. At the time, he didn't tell the veterans that his son had talked about a past life, saying instead that he was writing a book about the ship. He learned there that Jack Larsen, though not at the reunion, was still alive. He had not gone missing as Bruce had assumed; he had merely left *Natoma Bay* for another assignment. Bruce also learned that only one pilot from *Natoma Bay* had been killed during the Iwo Jima operation, a twenty-one-year-old from Pennsylvania named James Huston.

The statements I gave from James Leininger's talk with Bruce about Iwo Jima are from Bruce's *Primetime* interview with Chris Cuomo in 2004. At the time, he quoted James as saying, "That's where my plane was shot down." He now remembers James saying "That's *when* my plane got shot" rather than where. I don't expect every word to be identical this long after the events took place, but the difference is worth mentioning. James Huston's plane was shot down in the Iwo Jima operation but not actually over Iwo Jima itself. "When" would be more literally correct than "where" since the crash was during the Iwo Jima operation but not on Iwo Jima itself.

This seems a minor quibble even with "That's where my plane was shot down." James Huston might have said he was shot down at Iwo Jima if he could have told the story years later. The pilots of *Natoma Bay* made 123 flights in the Iwo Jima operation in the days before the start of the invasion and another fifty-two on February 19, 1945, the day the assault began. After that, its duties expanded as the battle to take Iwo Jima went on. As the Japanese were preparing a buildup of troop replacements and supplies, eight pilots from *Natoma Bay* took part in a strike against transport vessels in a harbor on Chichijima, an island about 165 miles from Iwo Jima.

The aircraft action report filed after the event notes the following: heavy antiaircraft fire put the planes under fire from both sides of the harbor. James Huston's plane was apparently hit by the fire as he approached the harbor entrance. None of the other pilots saw him hit, but his plane suddenly careened into a 45-degree glide and crashed in the water. It exploded and burned, and by the time two of the other pilots could get to the area, no wreckage of the plane was still afloat. Only a greenish yellow spot on the water marked where the crash had occurred. This happened on March 3, 1945, four days before *Natoma Bay* completed its work in the Iwo Jima operation.

Following the *Natoma Bay* reunion, Bruce visited Jack Larsen in Arkansas. Larsen was indeed very much alive. He remembered well the day that Huston was killed. He described the heavy flak the planes encountered as they arrived off of Futami-ko Harbor of Chichi-jima. Larsen didn't see Huston's plane go down, but he felt certain it had been hit by flak. Soon after Bruce got back home, *Natoma Bay*'s historian sent him a copy of the squadron war diary, which also described Huston's final flight. Bruce began to focus on Huston, seeing that all the pieces were starting to fit.

There appeared to be no way, however, to confirm James's claim that his plane had been shot in the engine. The aircraft action report from Huston's squadron stated that none of the ship's other pilots had seen his plane hit. But it turned out that the *Natoma Bay* crew wasn't the only source of information.

Bruce posted a query about Huston's crash on a Web site about Chichi-jima. Months later, he received a call from a veteran off another ship who had witnessed Huston's plane get hit. He had flown off USS *Sargent Bay*, which had also taken part in the attack. His plane had been hit that day, too, on its second run. On its first one, he had seen a fighter from *Natoma Bay* take "a direct hit on the nose," as he had written in an informal memoir.

Bruce talked to three other men who had seen Huston's plane get hit, and they all told the same story. One of them said Huston's plane was very close to his, and he and Huston actually made eye contact just before Huston's plane was hit in the engine and quickly engulfed by flames. Another one was interviewed for the *Primetime* segment. He said, "I saw the hit. I would say he was hit head-on, yeah, right on the middle of the engine."

All of this matched what James had described, as documented in the *Strange Mysteries* segment before the Leiningers knew anything about James Huston. In that interview, Bruce reported that when their James was two, he had nightmares about a plane crashing on fire and being unable to get out. Andrea said that one day, as James was playing in their sunroom, he told her, "Mama, before I was born, I was a pilot, and my airplane got shot in the engine and it crashed in the water, and that's how I died." Andrea also states on the segment that James had said his plane took off from a boat and that it was shot down by the Japanese. Shari Belafonte mentions Iwo Jima in the narration, saying James may have been one of the pilots during the battle there. That segment, along with the documentation that James said he flew from *Natoma*, produces a record that points to James having memories of James Huston's death.

James also said that Jack Larsen was there when his plane crashed. The aircraft action report for the day Huston was shot down includes a drawing of the paths each pilot took; Larsen's plane is shown next to Huston's. Bruce had found his man.

Along with the additional details that Bruce and Andrea report, we have definite documentation—from the *Strange Mysteries* interview and from printed records—of statements and behaviors from James Leininger, items that were recorded before James Huston was identified. Here are the statements and behaviors, compared to the details from James Huston:

James Leininger	James Huston
Signed drawings "James 3"	Was James, Jr.
Flew off Natoma	Pilot on *Natoma Bay*
Flew a Corsair	Had flown a Corsair
Shot down by the Japanese	Shot down by the Japanese
Died at Iwo Jima	The one *Natoma Bay* pilot killed in the Iwo Jima operation
"My airplane got shot in the engine and it crashed in the water and that's how I died."	Eyewitnesses reported Huston's plane "hit head-on right on the middle of the engine."
Nightmares of plane crashing and sinking in the water	Plane crashed in the water and quickly sank
Jack Larsen was there	Jack Larsen was pilot of plane next to Huston's

FAMILY FACTS

Andrea reports she asked James one day if Little Man had any brothers or sisters. James said he had a sister named Annie and another one named Ruth, or "Roof" as he said initially. He said Ruth was four years older than Annie, who was four years older than he was. Those details were correct for James Huston's family.

We do not have any verification of the conversation beyond Andrea's memory. When I first talked to Andrea after the *Primetime* segment aired, she told me she had made notes when James talked about these things so she could show them to Bruce, who was often away with his work. In the most disappointing part of my visit with them, I learned that after the Leiningers had written up the case for their book, Andrea either lost or threw out the spiral notebook she used to make notes. Though their book, along with the timeline and the detailed write-up they shared with me, relates the events, it doesn't constitute the same level of evidence that contemporaneous notes would have. Since verification is available for much of the story, the loss of the notes is certainly not a fatal flaw, but it would have been great to have them.

Regardless, Andrea eventually discovered through some clever detective work that James Huston's sister Anne was still alive. Andrea called Anne, who was eighty-four at the time, and then Bruce did as well. Afterward, Anne sent them some photos of her brother. Two of them solved a mystery for the Leiningers. Their James had talked repeatedly about flying a Corsair, as they described in the *Strange Mysteries* piece before James Huston was identified. This seemed to be incorrect for Huston. Bruce had learned that no Corsairs ever flew off *Natoma Bay*, and Huston had been killed flying an FM-2. The pictures Anne sent included two with Huston in front of a Corsair, one with a squadron and one by himself.

Bruce later discovered that before Huston joined squadron VC-81 on *Natoma Bay*, he had been part of a squadron, VF-301, that tested the Corsair for the Navy. The plane had been modified due to problems with landings. To test how well the modifications worked, the pilots in VF-301 took test flights with it, making 113 landings without difficulty. Bruce has several pictures of Huston with the squadron, and he talked to a veteran and the son of another veteran who served with him there. Following the testing, the Navy began using Corsairs, and Huston transferred to VC-81 on *Natoma Bay*. (An official history of the squadron documents that five fighter pilots transferred to VC-81 in October 1944, including ones from VF-301.) Though James Leininger was wrong when he seemed to say he was flying a Corsair when he was killed as James Huston, he was correct that Huston did indeed fly one. And getting to test an exciting new plane like the Corsair must have been quite memorable for Huston. Bruce talked with other pilots who had flown the Corsair, and they all felt demoted when they had to move down to more ordinary planes like the FM-2, the one in which Huston was killed.

Andrea reports that sometime later, she went into James's room one night carrying a glass of wine. James looked at the glass and said his father had been an alcoholic. His father would get drunk on liquor and tear up the house. When he was thirteen, the family had to put his father in the hospital for six weeks. His mother had to work as a maid during that time, and Ruth, his older sister, was "mortified." When their father got out of the hospital, Anne moved away.

At that point, though Andrea had talked with Anne on the phone, they hadn't met, and clearly James had no way of knowing such things. Andrea called Anne and asked her about what James had said. She confirmed the details. Her father had indeed gone into rehab. Ruth, who was working as a society columnist for the local paper, was definitely mortified when their mother had to work as a maid in the home of a family Ruth had written about. Anne, uncomfortable with their father when he returned, moved to their grandparents' home for her last year of high school.

I wanted to verify that phone conversation if I could. Andrea didn't have notes, but Anne was still alive. The Leiningers gave me her phone number, and I called her when I got back to Virginia. Unfortunately, I was asking a ninety-one-year-old woman to recall a phone conversation from more than five years before. She remembered that Andrea had asked about their father being an alcoholic at one time, but she couldn't recall any other specifics. Later, looking back through my file on

James, I came across a posting from July 2005 that Andrea made on the Reincarnation Forum, part of Carol Bowman's Web site. In it, she relates all the details of both of James's conversations about the family: the first one when he gave the names of Huston's sisters and the later one about their father's alcoholism. James was seven when Andrea posted that, so the events were relatively recent. And Andrea's memory of them had remained unchanged when I interviewed her five years later. Though that clearly wasn't perfect confirmation, it demonstrated consistency in the story over time.

SPECIAL KNOWLEDGE

James often surprised his parents with his knowledge of World War II planes. Around the time he turned two, Andrea bought him a toy plane and commented that there was a bomb on the bottom of it. James corrected her and said it was a drop tank.

During the filming of the *Strange Mysteries* segment soon after James's fourth birthday, one of the producers asked James about Corsairs, and he commented that they always got flat tires. The ABC crew then interviewed a military historian who stated that the Corsairs hit hard when they landed, often resulting in flat tires.

When James was six, Bruce made him a model of an FM-2, the plane Huston flew on *Natoma Bay*. James said something was missing. He said the planes had a small antenna on the side that people sometimes bumped into. The model didn't have one, but when Bruce researched the FM-2, he found that James was right.

Around the time James turned seven, he and his parents watched a History Channel program about Corsairs that showed footage of a Corsair chasing another plane the narrator called

a Zero. James said it was a Tony, not a Zero. Bruce had heard
of a Tony but couldn't identify one, certainly not as it shot across
a television screen in old war footage. James explained the
Tony was a Japanese fighter that was smaller and faster than a
Zero. He also explained that it was called a Tony because the
fighters were named after boys while the bombers were named
after girls. When Bruce consulted the war diary for Huston's
squadron, he found that the squadron had downed one Tony.
Six of the fighters cornered the Tony and attacked it. The aircraft action report documents that Huston was the one who
first spotted it.

James also seemed to remember details about life on
Natoma. When he was five, Bruce was repairing some rotting
trim when James picked up a sanding disc and said he had
been looking for one of those. Bruce asked him what he wanted
it for, and James said they never had enough records on *Natoma
Bay*. Sanding discs do indeed look like old vinyl music records,
and Bruce talked with a *Natoma Bay* veteran who said the ship
had a record player with only one record.

Also when James was five, Andrea cooked meat loaf for
the first time in James's life. When she told him what they
were having, he said he hadn't had it since he was on *Natoma
Bay*. He ate it up that night and said he had always enjoyed it
on the ship. Bruce reports several veterans told him meat loaf
was a regular meal there.

When James was six and a half, he attended his first *Natoma
Bay* reunion. As he and Andrea were touring the museum,
they came upon a five-inch cannon (which, despite the name,
is a large object, as the five inches refers to the diameter of the
projectiles it fires). Several veterans heard him say *Natoma Bay*
had one of those, which it did. When one of them asked him

where it was located, James correctly said on the fantail, which is on the back of the ship. Bruce isn't aware of any pictures of *Natoma* they might have seen that were taken from an angle that would show the cannon.

Also at the reunion, Andrea reports that she and James were stopped in the hotel hallway by Bob Greenwalt, a *Natoma Bay* veteran who had talked to Bruce on the phone but hadn't met any of the Leiningers. He asked James, "Do you know who I am?" James replied, "You're Bob Greenwalt." When Bruce asked him later how he knew that, James said he recognized Greenwalt's voice.

I wanted to get confirmation of the story from Greenwalt, so Bruce said he would contact him for me. After several unreturned phone calls, Bruce spoke to Greenwalt's wife and learned he was not doing well. In his late eighties, he was on oxygen with several severe health issues, so he was not available to interview.

When James was six, he was looking at the FM-2 model Bruce had made. He commented that they used to put oil in the drop tanks. The planes would drop them, and they would hit the ground and make a big fire. Bruce recalled a previous conversation with Jack Larsen. Larsen had been the assistant armament officer on *Natoma* and had described how they improvised napalm bombs by mixing napalm powder with gasoline in the drop tanks to form napalm jelly. They then included a hand grenade attached to a cable. When the tank was dropped, the cable would pull the pin of the grenade. If the timing was just right, the grenade would explode as the tank hit the ground, producing a remarkable explosion. Bruce hadn't read about that anywhere and knew of no way James could have learned about it.

PAST BEHAVIOR

The children in our cases often show behaviors that appear connected to their reports of past-life memories. This most often relates to the occupation of the previous person. That was certainly true for James. His fascination with airplanes seems to have been passionate to the point of being obsessive. Along with the countless toy planes he had, when he was four, he used an old car seat and pieces from various objects to create a play cockpit in the closet of Bruce's home office. Bruce would hear him pretending to be a pilot, and then James would come tumbling out, pretending to parachute after his plane had been hit.

Another behavior James showed was a ritual after getting into his car seat. He would raise his hands over the top of his head and pull them down to just over his ears. He would then move his right hand down in front of his face to his chin. His parents figured out the ritual when they took James to an airshow when he was three and a half. James was able to sit in the cockpit of a Piper Cub, where the pilot had his headgear with the earphones and microphone attached. Andrea watched James put on the headgear and use the same motions to put the earphones on his ears and the microphone in place at his chin that he used in his car seat ritual.

When James was four and a half, he and his parents visited some of Andrea's family in Dallas. They went to a community pool, where James and his cousin began playacting. James pretended to shoot at airplanes and talked about shooting "the Japs." After a short time, Andrea called him over and told him he shouldn't say that. She said the war was over anyway and we beat the Japanese. James was momentarily stunned and then became ecstatic, jumping up and down and screaming in celebration. Andrea told me about this the first time we talked on the phone, which was a year and a half after the incident occurred. Her sister and Bruce still remembered it well six years later. It was embarrassing for the adults but funny, and it was another demonstration of the emotional connection that James, like the children in many of our cases, had to the events he appeared to remember from long before.

When I was finally able to talk to James as he neared his twelfth birthday, those emotions were no longer apparent. As is usually the case, the memories themselves seemed to be gone by that age as well, though James had hinted he might still have some he could talk about when he was older. I was able to see him away from the actual interview, both at home and when we all went out to dinner. He presented as a typical boy his age. He was well-spoken but not formal or pseudo-mature. He could become silly at times when he was joking around, and he was close to his parents, but not too close. All in all, he seemed to be a fine young man, certainly not weird or disturbed in any way.

HEAVENLY MEMORIES

When James turned three, he got his first G.I. Joe and named it Billy (or Billie, as it turned out). When he received his second one that Christmas, he named it Leon. Two Christmases later, when he was five and a half, he received his third, which he named Walter. These G.I. Joes were his buddies, and he took them everywhere. He played with them in the tub and slept with them at night. Andrea's sister remembers him naming one immediately after he unwrapped the package. His parents were particularly struck by the names Leon and Walter, as they aren't common ones for a young child to use. When they asked him why he chose those, he told them because that was who met him when he got to heaven.

Ten men from Huston's squadron aboard *Natoma Bay* were

killed before he was. The names of three of them were Billie, Leon, and Walter. James's parents even discovered that the hair color for each of them matched the hair of the G.I. Joes. Billie Peeler had brown hair, Leon Conner had blond hair, and Walter Devlin had red hair, as did their respective G.I. Joe namesakes.

The day after James's comment about meeting them, Andrea brought up the topic again and asked James if there was really a heaven. When he said yes, she asked where it was, and he spread out his arms and said, "It's right here." She asked what it looked like, and he said it was the most beautiful place in the world.

Andrea asked him if there is really a God, and James said yes. She then asked if God is a man or a woman. I would guess that a lot of very young children from Protestant homes would imagine God as a man with a long white beard, perhaps looking like Charlton Heston, sitting on a throne. James's answer was that God is not a man or a woman; he is whoever you need him to be at the time.

Andrea also asked him if everyone comes back. James said no, that you get to choose. You don't have to come back. You can, but if you don't want to, you don't have to.

James also had an interesting story to tell about coming back. When he was four and a half, he was "helping" Bruce rake leaves one day when Bruce hugged him and told him how happy he was to have James as his son. James responded that when he picked Bruce he knew he would be a good daddy. Bruce asked what he meant, and James said that when he found Bruce and Andrea, he knew they would be good to him.

Bruce asked James where he had found them, and James said Hawaii. The three of them had gone to Hawaii that summer, so Bruce told James he didn't find them there because they were all there together. James said no, it wasn't that time; it was when only Bruce and Andrea were there. Bruce asked James where he had found them, and James said it was at the big pink hotel. He added that he found them on the beach when they were eating dinner.

Bruce and Andrea had indeed gone to Hawaii before James was born. They stayed at the Royal Hawaiian, a large pink hotel on Waikiki Beach, a different section of Honolulu than where they visited with James. That was their first week of trying to get pregnant, and Andrea had just gone off birth control pills. Bruce and Andrea finished their time there with a nighttime dinner on the beach. Though James was not conceived in Hawaii, Andrea was pregnant within a couple of months.

All in all, this is quite a remarkable case. Though I might have been able to corroborate parts of it more if I could have studied it sooner, it still stands up very, very well. In fact, I have trouble coming up with an ordinary explanation for it. You may say it was all a coincidence, but if so, it was one heck of a coincidence.

James appears to have had memories of James Huston's life. This little boy showed knowledge of events from the Pacific in World War II, and not just knowledge, but emotions from those events and the trauma of being killed there. Even so, he is now a happy, thriving young man, the trauma seemingly behind him. The third James is enjoying his new lease on life.

Chapter 5

HE CAME FROM HOLLYWOOD

Our office received a "To Whom It May Concern" letter one day from a mother in Oklahoma named Cyndi. She said she was hoping we might be able to help her solve a case of possible reincarnation. Her five-year-old son, Ryan, had been having memories of what his parents believed was a past life. She explained that she grew up in a Baptist church and that her husband was the son of a Church of Christ minister. They had never been taught to believe in reincarnation. They were ordinary people; her husband was a police officer and she was a county clerk deputy. Ryan was not ordinary and had lately had some extraordinary stories to tell.

About a year before, Ryan began talking about going home to Hollywood. He would cry and plead for Cyndi to take him home so he could see his other family. When this preschooler was playing, he would often shout "Action!" and begin to direct imaginary movies. His parents didn't take all this very seriously until a few months later, when he began having nightmares. He would wake up grabbing his chest and saying he couldn't breathe. He said that when he was in Hollywood his heart had exploded.

One night, Ryan said he wanted to tell Cyndi what it was like when you die. He began describing an awesome bright light and said you should go to the light. He said everyone comes back and that he knew Cyndi before. He claimed he picked her to be his mother.

Since Ryan seemed to be struggling with the memories, Cyndi went to their public library and picked up some books about Hollywood, in hopes that Ryan might see a landmark that would trigger memories that were more specific. As they looked through them, Ryan became excited when he saw a photograph of Rita Hayworth. He said he knew her and that she used to make "those ice drinks." He later said she called them Coke floats.

They came across a picture in another book from a 1932 movie called *Night After Night*. Ryan got excited again, and as he looked at the men in the photograph, he pointed to one of them and said, "Hey Mama, that's George. We did a picture together. And Mama, that guy's me. I found me." The photo shows six men, with all eyes on the two in the middle having a confrontation. The second man Ryan pointed to is on one side, wearing a black bow tie like the rest, along with a bowler hat and an overcoat.

The book didn't list the people in the picture, so Cyndi was unable to identify the man Ryan said he had been. She did verify that the first one was George Raft, a film star in the 1930s and '40s, primarily in gangster movies.

Ryan said he had been friends with a cowboy who was in the movie. He said this cowboy had a horse he did tricks with. He also said the cowboy had made cigarette commercials. With a little work, Ryan's parents discovered that an actor named Gordon Nance was in *Night After Night*. He later changed his name to Wild Bill Elliott. He starred in Westerns and was also a spokesman for Viceroy cigarettes.

Ryan described a scene in the movie that involved a closet full of guns. Later that night, Cyndi found *Night After Night* on YouTube. She saw that there was indeed a scene that included a closet full of guns. She pointed out that Ryan was only five and had never even seen a black-and-white movie, much less this one.

He also reacted to a picture of Marilyn Monroe, whom he called that Mary lady. He said he had been at a party one night and tried to talk to her. He laughed and said one of the studio guys punched him in the eye. He said you couldn't even get close enough to talk to her because those studio guys wouldn't let you. He said he liked being Ryan but he liked living in Hollywood, too. He said he had made films and that he had lived in a big house with a swimming pool outside.

Cyndi wrote that the most bizarre thing Ryan had done was describe some events that happened while she was pregnant with him. It was a story he shouldn't have known anything about, but he said he saw it all from heaven. She didn't provide any other details in the letter, but I learned more later.

Cyndi said she was writing because she really wanted help in identifying the man in the picture Ryan had pointed to. She said that he told her he was starting to forget about his life in Hollywood. That made him sad, but at the same time he just wanted to be Ryan. Cyndi finished by saying that Ryan was a great little boy and she wanted him to have answers to the questions he cried about at night.

We hear from American parents frequently, usually by e-mail these days but sometimes by postal mail as well, but it's rare to get that much detail from them. And having a picture of an unnamed man whom the child says was his previous identity is unprecedented. I watched *Night After Night* on YouTube myself. There was in fact a scene involving a closet full of guns. I also found the one that the photograph in the book was taken from. The problem was that the man Ryan said he had been had no lines in the movie; he was playing a henchman of one of the other characters. That would make identifying him quite a challenge. The movie itself is notable for being Mae West's film debut and includes a classic Mae West line. A hat check girl sees her and says, "Goodness, what beautiful diamonds!" West responds, "Goodness had nothing to do with it, dearie."

I wrote back to Cyndi and asked if she and her family would be open to a visit from me. She responded that they would greatly welcome a visit or any kind of information I could give them. She also mentioned that she had started keeping a journal about Ryan, which meant we would have documentation of the things he said.

Ryan didn't want to talk to anyone about Hollywood because he was afraid people would think he was crazy. I explained to Cyndi that it would be fine if Ryan didn't talk to me, but I was hoping he would warm up after I was there awhile. I said she could let him know I didn't think he was crazy, I was just really interested in the life he had described to Cyndi.

We exchanged e-mails leading up to our meeting. In one, Cyndi reported that Ryan said the reason he had to come back was that he didn't spend enough time with his family in his last life; he worked so much that he forgot that love was the most important thing. In another, she said Ryan had told her he had nightmares about a man they called Senator Five, whom he described as the nastiest villain that ever lived. He talked about an agency and going to a graveyard in New York with a buddy that worked for the agency. A week later, Cyndi said Ryan was resisting going to kindergarten because after he would tell the class about Hollywood and the agency in story time, kids would make fun of him when he said the stories were real.

I wasn't sure what to make of some of the stories myself. Ryan's talk about the agency and Senator Five sounded rather fantastic to me. The stories reminded me of a case a colleague of mine investigated in which a young boy gave startlingly accurate details about a man who had lived hundreds of miles away. He would then get wound up and begin talking about race car drivers and various make-believe topics. It was difficult to tell what counted as past-life report versus pure fantasy.

Ryan also talked some about Broadway. He began doing a tap dance routine and said he remembered it when he heard some music on a cartoon that sounded like the music he used to tap to. He said he had done it with two buddies. He hadn't taken formal lessons but had taught himself.

When the family was packing for a vacation trip to Branson, Missouri, a month before we met, Cyndi told Ryan he could dress up when they went to see a show there. He responded, "Oh Mom, I hate auditions." The play they went to was a variety show that included a tribute to veterans. During a piece on Pearl Harbor, Ryan became very emotional. He booed a clip of Franklin Roosevelt, and when his dad got on him about it, he turned to his mother and said, "Daddy doesn't know what an idiot that man is." Halfway through, he began muttering about "the damn Japs." He cried during the presentation and stood applauding at the end.

In planning my trip to meet the family, I would be taking along a small flip camera to record our interview. A month before I received Cyndi's letter, I had gotten a phone call from a television producer named Russ Stratton, who was interested in making a program about our work. Such calls are usually from producers hoping to pitch an idea to a cable network. In this case, Russ said that A&E was already on board. And one of the producers involved in the project was Doug Liman, the director of films such as *The Bourne Identity* and *Mr. and Mrs. Smith*. The plan was to have a first-rate director reboot an A&E series from the 1990s called *The Unexplained*.

Russ seemed sincerely interested in our work, and I agreed to participate in the project. The plan was to show a re-creation of a previous case, but in discussing recent ones, I mentioned that I was preparing to go to Oklahoma to meet a family. One of the producers sent me a camera to film the interview. The understanding was that the footage probably wouldn't be shown on television and certainly not without the family's permission. Even so, the producers thought the opportunity to have an initial interview on film was too good to pass up, and at the very least, it would give them a better understanding of what was involved in studying a case.

A VISIT TO OKLAHOMA

I flew to Oklahoma to meet Ryan and his parents early on a Saturday afternoon. Cyndi was warm and pleasant. Her husband, Kevin, a police officer, seemed out of central casting for an Oklahoma lawman with his stocky build, his closely cropped hair, and Southwestern drawl. He definitely did not come across as someone you would expect to promote the idea of past lives. Ryan, at that point three months short of his sixth birthday, was initially reticent as these children tend to be. He was clearly fascinated by the camera, which I set up on a small collapsible tripod the producers sent, and Kevin had to admonish him several times not to touch it. Ryan didn't touch it, but he sure wanted to.

We sat at the kitchen table to talk about the things Ryan

had said. He had usually made his statements at night, often right after his bath. His personality seemed different at times, with a more mature vocabulary. He might talk about his memories three days straight and then say nothing about them for three weeks. He initially would only talk to Cyndi about them but lately had begun talking to Kevin as well.

Cyndi had sent me a copy of the notes she was keeping. She was sometimes adding entries on a daily basis. This meant his comments were fresh in her mind when she recorded them. He once said, "I used to be big; now I'm little." Another time, he said, "I liked it better when I was big and I could go wherever and whenever I wanted to go. I hate being little." Cyndi reported that if Ryan saw a shot of the Hollywood Hills on television, he would always say, "That's my home. That's where I belong." At one point, he said, "I just can't live in these conditions. My last home was much better."

He made various statements about family. He said his mother had curly brown hair. He talked a lot about a sister, who was three years younger than he was. He talked about a daughter and said her mother liked to put her hair in either pigtails or a ponytail. At other times, he also talked about three children. He wasn't sure if they were his children or not, but he remembered bringing elaborate coloring books to them. He said he drove a green car, while his wife had a nice black one.

Ryan talked about traveling a lot. During the family's vacation to Branson, they were walking along the brick streets downtown when Ryan became excited and pointed to a small café with outdoor seating. He said the place reminded him of when he went to Paris. They had restaurants outside there and fountains in the middle of the street, and he went and saw the big tower. He asked Cyndi what the tower was called, and when she told him the Eiffel Tower, he said, "That's it, Mom. I have been to the Eiffel Tower in Paris." Cyndi asked if he had really been there, and he said, "Yes, Mommy, I have been to China, Paris, New York. When are you going to listen to me? I have seen the world."

One day he walked into the kitchen and asked if he and Cyndi could dance together. He said, "Mommy, I can't wait until I get big again and I get to go on those big boats, wear fancy clothes, and dance with all the pretty ladies. That's how you see the world, Mommy, from a big boat." He mimicked dancing what appeared to be a waltz and said that dipping was his favorite part of dancing on a ship.

He talked about visiting China and said you had to learn to use chopsticks there because they didn't have silverware. He said you got good at it if you wanted to eat. He also talked about Chinatown a lot and said they had the best food there. When he was in preschool, he asked one day if the family could go eat at a place where they used chopsticks. His parents took him to a Chinese restaurant. He loved the food, eating all of it while refusing to use silverware. Kevin said he was amazed at how proficient Ryan was with his chopsticks.

Ryan talked about how much he hated cats. He told Cyndi one time that when he was living in Hollywood, he tried to help an injured cat that didn't know him. The cat scratched him "something awful" and there was a lot of blood. He then showed her where the scratches had been on his arms. He said another time that he got his daughter a watchdog but she didn't like it.

One day, Ryan said he wanted to watch cartoons all day. Then he said, "Mom, just get me a Tru Ade." She said, "What?" and he replied, "I mean a Dr Pepper." She did an online search and found that Tru Ade was a noncarbonated soft drink that came in orange and grape flavors. It seems to have been made from the 1940s through the '60s or early '70s. Cyndi showed Ryan a picture of an ad for Tru Ade, and he laughed and said, "You can't get that stuff anymore. Now I just drink Dr Pepper."

I asked about Ryan's agency talk. I was thinking that Ryan was referring to being a secret agent, and Cyndi seemed to think so, too. But he never quite said that. He had said he worked in an agency where people changed their names. And he talked a lot about Senator Five and what a mean person he was. He once asked for a map of the United States. He pointed to New York and said that's where they went to see Senator Five. He said they saw him in a graveyard there. A few hours after pointing out New York as the place they met, Ryan told Cyndi that if she could find Senator Five on the computer, he could pick him out. He said he could pick him out because he saw his face at night when he was asleep.

Parents have often told me there is a distinct difference in their children when they are describing their purported past-life memories compared to when they are engaging in make-believe. They tend to be more serious and matter-of-fact talking about a past life. I asked Cyndi if there was any difference in how Ryan talked about the agency part compared to how he talked about Hollywood. She said he did seem a little different. I gathered he showed more sadness and longing talking about Hollywood, whereas he was more energetic discussing the agency.

Ryan also made comments about little things, often when triggers in the environment such as smells or music seemed to stir his memory. Cyndi was patting Ryan's leg one afternoon when he said it reminded him of when he was in Hollywood and he used to get "those skin burns." Cyndi asked if he was talking about sunburns, and he said he used to get them all the time in Hollywood.

One night at bedtime, Ryan said he didn't want to go to sleep because he didn't want to have nightmares again. He cried for about thirty minutes, saying repeatedly, "Mommy, I'm homesick. I'm just so homesick." Another time, he said he used to live somewhere with the word *Rock* or *Mount* in it. A while after the interview, I told Cyndi about my search for towns with those words in the name, but she said Ryan had talked as if Rock or Mount was part of the street address.

Ryan also made comments about his time between lives. At one point, he said he went somewhere after he died, but not to heaven. It was a waiting place. Another time, he said he saw his parents from heaven. He said he picked his mother but not his father and that he came back to take care of her.

When Ryan's parents married, they decided they would only have one child because Kevin already had two from his first marriage. Cyndi very much wanted a daughter. Ryan came over to Cyndi one night and asked why she had thought he was going to be a little girl. When she asked him who told him that, he said no one told him and that he saw it from heaven. He said, "This doctor guy did a test and told you I was a boy. You got mad and said he was wrong. You just knew that I was going to be a girl. Mommy, it was Daddy's birthday, you went to a restaurant afterward to eat and you cried for a very long time."

Cyndi reports everything happened just as Ryan said. She had always regretted the way she acted that day. It's hard to imagine she had ever told Ryan about it.

After the interview, we went out to dinner, which Kevin insisted on paying for even though I could put it on my expense report. He and Cyndi came across as completely sincere, and there seemed no chance they had put Ryan up to saying the things he had. The question remained, however, whether

Ryan had made it all up. He did appear to have an active imagination. The emotion he attached to his claims, however, indicated this was more than just make-believe to him.

The only way to answer the question was to find out if the man in the picture had done the things Ryan described. But figuring out the identity of a nameless face from a 1930s movie seemed a nearly impossible task. I looked into posting the picture on the Turner Classic Movies message board. That would be a real long shot, but I thought it might be worth a try.

A POSSIBLE IDENTIFICATION

A couple of weeks after my trip to Oklahoma, I received a telephone call that changed the search. One of the television producers called because the family they had planned to film for their program had backed out. So they wanted to use Ryan's case instead. This would mean that the television folks could use their resources to search for the man in the picture, which greatly increased our chances of identifying him. The question was whether Ryan's family would agree to participate in a program for television.

I e-mailed Cyndi and explained the situation. I made clear that it was completely up to them to decide if they were comfortable with the prospect of Ryan's story being told on television. If they decided they didn't want to do the program, that would have no effect whatsoever on our interactions. Cyndi wrote back to say she had watched a show about psychic children a few nights before and all she could think about was how much Ryan's story could help some other family going through a similar experience. She said she was interested in letting Ryan do the show, but she would want it done with them in shadow with different names.

Cyndi also asked if the producers would want to film Ryan

in Hollywood. I responded that they probably would if she and Kevin were agreeable to it. She said the reason she asked was that Ryan had been saying repeatedly that he was going to go to Hollywood for three days and that he was going on a big airplane. She reported he had been talking about that even before the family knew anything about our initial visit being filmed.

After one of the producers called and talked with Kevin, he and Cyndi decided they better tell Cyndi's father, the one remaining grandparent who didn't know what Ryan had been saying. They were surprised when he actually took the news better than the rest of the family; he said he had seen things on television about other children like Ryan. Ryan was excited about this news, saying his grandfather didn't think he was crazy and he could tell him about Hollywood now.

As Cyndi was getting Ryan ready for bed that night, she told him, "Ryan, you do know that you are not that man in the picture anymore. We just want you to be Ryan." He responded that he was not the same as the man in the picture on the outside but that on the inside he was still that man.

Cyndi e-mailed the following day to say that Ryan didn't want the interview done in shadow and didn't want his name changed. He said that what he was going through was real and that if his parents believed him they wouldn't want to be hidden. This put Cyndi and Kevin in a tough spot. They live in a small town, and they were concerned about what people would think of them if they went on television with Ryan's story. Cyndi's family was opposed to the idea, but since she didn't want Ryan to think she and Kevin were ashamed of him, she e-mailed the producer and told him they would agree to be on the program with their identities unconcealed.

The television crew then visited Ryan's family. Russ Stratton, the first producer I had talked to, was not part of the group.

He was still overseeing the project, but a separate team had been hired to do the filming. Cyndi reported that Ryan had a great time with them, and he enjoyed playing with all the equipment they brought in. The crew filmed interviews with the family. They showed Ryan the book with the picture from *Night After Night*, and they captured him on camera pointing to the man he had identified and saying, "That one's me."

The television folks then thought they might have figured out who that man was: an actor named Ralf Harolde. But they based this solely on their sense that Harolde looked like the man in *Night After Night*. After a little research, I wasn't so sure. Just looking at pictures of him, I wasn't convinced he was the same person. I also saw that Harolde's real name had been Ralph Wigger. When I found Wigger in the census records, I saw that he appeared to be an only child, even though Ryan had talked at length about having a sister. Records from when Wigger was one, ten, and twenty years old listed no siblings.

The television people decided to take Ryan to Hollywood to see what he might remember, making his prediction about taking a trip there come true. I wanted to accompany his family, but we couldn't get my schedule to line up with the director's. Since the crew was under time pressure, the group went ahead with the trip without me.

I received a report from Cyndi the day the family got back home, even though they arrived at two in the morning. The trip proved to be rather arduous for Ryan and his parents. It began with another interview in the hotel room. The problem was that while the television folks were trying to capture Ryan saying something extraordinary on camera, he was getting annoyed because he wanted to see Hollywood. He did enjoy the hotel, the Hollywood Roosevelt Hotel, which was built in 1927 and hosted the first Academy Awards two years later. He made comments to Cyndi and Kevin about remembering it, but only when he was away from the cameras.

The film crew took the family to see two homes where Ralf Harolde had lived. He had apparently lived in quite a few places, and they went to the first and last of his houses. Ryan showed no reaction at all. At the last one, Kevin asked him on camera if any of it looked familiar to him, and Ryan said no. Cyndi said that Ryan did recognize the house of Wild Bill Elliott, the actor from *Night After Night* he said he had been friends with. She also reported he loved seeing the ocean and said he used to bring his girlfriends there.

I responded to Cyndi that since Ryan showed a reaction to Bill Elliott's home but not Ralf Harolde's, I was again wondering if Harolde was the right guy. Ryan continued to talk about past memories, not only about Hollywood but New York as well, saying he played the piano there.

A BREAKTHROUGH

Six weeks after the family's trip to Hollywood, I received an e-mail from Russ Stratton, the producer overseeing the television project. It said, "Please call when you have a moment . . . we've had a breakthrough on Ryan's case . . . we've definitely identified who the actor was." That got my attention. When I called Russ, he gave me the update. He had been dissatisfied with the Hollywood trip. When he found out from the crew that their only method of identifying Ralf Harolde was to look at pictures, he was really dissatisfied.

Russ hired an archival footage consultant named Kate Coe to try to find out who the man in *Night After Night* was. She initially figured the job would be easy. Once she learned the details, however, she changed her mind. As she said on *The UneXplained*, she thought, "Oh, wait a second. It's an uncredited extra. It's some guy in a hat!" She sent the photo from the movie to other researchers, and no one could identify him.

Eventually, she went to the library of the Academy of Motion Picture Arts and Sciences, probably the largest film library in the world. She got all the material she could find on *Night After Night*. Most of it involved the stars of the movie. Then she spotted a picture of the man she was searching for. He was looking into the camera with a long cigar in his mouth and a bowler hat on his head. The caption of the picture just gave the name of the movie and the stars. On the back, however, was this description: "What the well-dressed racketeer will wear. Marty Martyn, playing a racketeer in Paramount's 'Night After Night', with George Raft, Constance Cummings, Wynne Gibson, Mae West and Alison Skipworth, gives a demonstration of underworld sartorial excellence."

What's odd is that Marty Martyn is listed in the credits at the end of *Night After Night* playing a character named Malloy, even though the man Ryan pointed to had no lines in the movie. This initially made me unsure if that man really was Marty Martyn, so I watched the movie again. No one is called Malloy in the film, and none of the other actors look like Marty Martyn. Only two characters wear bowler hats, the man Ryan pointed to and his boss, who was played by an actor named Bradley Page. The actor Ryan pointed to had to be Marty Martyn.

We finally had a definite name to go with the face. With a little work, Russ's team was able to find Marty Martyn's real name and some basic facts about his life. He only had one biological child, a daughter with his last wife. Russ's team was able to identify her and find her phone number. Russ called her up. Some of their conversation is on the *UneXplained* program that eventually aired. Russ tells her a little of the story and finishes by saying they think the man Ryan identified was Marty

Martyn. The daughter responds, "That's my father! Is this some kind of a joke?" She was understandably skittish about the whole thing. Russ sent her an e-mail detailing how they had found her, with the thread involving a family history volume in the New York Public Library as well as various online databases.

While she was processing it all, we had work to do. Now that we knew the identity of the man in the picture, I could test Ryan to see if he would recognize people Marty Martyn knew. In the Asian cases, families have often conducted informal tests that were completely uncontrolled. As Ian wrote, the tests often occur with a large group of people around. Someone asks a leading question such as, "Do you see your wife here?" When everyone looks expectantly at the previous person's widow, the child can hardly fail to point out the correct person. There have been exceptions, such as the case of a little girl in Sri Lanka named Gnanatilleka, who was presented various individuals from the previous person's life (and a couple of people whom the previous person never met) and asked if she knew the person. She correctly identified the ones the previous person knew and gave some details about them she could not have known based solely on their appearance.

In Ryan's case, it made no sense to try to bring in people Marty Martyn had known, since he died in 1964. But I could show Ryan pictures. Russ's group had photographs of a number of people from Marty Martyn's life, and at my request, they also produced similar ones of people Marty did not know.

With those in hand, I made a trip back to Oklahoma to see Ryan's family again, this time with a film crew joining me. Russ had taken over the hands-on work of making the program, and he and his producing partner, Amy Hobby, led the team. Before going, we told Cyndi that the man in the picture was not Ralf Harolde, as the previous production crew had guessed, and that we now knew his actual identity. We didn't tell her the correct name because I wanted to make sure the recognition tests were untainted. I didn't think she would start madly researching Marty Martyn's life, but I wanted to make sure that possibility didn't even exist. This was quite difficult for Cyndi. Russ had told her about a few items, which likely only tantalized her more, but no identifying details. She said she guessed Ryan's statements must be pretty accurate if all of us were flying to Oklahoma so quickly, but after dealing with this thing for months, she was dying to know all the facts.

Ryan was initially happy to hear that the man in the picture had been identified and that he wasn't Ralf Harolde. But in the days leading up to the visit, he became skeptical about being filmed again. He said he didn't want to deal with the television crew. He felt they had tried to make a joke out of him in Hollywood. He wanted to know why they didn't listen when he said he didn't know Ralf Harolde's houses and why they lied to him about what his previous name had been. He said it wasn't fair that he didn't remember his name.

Cyndi explained that a different film crew would be coming this time. She told Ryan that the crew didn't mean to lie about the man's name and that everyone makes mistakes. He was adamant that he would not cooperate. Cyndi told me she was hoping she and Kevin could get Ryan prepared before we all arrived that weekend. I told her we would certainly be gentle and that with luck, Ryan would warm up after a while.

When we arrived, Ryan was definitely in a mood. He had been sleeping poorly and was clearly uncomfortable about us being there. Russ apologized to him for the way the filming had gone in Hollywood. Even so, this was a lot to ask of a child.

Ryan had just turned six years old, which was a particularly difficult age for what we were trying to do. It can be hard for a child that young to cooperate with any activity for a significant period, especially as people are filming him. At the same time, he was getting a little old for the past-life images to still be prominent in his mind.

Adding to the difficulty was the frustration Cyndi was feeling because we would not tell her the name of the man in the picture. Ryan could feel her frustration, which she was then taking out on him when he had trouble cooperating. She said later she was acting so harshly toward him that she should have been filming an episode of *Supernanny*.

We attempted some recognition tests. Russ and his team had collected pictures of various people Marty Martyn had known. I may have made two mistakes when I showed Ryan the pictures. I showed him lineups, four pictures at a time, in which only one was someone Marty Martyn had known. This might have been too much for a six-year-old to take in. I could have shown him one picture at a time, some being people Marty knew and some not.

The other possible mistake was that when I showed him the pictures, I simply asked him if any of the people looked familiar. I was being intentionally vague in hopes that if Ryan did recognize anyone, he would then give details such as the relationship Marty had to the person. Ryan said later he didn't understand what I was asking. He thought I was asking if the pictures looked familiar rather than asking him to identify specific people.

Our initial tests did not go well. It was clear Ryan didn't want to do them and was pointing at pictures randomly. We took several breaks and after a while decided to give up for the day. We all went out for dinner at a barbecue restaurant and had a good time. When we got back to the house, Ryan said he wanted to try some more pictures. I was concerned he might be too tired, but he was clear that he wanted to try.

We sat at the kitchen table. I showed him pictures of four women, one of whom was Marty Martyn's last wife. When I asked Ryan if any of them meant anything to him, he pointed to the picture of Marty's wife. I asked him about her, and he only said that she looked familiar.

I told Ryan and his parents that I thought I might know who Senator Five was. I showed him pictures of four men. He pointed at one and said with apparent certainty, "That's Senator Five." I asked him, "Are you sure?" and he answered, "I'm sure." Ryan had said that he met Senator Five in New York. I checked records and found that New York didn't have a Senator Five but did have a Senator Ives. Irving Ives was a U.S. Senator for twelve years in the late 1940s and the 1950s. I thought Five and Ives sounded so much alike that a young child could easily mix them up. Senator Ives was the man Ryan pointed to.

I then showed Ryan pictures of four young men, one being Marty Martyn, who were all carrying tennis rackets. Ryan picked up the picture of Marty and said he remembered it, that it looked familiar. I asked him how, but he only said it was familiar. I then explained that this was the same man as the one in *Night After Night* Ryan had pointed to, only he was younger in this picture. Though this recognition may not be as impressive as the first two since Ryan had already seen the picture of Marty from *Night After Night*, Marty did not look identical in the two pictures, as they were taken at different angles and at different ages.

I tried a couple more tests. Ryan began missing again, and

we called it a night. We left some of the pictures, and Ryan looked at them with Cyndi after we were gone. One was a family picture that included Marty's last wife, his five stepchildren, and an inset of his daughter. Ryan pointed to the older stepdaughter and told Cyndi, "I used to talk to her and give her advice. She never wanted to listen to me. She had no respect." He didn't like the pictures of Marty when he was older, the bald pictures with the glasses as Ryan called them. He preferred the ones where he looked "young and handsome."

The next morning, we met again. I had typed out a list of four names. One was Marty Martyn. The others were similar kinds of names—John Johnson, Willie Wilson, and Robert Robertson—because I didn't want Ryan to pick Marty Martyn simply because that name stood out. I had Kevin read the names, since I knew the correct one. As he read the others, Ryan said no after each one but was silent on Marty Martyn. He then pointed to Marty Martyn's name, and when Kevin asked him, "Marty Martyn?" he confirmed his choice.

MEETING MARTY'S DAUGHTER

After that visit, Ryan was confused at times about Marty's daughter. People explained that she had grown up. He said he thought she was still little and that everyone was making up the idea that she was now old. He said he remembered her being not much bigger than he was then and that he really didn't think he had been gone that long.

Cyndi had hoped that solving the mystery of the man in the picture would enable Ryan to put his past life behind him. As she said, she kept praying the memories would diminish and Ryan could just be happy. At one point, he told her, "Mommy, I just want to be me, not the old me." He then got angry and said to tell Marty's daughter he didn't want to meet her. "She got old. Why didn't she wait for me?" He got upset and walked off.

Ryan eventually came around. He predicted he would get a chance to meet Marty's daughter. He planned on loving her instantly because he said you can feel love and it doesn't go away. Marty's daughter remained unsure about participating in the project. Russ sent her a DVD with some of the footage of Ryan and his parents and eventually met with her. After being assured that all of this was on the up and up, she agreed to a meeting. She would talk with me and meet Ryan, but she did not want to be filmed.

Since Marty's daughter lived in the Los Angeles area, the meeting meant another trip there for Ryan. Russ's team had arranged for us all to meet at a small house. Ryan's family dressed up more for the meeting than they had for previous events, which I thought was a way of showing respect for Marty's daughter and an appreciation for her willingness to meet. Despite Ryan's intention to love Marty's daughter instantly, he seemed intimidated by the experience. As the family walked into the house, Cyndi asked Ryan to introduce himself. Ryan stepped forward and shook hands with Marty's daughter. She said, "Hi Ryan, nice to meet you." Without responding, Ryan turned around and went back to Cyndi. He was standoffish for the rest of the meeting.

Afterward, Ryan told Cyndi that Marty's daughter wasn't like he thought she would be, that her energy had changed. Cyndi responded that when people grow up, they change. Ryan said, "Same face, but she didn't wait on me. She changed; her energy changed. I don't want to go back. I want to always keep this family." His response was like those many of the Asian children have shown following similar meetings. The intense longing for the previous family they have repeatedly expressed often dissipates (though not always) when they see that the people they have talked about have aged as their lives have gone on. The children's memories have been validated, but they also see that things have changed.

MARTY MARTYN'S LIFE

Before Ryan met Marty's daughter, I sat down with her to review his statements. She had only been eight years old when Marty died. She had fond memories of him, but there was a lot about his life she didn't know. In fact, she hadn't been aware of the existence of one of his sisters, who died at an early age.

Even so, between her memories and the records Russ's team had unearthed, we were able to piece together a picture of Marty Martyn's life, and we could compare it to Ryan's statements. In most of our cases, people have tried to see if a deceased person could be identified whose life matched the statements the child had made. Here, there was only one guy that Ryan could have been talking about, because he had pointed to him in a picture. We weren't trying to see if there was anyone whose life matched Ryan's statements; we were looking to see if Marty Martyn's did.

What we found was that though Ryan was off on some of the details, a lot of what he said was correct for Marty Martin. It had seemed unlikely that an extra with no lines would have danced on Broadway, had a big house with a swimming pool, and traveled the world on big boats. But Marty Martyn did.

Marty was born in Philadelphia in 1905. Ryan had talked a lot about a sister and also mentioned another one, and Marty had two sisters. His mother had curly brown hair, as Ryan had said. Ryan was right about dancing in New York, as Marty and one of his sisters went to New York to be dancers. He danced in various reviews on Broadway, and his sister became a well-known dancer there.

Marty then moved to Los Angeles, having a life in Hollywood as Ryan had described. He began as an extra as well as a dance director. He then became a Hollywood agent, not the secret agent kind but a talent agent. He set up the Marty Martyn Agency, where he had notable clients such as Glenn Ford. Ryan had talked about people changing their names with the agency, which would certainly be true for a talent agency. Marty had several connections to Rita Hayworth, and his daughter confirmed he probably did know her. He may well have interacted with Marilyn Monroe as well, as his wife's family knew her.

Marty was a big sunbather, getting sunburns as Ryan had mentioned. Ryan said he used to take girlfriends to see the ocean, and there are pictures of Marty with young women on the beach. He enjoyed going there and watching surfers, which Ryan had said as well.

Marty was married four times. He became quite wealthy, and he and his last wife enjoyed an upscale lifestyle. Ryan said he had driven around Hollywood in a green car and that his wife drove a nice black car. Well, Marty's wife didn't actually do the driving, but they had a custom-made Rolls-Royce that was presumably a nice car. Ryan remembered an African American maid, and Marty and his wife had a number of them. Ryan said he owned a piano, and Marty had pianos in his house. The family lived in a fine house with a large swimming pool, as Ryan had described. Ryan said his address had Rock or Mount in it. And Marty Martyn's last house, that fine home with the big swimming pool? It was located at 825 N. Roxbury.

Ryan said one time that when he was a little kid, his family didn't have a TV in their house; no one did. He said he was so excited when he got his first TV. That statement, while accurate for Marty, was quite general. It would have been true for anyone in Marty's generation, but I still found it notable that a six-year-old child would understand that people in that era didn't have televisions.

As Ryan had reported, Marty and his wife traveled the world. Marty's daughter doubted he ever went to China as Ryan had said, but there was a Chinese restaurant in Hollywood he really enjoyed. Marty and his wife did go to Paris a lot. In fact, his daughter showed us a picture of her parents in Paris. Ryan had spoken of traveling on a large ship and doing a dance like a waltz on it. Marty and his wife had traveled to Europe on the *Queen Mary*, where dancing took place.

Ryan had said that Theodore Roosevelt was the best president ever, and he had booed Franklin Roosevelt. Marty was a Republican, and his wife was a major Republican as well. As for politicians, Marty did indeed meet Senator Ives from New York. His daughter said she had a photograph of the two of them together. Though there is no evidence that Marty felt the animosity toward him that Ryan demonstrated toward Senator Five, the two men definitely met.

Ryan had talked about having a daughter as well as interacting with other children, but he was unsure if those were his. Marty had one biological daughter along with five stepchildren, and he did indeed have a difficult relationship with his older stepdaughter as Ryan had said. One item that was probably incorrect was that Ryan said that his wife enjoyed putting his daughter's hair in pigtails or a ponytail. If Marty's wife did, it was when his daughter was too young to remember it. She did say that her father hated cats, as Ryan had described. Ryan said he gave his daughter a watchdog that she didn't like. Marty Martyn got his family a dog—though since it was a Yorkshire

Terrier, it wouldn't have been much of a watchdog—and his daughter didn't like it. Ryan talked about bringing coloring books to a group of children. Marty's daughter said he brought her a lot of coloring books.

Ryan had asked for a Tru Ade to drink. Marty's daughter didn't remember seeing him drink those, but she did say that he liked Orangina soda, a similar drink. Ryan had said he loved bread in his last life, and at another time said he loved blueberries. Marty's daughter confirmed that rye bread and bagels were among her father's favorite foods, and he also loved fruit.

Ryan said he had been a smoker. Marty smoked cigars and had a monogrammed cigarette case. Ryan said he had died when his heart exploded, but this was apparently incorrect for Marty. He died on Christmas Day in 1964. He had leukemia, and his daughter reported he was in the hospital when he died of a cerebral hemorrhage. Ryan would wake up grabbing his chest and saying he couldn't breathe. Marty's death was apparently unwitnessed, so there is no way of knowing precisely what he experienced when he died. Ryan did say that he died in a room with numbers on the door, which was likely true for Marty's hospital room.

Some of the other things Ryan talked about did not match Marty Martyn's life. For example, he talked about a father who had raised corn and then died when Ryan was a child in his last life. There were many other items, scores of details, that we were unable to either prove or disprove for Marty, since our sole sources of information were public records and a daughter who was only eight when he died.

Even so, many of the details Ryan gave did fit the man he pointed to in the picture, who had a much more exciting life than anyone could have guessed a movie extra would have. Though that might seem like strong evidence for reincarnation—and it is—there is another factor in Ryan's case that complicates matters.

A CHILD PSYCHIC

Ryan has had a number of incidents in which he seemed to demonstrate special knowledge. He told Cyndi one night that there were supposed to be three babies in her family. When she said she didn't know what he was talking about, he repeated that there were supposed to be three babies in her family and said a baby was born in the first week of July but not on the first day as Cyndi was. The baby came early; he was supposed to wait to be born. He decided he wasn't ready to come back yet so God didn't make him stay. When Cyndi again said she wasn't sure what he was talking about, Ryan started to cry and asked her to call his grandmother so he could ask her about the third baby. He said his grandmother had been very sad and that she really thought she was going to get to take that baby home. Cyndi told him it was too late to call that night but she would call the next day.

Cyndi's mother had indeed had another baby besides Cyndi and her brother. With her first pregnancy, the baby was born premature and died minutes later. His birthday was July 8, and Cyndi stated with certainty that her mother had never talked about the baby around her grandsons. When Cyndi told her mother what Ryan had said, she started crying.

Another time, Ryan, Cyndi, and Cyndi's mother were shopping out of town when they took Ryan into a walk-in hair salon to get a haircut. Ryan told the woman cutting his hair that he wanted her to use her red scissors, the ones that had special meaning to her. She asked how he knew about those. He told her he was psychic and could see them in his mind. She then took a black case out of her drawer, unzipped it, and pulled out a pair of red scissors.

Ryan would sometimes touch people's faces with his fingers and say that he needed to feel their energy. He did that to his grandmother and told her she was going to get chicken pox. Two weeks later, she came down with shingles, an illness produced by the reemergence of the varicella zoster virus that causes chicken pox.

Ryan came by Cyndi's office with his dad one day on their way to see a movie. Cyndi's phone rang, and Ryan picked it up and handed it to her. When the man started talking, Ryan reached down and pushed the button to end the call. Cyndi, no doubt exasperated, asked Ryan why he had done that. He responded that the guy had the wrong number and was an idiot. The man called back, and sure enough, he had the wrong number and did act thoughtlessly, arguing with Cyndi about having the wrong phone number.

On Ryan's first trip to Los Angeles, Ryan told Cyndi as their plane was landing that they would have white cars when they got to Hollywood. When the traveling group got to the rental car lot, they received a white car and a white van.

Cyndi took Ryan to the store one night to pick out some pool toys to take with him to his grandparents' house the next day. He picked out water blasters, and Cyndi said he could get two, one for him and one for his cousin. Ryan insisted he needed three, but Cyndi told him two was enough. On the way to his grandparents' house, Ryan said his grandfather would break his cousin's before he even got to use it. Cyndi responded that Ryan's grandfather probably wouldn't be in the pool. When they got to the house, Ryan's grandfather was in shorts and ready to swim. Before Ryan's cousin arrived, his grandfather accidentally broke the water blaster Ryan had gotten for him. They needed a third one, as Ryan had said.

Cyndi e-mailed me the day after Father's Day to say that a couple of weeks before, Ryan had gone on and on about wanting to buy Kevin a watch. When Cyndi told him Kevin already had a watch, Ryan insisted he would need one by Father's Day. When Kevin came home from work on the morning of Father's Day, he explained that during a fight with a drunk man that night, his watch had been broken.

Cyndi went on to say that later that day, she and Ryan went shopping so Ryan could get his grandfather a present. His grandfather is a diesel mechanic, and Ryan said he wanted to get him a special wrench. He said he wasn't sure if his grandfather would need a wrench that he didn't have or if his would get broken, but he knew his grandfather would have to buy a new one.

A few days later, Cyndi e-mailed again to report that Ryan's grandfather had to leave a job site the previous day before he was completely finished with his work. He asked a man who worked for him to drive his truck home while he rode with someone else. The man didn't put all the tools back in the toolboxes, and when Ryan's grandfather got home, he noticed that they were scattered on the back of the flatbed truck. He thought some of the tools had probably fallen off onto the road, and sure enough, by the end of the week, he had bought some new wrenches.

Cyndi also said in the Father's Day e-mail that Ryan told his grandmother that day that she was going to hurt her back and have to go to the chiropractor. Four days later, Cyndi e-mailed again to say she had just gotten off the phone with her mother, who had been in the kitchen putting up dishes when she turned wrong and threw out her back.

That August, Cyndi reported that Ryan was predicting who his teacher was going to be for the second grade. He told her he had seen the list in his mind and knew which teacher he would be getting. When Cyndi told him they would need to wait until the next week to find out, he wanted to bet an Xbox on it. Cyndi wouldn't bet him, which turned out to be wise because the following week she e-mailed me a picture of the post card he had gotten from his new teacher, the one he had predicted.

I called Ryan's grandmother and confirmed with her all the incidents that involved his grandparents. I might be able to write off one or two of these, but with so many happening, Ryan appears to have some psychic abilities. (I realize this is a controversial area, but if you're this far into a book on past-life memories, I hope the possibility of extrasensory perception isn't too much of a stretch.) This raises the question of where Ryan's knowledge of Marty Martyn came from. Was it all memories, or did his psychic abilities lead him to know about events he didn't personally experience? And did seeing the picture of Marty Martyn connect Ryan with information about his life that Ryan then interpreted as memories? For that matter, were some of the details that Ryan gave that didn't match Marty Martyn part of a flood of information about other people's lives that Ryan perceives because of his psychic abilities?

Most of the children we study have not demonstrated special knowledge about anything other than the life of one deceased person. And the details they report are not just objective information but seem to be memories from the viewpoint of that person. When Ryan cried about missing his old life, he was showing an emotional connection to material that he felt he had experienced, not just events he knew about. Still, a special case like Ryan's may give us clues that knowledge is not always completely isolated in each of our brains, as he seemed to have access to information he could not have gained through the usual functioning of his brain. There may be a more diffuse field of knowledge rather than just individual points where it resides. Similarly, it's easy to think of past lives in a linear fashion, with separate souls moving from one life, to another, and then another in a straightforward progression. The reality may be more complicated than that, as I'll discuss at the end of the book.

RYAN'S POSTSCRIPT

After the meeting with Marty Martyn's daughter, I had a plane to catch. The TV producers took Ryan and his parents to some of the sites Marty Martyn had known. They went by Marty's last house on Roxbury, the one with a big swimming pool. Unfortunately, the house had recently been torn down, and a new one was being built in its place. Ryan seemed okay with that. They visited the building where the Marty Martyn Agency had been. Ryan walked all the floors of the building and even asked if he could stay longer. He also enjoyed going to an apartment complex Marty had stayed in, as well as the Beverly Hills Hotel, where Marty once had a bungalow. The next day, they went to the beach, and Ryan enjoyed playing in the sand and watching the surfers.

Following that trip, Ryan's talk about Marty Martyn's life became infrequent unless something reminded him of it. Cyndi found that he did much better with showers in the morning than baths at night, which often seemed to bring out longings for the past. She was pleased that he had learned to live more in the here and now. Ryan did continue to say he wanted to see Marty's youngest stepson. He wanted to tell him that he knew he had turned out well. He was sorry he hadn't visited him during his trip to Hollywood, but he didn't know where the man lived.

Cyndi was understandably nervous about the television program that would show Ryan's case, both about the program itself and about people's reactions to it. But everything turned out well. *The UneXplained: A Life in the Movies* aired on April 30, 2011 (on the Biography Channel rather than A&E as originally planned). Cyndi, Kevin, and Ryan all felt that the producers did a great job with it.

Cyndi soon received a telephone call from a Baptist minister, after someone lent him a copy of the program. As it happened, Kevin had previously had conflict with him. Cyndi saw him occasionally because he was the pastor of one of her co-workers, and he had always been pleasant. He called to tell Cyndi not to let anyone keep her from helping Ryan reach his full destiny. He said how inspiring Ryan's story was and how it proved that God could do big things. He told Cyndi he couldn't wait for his wife to get home so she could watch the program, and he planned on showing it at the next Bible study meeting at his church. Cyndi was so stunned that this Baptist minister, who had clashed with her husband, was calling to offer her encouragement about Ryan's past-life story that she could barely speak. Though not everyone Cyndi and Kevin knew was as open-minded, most people's reactions were positive.

While Ryan continues to make spiritual remarks and to have psychic impressions, his talk of Marty Martyn has stopped almost completely. Six months after *The UneXplained* aired,

Cyndi walked in his room one night to find that he had taken down all of his wall decorations, including his iron Eiffel Tower and his pictures of New York. He told her it was time to just be a regular kid. He wanted to know if his dad could paint his room and if they could get him some Oklahoma Sooners bedding and sheets. His parents were thrilled.

Chapter 6

FAMOUS NAMES FROM THE PAST

We occasionally get e-mails or letters from people who think they were famous in their past lives. This typically begins when they feel a connection to a historical figure. They then see things they have in common with that person, such as interests or abilities, or parallels in their lives such as both having absent fathers or attending boarding schools or traveling to other countries. At times, hypnotic regression or a "past-life reading" is involved in identifying the famous individual. Even though many of the people who write us do not claim to have specific memories from their famous past, they have become convinced nonetheless that they were significant historical figures.

Some of these people are leading quite accomplished lives and show no signs of being mentally ill or excessively fantasy prone. Even so, we view such reports with great skepticism. First, there is the matter of statistics. The number of people from the past who were famous is such a small proportion of the overall population that it is unlikely that any given living person was someone famous in the past. It is beyond unlikely that among our correspondents would be five people who were Mary Queen of Scots, five who were Thomas Jefferson, two who were Amelia Earhart, and so on. But as a correspondent once remarked to Ian, if we've all had past lives, *some* of us must have been famous before.

Apart from the statistics, there is the more critical issue of how to tell who someone might have been in a past life. Unless the person has actual memories that can be verified, trying to identify the past life of a present-day individual becomes little more than pure speculation. We have always focused on young children because they are the ones who spontaneously report specific memories of previous lives that can be checked for verification. For famous figures, the young age is important for another reason. The most impressive memories in our cases involve information the children could not have learned through normal means. It would be very difficult for an adult to recall details of a famous figure's life that he or she could not have known before but that could nonetheless be verified as accurate.

The reports about famous past lives almost always come from adults, but there have been occasional exceptions. Ian and two colleagues wrote a paper about seven purported past-life cases that involved deception or self-deception. In one of them, a man in Turkey greatly admired John Kennedy. Just before his son was born in 1965, he had a dream in which President Kennedy came to his house and said he wanted to stay with him. The man then named his newborn son Kenedi, giving it a Turkish spelling. When Ian interviewed the man as his son was turning two years old, the father reported that the boy would say he was President Kennedy when he was asked his name.

Ian was amused by the case but thought no more of it until an associate happened upon it again when Kenedi was nineteen. At that point, his father said that Kenedi had added that he lived in America, was married, had two children, and was rich, facts that were presumably common knowledge every-where. Kenedi himself was convinced at age nineteen that he really had been President Kennedy. Ian, on the other hand, thought the case illustrated how a parent can unintentionally impose an identification of an admired individual onto a child.

I now present two cases in which the previous person was famous, or at least quite well known, in his day. These two have distinct differences from the ones above. They involve very young children whose statements about being a previous indi-vidual were completely unexpected by their parents. Though any claims regarding a famous person may raise certain con-cerns, these two cases also include some intriguing features.

HE CAME FROM HOLLYWOOD TOO

A month after Ryan's mom first wrote me, I received an e-mail from another mother, named Jennifer. She began by saying, "Forgive me for contacting you out of the blue." (No forgive-ness was necessary since I'm always looking for new cases.) She said she had been searching the Internet for days for some-one who might be able to help her.

She thought her son Lee, who was three and a half years old, might be remembering a previous life. She said things had begun about a year before with small incidents such as argu-ments over his middle name and the date of his birthday. From there, he had made other comments. Jennifer said he was grow-ing increasingly angry because she wouldn't take him to his "other house." He was upset because he hadn't been there in a long time and he needed to go to work. Jennifer was worried Lee might try to run away and get there on his own.

She believed she knew the identity of the man whose life Lee was talking about. She was reluctant to give the name, be-cause the man had achieved some amount of fame and success, and the last thing she wanted anyone to think was that she was somehow looking for money.

We soon talked, and six weeks later, I flew out to the family's home to meet them. They live in a small Midwestern town of less than two thousand people that is fortunately only about twenty-five miles from a major airport. I sat down with Lee, his parents, and his fourteen-year-old sister. Jennifer's husband, William, a nonpracticing Catholic, was a truck driver, while Jennifer, a stay-at-home mother of three, including an eighteen-month-old, was somehow finding the time to return to college. She described herself as a nondenominational Christian and as "New Age." She reported a belief in reincarnation, but she felt this belief made her want to be extra cautious about Lee's statements. She had been careful not to ask him leading questions and not to automatically assume he was talking about a past life.

When Lee was about two and a half, he began mentioning his "other mommy." Initially, his parents didn't think much of it. Around that time, he insisted his middle name was Coe and said Coe was his mother's name as well. When his mother said her name was Jennifer, he said that was his daughter's name. For close to a year after that, he continued to insist his middle name was Coe whenever anyone mentioned his full name.

Lee then developed what Jennifer called an "obscene fascination" with Hollywood. He talked about it a lot and about his "other house." He said he had to go to Hollywood to go to work. William thought he might be talking about a past life. One day when Lee was three years and three months old, his family was sitting together and William asked Lee what he did in Hollywood. Lee said he worked on movies. William asked if he acted in movies, and Lee said no, he wrote movies.

Lee's parents began naming movies and asking if he had

written them. They report that when they got to the fifth or sixth one, *Gone with the Wind*, Lee said, "Yes, that was my movie. I wrote that movie." As Jennifer was looking up *Gone with the Wind* on the IMDb Web site, Lee's sister asked him how old he was when he died, and he said forty-eight. Jennifer then saw that the screenplay for *Gone with the Wind* was written by Sidney Coe Howard, who died when he was forty-eight. Lee's parents and his sister all remembered the conversation happening that way.

The idea that Lee had been Sidney Coe Howard in a past life explained other behaviors and statements he had made. As his third birthday was approaching in early June, Lee had insisted that his birthday was June 26, not June 21, which is his actual birthday. Children may want to celebrate their birthdays early, but few would insist their birthdays were later. Sidney Coe Howard was born on June 26, 1891. His mother's maiden name was Coe. His eldest child, his daughter from his first marriage, was named Jennifer.

One day, Jennifer, Lee's mother, asked him to tell her about Hollywood, but he refused. He said something that sounded like "Ohlawn." Jennifer asked what that was, and he said that was where his parents were. She asked him about his parents (whom he called his "other parents"), and he told a story about breaking a wheel on his mother's truck. He then started talking about Hollywood and said something about "Junai" (as Jennifer wrote, June eye? June nine?). When she couldn't figure out what he was trying to say, he got frustrated and stopped talking.

We never did figure out what "Junai" meant, but "Ohlawn" sounds pretty close to Oakland. Howard was born in Oakland, California, and his parents lived there until his father's death in 1915. His mother then moved to Berkeley, California, and eventually to New York City.

Lee would talk about his house in Hollywood and also said he had another house. He once told Jennifer that he had a tractor at his other house but that his people didn't take care of it. This seemed to refer to Howard's death, which was tragic. It happened on his farm in Massachusetts. He was planning to take his tractor, a Cleveland Cletrac crawler-type tractor that was a large piece of heavy machinery, out of the garage to work on a field he had recently purchased to extend his property. A hired hand had accidentally left the tractor in gear, and when Howard turned on the ignition switch and cranked it from the front, it lurched forward, pinning him against the stone foundation of the garage and crushing him.

Lee showed an aversion to anything tight around his upper body from the time he was a toddler. He hated being caught between Jennifer and a piece of furniture and even disliked being hugged tightly. He was also afraid of tractors. He was interested in them and thought they were cool, but he liked to keep his distance. When a neighbor got a new one, Lee didn't want to get close to it and wouldn't get on it even when it was turned off.

Lee also had nightmares, often on a nightly basis, that he usually couldn't describe. Jennifer e-mailed me the day after one of them. She had found him crying during the night, and when she asked him what was wrong, he said, "My arms are broken!" She said they were fine, but he insisted they were broken. When she asked him what happened, he said something that sounded like "cars on my arms." She asked, "A car is on your arms?" He said, "No, cars on my arms!" She asked again, and he yelled "No!" and then began waking up more.

At the end of my meeting with the family, I mentioned yet another television production. Thomas Breinholt, a Danish filmmaker, was working on a multipart series for Danish public television called *Soul and Science*. He interviewed me a week before my trip to see Lee's family. He asked if he could film me as I investigated a case, and I told him I would ask Lee's parents when I met them. When I brought it up with them, I explained that while the series would only be broadcast in Scandinavia, it was certainly possible clips could end up on YouTube or other sites. Lee's father said filming would be fine with him. I had the sense he didn't really care what people thought about him.

Jennifer was more hesitant. She was concerned about any effects that being on television talking about a past life might have on Lee down the line. She didn't mind the family's faces being shown, but she didn't want their names to appear on an Internet search. Afterward, Thomas Breinholt said he would be happy to withhold the family's full names and their location. Reassured, Jennifer agreed to be filmed, and we made plans for another interview. I would meet Thomas at the airport on a Monday morning, and we would go to the family's home for a noon meeting.

This meant I would leave Charlottesville on an early morning flight. Except that I then received a *very* early morning telephone call from the airline with an automated message that my flight had been canceled. When I was able to track down Thomas and tell him the news, he was understandably upset, since a major reason why he had flown over from Denmark was to film my interview with the family. That meant moving to Plan B, which was that Thomas would film the family talking about their experiences without me. Except that William's truck broke down in Missouri, so he wasn't there for the interview either. Even so, Thomas's meeting with the rest of the family went fine, and he seemed pleased with the footage he was able to get. At one point during the day, Lee's sister pulled up a clip of me on YouTube. Lee, who had just turned four, exclaimed, "Why is Dr. Tucker on the computer? He's supposed to be here!"

Thomas asked Jennifer about the possibility of taking Lee to places where Sidney Coe Howard had lived to see what his reactions would be, and she agreed. That meant we needed to do some research. Thomas was able to find some information online about places where Howard had lived and about his children. I then discovered that one of his daughters was living in the tiny Massachusetts village where Howard had died. It was fairly easy to find her address and phone number.

With some trepidation about bothering a seventy-seven-year-old woman with an admittedly unusual request, I wrote to her. I told her about Lee's statements and said I would love the opportunity to review all of them with her to find out how well they matched her father's life. I also wanted to take Lee to places that were meaningful to her father to observe any reactions he might have. I explained how I had found her, apologized for the intrusion, and said I hoped the letter was not disturbing to her and hoped to hear back from her soon.

A few days later, Howard's daughter called. She stated up front that she felt ninety percent skeptical about the situation, but she also seemed intrigued because, as she said, no one knew about her father anymore. She wrote afterward that she was reassured by our conversation. She also supplied personal information about her father that was not available online, such as pets he had as well as people who worked for him. I then sent Jennifer some topics to ask Lee about if she caught him in the mood to talk about Howard.

Howard's daughter was living on the farm where her father had died. She was open to letting us visit, and she mentioned that a summer theater her father had been very connected with was in nearby Stockbridge. I thought a trip to Massachusetts made more sense than taking Lee to Los Angeles. Howard had not actually owned a home in Hollywood, though he had rented particular places when he was there working. In addition, we would have full access to the Massachusetts house. One potential hitch was that Howard's daughter and her family always closed up the farmhouse in the fall and spent winters in New York City, where the weather was better. With it being September at the time, we had a fairly narrow window for a meeting.

We picked out a date, but as we were discussing arrangements, a new issue surfaced. Lee's father, William, was offered a job at the airport nearby. His training would end just before our planned trip, but he didn't know his work schedule after that. We planned a trip but William's schedule kept getting changed so much that we eventually had to cancel it. That was probably for the best because Howard's daughter e-mailed afterward to say a nor'easter hit the day we had planned to arrive, with fierce winds and lashing rains all day. She was open to a visit six months down the line, after cold weather and some renovations on the house were over.

In the intervening months, Lee became more reluctant to talk about Hollywood. Jennifer sensed he was embarrassed if her family asked him about it, as he thought they were making fun of him. Even so, he would often make minor comments to his mother about when he was big, things like, "When I was big, I had a blue shirt like this."

We were eventually able to make the trip to Massachusetts in the spring. At that point, Lee was about to turn five, and his talk about Hollywood had trailed off considerably. I met up with Lee and his parents at the airport, and we drove to the Howard farm on a pleasant Saturday morning. We met Howard's daughter along with her husband and her sister, Howard's youngest, who was only ten months old when he died. All three of them were wonderful—dignified but quite friendly. I don't know what they thought of the whole exercise, but they were respectful of the process and completely forthcoming.

We met at the house. Renovations to the kitchen were still ongoing, though they were largely done and looked beautiful. Howard's daughter showed us the interior of the home, pointing out changes that had been made over the years. Lee showed no reaction to meeting the family or seeing the house. We saw the grounds and then all spent some time talking by the pond. Howard's daughter also took us by nearby sites that Howard had frequented, including the place where he was killed, but again, Lee showed no response.

The family served us a picnic lunch on their large back porch. Afterward, I showed Lee some pictures of people from Howard's life. One was of Howard himself, but the others were pictures of people I thought Lee and his parents would not have stumbled across by accident, such as Howard's first wife, a couple of people he had worked with, and his father-in-law, a conductor named Walter Damrosch. Lee's parents could have helped him cram for the visit, but after meeting them, I didn't doubt their sincerity. Short of fraud, routine explanations would be difficult to come by if Lee recognized the people in the pictures. I didn't show him lineups as I had Ryan but rather just presented him one picture at a time to see if he recognized anyone. He did not.

All in all, the visit was uneventful. Perhaps if we had gotten there six months earlier, things would have been different, though of course we have no way of knowing. We do know that by the time of our trip, Lee was not talking about Hollywood as he had earlier.

If Lee's family is remembering his early comments correctly—that his middle name was Coe, that he wrote *Gone with the Wind*, had a daughter named Jennifer, and died when he was forty-eight—then he showed unusual knowledge about Sidney Howard's life. He talked about some smaller details as well, but Howard's daughter was not able to confirm them. For instance, Lee said he had a red tractor at his other house. Howard had a John Deere that was presumably green, but his daughter did not know the color of the Cleveland Cletrac that killed him. I looked online and found pictures of models made at the time Howard died that were indeed red, but there is no record of the color of his particular tractor. Howard's daughter did say she felt sure his mother had never owned a truck, as Lee had described, but that perhaps there was one that belonged to a gardener.

Since Lee did not give any personal information that could be verified to match Howard's life but that was not readily available online, his case does not provide the level of evidence of a past-life connection that James's and Ryan's do. Even so, in considering his statements as well as his behaviors, I can't dismiss it either. The case as a whole remains somewhat unresolved but intriguing nonetheless.

A GOLF CHANNEL

This next case is most notable for the child's behavior and abilities. I first heard from his father when the boy was three. He reported that his son Hunter had received a set of plastic golf clubs when he turned two. He loved the clubs and played with them incessantly. A few months later, Hunter's father was running through the television channels when he passed the Golf Channel. Neither of Hunter's parents played golf, and his father hadn't even known the family got the Golf Channel. Once Hunter saw it, he told his parents to go back to it. From then on, he had no interest in children's shows and wanted to watch nothing but the Golf Channel. His parents had to limit him to thirty minutes in the morning and again at night.

One day, there was an infomercial about Bobby Jones, a famous golfer in the 1920s whose name is now used by a company that makes golf equipment and accessories. When Hunter saw the program, he told his parents he had been Bobby Jones when he was big. He said this repeatedly, and when someone would ask him what his name was, he would say Bobby Jones. He wanted to be called Bobby and would correct people if they called him Hunter. He would also correct them if they called him Tiger or any other name. He knew of Tiger Woods and other golfers from the Golf Channel, and though he liked them, he was much more passionate about Bobby Jones.

His parents initially laughed about all this. They were both raised Christian. His father had read some about Buddhism, however, and was intrigued by the idea of rebirth. He decided to test Hunter. He showed Hunter pictures of six golfers from the 1920s and asked him which one was Bobby Jones. Hunter pointed at the picture of Bobby Jones and said, "This me." That might not be so surprising, but he then pointed to the picture of another golfer, Harry Vardon. Hunter said, "This, Harry Garden. My friend." Hunter's father printed pictures off the Internet of several houses, including Bobby Jones's childhood home. When he showed them to Hunter, he said, "House, house, house" as he pointed to each picture until he got to

Bobby Jones's home. He suddenly appeared wistful as he said, "Home." His dad thought Hunter had not seen either Harry Vardon or Bobby Jones's childhood home before, and was shocked.

Hunter would take his little golf clubs wherever he went. When he practiced at the beach, he would call it the sand trap. Golfers would see him practicing and comment on what a great swing he had. His parents gave him a set of real golf clubs for Christmas, and he then began taking lessons at a golf club. The usual starting age for lessons was five, but when the staff saw Hunter's swing, they accepted him while he was still two. His instructor called him a golf prodigy. Several older golfers commented that Hunter's swing reminded them of Bobby Jones. Not being a golfer, I'm not in a position to judge any resemblance, but he seemed to show a similar front leg move.

When Hunter was three, his mother was putting him to bed one night as they talked about him being his parents' child. He said, "Just like my child?" When his mother asked him his child's name, Hunter answered, "Bobby Jones. He was my son." Bobby Jones did indeed have a son named after him, Robert Tyre Jones III, and I later found a mention from a *Time* magazine article that referred to the son as "young Bobby" when he was fourteen.

When I got the report from Hunter's father, I quickly asked about visiting the family. His parents were agreeable to a meeting, and we soon worked out a time for me to visit them at their home in sunny Southern California. Hunter's parents were very pleasant and cooperative, and Hunter, a few months past his third birthday, was very cute. I brought along some pictures of Bobby Jones with other golfers, but I wasn't able to get Hunter engaged enough in looking at them to give me any feedback.

We finished out in the yard as I watched Hunter hitting golf balls into a net. Even if the visit didn't produce new information, it was useful in that it gave me the chance to review the history with Hunter's parents and to see that they came across as reasonable, responsible people.

I received an update from Hunter's father a year later. Hunter had said very little in the interim about Bobby Jones or any memories, but he remained obsessed with golf. Not only did he enjoy playing it, he would also spend time at night designing golf courses with his blankets, which he would then show to his parents. His favorite real course was Augusta National, home of the Masters Tournament. Bobby Jones founded the Augusta National Golf Club and helped design the course.

When Hunter was three and a half, a friend of the president of the local GolfTEC, an outfit with numerous centers around the country, saw Hunter playing golf and was impressed. He connected the family to GolfTEC, which let Hunter begin weekly lessons with a PGA Golf pro. They called him a prodigy there and said he had a natural swing. His father emphasized to me that he and his wife weren't pushing Hunter to play golf. They had him in a soccer league, and he enjoyed various activities. But he continued to ask to go to the driving range and to golf courses.

After another year passed, Hunter's father sent me a video of Hunter playing golf. Although I'm not a golfer, even I could tell he was exceptional. It was hard to believe that this smooth swing was coming from a five-year-old.

Hunter is now seven. At last count, he had won forty-one out of fifty junior golf tournaments, including twenty-one in a row. During the week his father wrote me with an update, Hunter had just competed in the six- to-nine-year-old division of a local tournament and won it by ten strokes. He was doing well in other areas, too. As he was completing the first grade, he was reading, writing, and doing math at a third grade level.

Hunter's obsession with golf is reminiscent of James Leininger's obsession with planes. Such behavior is common in our cases. Many of the children show themes in their play that appear connected to the past-life memories they report, most often related to the occupation of the previous person. That doesn't often allow them to show special skill at the occupation; for instance, a toddler like James could hardly show proficiency in flying a plane. In Hunter's case, golf is an area that has allowed him to show exceptional ability.

In nine percent of our cases, the children are said to have unusual skills related to the previous life. This often involves the family's subjective opinion that their child was able to perform an activity better than children would normally be expected to. In Hunter's case, winning twenty-one golf tournaments in a row is more than a subjective opinion. He clearly has unusual ability in golf.

Some people have wondered if the talents that prodigies show come from previous lives. We certainly have little understanding about where they do come from. How does a Mozart come along, composing by age five and performing exhibitions by age six? In his case, his father was a music teacher, but there have presumably been countless music teacher parents who tried to groom their children but didn't produce Mozarts.

I've always resisted ascribing a past life to prodigies, because unless they talk about prior memories, I wouldn't make the leap that this poorly understood phenomenon is due to past lives. Ian likewise never made that claim. When he wrote a paper on abnormalities that are not fully explicable by genetics and/or environmental influences, he did discuss precociously expressed interests and goals that some children have had without an obvious stimulus. His examples included Georg Friedrich Händel the composer and Florence Nightingale, the founder of modern nursing. He noted that as far as he knew, none of the people he listed ever remembered having a previous life, but he argued that the early intensity of their striving toward unusual goals had no explanation in their genetics or early environments. He also pointed out that the children we've studied have sometimes shown unusual aptitudes, but not fully formed skills that geniuses like Mozart manifested as children.

Hunter may be an exception. I suppose the difference between unusual aptitudes and fully formed skills can be in the eye of the beholder, but to say that Hunter showed an unusual aptitude for golf at a young age seems to be an understatement. He has received coaching early on, but only because of the skill he showed before that. While he hasn't accomplished anything comparable to what Mozart did as a child, he seems to be, if not a prodigy, one really good golfer at an early age. And his skills correspond to his very early claims about a past life.

Lee and Hunter both claimed to be well-known figures. Though Sidney Coe Howard is no longer remembered by the general public, Bobby Jones remains a familiar name to many people. That may cause you to doubt Hunter's statements. Both of these cases, however, show little in common with the case of Kenedi, the boy in Turkey. Kenedi's father admired John Kennedy greatly, whereas Hunter's parents had little interest in golf and Lee's parents had never heard of Sidney Coe Howard. Despite my own hesitancy about cases involving well-known figures, I think these two demonstrate that some of them should be taken seriously.

•   •   •

Along with the well-known figures, another characteristic these cases share is that both of the children reporting the memories were boys. This is not surprising, as sixty-two percent of our subjects are male. We have wondered why more boys than girls talk about past lives. Since ninety percent of the children talk about a life as a member of the same sex, another way of considering the question is to ask why more of the past lives involve males. Ian speculated that women's lives on the whole might not have as much variety and excitement—and thus be as memorable—as men's lives in the cultures where he studied cases (he was specifically referring to cases in Burma). This would lead to fewer female lives being remembered. That's a reasonable possibility but not, it turns out, the correct explanation. We no longer have to speculate because now that we have two thousand cases coded and entered into our database, I think we have a definite answer.

In cases in which the cause of death is known, only thirty percent of the previous individuals died by natural causes. Those cases include roughly fifty percent males and fifty percent females, there being slightly more male deaths than female ones (which seems to also be true in the general population).

The other seventy percent of our cases involve unnatural deaths, including murders, suicides, and accidental deaths. (I'll discuss the issue of unnatural deaths more in an upcoming chapter.) It's in those cases where the difference in the sexes shows up. Seventy-three percent of the time, the cases involved males.

Unnatural deaths in the general population show the same pattern. Men are more likely to die an unnatural death than women because they engage more in high-risk behaviors such as driving too fast, getting into drunken knife fights, and so forth. I found statistics for five years of deaths in the United States and checked the male-to-female ratio. I discovered that males accounted for seventy-two percent of the unnatural deaths.

I was quite impressed by how the male/female percentages in our cases match up with those in the general population. If the children are fantasizing about past lives I can think of no reason why this would be the case, why the types of death broken down by gender would have the exact same percentages as the general population. On the other hand, if the children really are recalling past lives, you would expect a random sample of two thousand to have the same percentage of males and females as the total population. We have more males overall because so many of our cases involve unnatural deaths. But within the categories of causes of death, the ratio of males to females matches perfectly with the general population, which I take as further evidence that the children's memories may well be valid.

Chapter 7

IDENTITY UNKNOWN

In our strongest cases, a deceased individual has been found whose life matches the details the child has given. In that situation, we say it is a solved case. We also have a number in which no one has identified one particular person from the past whose life the child appears to be remembering. Those we call unsolved, and they make up almost thirty percent of our collection. With the unsolved ones, we have to consider more the possibility that the children are either experiencing a fantasy or even making up stories intentionally. But I don't think we should dismiss these cases out of hand. Some can be quite compelling. At the very least, they raise the question of what could possibly lead young children to believe they remember the events some of these children report.

A TRAUMATIC WALK DOWN A DUSTY ROAD

I met a woman at a conference a while back who has had a memory of another life since she was a child. Susan, an accomplished clinical psychologist, has told no one about this except her husband. He was accepting, feeling that reincarnation is as likely as anything else, but they take their children to a Protestant church. She does not remember if she even told her mother about the memory, but she knows she told no one else.

Beginning at a very early age, Susan, who is Caucasian, remembers being an African American girl of seven or eight walking down a dirt road. Susan grew up in a mountainous area, but the environment in her memory is different. It is hot, humid, flat, and very dusty; Susan thinks it is probably in the Southeast United States. As she is walking, she looks down at the dry skin of her hands and thinks they look "ashy."

A car comes up, one perhaps from the 1940s, and she is suddenly yanked into it. There are two white men in the car, grown men in their twenties or thirties, the driver and the one who pulled her in. She remembers the bench seat, the lines of the upholstery, the dusty floorboard. There, in the car, she is raped and murdered.

Susan's recall of this was as much a memory for her as anything from her childhood. She also had repetitive dreams about the event. In some of them, she re-experienced it. In others, she observed what happened from above. She didn't think of the dreams as nightmares, but they did wake her up frequently.

Susan also had, and still has, an exaggerated startle response, meaning that a little noise that surprises her can make her jump much more than most people. She doesn't remember being excessively anxious about her safety as a child, but she did worry a lot about her father. He was a surgeon who worked long hours, and Susan would irritate her mother when she delayed dinner by insisting on watching for his car to come down the road, which meant that he was safe. Her mother took her to a counselor at one point for psychotherapy. Susan was quite young and does not remember anything about the treatment. She thinks that perhaps she had told her mother about her memory, leading her mother to take her to the therapist.

Susan knows of no stimulus in her environment that would have caused her to have such a memory. There were African Americans living in her town but no particular racial unrest. It was only later when she was cheerleading that a black friend on the squad told her that when African Americans' skin gets so dry that it looks gray, they call it "ashy."

Susan attended a Methodist church growing up, where she presumably was not taught about past-life memories. Her mother was raised Catholic, though she was open to various ideas about religion. Susan definitely did not learn about past lives from her father. The son of a minister, he said he had gotten his fill of church as a child, and he was resolutely a man of logic and science. When Susan asked him why we are here, he said to reproduce. When she asked what happens when we die, he explained how the body decomposes.

Susan took a philosophy class in high school and did a project on Emanuel Swedenborg, the scientist turned mystic. Though Swedenborg did not believe in reincarnation, his ideas about how people create their afterlife by the way they live their lives here were ones she found quite meaningful. Her subsequent work as a psychologist, however, has been more behaviorally based and completely mainstream. She feels her memories had no negative effects on her as she grew older, causing no impact on her sexual relationships and no ongoing anxiety problems other than the continuation of her exaggerated startle response.

Susan has also experienced migraines all her life. Even though people have told her it's impossible, she remembers seeing the visual phenomena that can precede migraines—flashing lines of light—through the slats of her crib. She has thus maintained some very early memories. Along with those, she has apparently maintained some memories of a past life as well, not some happy fantasy to be sure but rather the mundane details of a horrific event.

Erlendur Haraldsson, a colleague, has suggested that some of these children might be experiencing posttraumatic stress disorder (PTSD). Many do have persistent images of a violent death, and some groups of children Erlendur has studied in Asia showed more symptoms of anxiety and aggression than samples of children without past-life memories. The symptoms, however, were mild, and many of the individual children did not show them.

In general, though I wouldn't say that most of the children have PTSD, many do talk repeatedly about a traumatic memory. Also, in the cases in which the previous person died an unnatural death, over thirty-five percent of the children show an intense fear of the mode of death, the kind of avoidant behavior that is part of the official DSM criteria for PTSD. Susan showed some post-traumatic symptoms. Along with her persistent daytime memories, she had repeated dreams about the traumatic event. She also had some anxiety and an exaggerated startle response, another criterion for PTSD. She may not have had enough difficulties to warrant the full diagnosis, but she did show symptoms of it, just as James Leininger showed post-traumatic symptoms related to a plane crash. There seemed to be no reason for Susan to develop a fantasy that she was raped and murdered as an African American girl in another part of the country, and certainly no reason for her to develop post-traumatic symptoms from it. If the images she experienced were what they seem to be, it was not a fantasy that traumatized her; it was a memory.

In the following two groups of cases, I've corresponded with the parents or subjects but not met them face to face. Though the children involved haven't given details that could lead to a successful search for a previous person, each case has notable facets. The cases serve as examples of what numerous families are experiencing, as we get these kinds of reports all the time. I could choose many other similar ones to present, but these are some that have recently caught my attention.

THE THINGS LITTLE GIRLS SAY

A father from Canada e-mailed me about his daughter. He explained that during his own childhood, he never had any interest in hockey. This was a great source of disappointment to his father, who was quite passionate about it and wanted to share that passion with his son. Because of the difference, the son never felt his father's love, and they never became close.

As an adult, this man not only disliked hockey but resented it, because of the difficulties it had caused him. When he met his future wife, he told her they would get along fine as long as she never talked to him about hockey or wanted to watch a hockey game on television.

They had a daughter named Hannah. They tended to be overprotective parents, and since their work schedules were different—the wife working days while her husband had his own business and worked nights—they never used a sitter until Hannah was nine years old, when her grandmother began to watch her.

Like her parents, Hannah had never expressed any interest

in hockey before a conversation when she was three years old. She asked her father that day why her son didn't come around to take her to hockey games anymore. He asked her when her son had done this, and she said, "You know, Daddy, when I was an old lady." For a couple of months, she asked about her son and seemed frustrated that he wasn't coming around.

Hannah gave details about her son. She said he was skinny and had curly, red hair. Though Hannah's parents were vegetarian and didn't wear leather, she talked about how her son wore a leather coat that, based on where she pointed on her father as she told him about it, was a three-quarter length coat. She said he drove a white car that had some rust on it. She also used the word *arena*, which her father found remarkable, as Hannah had never been to an arena and he thought no one would have had a reason to talk about one around her.

Hannah then stopped talking about her son and hockey games. When her father asked her about those things a few months later, she seemed to have no memory of them.

Even though the child's statements can't be verified in this case, I find it quite striking. What would possess a three-year-old, especially one whose family didn't even like hockey, to imagine she had been an elderly woman wanting her son to take her to hockey games?

The same month that I first heard from Hannah's dad, I received a letter from a father in the Midwest. He reported that when his daughter Chelsea was around three years old, she talked about a friend named Dorn, telling her mother first and a day or two later her father. She said that she and Dorn were playing in a muddy street when some bad men rode up on horses and killed her friend. Some policemen in round hats showed up later to talk about it.

This story was quite unlike the things she normally talked about, in the level of detail as well as the subject matter. Her father noted that the images certainly didn't match any events she had experienced and that she was never left unattended to watch television on her own. When he asked her a question about it a few weeks later, she answered in a way that made him think the memories were in her mind to stay. When he brought it up again after a much longer interval, however, she seemed to have no idea what he was talking about.

Chelsea is a young adult now. Her father says she has no recollection of her story about Dorn and thinks it sounds a bit odd. Though it may, it fits the patterns we see in a lot of our cases. While most of the children describe suffering a traumatic death themselves, some talk of witnessing violence or experiencing nonfatal trauma. Her age fits the typical case, and like most of our subjects, she seemed to forget all about her previous report as she got older.

The next case has a couple of strengths. Not only did the girl's mother keep notes of her statements, she also performed a test that the girl passed.

Olivia is a British girl whose family has lived in various parts of the world. Her mother was raised Catholic but was uninterested in religion as an adult, describing herself as an "agnostic atheist." Olivia seemed to talk about two past lives, but I want to focus on one of them. When Olivia was two years old, she and her mother were out walking when her mother asked Olivia what time she thought it was. Olivia said, "seven o'clock" then added, "1789." Her mother repeated, "1789?" Olivia thought for a minute and said with conviction, "No, 1787."

The following month, Olivia and her parents were riding on a bus when her mother commented that Olivia's furry white hat with ears made her look like a lamb. Olivia began talking about taking all the "fur off a lamb." She said that after taking off the fur, you brush all the dust out of the hair. She added that this was very important.

While still two years old, Olivia came to her mother one day and told her quite matter-of-factly that her name used to be Daisy. Some time later, she approached her mother again and out of the blue said, "Robinson." Her mother asked what that meant, and Olivia said, "It's a name." Her mother asked her whose name, and Olivia replied, "It was *my* name." She told her mother that she used to be Daisy Robinson.

Olivia talked about past events a number of times when she was two and a half. Her father began to wonder if she was remembering a past life, but when he would ask her, "Have you got another mummy and daddy?" she always looked puzzled and said no. When he asked her one time if she *used to* have a different mummy and daddy, she became excited and said yes. Her parents asked about any brothers or sisters, and she said she didn't have any. They mentioned the sheep shearing and asked what she used to make. She answered, "blankets," which her mother found striking since Olivia had seen sheep skin rugs before but never a woolen blanket.

Olivia came up to her mother one day as she was doing housework. Olivia told her, "All the air came out of here." Her mother didn't know what she was talking about and asked, "Out of where?" Olivia pointed to the middle of her body and said, "Here. And I died. But I don't like talking about it." She looked sad and turned around and left the room. Her mother was stunned by this. Olivia had had no contact with death, other than seeing a dead frog once that her parents hadn't even told her was dead.

One day after waking up from a nap, Olivia was sitting up

on her cot and began telling her mother again about 1787. Her mother asked if she had known any songs back then, and Olivia immediately said, "London Bridge Is Falling Down," which was a favorite of hers. It turns out that "London Bridge Is Falling Down" was in fact around in 1787. The words of an early version appeared in *Tommy Thumb's Pretty Song Book* around 1744, and it may well be much older than that. The dance "London Bridge" was mentioned in a 1659 play, and "London Bridge Is Broken Down" was associated with children in a 1725 publication and mentioned in a London opera in 1730.

Another time, Olivia approached her mother and out of the blue said, "Thirty years old." When her mother asked who was thirty years old, she said, "I was. When I died. I died because I didn't eat anything." She then wandered away. After her mother got over the shock of what her two-and-a-half-year-old had just said, she began thinking that the voracious appetite Olivia had shown from the time she was a newborn could be explained by starvation she had experienced in a previous life.

Olivia was eating a green apple one day when she began giggling to herself. She told her mother that Daisy Robinson had only eaten red apples but that she only liked green apples now. This seemed funny to her. Another time, she said that Daisy Robinson's mother had been named Kitty. Olivia didn't know anyone named Kitty, and her mother felt sure she had never heard the name used for a person before.

Olivia's talk about past lives then stopped for a long time. Her mother thought she had forgotten about them until a conversation after the family's dog died. Olivia was four at that point, and her comments were interesting enough that her mother grabbed a pen and paper and made notes as she talked. Olivia wondered if the dog would come back as another dog and said she thought it would because she had had past lives herself. But she didn't think their dog was a new doggy yet because, she said, "you spend a bit of time dead first, like a few weeks or a few months or something."

Her mom asked if that happened to her, and Olivia said yes. When her mother asked where she was after she died, she said she didn't exist. She said that it was hard to explain but that she went into thin air. She went up into the sky and broke up into bits of dust. The dust then floated all over the place. She said dying wasn't scary, and when she was dust, other people made friends with her. They were dust as well. Her mother asked if she was scared of dying now. Olivia said no, she wasn't scared, but the thought of dying did make her sad because she liked being on Earth. Olivia was extremely serious throughout the conversation. In fact, her mother said Olivia had such a serious look in her eyes that it made her uncomfortable.

Olivia then seemed to move on, and her mother didn't hear about past lives again until one day when Olivia was five years and nine months old. Olivia began a conversation by asking her mother if it was silly to believe in something if there isn't any proof. They discussed that question, with her mom using the belief in God as an example of something that some people can't believe without proof while others do so easily.

Olivia then said that when she was Daisy, she believed in God and she went to church. Her mother wondered why she used to believe in God but didn't now. Olivia said that was because she was a different person now. Her mother told her she thought that Olivia might have the same personality that Daisy had, but Olivia said no, the personality was gone but the person was still there. Her mom asked if she meant that a "person" and a "personality" are two different things, and Olivia said yes.

As they talked about Daisy's life, Olivia said she lived in a little town. She didn't remember the name of it but did remember it was in England. She said most people lived in little villages where everybody knew each other. She said there were a few shops, and you could buy bread, cheese, and meat. Her mother, with a straight face, asked her if there was a McDonald's in the town. Olivia laughed and said it wasn't invented yet. She said they didn't even have cars, only horses. Olivia then said she remembered the money they used had the king on it. She said the coins were bumpy on the edges and very flat.

Olivia's mother investigated English coins from 1787, the year Olivia had previously given for Daisy. They all had the picture of King George III on them. They had serrated edges and were flatter than the modern-day £2 coin. She decided to show Olivia pictures of various coins, fifty-two in all, that ranged from ancient Celtic and Roman coins all the way to modern-day ones. She asked Olivia if any of them were familiar to her. Olivia looked through them all, quickly dismissing ancient hammered ones as well as modern-day coins. When she saw a page of milled coins, machine-made as all English coins have been since the 1600s, she pointed to the dots around the edges of one of them and said that was what she meant when she said the coins were bumpy.

Olivia then pointed to a 1787 George III shilling and said she definitely recognized the coin and the picture of the king on it. She pointed to three other coins she said she remembered. All of them were George III coins: a spade guinea from 1793, a Somerset Bristol halfpenny token from 1793, and a farthing from 1799 that she said was vaguely familiar.

Olivia's mother once told her she thought her past lives must be some kind of game she was playing. Olivia became upset and vehemently denied it. When her mother saw her engaging in role-play make-believe another time, she asked Olivia if it was only a game, and Olivia said yes. Her mother noted how different the two activities were: how she could identify elements from a favorite movie or book or play in the role-play but not in the past-life talk; how the details changed frequently, sometimes in seconds, in the role-play but never in the past-life talk, even over months and years. She knew Olivia believed her memories were real, and after a while, she struggled to find any reason to doubt her.

IN DREAMS

I tend to be leery of claims that someone's dreams are events from a past life. Dreams are complex things, often puzzling and frequently nonsensical. Some of the cases I've described have included dreams, of course, but they also involved waking statements as well. If a case only involves dreams, I don't tend to make too much of it. Occasionally, however, we get reports that impress me.

One came from a man who reported that he had the same dream over and over from age three to around age seven. It involved being a little boy playing at the seashore where there were crowds of people. In the dream, the ocean began to recede, and as it did, he could see fish flopping on the wet sand where the ocean had been moments before. He and others began wandering out onto the wet sand, amazed that the ocean had pulled back for what appeared to be miles.

He continued to walk farther and farther out, picking up giant shells, some of which still had living creatures wiggling inside. He then began hearing screams, lots of screams, coming from men, women, and children who were running back toward the beach. He looked up and saw the ocean, which was still far away but now appeared as a giant wall of water. It was rushing forward as people frantically tried to escape it. He remembered seeing it over his shoulder as it got closer and closer until it finally loomed over him and crashed down on him. He would drown in the dream and then wake up in his bed.

For a long time, the man didn't make much of the dream. His family often went to the beach when he was growing up, and though the dreams were terrifying, he had no fear of the ocean. When he was around the age of twenty-five, he was shocked to learn that the ocean really can recede, as it does before a tsunami. It was only then, as he wondered how he could have possibly known about a receding ocean as a three-year-old in the early 1950s, that he began to view the events he experienced not only as a dream but also as memories from a previous life.

Another man recently emailed me with similar dream experiences. Like the previous one, he repeatedly had the dream when he was a little boy, dreaming the identical scene dozens of times until he was five or six years old. It was always exactly the same, and he reported that even now in his fifties, he can still remember the details vividly.

In the dream, he appears to be storming the beach with a group of soldiers or warriors. They are in waist-deep water moving toward the shore, where there is a large stone wall or fortress. People are on top of the wall shooting arrows at the incoming force. He remembers seeing the arrows moving like dark sticks against the light blue sky. One is then speeding toward him and hits him in the chest. It knocks him backward, and the next thing he remembers is being dragged onto the beach by two other men. He can see the end of the arrow sticking out of his chest as one of the men attempts to pull it out. There is chaos around him as he slowly fades away. He remembers seeing the blue sky with small, white clouds, until his vision closes in and the world goes dark.

The man had sensed as a child that he was big in the dream. He feels he was bigger then than he is now as an adult. He also reports that even though the dream was entirely from a first-person point of view, he can picture the face of the man in it, one with long, reddish hair and a beard. The image reminds him of a Viking warrior, and he is convinced that he remembered his death from a previous life.

A FIRE ON C STREET

With this last case, I did meet the girl and her parents. Even though I wasn't able to verify that she was remembering the life of a particular individual, some of the things she said and did were definitely out of the ordinary.

My first contact with the family was an e-mail from the girl's mother, Kathleen. At the time, Nicole was twenty-two months old. Her first unusual behavior had been at thirteen months of age when her parents placed her on a horse. She grabbed the saddle horn with her left hand and the reins with her right, sat upright, and began kicking. Her parents didn't own horses and knew little about them. At seventeen months of age, Nicole began making the clicking sound in her throat that riders often do to get their horses to walk. At twenty-two months, she verbalized a series of equestrian commands that she could not have learned from her parents.

Kathleen, while confessing she was hesitant to mention it since I was a psychiatrist, also noted that Nicole often had conversations with people who weren't there. After I wrote back and assured her that I didn't think such behavior in a twenty-two-month-old indicated a psychiatric disturbance, she shared more.

Kathleen's brother Mike had died about six months before. For the last twenty-five years of his life, he had been wheelchair bound after being hit by a train and losing his legs. Kathleen, the only person to ever call him Mikey, saw him very little during the twenty years before his death.

Nicole has two mothers, Kathleen and her partner Lynn. A few weeks before Kathleen first contacted me, Nicole was at the breakfast table one morning when Lynn noticed her staring outside. Lynn asked her what she saw, and Nicole began yelling something Lynn couldn't make out. Lynn said she didn't understand and asked again what Nicole saw. Nicole started yelling, "Mikey, Mikey, Mikey!" Lynn asked if Nicole saw Uncle Mikey and asked where he was. Nicole yelled, "Right dere, outside." Lynn could see that no one was outside and asked again where Mikey was. Nicole responded, "Right dere, in chair."

A couple of weeks later, Nicole was recounting her day's events with her parents, and she again talked about seeing Mikey outside in his chair. This unnerved her parents, and Kathleen wrote to me a few days later. She said she and Lynn wanted to be careful not to lead Nicole to make up things while at the same time encouraging her to feel safe sharing any experiences she was having.

Nicole mentioned Mike several more times, saying he was in a chair. She had never met him, so Kathleen showed her a few photographs of him. Nicole showed no signs at all of recognizing him. If she was seeing visions of him, he looked different in some way than he did in the pictures.

I didn't hear from Kathleen for a while, until soon after Nicole's third birthday. She reported that Nicole had stopped talking about Mike. When Kathleen had asked her a few months before if she saw Mike anymore, she said no, but that she still remembered him. Kathleen asked what she remembered, and she said solemnly, "I remember the train." Kathleen had never talked to Nicole about the accident, and when she asked what she remembered about the train, Nicole said the sound of the wheels on the track. Kathleen was struck by this because Mike had described that sound as one of his last recollections before being hit. He said he was haunted by it. Kathleen noted that Nicole had never liked trains from infancy on. When she was a year or so old, her parents had to remove her from a room after she began wailing at the sounds that a model train was making.

While Nicole's talk about Mike receded, she began talking more about a time when she lived on C Street (or perhaps, Sea or even Seay Street). Her first comments began before she was two years old and then increased over time. She said the house on C Street was in an area that was sunny, not like the Pacific Northwest where her family lived. She said she lived there with her father, her sisters, and her best friend, a man. She had been the middle of three sisters, with the youngest being named Jackie. At one point, she described her father dancing in a suit at a wedding. She also said her father cut the branches off of trees and cut down the big old trees and made them float in the water. She talked repeatedly about the house on C Street burning down. Kathleen noted that Nicole seemed to go back and forth between memories and make-believe, but both Kathleen and Lynn could tell a difference when she would switch to make-believe. Her voice would change, and she would begin to give fanciful names for people, like Kuka and Lala and Hoopty.

I asked Kathleen if the family would be open to a visit from me to learn more about what Nicole was saying. She and Lynn considered it for a while and then agreed. They asked

Nicole if she wanted to speak to me. She said, "Yes, but I will be a little shy of him." They told her she didn't have to talk to me if she didn't want to, and she then became emphatic, saying, "No, no, I want to talk to him. I will *not* be shy!" And she was right. Kathleen was concerned Nicole might become oppositional and not talk to me, but she needn't have worried. Nicole proved to be quite engaging, though she didn't share any new information about C Street with me.

I met the three of them in their home. At that point, Nicole was thirty-nine months old. Her parents talked about how she would often say she just wanted to go home. They would tell her she was home, and she would say, "Oh yeah, I am home." At times, she would appear very sad talking about people from C Street and had recently asked if her parents could take her to her "little house on C Street." She said the top of it was kind of orange and that it was right down the street from a church.

Nicole would talk about these things at various times, sometimes after waking up from a nap. She had also dreamed about something happening to her sisters from C Street. She spoke a lot about the fire there. She said she didn't die in it. She would make the sound of a fire and said how the backyard was all that was left afterward.

She once said that when she was twenty-eight, she had gotten covered in dirt and got in the water. She then rowed her dinghy across the water and landed in some trees but didn't get hurt (or "didn't have any owies" as she put it). Kathleen asked if she had said "thingy," and Nicole answered, "No, Momma, dinghy! It's a little boat!"

We had a very pleasant visit. The next day, the family was riding in their car when Nicole said she couldn't find her picture book. Kathleen asked what picture book, and Nicole said her picture album. Kathleen said the picture album she had made for Nicole was in her room, but Nicole said no, the picture album from her house on C Street, it got all burned up in the fire. She talked about a burnt picture album with the edges curled.

The impression that emerged was that Nicole seemed to be describing a life in which she had experienced a traumatic fire, probably when she was a child. She had survived the fire and lived to be an adult. In fact, she had talked of being a doctor.

If Nicole was remembering a past life, the big question was where C Street was. An online search reveals numerous towns with C Streets or Sea Streets or Seay Streets. In particular, it shows that C Street in Virginia City, Nevada, was destroyed along with most of the town in a large fire in 1875. I found an account of the fire that listed the buildings destroyed on C Street. Though they appear to have been primarily commercial, there were several lodging houses lost, and the list concludes with "and many other buildings."

Kathleen contacted a historian to learn more about the town. She asked about timber work and bodies of water, since Nicole had mentioned those. The answers were inconclusive. The historian reported that the hills there had been covered with ponderosa pine and cedar at one point, but all of it was clear cut. Wood was brought from Tahoe to run a gold mill, brought partially by flume, man-made canals that logs were floated down. There are lakes nearby, but no significant ones in the immediate area.

Virginia City was certainly a possibility. The problem was that we didn't know if Nicole was describing a great conflagration like the one there or a simple house fire. For instance, I found a news story about a wildfire that destroyed one house on C Street in Martinez, California, in 2004. Since there might have been numerous other fires of this sort, I decided that rather than taking Nicole to Virginia City to see if she recognized any buildings still there from the 1800s, I would wait to see if she came out with more information identifying a specific town. But she never did.

I heard from Kathleen intermittently over the next few months. As Nicole was nearing her fourth birthday, she said one day that remembering her C Street family took a lot out of her. A week or so later, she appeared sad, almost despondent, and said, "Maybe I never had a C Street family. Maybe I just made them all up." Her C Street family may have been her imagination—there is no way of knowing with certainty since I wasn't able to find a family that matched her statements—but she may also have been voicing confusion because her memories didn't fit with her increasing awareness of how life appears to go. She had begun to feel perhaps that since she couldn't have had a family previously, what she thought she remembered must not have happened. Kathleen and Lynn were sad that with Nicole's memories fading, she seemed to be disconnecting from the spiritual realm she had access to before.

The disconnection, however, was not complete, as Nicole occasionally talked about C Street for some time. When she was five, she rarely mentioned it, but if her parents asked if it was real, she would emphatically respond, "Is real! C Street is still there!" She maintained that there was a fire but that she didn't die in it, and she would mention images from time to time, most often involving her father, the church nearby, and incidents with water and logging. She also gave little snippets about her life after the fire.

When Nicole was five and a half, the family visited a small gallery in another town. Nicole noticed a handcrafted black box with a Victrola speaker horn on top. She stopped suddenly and said, "Oh my gosh, I haven't seen one of these in years!" Kathleen asked if she knew what it was, and Nicole said, "Yes, Momma, it's a record player." Kathleen asked where she might have seen one, and Nicole answered, "C Street. We had one in the '30s." For the next twenty minutes, she was humming songs that she said she recalled hearing on her record player. Her parents were impressed by how pretty the tunes were, as well as by the sophistication of Nicole's humming. Several times, her voice got a tremolo, a trembling effect, in it. A couple of days later, Nicole said she used to go to sleep listening to music on that old record player.

Though I'm not sure of Nicole's timing when she said she had a record player like that in the '30s, as I gather phonographs with horn speakers were passé by then, the incident as a whole is impressive. Nicole's startled recognition upon seeing the phonograph, followed by her becoming engrossed in music she felt was from long ago, suggests to me that she was connecting with some kind of memory.

A month later, she talked about getting from C Street to her current life. She said she was just walking on C Street and then was in another world, where there was something blocking her and she couldn't get through. She was then suddenly in her mother's tummy. Nicole said, "I was like, 'This is weird, I'm little and I'm going to get born again. I'm a baby. This is so weird.'" She talked about feeling very small in the womb, and how it was dark and odd there.

When Nicole was six, she told Kathleen, "Mom, you know when I came out of your tummy, this life turned out to be way more fun and laughter than I was expecting."

When Nicole was seven, she was getting in the car to go to school one day when she stopped, closed her eyes, and tilted her head back. "I feel there's an earthquake coming," she said. She said it wouldn't be in her state (in the Pacific Northwest) but very close. Kathleen told some colleagues at work about it. That evening, Nicole was puzzled that there hadn't been an earthquake. The next day, one of Kathleen's co-workers came running up and asked if she had heard about the 6.0 earthquake that hit off the Oregon coast the night before.

Such incidents suggest that Nicole, like Ryan in chapter 5, has some psychic abilities, again raising the question of where her past-life images came from. Were they actual memories, or were they material Nicole saw psychically? And more important, could psychic abilities explain all apparent past-life memories? Since I reviewed this issue in my first book, I won't go through the whole discussion again, except to point out that most of the children in our cases do not show any psychic abilities. At last count, only twenty-six percent of the families have said the children displayed any ESP other than their past-life memories, with nearly three quarters of those showing just a slight amount. If the past-life memories are examples of psychic abilities, those abilities are for the most part oddly limited to the memories and perspective of one specific deceased individual.

A FIRE ON C STREET, PART II

I sent the above write-up to Kathleen to check for any errors in my telling. She wrote back that Nicole, now seven, picked up the printout of the story and began reading out loud. When she read "A Fire on C Street," she yelled, "Yeah, that's how it was spelled!" She made little comments as the family read it but none that seemed heartfelt until they came to the mention of Virginia City, Nevada. Nicole grabbed the paper and said, "Let me see that. Where did you say that was?" Kathleen answered

Nevada. Nicole repeated "Nevada" and then started yelling, "Nevada, that's it! That's it! It's Nevada! We have to go to Nevada!" Kathleen tried to put her off, but Nicole persisted, saying, "Mom, that's it, that's it!"

I was surprised by Nicole's reaction, because she wasn't really talking about C Street anymore. Given her positive response to Nevada, I suggested we go to Virginia City to check it out. It would be expensive, with four of us flying there, but a generous donation we had received a few months before meant we had the funds to undertake the trip.

Kathleen responded hesitantly but said that if it might be beneficial to Nicole to go at some point, she would welcome the opportunity. I told her that if we were going to go, we should do so before Nicole got any older since the memories in these children usually fade. We also discussed the potential effects of a trip on Nicole, both positive and negative. When the family talked about it, both Kathleen and Lynn were unsure, but Nicole was emphatic about going. She told Kathleen, "Mom, what are you guys afraid of? What do you think might happen?" Kathleen told her she was afraid that C Street wouldn't be as she remembered it. Nicole said she understood that was possible but kept repeating that she needed to go.

And so we went to Virginia City. We were corresponding over the summer, and though it made sense to go before Nicole started back to school, August is not necessarily the most pleasant time to visit Nevada. The trip did not result in any definitive discoveries but did have some interesting parts.

I met Nicole and her mothers at the Reno airport. Our flights were supposed to arrive at the same time. As my connecting flight was rolling down the runway, however, an alarm went off in the cockpit because of a mechanical problem. After a long delay to determine if the issue could be resolved, the airline eventually found another plane for us, and we finally flew to Reno. This made me hours late to meet Nicole and her parents, who were stuck at the airport waiting for me. Nicole and Kathleen put the time to good use by taking a long nap, and they were all understanding about the delay.

I hadn't seen Nicole for four years, since she was three years old, and yet she seemed to remember me. After a brief initial period of shyness, she was very friendly and outgoing. We got the rental car and then took quite a winding road to Virginia City. As we rode on the asphalt surface, Nicole at one point said, "They didn't have these black roads when I lived here before." Because of the flight delay, it was near the end of the day by the time we got to Virginia City, and since we had the whole next day to explore, we just had dinner and called it a day. The inn where we stayed was made up of three different buildings, at least one of which was built before the fire in 1875, but Nicole showed no particular reaction to it.

The next morning, it was time to explore. We had explained to Nicole that we were trying to determine if Virginia City was the place she remembered, but that since the fire was a long time ago, things would look different now than they did back then. Virginia City had been a boomtown in the late 1800s because of mining. It began with mining for gold. After workers complained of all the blue mud that would stick to their shovels, some of which was used to pave streets, someone figured out that the blue was due to silver. Silver mining then became a huge operation there. Those days are long gone now, and the city has a population of under a thousand people. It's still a tourist attraction, though, and some people remember it as the town the Cartwrights frequented on the *Bonanza* television show.

It turns out that C Street is the center of activity in Virginia City and always has been. We learned that there were some small houses and some boarding houses there before the fire, but it was also the major commercial street. We started at the visitor center, which was located on C Street. Nicole had talked a lot about a church that was near her house. There was the Presbyterian church on C Street that had been the one church in town left undamaged by the fire. It was a few blocks from the visitor center, so we walked down to it. I saw no way to disguise what we were doing, so I simply asked Nicole if this was the church she remembered. She said it was not; the church she remembered was more pointed at the top. Being right in front of the church, the top of it was hard to see from her vantage point. We walked across the street so we could see it better. It had a small steeple at the top, and from the new angle Nicole said, not very convincingly, that it might be the one she remembered.

Nicole had also said the church was on a corner, which this one was not. I soon noticed another church that was just off of C Street. It was a large, more ornate Catholic church that had a sizable steeple. As we approached it on a town tour, Nicole said, "They did a good job of repairing it. It looks almost like it did before." After the tour, we walked back to the church. Nicole had told her parents that her father got married in a church that took up a whole block. This church was indeed that large. She had described her father in a black suit, dancing at a wedding, and her parents had the sense she was talking about the wedding when he married her stepmother.

We went inside the church and its impressive sanctuary. We learned that the wooden interior had been destroyed in the fire but that the exterior walls were the original ones from

1868. Nicole had mentioned a church near her home a number of times. She had said it was on a corner and that it hadn't burned down in the fire. It wasn't clear if those descriptions were of the same church where her father was married, but this church could fit all the details. Nicole didn't show any obvious reaction to it. Inside, I asked her if this was the one she remembered, but she didn't respond. Throughout the visit, in fact, she was reluctant to discuss any memories, particularly with her parents.

We went to a museum to learn more about the town's history. We found out that when the mines were being created, special wood frames were designed for the tunnel interiors to keep them from collapsing. This led to a tremendous need for timber, but there were no forests right by Virginia City. As a result, lumber mills were built where the forests were, and the lumber was transported from the mills to the mines. Water pathways or flume were constructed on which the wood could be floated to the city. The longest flume was nearly twenty-five miles in length, and by 1879, there were eighty miles of flume in the Sierra. That year, more than thirty-three million feet of lumber were transported by flume. At the museum, we saw pictures of a lumber mill and a large flume. Nicole's talk about her father floating trees in water thus fit for Virginia City, much more than it would for most places. It was an odd detail, but one appropriate for that area.

Another detail that fit for Virginia City involved horses. Nicole had talked about horses that would walk through town and into her yard. She said that boys would chase them and try to jump on them to ride them. That sounded like nonsense to Kathleen and she dismissed it. We learned in Virginia City that wild horses had been in the area for a long time and are there to this day. In fact, we saw one walking through town.

One detail Nicole had given that I had largely dismissed was a name she pronounced O'Manny. That sounded made up to me, but Nicole said that a friend who lived next to her had that name. Kathleen discovered online that the Irish surname O'Mahony is pronounced O'Manny. (I also learned later that a reality television personality had the name Ommanney, as did Admiral Erasmus Ommanney in the British Royal Navy.) There was a large Irish population in Virginia City, which also fit with a comment Nicole had made when she was younger. She said her sister had taught her how to put on makeup and had also taught her how to hooley dance. Kathleen didn't know what a hooley dance was (and neither did I), but *hooley* is an Irish word that the *OED* defines as "a noisy party." Another source describes it as an evening of traditional music and dance.

Kathleen and I decided to check out the Irish cemetery for any O'Mahonys. I initially suggested taking Nicole to the cemeteries to see if any names were familiar to her. She wanted no part of that, and once Kathleen and I visited the Irish one, I was glad Nicole wasn't with us. In the ninety-five-degree Nevada heat, we had a long walk past various cemeteries just to get to the Irish section. Once there, we discovered a sprawling collection of graves on uneven ground, some that were hard to get to and some that appeared completely untended. We did not see any O'Mahonys, and after a long, hot search, we were both happy to make it back to the car more or less intact.

Throughout the trip, Nicole was an engaging, happy seven-year-old. She didn't appear to have any emotional reactions to the sights we saw, though admittedly many things looked different that they did over a hundred years ago. We did not find definite evidence that Virginia City was the place of her memories. It was consistent with her statements in a fairly striking way at times, but I couldn't be one hundred percent sure it was the right place. Nicole had no such doubts. Her one show of emotion came at the end of the trip. Kathleen related to me that as the family's plane was lifting off from the Reno airport, Nicole suddenly burst into tears. She said, "I don't want to leave here. This was more than just a trip." Kathleen asked if she really thought Virginia City was her home before, and Nicole responded, "No, I *know* it was."

Though none of the cases in this chapter conclude with an identification of the previous person, they are good examples of this phenomenon. It is not just some strange thing that happens in faraway places—these cases have occurred in typical American families, most of whom say they had no belief in past lives before the children started reporting their memories. And these are just the tip of the iceberg, as we've heard from scores of other families reporting similar events. Families may not tell many people about them, but they are happening nonetheless.

When I was in private practice, I once treated a boy for attention-deficit/hyperactivity disorder. I later learned that his family had previously contacted Ian because the boy was talking about a past life. They hadn't told me, his treating psychiatrist, about it, so I'm sure they kept it from a lot of people. The parents in some cases haven't even told the child's grandparents about the statements because in our culture, they can sound pretty weird. So even if you never hear about it, your neighbors or co-workers or distant family members may have a child who talks about a past life. That doesn't mean the child has given details that can be traced to one deceased individual. But after hearing story after story after story, I've become convinced that we should take such reports seriously.

Chapter 8

MIND OVER MATTER

After studying the cases I have and reviewing the notes of Ian's investigations, I have concluded that some young children do appear to possess memories and emotions that come from a deceased individual. How does a reasonable person make sense of this? Something extraordinary seems to be going on, but how can an idea like past lives mesh with the world of science and all that we have learned through the scientific method?

The answer lies in being aware that science involves more than just scientific materialism, the concept that the world consists entirely of physical matter. On the basis of materialism, most mainstream scientists would dismiss the cases out of hand because they say that no part of us can continue after our bodies die. As I've learned more about scientific knowledge as it exists today, however, I have discovered that the picture is actually much more complex.

Findings in physics over the last hundred years—particularly in quantum physics or quantum mechanics, the study of the universe's smallest particles—have shown that the physical universe is much more complicated than it appears. They strengthen my view that there is a consciousness that exists separate from the material world. I now believe that the physical grows out of the mental, meaning that the physical world is created out of something you can think of as Mind or consciousness or the spiritual. Our cases, and the possibility of children remembering past lives, then fit in nicely with a new understanding of existence.

Materialism—the belief that physical matter is all there is—has become practically synonymous with modern science, and it is unquestioned by many, though certainly not all, scientists. It relegates religion to antiquated folk belief and consciousness to purely a product of a physical brain. Any consideration of the nonphysical is akin to a belief in fairies or leprechauns.

Modern science was not always so certain of materialism. Isaac Newton, one of its founders, wrote numerous religious tracts. Alfred Russel Wallace, the co-discoverer of the theory of natural selection with Charles Darwin, was impressed by séances he attended and publicly advocated spiritualism. Many other scientists open to religious or spiritual ideas could be mentioned as well. The point is that the worldview currently presented by mainstream science that the physical universe is all there is conflicts with views that many esteemed scientists have held.

Such views continue to be held quietly by a minority of scientists today. A recent study found that a quarter of scientists from top research universities regarded themselves as spiritual, which many viewed as separate from religious. Even twenty percent of the atheist scientists considered themselves "spiritual atheists." Many of the scientists in various fields who are religious tend to keep their faith—or in some cases, their other anomalous beliefs—separate from their scientific outlooks, and private as well. There are exceptions. Francis

S. Collins, the geneticist who served as director of the Human Genome Project and is currently the director of the National Institutes of Health, wrote a book entitled *The Language of God: A Scientist Presents Evidence for Belief,* pushing for harmony between science and religious faith. Brian Josephson, a Nobel laureate physicist, created a controversy when his contribution to a booklet accompanying a set of stamps that commemorated the one hundredth anniversary of the Nobel Prizes included a statement about developments that "may lead to an explanation of processes still not understood within conventional science, such as telepathy."

What most mainstream scientists seem unaware of, or at most only vaguely aware of, is that the most fundamental findings of physics have now disproven materialism. Valuing a special place for consciousness or spirituality can be incorporated into an overall understanding that includes the insights gained through science. Work in quantum mechanics has undermined many of the basics of what we thought we knew.

When the findings of Newton and others in classical physics explained so many of the world's happenings so well, it was logical to conclude that they were all that was needed to understand everything in the world, from the smallest particle to the largest galaxy. Then came relativity and, with perhaps even more paradigm-shattering effect, quantum mechanics. As Henry Stapp, a physicist at the Lawrence Berkeley National Laboratory, has said, "We have known for almost a century that this theoretical creation of the human mind called 'classical physics' is a fiction of our imagination." Classical physics is a close approximation of reality, in most cases one of such remarkable accuracy that it is sufficient for all practical purposes. But while classical physics works most of the time, the inferences that we draw from it may not be correct. And in fact you will see that one of these—materialism—has now been shown to be wrong.

The universe gives the appearance that it sprang into existence approximately 13.8 billion years ago. According to the Big Bang theory, all matter and energy present in the universe today began then as a single point. They expanded with the Big Bang to create the still expanding universe of today. After 300,000 years or so, hydrogen and helium molecules began to form. Another 300,000 years later, clumps of matter formed and began coalescing into galaxies. Our sun was formed around 4.5 billion years ago, and the planets followed after that.

By appearances, eukaryotic cell organisms developed one and a half to two billion years ago, followed by multicellular life. More complex organisms developed, leading eventually to the variety of plants and animals present today. Humans were the accidental result of natural selection. As their brains evolved, their frontal lobes grew and produced the experience of consciousness. As conscious observers, humans were eventually able to examine the world and learn how it came into existence.

I now believe this story is seriously incomplete. Consciousness is not merely an incidental byproduct of evolution. The logical conclusion from various findings in physics is that consciousness actually creates the universe. And its creative process continues to occur in every instant. As Max Planck, a founder of quantum theory, said, "I regard consciousness as fundamental. I regard matter as derivative from consciousness. We cannot get behind consciousness."

Work in quantum mechanics has revealed what is known as the measurement problem. This unassuming name describes a challenge that shakes our understanding of the world to its core. Quantum theory says that particles on the small quantum scale exist less as solid objects and more as probability waves. Only when an object is measured, it seems, does its probability wave collapse to produce one outcome.

Being aware of the critical role that measurement—or more to the point, observation—plays can lead to new understandings about the true nature of the world, ones that are both more wondrous and more accurate than the previous mechanistic view of the universe. To get to those, I need to take a detour into the world of physics, which I now believe provides crucial insights about the spiritual realm and the ultimate nature of reality. Despite any rough terrain along the way, you'll see that the destination is worth the trip.

TURNING THE PROBABLE INTO THE ACTUAL

There is a frequently cited work in physics called the double-slit experiment, which I touched on briefly in my first book. In the experiment, you have a light source, along with a photographic plate that records the light that's emitted. Between them, you place a screen that blocks the light. If you cut a slit in the screen for the light to pass through, then a fuzzy image is created on the photographic plate that corresponds to the location of the slit.

What happens if you cut a second slit in the screen? You might think you would get two fuzzy images, matching the two slits, but you don't. Instead, the light appears to pass through the slits as waves, producing an interference pattern on the photographic plate, of alternating light and dark bands. An analogy would be the waves you get if you throw two large objects into a lake. Where waves from the objects collide, you get a large peak in the water, whereas two troughs combine to produce a deeper depression, and a wave from one and a trough from the other cancel each other out. It's not water waves in the double-slit experiment, but light waves seem to come out of the slits and interfere with each other, producing this pattern of light and dark bands.

Light sometimes acts as if it's made up of particles called photons, and other times it acts like waves. But here's the thing about the double-slit experiment: when you turn down the light source so low that the light goes through the screen one photon at a time, guess what happens? Somehow, you still get the interference pattern. As Paul Dirac said, "Each photon then interferes only with itself." It's as if each photon hasn't made up its mind which slit to choose and goes through both of them simultaneously.

In case you think these results are simply due to the strangeness of light, its particle-wave duality, you should know that the double-slit experiment has now been done with electrons as well. In fact, similar experiments have been done with neutrons, atoms, and even larger molecules. Not just light but actual matter also acts like waves, seeming to go in two places at once and interfering with itself.

The famed physicist Richard Feynman said the double-slit experiment was "impossible, *absolutely* impossible, to explain in any classical way" and it "has in it the heart of quantum mechanics." I hope I've conveyed just how strange the results are. Particles act like waves, being in two places at once. But waves of what, exactly? It now appears that matter should be thought of as waves of probability.

Most of us learned in science class that atoms, the building blocks of the universe, consist of electrons circling a nucleus like small billiard balls. Quantum physicists tell us instead that electrons are better seen as smears of probability, with their locations being potentials rather than definite places. As strange as it may seem, it is only when an electron is measured that its location goes from a smear to a specific spot.

In the double-slit experiment, there is one thing that can force the photons to make up their minds and go through one slit or the other. If you set up sensors to observe them as they travel, each photon is seen going through just one of the slits. The interference pattern on the photographic plate disappears, and you get two fuzzy images corresponding to the two slits instead. The observation leads to one path, one definite outcome, rather than the two potential outcomes that existed before.

Similarly, take a small particle that can travel down one of two paths, with a fifty-fifty chance of going down each one. According to quantum theory, until someone looks to see which path it goes down, with a measuring device for instance, all that can be said about the particle is that it has the two probabilities. Common sense says it goes down a path but we just don't know which one until someone checks. Common sense, however, can be misleading at the quantum level. Until the particle is observed, it does not actually go down either path. It simply exists as a fifty-fifty probability wave for going down each one.

To say that light and matter only exist as probability waves until they are observed raises the question of what existence in such a state would mean. As Werner Heisenberg, one of the founders of quantum physics, noted, "The atoms or the elementary particles themselves are not as real [as any phenomena in daily life]; they form a world of potentialities or possibilities rather than one of things or facts." With a measurement, one outcome snaps into place. "The transition from the 'possible' to the 'actual' takes place during the act of observation," to quote Heisenberg again. The measurement somehow causes one of the two possibilities—or in other situations one of many possibilities—to become the reality that is seen. Measuring something thus creates a reality that did not exist before.

The findings from the double-slit experiment are an example of superposition, the idea of a particle being in multiple states simultaneously. This concept applies not only to the location of particles but to other attributes as well, such as velocity and spin. In all of these, multiple possibilities exist. Heisenberg called the potential outcomes *potentia*, and all the potentia add up to produce a probability wave. A photon may go through one slit or the other, and both possibilities coexist as superpositions of possibility. When a photon, or an electron, is detected, the probability wave reduces down to the one outcome that is observed. It is only with measurement that the various possibilities are collapsed down to one actuality, and physicists refer to this as the collapse of the wave function.

A MEASUREMENT OR AN OBSERVATION?

When a measurement produces an outcome, is it the change in the measuring device that collapses the wave function, or does it collapse when the scientist observes the result? One person who considered this question was John von Neumann, a brilliant mathematician who wrote a book called *Mathematische Grundlagen der Quantenmechanik* (*Mathematical Foundations of Quantum Mechanics*). It provided, as its title said, rigorous mathematical foundations for the theories of the quantum physicists. Physicist Nick Herbert calls it the "quantum bible" and says that like many sacred texts, it is revered by many but read by few (the latter perhaps because it is filled with an astounding number of mathematical equations).

In the book, von Neumann discusses how the world must

be divided into two parts, the observed system and the observer. He shows that where we consider the cut between the two can be in various places. The measuring instrument can be considered part of the observed system or part of the observer; the mathematical result is the same. In fact, the changes in the retina of the observer as he looks at the measuring instrument can be considered part of the observed system. Even the chemical changes of his brain cells can be considered part of the observed system, until all that counts as the observer is "his abstract 'ego.' " The one essential part of the observer—in the critical interaction of observed system and observer that produces events in the world—is the observer's abstract ego, or "the intellectual inner life of the individual." No result in a measurement actually occurs until, as Herbert summarizes, a physical signal in the brain becomes an experience in the human mind.

Another guide to this question came from physicist Mauritius Renninger. He produced a thought experiment that involves finding a negative result. For an example that's simpler than Renninger's original, imagine that you do an experiment in which a photon can take one of two paths, and a measuring device can be set up on one of the paths to determine if the photon goes down it. The device failing to detect it on that path would mean that the photon must have taken the other one. As Renninger and others examined this situation, they found that observing the absence of a photon on the first path collapses the wave function just as much as observing the presence of it would. Since nothing is actually measured and only an absence is observed, this indicates that the observation—not the measurement itself—is the critical process in wave function collapse. As Johns Hopkins physicist Richard Conn Henry wrote in the journal *Nature*, "The wave function is collapsed simply by your human mind seeing nothing." This led him to conclude, "The Universe is entirely mental."

Experimental evidence along these lines has come from the world of parapsychology. Researchers have used devices called random number generators or random event generators that produce output in a completely random pattern. For example, a device might put out a series of light flashes, either green ones or red ones. There would be a fifty percent chance each time of the flash being either red or green. In studies, people then try to use their minds to change the output in one direction or the other so that more red flashes or more green flashes are produced than you would expect by chance. A considerable amount of data using random event generators has indicated that willful conscious effort can indeed cause a slight but significant deviation in the output of the devices so that it's no longer random.

A researcher named Helmut Schmidt, who was a physicist as well as a parapsychologist, took the work a step further to see if conscious effort could produce nonrandom results *even if the effort occurred after the events had already been recorded*. He got positive results in the five studies he did, with odds against chance of 8,000 to 1. He recorded random events such as the red and green light flashes, and the series of flashes was then stored on a floppy disk. Days or months later, the sequence was shown on a computer while a test subject tried to mentally cause one of the colors to flash more. As long as no one inspected the recordings beforehand, the mental efforts of the test subjects could cause the results to be nonrandom, with more of one color appearing than would be expected by chance. The test subjects' success means that the collapse of the wave function did not occur when the flashes of light were initially measured by the recording device; it only happened when the recordings were later observed. French physicist Olivier Costa de Beauregard wrote that the experiments "may herald a scientific revolution akin to the Rotating Earth one."

Thus, Renninger-type experiments show that observation can collapse the wave function even when nothing physical is actually measured. Schmidt's research demonstrated that interaction with a recording device fails to collapse the wave function; the collapse only occurs when the result is later observed. Von Neumann was therefore right that a change in a measuring device is not the critical factor. It is the awareness by the observer that appears to complete the process and produce a single reality out of the various possibilities.

It also seems that it's not the observing per se that produces a result, it is the knowing produced by the observing that does. By seeing that a particle doesn't go down one path, an observer in the Renninger-type experiments can deduce that it must have gone down the other one. Since no other result is possible, the observer "knows" which path the particle took, thereby collapsing the wave function and producing the result. It is not the act of measuring that produces a result, it is the act of knowing—the interaction of the world with von Neumann's "intellectual interlife of the individual."

THE LARGER WORLD

If you're telling yourself that all this weirdness is just limited to the tiny quantum world, then you're mistaken. You're in good company, to be sure, as physicists for a long time thought that while quantum mechanics ruled the microworld, classical physics controlled the larger one. They assumed there was some kind of border between the two. But not anymore. Few physicists would still give classical physics equal billing with quantum mechanics. Classical physics is a useful approximation, but the world is ultimately quantum at all levels.

Physicist Brian Greene has written that quantum mechanics "shows that the universe is founded on principles that, from the standpoint of our day-to-day experiences, are bizarre." These principles must extend beyond the microscopic quantum world since quantum events can have macroscopic consequences, as large objects can be dependent on the quantum behaviors of their atomic parts.

This effect of the quantum on the larger world is colorfully exemplified by Schrödinger's famous cat. Intending to show the absurdity of quantum theory's dependence on measurement, Erwin Schrödinger suggested a thought experiment in which a cat is put in a chamber with a vial of poison, a hammer, and a small amount of a radioactive substance. A device is set up so that the decay of a single radioactive atom will cause the hammer to fall, breaking the vial, releasing the poison, and killing the cat. There is so little of the radioactive substance that over an hour, there is only a fifty percent chance that an atom disintegrates and sets off the device.

If the contraption is left alone for an hour, the atom is in a superposition of both having decayed and having not decayed as long as it remains unobserved. This would mean that the cat is also in a superposition of being simultaneously both dead and alive—not the kind of result you want your theory to produce. One might conclude from this that quantum mechanics fails when systems get large enough or complex enough. Experimental findings now show, however, that superposition can indeed occur with macroscopic objects. A paper in the journal *Nature* in the year 2000 showed that an instrument called a superconducting quantum interference device (or SQUID) could be put in a superposition of two states simultaneously: one with current flowing clockwise and the other with current flowing counterclockwise. This led to commentaries with titles like "Schrödinger's SQUID," "Schrödinger's cat is now fat," and "New life for Schrödinger's cat." Work has advanced to the point that physicists at University of California, Santa Barbara, achieved superposition in an object that's even visible to the naked eye. After *Nature* published their study, the journal *Science* named it the Breakthrough of the Year for 2010.

Quantum effects can be present in the larger world, even if they are hard to see. As physicist Anton Zeilinger has said, "A transition from quantum to classical as you go from micro- to macroscopic . . . is not going to happen in my expectation. It's just a question of the skill of the experimenter and how much money [there is] to perform the experiment." Numerous experiments, from Zeilinger and others, have now demonstrated quantum effects in increasingly larger objects, and it appears clear that there is no definite border between the two worlds. The world at the quantum level and the larger one at the classical level are not two separate systems. Even though it's usually not apparent, the larger grows out of the quantum with all its strange patterns.

OBSERVING THE PAST

The quantum world not only can affect the larger one, it can even affect the past. Observation in particular is necessary to determine the past. Recall the double-slit experiment, in which light particles travel through two slits at once unless observation forces them to go through one or the other. John Wheeler, a notable figure in physics who among numerous other accomplishments gave black holes their name, imagined a thought experiment in which the double-slit experiment is done with a twist. You have the sensors set up to observe the photons going through the slits as before, but you also have a barrier that blocks the sensors from "seeing" the photons and the slits. If you leave the barrier up, the photons seem to go through both slits simultaneously and produce an interference wave pattern. If you lower the barrier, the sensors measure the photons, which then go through one slit or the other as discrete particles.

Wheeler suggested that you could wait and lower the barrier just after the photons went through the slits. The sensors would observe the particles as they continued to travel, producing definite paths coming from one slit or the other. In this way, the decision of whether to lower the barrier would determine if the photons were acting like waves or particles when they passed through the slits—even though that decision wouldn't be made until after they did. Thus, the decision would determine what kind of path the photons had taken as they went through the slits *in the past*.

This kind of delayed-choice experiment has now been carried out experimentally by several groups. They confirm that the later choice determines the earlier behavior of the photons.

Wheeler wasn't content to stop there. He advanced his line of reasoning to near mind-boggling proportions when he proposed a similar thought experiment on a galactic scale. Imagine a distant quasar that is emitting light. Between it and Earth would be two large galaxies, whose gravity could bend the light as it headed toward Earth. In this huge version of the double-slit experiment, the quasar would be the light source, and the galaxies would substitute for the slits. Astronomers on Earth could point telescopes at the galaxies to observe light photons as they were deflected by the galaxies. Or, they could set up mirrors in such a way that photons deflected by the two galaxies would not be observed but would instead hit a piece of film, producing the alternating light and dark bands produced by waves, even if the quasar was so far away that light from it would hit the film one photon at a time. The alternating interference bands would mean that the photons had seemingly traveled through both galaxies simultaneously, even though they would be light-years apart.

More amazing still is that since this would just be a really large version of the double-slit experiment, it would be the astronomers' actions that determined the kind of path the photons took. The astronomers would force each photon to go through one galaxy or the other if they observed it with a telescope as it did so, or the photons would act like waves, going through both galaxies simultaneously and producing the alternating bands on the film. Since the quasar would be so far from Earth, however, the photons would have begun their travels billions of years before.

Observers on Earth could thus determine the kind of path that a photon started *billions of years before*. They could do this, not because they reach billions of years into the past, but because the probability wave function for that path, even the part of it in the long ago past, does not collapse until an observation is made. The wave function, consisting of all the possible paths the photons could have taken, continues to exist even for billions of years, until an observation finally collapses it and produces one outcome. Another way of saying this is that the histories of the photons aren't determined until they are known by observers.

BECOMING ENTANGLED

Another example of the interplay between knowledge and time is the concept of entanglement, a problem that has puzzled physicists for nearly eighty years. Albert Einstein was unhappy with quantum theory in 1935. It held that attributes of particles were just potentials until one outcome was observed. Einstein felt this must be wrong, that the attributes existed before they were observed, they were just hidden. He published a paper with two young colleagues, Boris Podolsky and Nathan Rosen, based on discussions they had about a thought experiment, with Podolsky writing the manuscript. Einstein was subsequently unhappy with the particulars of the paper itself, and it's not clear he even read the final draft before Podolsky submitted it.

Even so, this little paper—not quite four pages long, without references, and with its famous author dissatisfied—has had a profound impact on the course of physics, being cited in physics journals far more than any other paper Einstein ever wrote. It is known simply as EPR, the initials of its authors. The setup of the EPR thought experiment usually cited today is an alternative proposed by David Bohm, since Podolsky's original fairly obscured its central point. In the Bohm version, two particles interact in a way that causes them to have opposite results for a given attribute; for instance, if one particle is "spin-up" the other is "spin-down." After that interaction, the particles go in different directions. When someone later measures the spin of one of the particles, the spin of the other one is automatically known since the two spins are opposites.

Einstein thought EPR proved that quantum theory was an incomplete description of reality. It said that the spin of the particles only becomes definite when a measurement is made. Further, the theory said that no matter how far apart the particles go, measuring the spin of the first one would cause the spin of the second to suddenly snap into existence, even though the two particles would be completely separated by a great distance.

The EPR authors pointed out that the experiment would make the reality of the second particle "depend upon the process of measurement carried out on the first [particle], which does not disturb the second [particle] in any way." They then stated, "No reasonable definition of reality could be expected to permit this."

Perhaps that means that reality is not reasonable, because as subsequent events have demonstrated, that turns out to be the way the world is. John Bell published a discussion of EPR in 1964 that led to this realization. Bell's theorem takes two assumptions. One is that objects have separability: in Bohm's EPR example, the assumption is that measuring the spin orientation of one particle doesn't affect the orientation of the second particle in a remote location. The other assumption is that objects are real: the second particle had a predetermined orientation before the first particle was measured. Bell showed mathematically that any theory that exactly reproduced the predictions of quantum mechanics would violate one of the two assumptions. Thus, any interpretation based on realism would have to be "grossly non-local."

Following Bell's paper, experiments using entangled pairs of particles were carried out, most notably by Alain Aspect and colleagues, but by others as well. The setups for the actual lab experiments were different than the Bohm EPR example, but the principles were the same. The results were consistent with quantum mechanics and not with local reality, demonstrating that EPR does not show that quantum theory is incomplete. Instead, EPR led the way to the discovery that the idea of a local reality is incorrect.

Bell wrote that requiring locality—requiring that measuring one particle wouldn't affect the distant second particle—was the essential problem. But that was only one assumption in his theorem. The other one—requiring a physical reality to exist before any observation—could instead be faulty. Though such a possibility appears more consistent with the rest of quantum theory, it seems so illogical that many physicists have tended to avoid addressing it. Bruce Rosenblum and Fred Kuttner are two physicists who, despite being open to considering consciousness alongside quantum physics, recently wrote about Bell's theorem, "Our world therefore does *not* have both reality and separability. (And we immediately admit to having little understanding of what the world being unreal might mean.)" Even so, the nonlocality explanation has recently been falling out of favor.

In 2007, a group of physicists in Vienna published a study in *Nature*. They conducted a Bell-type experiment, except in this case, it relied only on realism and not so much on locality. They found that just assuming realism—that there is an objective reality separate from observation—would still produce results that differed from quantum mechanical predictions and from those that occurred during the experiment. The study thus refuted realism, leading the *Physics World* Web site to produce a headline proclaiming, "Quantum physics says goodbye to reality." The researchers couldn't exclude all classes of nonlocal theories but felt their results indicated that any nonlocal extension of quantum theory would have to be "highly counterintuitive." And if you don't accept a nonlocal explanation, you're left with the denial of objective reality.

This leads to a way to understand entanglement that was first proposed by Costa de Beauregard back in 1953. In EPR, an interaction produces opposite spins in two particles. Whether the spin of each of them is up or down isn't known until one of them is measured in the future. More important, not only are the spins not known, they aren't even real until one of the particles is measured. Likewise, the original interaction that produced the opposite spins isn't real either; it remains a collection of ghostly potentia until the results of it are known.

When the spin of one of the particles is eventually observed, it becomes definite. This causes its previous interaction with the second particle, when it acquired its spin direction, to become definite, too, because the interaction had to go in a particular way to produce that outcome. With the original interaction being definite, the spin of the second particle becomes definite as well, since it was also established in that interaction. The observation thus produces not only the present of the particles (their spins), but their past as well. Making the past definite, by looking at the spin of one of the particles, creates the illusion that measuring one particle suddenly affects the other one a great distance away. It does in a way, but only because it affects the particle's past. Entanglement occurs because the initial interaction between the two particles that created their opposite spin directions doesn't become actualized—the wave function doesn't collapse—until an observer later measures the spin of one of them.

A MATTER OF TIME

Entanglement makes clear that until their outcomes are known, *events in the past haven't happened yet*. With his theory of special relativity, Einstein showed that time is not the constant it seems to be. Two clocks moving through space at different speeds will tick at different rates, meaning that time as we think of it can move at different rates. The findings of quantum physics lead to a conclusion that time is even stranger than that. In essence, until the results of an event are known, it hasn't really happened yet, even though it may occur on a date we think of as being in the past.

Events do occur in a timeline but not necessarily in order. I can draw a timeline with four events on it labeled A through D:

BEGINNING   END

My common sense tells me that Event A happens first, then Event B, then Event C, and then Event D. Quantum physics tells a different story. It says that Event A doesn't occur until its outcome is known, so Event B could actually happen—it could become definite when its wave function collapses—before Event A does. If I place myself at the end of the timeline and say that I'm at the present, Event A from what seems like the distant past may not have even happened yet. It may still only be a number of potential outcomes.

If the terms weren't so ingrained in our minds, it might be more accurate to think that events whose outcomes have been observed (or are at least known) are in the past, events being observed now are the present, and events that have not yet been observed are still in the future. Those "future events" could be anywhere along a timeline, from the year 2525 to the year 1776 to the time when photons from a distant quasar began their paths toward Earth. Some people talk about backward causation or retrocausality, of reaching back in time to change a previous event. But observing previous events doesn't change the past—because the unobserved past hasn't happened yet.

There is a well-known paradox about time travel, that if such a thing were possible, a time traveler could go back and kill his grandfather before he had fathered children, thus preventing the time traveler from existing in the first place. (But since he then wouldn't have existed to go back, his grandfather would still be alive, and on and on. Stephen King dispensed with the paradox in his recent time-travel novel *11/22/63* when one character is talking about going back in time and another one asks what would happen if you went back and killed your grandfather. The first character stares at him baffled and asks, "Why the [heck] would you do that?" and the conversation moves on.) With the model I'm describing, the existence of the time traveler means his grandfather definitely lived to have children, so that part of his life couldn't be undone (its wave function has already collapsed). I'm not talking about going back into a past that's happened; I'm saying that events that we think of as occurring in the past don't actually happen until observation creates a particular outcome. As Wheeler wrote, "It is wrong to think of [the] past as 'already existing' in all detail. The 'past' is theory. The past has no existence except as it is recorded in the present."

There is no limit to how far in the past events can be and still be undetermined. Remember that Wheeler pointed out that how astronomers choose to make measurements on Earth can affect the path a photon takes to get here—even the path it took billions of years before the astronomers were around to make their measurements. He wrote that since equipment operating in the present plays a part in bringing about things that appear to have already happened, the idea that the world exists "out there" independent of us can no longer be upheld. He wrote that "in some strange sense this is a 'participatory universe'" and that "there is a sense in which what the observer will do in the future defines what happens in the past— even a past so remote that life did not then exist." He added that quantum physics shows that " 'observership' is a prerequisite for any useful version of 'reality,' " saying this leads one "to explore the working hypothesis that 'observership is the mechanism of genesis.' " Observership is the mechanism of genesis: that's quite an idea, that the observer is the creator. Wheeler suggested that "acts of observer-participancy" could give "tangible 'reality' " to even the beginnings of the universe.

Despite appearances, the universe was not created in one fell swoop in the Big Bang. Instead, it continues to be created, one observation at a time. Events in the distant past such as the paths of photons billions of years ago—even events all the way back to the Big Bang—remain in suspended animation until they are observed, at which point one particular outcome occurs. Stanford physicist Andrei Linde has said, "You may ask whether the universe really existed before you start looking at it. . . . And my answer would be that the universe *looks* as if it existed before I started looking at it. . . . When we look at the universe, the best we can say is that it looks as if it were there 10 billion years ago."

This does not mean that we human observers had to come into existence. Different life forms might have evolved here or in other places in the universe. Observers had to develop somewhere, however, in order for the world to exist. This idea explains how the universe appears so finely tuned to support life. If some of the physical constants or initial conditions of the universe had been different, not only would life have been impossible, planets couldn't even have formed. Some have argued that the odds of a low-entropy universe with formed matter, not to mention intelligent life, are so infinitesimally small as to be almost zero. Since such a universe does in fact exist, some people say it is evidence for the existence of God. There are two responses against this. The first is that any universe we could be in would obviously have to be able to support life. The second is a concept called the multiverse, the idea that there could be an infinite number of universes that bubble into existence, so many that very rarely one would occur that could support life. Thus, there is nothing miraculous about our universe being the way it is.

With Wheeler's genesis through observership comes a different view, which is known as the strong anthropic principle. A universe that supports the development of observers is the only kind that ever *could* come into existence. The universe, our universe, was only in a state of countless potentia until observation caused a past to snap into existence, and that past clearly had to be one that would eventually produce observers. As Wheeler said, "Unless the blind dice of mutation and natural selection lead to life and consciousness and observership at some point down the road, the universe could not have come into being in the first place, according to the views under exploration here." There might have been nothing rather than something perhaps, but since "something" has to be observed before it can exist, a universe has to have observers. There are no lifeless, empty universes, because such a universe could never be observed into existence.

It might seem that humans on this little planet, or observers anywhere in any galaxy, are far too small and unimportant to have any significant function in the universe, much less bring it into existence. Observation, however, couldn't create a smaller universe, not because of size per se but because of the time required to produce life. An observed universe would have to be old enough for there to be elements other than hydrogen, since as Dicke said, "It is well known that carbon is required to make physicists." This is not entirely humorous, since the measurements by physicists to determine the age of the universe help determine that age. As Wheeler pointed out, to produce heavy elements like carbon out of hydrogen, thermonuclear combustion is required, and it needs several billion years to cook inside a star. And for the universe to provide several billion years of time, general relativity says it must extend in space several billion light-years. Any observed universe would have to be as big as ours is, in order to have observers. Though our tiny size in relation to the enormity of the universe may make living things appear insignificant, tiny living things can't produce a universe that's any smaller. And the universe can't exist without tiny living things to observe it.

THE WORLD OF CONSCIOUSNESS

Wheeler resisted the seemingly obvious connection between observation and *conscious* observation. He was quick to say that " 'consciousness' has nothing whatsoever to do with the quantum process," which involves only an event making itself known by being registered or recorded in some way. He did add that if that record then enters into someone's consciousness and is the first step in giving the measurement meaning, then that part of the story is important, but is not a "quantum phenomenon."

Others have not been so reluctant to consider consciousness in the quantum process. The issue started with von Neumann's mathematical work I described earlier. Though he only hinted at a consciousness-created reality, others have been more straightforward about it. Eugene Wigner, a Nobel laureate, proposed a thought experiment that came to be known as Wigner's friend. In it, a light may or may not flash at a given time. Wigner sets up a device in which, for example, an atom is excited if the light flashes. If he is out of the room, the wave function for the event does not collapse until Wigner comes back and checks the device. If instead of the device, Wigner's friend is in the room seeing if there is a flash, the wave function must collapse before he tells Wigner whether he saw one. It collapses when the friend observes the flash; otherwise, he would be in suspended animation until he gave Wigner the result. Because of this difference, Wigner wrote that "the being with a consciousness must have a different role in quantum mechanics than the inanimate measuring device." He said "it is the entering of an impression into our consciousness which alters the wave function" and that "it is at this point that the consciousness enters the theory unavoidably and unalterably."

The ideas of von Neumann and Wigner led to the Consciousness Causes Collapse (of the wave function) school of thought. One person identified with it more recently is Berkeley physicist Henry Stapp. He has written books with titles such as *Mindful Universe* and *Mind, Matter and Quantum Mechanics*. Stanford physicist Andrei Linde has also said, "I do not know any sense in which I could claim that the universe is here in the absence of observers. We are together, the universe and us. . . . I cannot imagine a consistent theory of everything that ignores consciousness."

Back in the 1930s, Sir James Jeans, a well-known British physicist and astronomer, made the oft-quoted statement, "The universe begins to look more like a great thought than like a great machine." He added, "Mind no longer appears as an accidental intruder into the realm of matter; we are beginning to suspect that we ought rather to hail it as the creator and governor of the realm of matter." French physicist Bernard d'Espagnat has written, "The doctrine that the world is made up of objects whose existence is independent of human consciousness turns out to be in conflict with quantum mechanics and with facts established by experiment."

I quote the various scientists to show that these ideas are part of mainstream physics. Since it has been said that there are as many interpretations of quantum theory as there are quantum physicists, I don't mean to say that this is the consensus view, or even the majority opinion. At the same time, these ideas are not merely New Age woo-woo physics. When a giant such as von Neumann points in a particular direction, it warrants serious consideration.

I hope I've shown that these ideas are a natural conclusion of the findings in quantum physics. If you think they are wild, you should hear some of the alternatives. One of the leading explanations proposed for the measurement problem is Everett's many-worlds interpretation. It says that when a measurement is made, the wave function doesn't collapse and produce one result. Instead, all possible results occur, each in its own parallel universe as the world branches into different versions of itself. The observer only sees one result, but other versions of the observer see the other possible results. The branches have no effect on each other, so no observer is ever aware that the split occurred.

Since every measurement creates separate universes in this hypothesis, the "many" in many-worlds quickly becomes a gross understatement. "An infinite number raised to an infinite power" might be more accurate. Yet this idea is taken seriously by a lot of physicists as a way to keep the observer out of quantum theory.

Wheeler's stated reason for denying the importance of consciousness, and I suspect the reason for many physicists, is that he saw it as one more physical process. He believed that "brain function"—the mind—"will someday be explained entirely in terms of physical chemistry and electrochemical potentials." This materialist worldview meant that Wheeler could see the importance of the observer—he had astounding insights about how observation could even create the distant past—but he was unable to accept that the consciousness of that observer was critical.

There is a paradox here to be sure. As Wheeler said, quantum mechanics leads us to consider the idea that "the observer is as essential to the creation of the universe as the universe is to the creation of the observer." Conscious observers eventually evolved in the universe . . . and then created that very same universe. How does that make sense? One answer is that individual observers are the result of evolution, it's true, but that doesn't mean that consciousness itself is. For people like me who are open to the possibility that consciousness is more than just the result of physical chemistry and electrochemical potentials—that there might be more to existence than just the physical universe—the way out of the paradox is for consciousness to be primary. The physical world grows out of it. The findings of quantum physics have challenged the worldview of materialism from the outset; at the very least, they have undeniably shown that the world does not function at the smallest level in a way that common sense suggests it does. The findings point, not just for me but for a number of physicists as well, to the fundamental importance of consciousness. Something has to be outside the quantum system to register it, to observe it. My answer is that consciousness is outside the quantum system, interacting with the physical universe but also existing beyond it, as it registers and creates that universe. Consciousness does not exist because the physical world does; the physical world exists because consciousness does. As Max Planck said, we cannot get behind consciousness.

A SHARED DREAM

The picture that emerges from quantum physics is a world in which events do not occur until conscious beings observe them. One way to comprehend this is to realize that it is quite similar to another world we know very well—the world of our dreams. When we are dreaming, people only come into existence there when we interact with them. They snap into existence the instant we observe them. Otherwise, the various people from our waking lives exist only as possibilities in the backs of our minds, figures who could exist in our dream world but so far remain mere potentials. Even though we are not aware of the similarity as we experience our lives, quantum physics has shown that the physical world works in the same way.

There are differences, to be sure. All sorts of nonsensical things happen in the dream world. We can suddenly fly in some dreams, but we are unlikely to do so in the physical world. It is undeniable that the possibilities are more limited in the physical world. Events that begin through observation become fixed, unable to be altered by other observations. The overall process, however, is very similar. Possibilities exist, and one of them becomes a fact when it is observed.

The analogy to dreams is so apt that the world can be thought of, not as the giant clockworks of Isaac Newton's mechanistic universe, but as a dream that all its observers share. Its pieces only come into existence when one of its dreamers experiences them. When something is not being observed, it may as well not exist.

Becoming aware that the universe at its most basic level depends on consciousness in order to exist requires us to alter our understandings of the world. The findings in quantum mechanics are so startling and, frankly, so hard to comprehend, that many scientists in other areas have not yet incorporated them into their fields. Biologists, for example, still tend to think of consciousness as being simply a byproduct of the brain as it evolved to help organisms survive in the natural world—an epiphenomenon, as it is called.

This view needs to change. A more accurate understanding is more optimistic: the universe is not a purposeless place that we came to exist in by random accident. Consciousness is the primary force of existence, and the physical universe is secondary to it. It exists because we exist, a product of our group imagination. We think of our minds existing in this world, but it's actually the world that exists in our minds.

We are the physical beings living in a physical world that mainstream science tells us we are. But we also have consciousness that is more than just a product of our brains. Though we have physical bodies with limited life spans, we also have a conscious piece that is part of something bigger. Consciousness is independent of the physical world and even the creator of the physical world. And a portion of it is in each of us.

Seeing that the world is like a shared dream can help us understand more about the interaction between mind and matter in our lives. In my dreams, I can't control what happens or what other people are doing. But some people do develop more control over their dreams. They have what are known as lucid dreams, in which they become aware they are dreaming. They then have more ability to shape what happens.

Perhaps we can develop more control over the physical world in the same way. Gertrude Schmeidler was an experimental psychologist working at Harvard in 1942 when she found repeatedly that people who rejected any possibility of psychic abilities did worse on ESP tests than people who were at least open to the idea. This finding has since been confirmed by numerous other researchers and has been termed the sheep-goat effect (with nonbelievers being the goats). What people believe is possible helps determine what is indeed possible for them, and being aware of the mental foundation of the world may open us up to new possibilities.

One possibility that I hope you are now open to is the prospect of life after death that our cases of past-life memories suggest. Each of the children seems to have a consciousness that existed before in another person. Though this may seem ludicrous from a materialist standpoint, the situation gets much more interesting when we take the findings from quantum physicists into account. If the physical universe grows out of consciousness, there is no reason to think that a person's individual consciousness ends when the physical brain dies. It may continue after death and return in a future life.

Chapter 9

WORKING ON A DREAM

Being open to the possibility of life after death naturally makes me curious about what it might involve. With the idea that the world exists as a shared dream, my thinking about it has changed. I no longer imagine that we go to another place when we die. Instead, we have another dream. The idea of some entity—a soul or a consciousness—moving from one world to another places too much emphasis on the physical worlds. Instead, the new experiences continue to be creations of the mind. If the shared dream model is correct, there need not be just one afterlife. Each individual starts another dream at the point of death, and the nature of the dream can vary from person to person.

EXPERIENCES NEAR DEATH

The immediate dream often seems to be a transition dream, involving an awareness of dying and moving on to another kind of existence. Near-death experiences (or NDEs) are, as the name suggests, the events that people report having when they come very close to death before being revived. I mentioned earlier the details they report, of floating above their bodies, going through a tunnel to another place, and often having a life review, seeing deceased relatives, and encountering a being of light.

The specifics of these experiences can vary. Just as people's nighttime dreams are affected by their previous experiences, I would expect afterlife events to be affected by experiences in life, and this seems to be the case. In particular, though there are common features of NDEs across cultures, there are also cultural differences.

Allan Kellehear reviewed reports of NDEs that had been published from a number of countries. Looking at the parts of NDEs that are common in the Western cases, he found that the major features seen across cultures were going to other worlds and encountering other beings. The tunnel experience was not reported in any of the non-Western NDEs, though times in darkness were often described. An out-of-body experience was present in the NDEs of most cultures, and the life review was present in several.

Satwant Pasricha likewise found both similarities and differences between accounts of NDEs in India and ones in the U.S. Both Indian and American subjects reported meeting dead relatives and acquaintances, seeing religious figures or beings of light, being revived through the thoughts of loved living persons, being sent back from the other realm by a loved one, and seeing their own physical body while seemingly dead.

She also reported features of Indian NDEs that were not seen in American ones, as the Indian subjects often told a different narrative from the typical American experience. Many of the Indian subjects described being taken to another realm by messengers, who then passed the subjects on to Yama, the god of death. When Yama's book containing a list of deeds and misdeeds was opened, it was discovered that the messengers had brought the wrong person. Someone else was due to die, not the subject, who then came back to this world and lived.

Todd Murphy collected ten NDE cases from Thai popular literature. The imagery people reported seemed to be culturally influenced, though Murphy argued that it should actually be considered a reflection of the individuals' expectations of what death would be like rather than their culture per se. The themes he reported were Yamatoots (the messengers Pasricha described in the Indian cases), the importance of merit accumulated during life, and, as in the Indian cases, the presence of cases of mistaken identity. The universal features pointed out by Kellehear and Pasricha were also present in the Thai NDEs. For example, dead friends and relatives were seen in four of Murphy's ten cases.

The overall message from these reports is that people from many parts of the world who come close to death describe having experiences as their bodies are in the process of dying. Such experiences seem to occur everywhere, but the ones people have are certainly not identical. Some people take the differences to mean that NDEs are not real events and that they do not provide evidence that consciousness can exist independently of the brain. Author Sam Harris recently made this argument regarding an NDE that Eben Alexander, a neurosurgeon for many years at Harvard Medical School, experienced and then wrote about in his book, *Proof of Heaven*. Harris noted that Alexander's account differed from another recent one, that of a four-year-old boy described in the book *Heaven Is for Real*, commenting that Alexander doesn't mention that Jesus rides a rainbow-colored horse or that souls of dead children must still do homework in heaven.

The fallacy of Harris's argument is that it's based on the premise that, as he says, "if a nonphysical domain were truly being explored, some universal characteristics would stand out." As I've just described, some universal characteristics do stand out, but beyond that, the bigger issue is that there is not just a single place where people go after they die. With the model I'm presenting, differences would be expected when people experience their next consciousness-created reality, their next dream. Just as an American Christian is unlikely to dream at night about Yama, the god of death, and an Indian Hindu is unlikely to dream about Jesus, a four-year-old's next consciousness-created reality may have little in common with that of a neurosurgeon.

The differences in the reports do argue against there being one afterlife place where everyone goes, as Harris says. But I would argue against that, too. The reports of NDEs from different people and different places show the variations I would expect to see. It appears that expectations and experiences play a role in the next reality that a person encounters (or helps create), just as our experiences and thoughts prior to going to sleep can shape our nighttime dreams.

The distinct differences among the experiences of various individuals also argue against the idea that NDEs are merely the result of the firings of dying brains, which might be expected to produce more uniform images. Arguing against this as well are the reports that many of the past-life children make about events between lives. About twenty percent of the children say they remember either observing earthly events such as the previous person's funeral, going to another realm, or having experiences related to conception or gestation to begin their current life.

Poonam Sharma, a medical student who worked with us one summer before heading to great things in internal medicine, compared published NDE reports to the children's descriptions in our cases of the time between lives, looking particularly at the Burmese cases she was coding for us to include in our database. She found significant overlap. For the Western NDEs, this was especially true for the transcendental aspects. For NDE reports from other parts of the world, the universal features of NDEs were seen in the children's intermission descriptions. The Burmese intermission reports were similar, though not identical, to the NDE reports from neighboring India and Thailand. These similarities indicated that the intermission memories need to be considered part of the same overall phenomenon—reports of the afterlife—that includes NDEs.

American children also describe memories of the time between lives that sound very much like NDEs. Patrick, the little boy in Chapter 1, reported encountering a relative in heaven—"Billy the Pirate," who was upset that no one talked about him after his death—in the same way many NDE patients describe seeing deceased relatives. Likewise, just as NDE patients report going to another realm, Lee, the boy who seemed to remember Sidney Coe Howard's life, described being in a castle up in the clouds somewhere. He said the castle didn't have lights or a potty, but it did have windows. When his mother asked how he went from a castle up in the sky to being Lee, he said he climbed down a ladder to become Lee. Though a castle in the sky may seem rather fantastic, it could have been part of the dream world Lee experienced before re-entering this dream world, what we think of as reality.

The idea that NDEs are merely the product of the final firings of dying brains, which some people offer as a way to explain them, can't possibly work for these similar reports from healthy, young children. The intermission reports also weaken the argument that people who have NDEs create fantasies of an afterlife as a defense to avoid confronting the end of their existence. Our cases involve young children who have not been close to death and in fact usually aren't old enough to fully comprehend the concept of death, yet their reports can be quite similar to NDE reports—thus posing a problem for psychological explanations offered for NDEs. Both phenomena—near-death experiences and intermission reports from young children—may in fact be glimpses of the afterlife, and they are both consistent with the model of consciousness-created reality.

THE DREAM CONTINUES

With the past-life memories they report, the children in our cases seem to be returning to the world in which they lived a previous life. A better way of describing this is to say that regardless of whether the children have an intermission experience, they fall back into the same dream they were in before—meaning this world. They have to be a new character as they continue, since the previous person has died in the dream at that point. Imagine that you are sleeping at night; you are awakened in the middle of a dream—perhaps you are startled awake by something traumatic that happens in it—but then you fall back asleep quickly and continue on in the same dream. This is completely analogous to what happens in our cases.

First, the new life usually starts very soon after the last one ended. The median interval—meaning half the cases have a shorter interval and half have a longer one—between the death of the previous person and the birth of the child is only sixteen months. Though most of the cases in this book are exceptions, the interval is typically very short. Thus, these cases are like waking up from a dream and then falling back asleep quickly and continuing in the same dream.

The endings of the past lives tend to be like dreams that end prematurely. In seventy percent of our cases, the previous person died by unnatural means, either by murder, suicide, or accident. James Huston's death in the Pacific and Sidney Coe Howard's fatal tractor accident are typical examples. The previous individuals also tend to die quite young, with the median age at death being only twenty-eight years old. Even when the previous people died from natural causes, their median age was only thirty-five, with a quarter of those deaths occurring when the person was fifteen or less. Thus, the death of Patrick's half brother at age two is unusual in the general population, but not so in our cases.

If you look at a graph of the number of deaths in the general population by the age when people die, what you see is a curve that gradually slopes up as more and more die with each older age group. In our cases, even when you look just at ones in which the previous person died naturally, what you see is the reverse, with the curve sloping down:

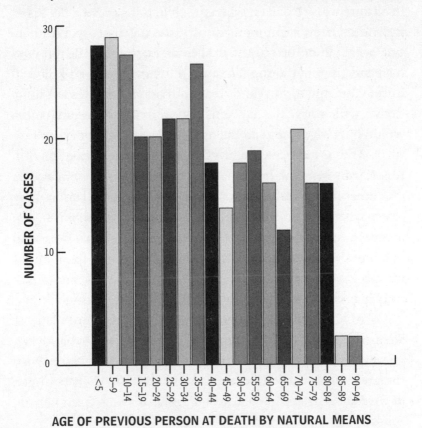

AGE OF PREVIOUS PERSON AT DEATH BY NATURAL MEANS

Dying young increases the likelihood that a child will later report memories of your life. With the model I'm proposing, this makes sense. Individuals whose dreams end prematurely—by being brief or through an abrupt ending—are more likely to return quickly to the same dream. Meaning, people who die young or by unnatural means are more likely to return to our mind-created world to start another life.

This idea of returning to the same dream also explains another pattern. The previous person was from the same country as the child in over ninety percent of our cases, often having lived fairly close by. Even when the child talks about a deceased individual from a different country, there is usually a connection with the child's country, such as Burmese children who have talked about being Japanese soldiers who were killed in Burma during World War II. If an individual resumes the same dream with a new life, it seems logical that the circumstances would be fairly similar to the original ones. He or she can't return as the same person since the previous individual died in this dream, but usually comes back in the same general area.

Emotional connections or unresolved emotional issues may affect where the individual comes back in the dream. If you compare cases in which the previous person was a deceased member of the child's family with ones in which the families were complete strangers, you find that there are some statistically significant differences regarding how the previous person died. Cases involving ordinary deaths are more likely to be same-family cases. The families are more likely to be strangers when more exceptional deaths were involved, meaning when the previous person died an unnatural death, died younger, or died unexpectedly even when the death was from natural causes.

My interpretation of this is that individuals with strong or unresolved emotional connections to their families—such as Patrick's half brother with his mother Lisa—come back to the same dream to continue the story with them. In situations without those emotional issues, these other factors—the unnatural or early or unexpected deaths—cause the individual to quickly fall back into the same dream as before, but not necessarily into the same family.

OTHER WORLDS

With our nighttime dreams, it's unusual of course to return to the same dream. I wonder if that's the case with our lives as well. Past-life memories, as far as anyone can tell, are not common. Only one systematic survey has been done looking at their frequency. It involved people in one section of India, and the researchers found that one case occurred for every 450 inhabitants, though they acknowledged they may have missed some cases. It's at least conceivable that many more children come into the world with past-life memories but that they either lose the memories before they are verbal enough to convey them or that their attempts to convey them are ignored or rebuffed strongly enough by their parents to quash them.

Nonetheless, there is no evidence that most children have such memories and thus no evidence, even if you accept our cases, that everyone is reborn back into this world. I see no reason to think that other mind-created worlds, other shared dreams, wouldn't exist in addition to the world we know here. Just as we don't usually return to the same dream when we sleep at night, the same pattern may well be true for our lives. Though individuals occasionally return to this shared dream, it might be more common to begin participating in a different shared dream after we die.

What might these other consciousness-created worlds be like? I suspect that depends on the experiences we've had in this life. Our nighttime dreams are certainly affected by our experiences during the day. The themes of your day may repeat themselves in your dreams at night. If you watch a horror movie, you may regret doing so later when you have bad dreams. Your experiences matter; they affect the dreams that follow.

Likewise, your life experiences could affect the mind-created worlds that follow after you die. Many Christians say your actions or beliefs determine whether you go to Heaven or Hell. But if I am right about existence being like a shared dream, then there might not be just one Heaven or just one Hell. There might be an infinite number of shared dreams, some heavenly, some hellish, and some like this world—heavenly at times, hellish at times, and most of the time somewhere in between. I do find it notable, however, that in this model I'm suggesting, the religions are right that the decisions and actions you make in this life help determine the kind of existence you have next. Though this would not involve a Judgment Day of any kind, you could experience a "good" afterlife or a "bad" one based on your life now, in what would be a purely naturalistic process.

This process also seems similar to karma, the Eastern concept that your actions determine your future circumstances. I don't mean karmic retribution or any sort of orchestrated punishments or rewards, but there could be consequences that would flow naturally from your prior experiences. Tibetan Buddhists feel that in addition to how you live your life, the state of mind you are in at the moment of death—your last thoughts and emotions—are critical in determining the existence you have next. This would be consistent with this model in which what your mind creates next is affected by the thoughts that lead up to each moment.

The afterlife environment might be surprisingly similar to this one. Though we don't typically return to the same dream at night, our dreams usually involve a fairly similar setting. There could be differences, to be sure, perhaps as many as the mind can imagine, and the physics might be distinctly different in one world compared to another. But at the very least, I think there would still be a space-time kind of experience and not purely thought or spirit. For there to be a sequence of events—for things to happen—there has to be, it seems to me, some kind of space-time world.

An illustration of this comes from the mediumship literature. Mediumship, the idea that certain individuals can communicate with the deceased, is a topic for another book, or really a library full of books. Suffice it to say that a number of renowned scientists such as William James and a couple of Nobel Prize winners tested mediums a century ago and concluded that some of them had access to information through some extraordinary ability of the mind, material that appeared to come from the deceased. (The researchers also found that many other mediums had no talent at all.)

Numerous descriptions of the afterlife were given by mediums, but the example I want to share comes from Reverend C. Drayton Thomas, or more precisely from his deceased wife. Reverend Thomas wrote books about mediumship in the 1920s and '30s. Our office has a photocopy of a rough-draft manuscript he wrote at some point. It includes various corrections, some handwritten. I don't know that it was ever published, but at the end is a three-page description that really struck me. Entitled "An account of her passing given by my wife through the mediumship of Mrs. Osborne Leonard," it purports to be a description by Thomas's wife of events in the afterlife. It concludes with "What I am so astonished about is the reality

and substance of things here. . . . In the garden I . . . tried feeling the trees, and found that their bark felt just as solid as the
trees in our garden at home. I even tried to shake the trees but
could not; they were large trees and felt firm to my hand.
When I touch other people their hands, too, feel firm. There is
nothing vague or vapoury about us."

I don't think there is our world and then the real spiritual
world. Our world is as real as it gets. It is created by Mind, but
that is also true for all other worlds. Existence grows out of
consciousness. I don't think, for example, that reality is like the
movie *The Matrix*, where human beings interact in a computer
simulation of the world, completely unaware that in actuality
they are in constant sleep in pods while machines use their
bodies as energy sources. The world is indeed like a mind-
simulated virtual reality, in a way, but it's as real as reality gets.

Who is with us in the shared dreams of the afterlife? When I
dream at night, people who are meaningful to me tend to pop
up repeatedly. Characters in my dreams include people who
are around me a lot—my wife, of course, as well as friends or
co-workers—along with people I happened to run into during
the preceding day or even just had occasion to think about that
day. But then there are also those I haven't seen or thought
about for some time but with whom I still feel an emotional
connection. This is particularly true for people I've known, or
even pets I've had, who are deceased, some of whom I've
dreamed about periodically for years after their deaths. I may
dream about them even more than I did when they were alive,
because their absence leaves an emotional tie that can no longer be fulfilled.

Our consciousness-created worlds may be populated in a
similar way. Certainly the initial ones are, as people who have

near-death experiences often report seeing deceased relatives on the other side. (Some even report seeing deceased relatives they hadn't known were dead before they had their NDEs, producing some very impressive cases.) I would hate to think of getting to the afterlife and not being able to see my loved ones again, and I think those connections would cause them to be with me again in the next world. Eventually the emotional ties may be resolved so those individuals would no longer be present, but my emotional need initially would keep them with me, causing them to appear in my next shared dream.

It's unclear how time would work across mind-created worlds. It's easiest to conceptualize lifetimes as being sequential—first I have one life, then another, then another—but I don't know if that makes complete sense when the lives involve different dream worlds. The different worlds or different dreams—while being space-time worlds—would themselves transcend space-time. While I think any world where things happen has to involve space and time, I'm not sure they would have to follow each other sequentially. They certainly appear to in some instances, such as when people report encountering other realms in NDEs. But I suspect the process is complex. For example, perhaps individuals can be characters in more than one dream. Perhaps you will see your deceased grandmother after you die one day, while "at the same time" she has also been reborn into another life here. Things may not be linear in a way we can easily understand.

Other examples of when one dream seems to follow another occur when children say they watched events in their parents' lives from heaven, such as James Leininger recalling his parents' trip to Hawaii or Ryan describing his mother's reaction when her ultrasound revealed she was having a little boy. These are a bit more challenging to explain with the dream model. They suggest individuals may occasionally be able to see across dreams or worlds, to view one dream while experiencing another one. This would be similar to reports in mediumship, where individuals in the afterlife—in a different dream—appear able to communicate with individuals in this world. At times, some people seem able to cross boundaries of consciousness. I make no claim to fully understand how they do it, but this ability may illustrate that consciousness and consciousness-created realities are more fluid and interconnected than we might think.

THE DREAMER

If we can move from one dream to another when we die, then some part of us would transcend the worlds we experience. We would have a larger self existing across our lives. To go back to the dream model, I exist as a character in my nighttime dreams, usually my daytime self but occasionally someone else. Along with my character in the short-lived dream, I as a dreamer also have my real self that exists apart from the dream. Likewise, I think we each have a larger part of us that transcends the individual dream—the individual lifetime—and continues to take part in creating other dreams, other lifetimes or worlds.

I suspect our roles in life are much like an actor's roles in movies. As we go from one life to another, or more accurately have one dream and then another, our characteristics in each life may vary quite a bit. We have different traits in each life, affected in this world by our genetic makeup and our upbringing. But a larger aspect of each of us would also carry over from one life to the next. Jimmy Stewart played many characters during his long acting career—most of them nice, some not so nice, some simple, some complex—but regardless of the character, it was always unmistakably Jimmy Stewart who was playing the role. There was this entity, this actor, who existed in each of his characters but also existed outside of them. The same might be true for us across lives. There would be a larger entity than just the person—or going back to the second chapter, the snake—we were in our previous life.

Jimmy Stewart brought something that informed and shaped each character he played. A character played by Jimmy Stewart turned out differently than one played by Cary Grant. I suspect the same holds true for any multiple lives we lead, that our consciousness brings something unique to each life. We start a life with a tendency for certain traits or patterns.

We have some evidence in our past-life cases that supports this. Among the variables we code for each case in our database, we include six personality or behavioral items for both the child and the previous person. (They were established a long time ago and may sound a bit archaic.) They are: Is/Was the person attached to wealth? Does the subject show a tendency toward criminality, and was the previous person a criminal? Is/Was the person philanthropic or generous? Is/Was the person active in religious observances? Does/Did the person meditate? Is/was the person saintly?

We don't have this information for most of our cases, so only a small number are included in the analysis for each item. Even so, there is a statistically significant correlation between the amount of every feature in the previous person and the amount in the child, meaning the more the previous person showed a feature, the more likely the child is to show it as well. This correlation is strong enough for each of the features so that the odds of it occurring by chance are no more than one in a hundred. The personalities of the two people are not identical by any means—we know genetics and environment have a large impact on personality development—but there does seem to be an effect. Certain tendencies have carried over.

I also suspect that not only does the individual bring something to each life but that each life also informs the individual, just as our experiences shape our development in this life. This larger self is not static but can change or grow. In this way, each individual does make progress (or at times may fall back) in what can be called spiritual development. My view is that this occurs in a natural way, not through some orchestrated effort. I don't believe that between lives, individuals meet with guides or some sort of council to learn what issues they will work on in their upcoming lives (as some hypnotic regression proponents suggest). Some individuals may have dreams like that before beginning this dream, but I doubt the true process is so literal. Rather, our next lives, whether in this world or another, will involve previously unresolved issues, just as our night-time dreams are attempts by our minds to process unresolved emotional material.

To speculate about an example, a person who focuses on hoarding his wealth in one lifetime may have a "nightmare" in his next life in which he is poor. Over the course of several lifetimes, he may come to see that wealth is not critical to having a satisfying life, so it will fade as an issue for him. As we make progress through some of our patterns, those will fall away, and we will move on to work on others. Progress is thus made as the content of each "dream" evolves. This seems similar to how species on Earth make progress when they evolve through natural selection. Just as the accidental changes in species ultimately lead to ever more successful adaptations to the environment, there may be side steps or steps in the wrong direction, but with the dream content changing as issues are resolved, spiritual progress is ultimately made in a naturalistic way.

Working through issues may involve difficult experiences, and certainly some people endure terrible pain and suffering in this life. On a smaller scale, we experience difficult events in nightmares as our minds attempt to process various emotions in our unconscious. Likewise, I hope that the traumas people suffer in life are part of a working-through process that across lifetimes may ultimately lead to resolution and progress.

MIND AND LIFE

One big difference between our nighttime dreams and our life experiences is that in our dreams, the other characters don't have an internal existence. They only exist because we observe them. In life, every conscious being presumably has an internal existence (unless you want to fall into solipsism and decide you're the only one who really exists). We are all co-creators of this shared dream, not our characters or personalities, but the conscious part of us that transcends the particular dream, the particular lifetime.

How might the larger part of each of us—the Dreamer—be connected to the other dreamers? In looking at the way our world works so seamlessly—once I observe the outcome of an event, the result is set for any future observers—I think the unique consciousness in each of us must be part of a larger whole. Each of us is contributing to a tapestry of existence rather than creating our own individual work.

The I in my nighttime dreams, my character in the dreams, is part of a bigger I, my larger mind out of which my dream world arises. All the people in the dream are arising from the same consciousness, in the case of my nighttime dreams, from mine. In the same way, all the individuals in the physical world may also arise from the same consciousness, from some larger conscious force.

Work that may be relevant to this came from Carl Jung. He explored the connection between the mental and the physical with his concept of synchronicity or meaningful coincidences, which involves correspondences between mental images and objective situations. He included three types of synchronistic events. The first is the one people usually focus on. In it, the mental state of an observer corresponds with a simultaneous external event in a meaningful way. He shares an example from his psychotherapy work with a woman who was too rational and intellectual to fully engage in therapy. As she was telling him one day about a dream in which she was given a golden scarab, an expensive piece of jewelry, Jung heard a tapping on the window behind him. He opened it and grabbed the insect that flew in. It was a scarabaeid beetle, whose gold-green color made it as close to a golden scarab as anything in that part of the world. He handed it to the patient and said, "Here is your scarab." The incident helped them push through her defenses and led to more productive psychotherapy.

Bernard Beitman, a friend and colleague of mine, has recently been studying synchronicities and coincidences. He points out that Jung was an active agent in this story. Not only did he get up and take the beetle to the patient, but Bernie feels Jung's emotions were important in producing the events, that his frustration with the patient's intellectualizing somehow helped cause that beetle to appear.

Jung's second type of synchronicity was a coincidence between a mental state and a corresponding physical event taking place away from the observer. An example he gave was when Emanuel Swedenborg had a vision of a great fire that was burning at the time in Stockholm, 250 miles away. The third type was a coincidence between a mental state and an event in the future that can only be verified later. With this, he discussed J. B. Rhine's ESP studies in which subjects guessed a series of cards that were not laid out until minutes or even weeks after the subjects made their picks. The results of the experiments showed odds that the subjects' correct answers occurred by chance were only one in 400,000.

With all of these, Jung argued that there was no physical cause that could have conceivably produced them, that they were "acausal." He said that, along with the connection between cause and effect, synchronicity was another factor in nature that the arrangement of certain events demonstrated. He noted that it could be dependent on the affective state—the mood—of the observer, that a positive state of faith and optimism led, in the ESP tests for example, to better results.

Bernie also related a story from another writer on coincidences, Roderick Main, about a man who was intensely studying the Biblical Book of Zechariah, in which Zechariah has a vision of four horsemen whose horses are red, black, white, and dappled. The man took a break, walked out onto the balcony of his hotel room, and saw four horses below: a red one, a black one, a white one, and a dappled one. He was stunned.

When Bernie told the story, I suggested the explanation for it involved affecting the collapse of a wave function, that the man's focus on the imagery of four horses of different colors had increased the likelihood that four horses of different color might separate themselves from other horses grazing nearby and end up by his hotel balcony. This would be producing one outcome from a fairly random group of possibilities, and the repeated imagery of the horses would be analogous to focusing on a particular scene one day and then dreaming about it that night.

Bernie's reaction to my suggestion, as I recall, was to laugh. And he is certainly right that this would not be a simple case of collapsing the wave function like observing an electron to see which slit it goes through. But I do think some similar inter-action between inward consciousness and outward physical events could be involved.

An example in my own life points out that this idea of a connection may be applied more broadly to other events, but also that the connection is complex. When I was fervently try-ing to get my first book published, I sent query letters out to numerous literary agents, including one to Patricia van der Leun. What I didn't know at the time—what I couldn't have known at the time—was that Patricia had just had a conversa-tion with one of her authors, B. Alan Wallace, a scholar of Ti-betan Buddhism and president of the Santa Barbara Institute for Consciousness Studies. Alan, whom I only met later, told Patricia about Ian Stevenson's work here at the University of Virginia. She was therefore intrigued when she received my letter soon thereafter. She asked me to send a book proposal, which she then took with her to a lunch she had planned with an editor at St. Martin's Press, Diane Reverand. Diane liked the proposal, so before I knew anything about it, I was close to having a publisher. In fact, we got an offer from St. Martin's before Patricia and I had even signed our agent/author agree-ment. And so the book was on its way.

You can decide I was simply lucky. But if you consider that consciousness may be involved in apparent luck, these events demonstrate what a complex process it can be. My wish to find a publisher didn't make Alan Wallace devote many years of his life to the study of Buddhism or hire Patricia as his agent. It didn't cause Patricia and Diane Reverand to be friends or create Diane's interest in such topics, as she had served as editor for a number of books on near-death experiences. The pieces nonetheless all fit together to create an outcome that was quite meaningful to me. Jung would not have counted this as a synchronicity, because the series of events was not so unlikely that they couldn't have occurred by chance. But I am struck by the possibility that the connection between the goal in my mind and a series of events that occurred largely out of my control involved something more than chance. This would not necessarily mean that my wish produced the outcome exactly, but consciousness may have been involved—in some complex way—in creating the physical reality that resulted. If so, this suggests that our thoughts—the images in our minds, our wishes and goals—are linked to each other's and to outcomes in the physical world. These thoughts and the subsequent realities may not only be linked but may emanate from the same source. In that way, the various pieces from my series of events in finding a publisher—or from the golden scarab story or the four horse story—fit together because they are all coming ultimately from one Mind.

This doesn't necessarily mean that everything that happens is planned or intended by this Mind. I don't control or plan the events in my nighttime dreams, and I know my mind creates those. The physical world may work the same way. This consciousness-created reality may include painful or negative events that happen randomly without any conscious intent or control. Even so, we may be able to reduce them by appealing to the benign aspect of this larger Mind.

If I accidentally touch a hot object, I am not burning my

hand to make it stronger; the event was just incidental. My immediate reaction is to move my hand away. The nerves from my fingers instantly send pain impulses to my central nervous system, which reacts quickly to send nerve impulses back to my arm telling it to move my hand. Each of us may be like a single nerve cell in one large nervous system, so every thought made with intention such as a wish or prayer may be like a pain sensation reaching the brain. Though the brain and the larger organism may or may not respond to the pain signal, there would be a natural tendency to remove the negative sensation, just as we do with our own bodies. At times, however, people override uncomfortable sensations—of pain as they are working out, or cold as they are traveling outside in the wintertime, for example—for their larger overall goals. So it might be with existence, that what looks from our individual, close-up perspectives like negative sensation we wish we could avoid—such as pain or disappointment—might help us make progress in the long run, just as an aching muscle during a workout becomes bigger and stronger over time.

I have no idea why my wish to get a publisher might have effected that outcome when similar goals in other circumstances do not. The world doesn't seem to function as Rhonda Byrne's book *The Secret* describes, with its idea that positive thoughts work as powerful magnets to attract positive outcomes like good health and great wealth. If only life were that simple. I do think that our hopes and wishes can affect outcomes, that we may be able to produce change by applying conscious intention to the world's happenings—it's just not as easy or straightforward as *The Secret* makes it out to be. I think exploring how to increase this effect—through prayer, meditation, insight, or as Jung's writings on synchronicity suggest, a state of faith and optimism—could be useful if the goal is to have more control over the events in this consciousness-created existence. We can try to improve the dream and make this a better world. At the same time, our hopes and wishes may be able to do only so much to override the creation—or perhaps the plan—of the Ultimate Source of both consciousness and the physical world. Religious people sometimes pray, "Thy will be done," which is a way to appeal to the benign aspect of this larger Mind, along with a recognition that there may be much that we do not understand.

THE BIG PICTURE

Since part of us seems able to transcend the various dream worlds as we move from one to another in different lifetimes, there must also be existence outside of these worlds and outside of space-time—an existence of pure Mind. Each of us may be like a single train of thought in one large Mind. We seem to be like a chain of islands as William James suggested, separate when seen above the water but connected at the ocean floor. More than just connected, islands turn out to be projections that are so many small parts of a single larger object, the planet. Likewise, each of our minds may turn out to be small streams of consciousness that are all part of a larger Mind, a "cosmic consciousness" as James said. This is not to deny our individualism; each island in the sea is an individual thing. But it is also part of something bigger.

In the same way, we may exist as individuals on the surface, while being part of something much bigger. Bigger than we can conceive, since we are not considering one sea but rather all thought. Imagine every train of thought you have had in your life multiplied by the billions of people who have lived on this one planet in this one galaxy multiplied by thoughts from countless other dream worlds, and suddenly the cosmic consciousness seems far bigger than even the physical cosmos.

Beneath the waterline of our individual existences, we may be part of this endless consciousness, something I am tempted to call the Mind of God. This is a far, far cry from my Southern Baptist roots, and yet this infinite realm of thought from which all worlds, all emotions, all events from the coalescence of a new planet to the fading glow of a dying star, from the first breath of a newborn baby to the final sigh of a long life well-lived flow, this Ultimate Source of all existence must be the thing that our feeble minds can only comprehend in some shrunken, anthropomorphized, clouded facsimile we call God. We think we can make out the vague outline, but the enormity of the thing makes it so much greater than we can imagine.

I know this is a long way from children's past-life memories. But as each step has followed the other, this is where the journey has led. A little boy who repeatedly relives the exact details of the terrible death of a young World War II pilot challenges the mainstream understanding that consciousness is always created by—and confined to—a physical brain. Exploring quantum physics then produces a way to understand such events because it leads to a rational conclusion that the physical world grows out of consciousness, meaning that consciousness must not be limited by the physical. A child in Louisiana remembering events from the life of a pilot from Pennsylvania offers a glimpse that consciousness survives across lifetimes and that experiences separated by great distances and many years can nonetheless be connected and intertwined.

This connection, along with the seamless way in which observations from countless observers create our holistic world, indicates that a single individual consciousness is only a tiny piece in the act of creation, that all the pieces work in concert as part of a bigger whole, and just as our physical world grows out of consciousness, so the entirety of existence grows out of this bigger whole, this Ultimate Source. As mere streams of thoughts from one large Mind, we are not separate; we are all in this together. And just as our experiences in life can enrich our individual minds, if this awareness that we are all part of the Ultimate helps us be a little more patient, a little more accepting, a little more loving, if it helps us to focus more on our shared experiences and less on our differences, then perhaps in some small way, we will be better able to enrich the Ultimate and, with it, all of existence.

Acknowledgments

I am very grateful to the families described in this book, for sharing both their stories and their time with me. Needless to say, *Return to Life* would not have been possible without them. I have changed most of their names, but fortunately, they know who they are.

The trips to Asia I discuss in Chapter 2 would clearly have been fruitless without the able help of translators, Sutdya Vajrabhaya and Wichian Sittiprapaporn in Thailand and U Myint Aung in Myanmar.

I also want to thank Greyson and Ariana Williams. Their generous donation enabled me to dedicate more of my time to completing the book. It also funded the research trip described in Chapter 7.

Patricia van der Leun, my literary agent, and Daniela Rapp, my editor at St. Martin's, helped make this a much better book than it would have been otherwise. Copy editor Eric Meyer added numerous improvements. Suggestions from Lori Derr and David Sauvage were also quite helpful.

Finally, I want to thank the love of my life, my wife,

Chris. She has again served as my unofficial editor. More important, being with her continues to energize my exploration of life and my appreciation of what it has to offer each and every day.

Notes

CHAPTER 1

p. 10: Ian had previously determined: Stevenson, 1993.

p. 10: *Reincarnation and Biology*: Stevenson, 1997.

p. 11: a man who vividly recalled: Moody, 1946.

p. 12: Carol Bowman: Bowman, 1997 and 2001.

p. 13: "If the vapid writings": Stevenson, 1978, p. 323.

p. 13: In a review of one of his books: King, 1975.

p. 14: We eventually included: Pasricha, et al., 2005.

p. 15: it published a letter: Stevenson, 1999.

p. 15: One was from Tom Shroder: Shroder, 2008.

p. 15: wrote a book about them: Shroder, 1999.

p. 15: "Scientists with Half-closed Minds": Stevenson, 1958.

p. 16: His final paper: Stevenson, 2006.

CHAPTER 2

p. 27: Ian and Satwant published a paper: Stevenson & Pasricha, 1980.

p. 27: Ian also wrote it up: Stevenson, 1984.

p. 28: Samuel Johnson's line: Bartlett, 1968, p. 430.

p. 28: a young woman named Sumitra: Stevenson, Pasricha, and McClean-Rice, 1989.

pp. 28–29: "from that of a simple village girl": ibid., p. 84.

p. 29: a follow-up investigation: Mills & Dhiman, 2011.

p. 30: "although we do not dogmatically assert": Stevenson, Pasricha, and McClean-Rice, 1989, p. 100.

p. 31: As William James said: James, 1896, p. 5.

p. 37: They fed her eggs: Foll, 1959, and Khaing, 1962.

p. 37: a boy in Sri Lanka named Sujith: Stevenson, 1977.

p. 38: Ian wrote that he had to overcome: Stevenson, 2000a, p. 209.

p. 41: ones whose specifics: For a good example, see Sabom, 1998, chapter 3.

CHAPTER 3

p. 51: The airport claims: http://isleofbarra.com/for-visitors/the-airport/plane-landing-on-the-beach.html. Accessed 8/16/11.

p. 54: I developed a scale: Tucker, 2000.

p. 56: Child Dissociative Checklist: Putnam, Helmers, & Trickett, 1993.

p. 57: When our colleague Erlendur Haraldsson: Haraldsson, 1995 and 2003, and Haraldsson, Fowler, & Periyannanpillai, 2000.

p. 58: Swarnlata Mishra: Stevenson, 1974, pp. 67–91.

p. 61: when children report memories of two lives: Stevenson, 2000a, p. 218.

p. 61: in four of Ian's cases: ibid.

p. 61: F. W. H. Myers's: For a remarkable review of Myers, see Kelly, et al., 2007, chapter 2.

p. 62: a soul that originated in a spiritual environment: Myers, 1903, volume I, p. 34. I learned of Myers's model of the mind from a presentation by Adam Crabtree.

CHAPTER 4

p. 66: *Soul Survivor*: Leininger & Leininger, 2009.

p. 72: *The Battle for Iwo Jima 1945*: Wright, 1999.

p. 73: post-traumatic play: See American Academy of Child and Adolescent Psychiatry Staff, 2000; Wälder, 1933; and, most notably, Terr, 1981. For post-traumatic symptoms in children who report past-life memories, see Haraldsson, 2003.

p. 75: *Natoma Bay's* involvement in Iwo Jima: *Dictionary of American Naval Fighting Ships* (1970), pp. 22-23.

p. 75: eight pilots from *Natoma Bay* took part: This is taken from the *Natoma Bay* Iwo Jima Operations Report War Diary.

p. 79: 113 landings: Tillman, 1979.

CHAPTER 5

p. 103: families have often conducted: Stevenson, 2000a, pp. 113–115.

p. 103: Gnanatilleka: ibid. See also Tucker, 2005, pp. 151–156, and most definitively, Nissanka, 2001.

CHAPTER 6

p. 121: Ian and two colleagues wrote a paper: Stevenson, Pasricha, & Samararatne, 1988.

p. 125: Howard's death: White, 1977.

p. 132: "young Bobby": Reported at http://www.cnn.com /2011/US/04/07/bobby.jones.iv.grandfather.legacy/index .html. Retrieved on 8/12/12.

p. 134: a paper on abnormalities: Stevenson, 2000b.

p. 136: Ian speculated that women's lives: Stevenson, 1983, p. 223.

p. 137: five years of deaths in the United States: www.cdc .gov/nchs/data/misc/atlasres.pdf. Retrieved 9/24/12.

CHAPTER 7

p. 141: Erlendur Haraldsson, a colleague, has suggested: Haraldsson, 2003.

p. 146: "London Bridge Is Falling Down": *The Oxford Dictionary of Nursery Rhymes,* 1952, pp. 270–78.

p. 162: a tremendous need for timber: See McLaughlin, 1998, chapter 7.

p. 163: hooley: another source is http://en.wiktionary.org/wiki/hooley.

CHAPTER 8

p. 166: A recent study found that a quarter of scientists: Ecklund & Long, 2011.

p. 167: *The Language of God*: Collins, 2006.

p. 167: Brian Josephson: Klarreich, 2001.

p. 167: "We have known": http://wwwphysics.lbl.gov/~stapp/UCSF050509.docA, p. 3.

p. 168: "I regard consciousness as fundamental": *The Observer* (January 25, 1931). Cited in Stromberg, 1942, p. 329.

p. 169: called the double-slit experiment: For discussions of the double-slit experiment, see Greene, 1999; Davies, 1983; and The Double-Slit Experiment, 2002.

p. 169: An analogy would be the waves: Greene, 1999, p. 99.

p. 170: As Paul Dirac said: Dirac, 1958, p. 9.

p. 170: The double-slit experiment has now been done with electrons: See The Double-Slit Experiment, 2002, for details of the history of the experiments.

p. 170: neutrons, atoms, and even larger molecules: ibid.

p. 170: "impossible, *absolutely* impossible, to explain in any classical way": Feynman, Leighton, & Sands, 1963, volume 3, p. 1-1.

p. 170: "has in it the heart of quantum mechanics": ibid.

p. 171: "the atoms or the elementary particles themselves": Herbert, 1985, p. 195.

p. 171: "the transition from the 'possible' ": Stapp, 2007, p. 90.

p. 172: Heisenberg called the potential outcomes *potentia*: Herbert, 1985, p. 195.

p. 172: John von Neumann, a brilliant mathematician who wrote a book: von Neumann, 1955 (original published in 1932).

p. 172: "quantum bible": Herbert, 1985, p. 25.

p. 172: Von Neumann discusses: For discussions of von Neumann's work, see Rosenblum & Kuttner, 2006, p. 184, and Herbert, 1985, pp. 145–149.

p. 173: "his abstract 'ego' ": von Neumann, 1955, p. 421.

p. 173: "the intellectual inner life of the individual": ibid., p. 418.

p. 173: a physical signal in the brain: Herbert, 1985, p. 148.

p. 173: He produced a thought experiment: ibid., p. 160.

p. 174: "The wave function is collapsed": Henry, 2005.

p. 174: random event generators: Radin & Nelson, 1989.

p. 174: A researcher named Helmut Schmidt: Schmidt, 1993.

p. 175: French physicist Olivier Costa de Beauregard: Costa de Beauregard, 1995, p. 290.

p. 175: Few physicists would still give classical physics: Vedral, 2011.

p. 176: "shows that the universe is founded": Greene, 1999, p. 108.

p. 176: Schrödinger's famous cat: Gilder, 2008, p. 173, and Schrödinger, 1935.

p. 176: SQUID: Friedman, et al., 2000.

p. 177: "Schrödinger's SQUID": Collins, 2000.

p. 177: "Schrödinger's cat is now fat": Blatter, 2000.

p. 177: "New life for Schrödinger's cat": Leggett, 2000.

p. 177: physicists at University of California, Santa Barbara: O'Connell, et al., 2010.

p. 177: *Science* named it the Breakthrough of the Year: Cho, 2010.

p. 177: "A transition from quantum to classical": Seife, 2001.

p. 177: Numerous experiments, from Zeilinger and others: For example, see Arndt, et al., 1999; Nairz, et al., 2002; Friedman, et al., 2000; van der Wal, et al., 2000; Hackermüller, et al., 2003. Further examples are shown in Vedral, 2011, p. 42.

pp. 177–78: John Wheeler . . . imagined a thought experiment: Folger, 2002.

p. 178: This kind of delayed-choice experiment: See Jacques, et al., 2007, which also references previous studies.

p. 178: a similar thought experiment on a galactic scale: Folger, 2002.

p. 180: Albert Einstein was unhappy with quantum theory: Fine, 2011.

p. 180: not clear he even read the final draft: ibid.

p. 180: cited in physics journals far more than any other paper Einstein ever wrote: Gilder, 2008, pp. 3–4.

p. 180: EPR: Einstein, Podolsky, & Rosen, 1935. Quotes from p. 780.

p. 181: John Bell published a discussion: Bell, 1964.

p. 181: Bell's theorem: For a discussion, see Rosenblum & Kuttner, 2006, pp. 142–152.

p. 181: "Grossly non-local": Bell, 1964, p. 195.

p. 181: most notably by Alain Aspect: Aspect, Grangier, & Roger, 1981; Aspect, Dalibard, & Roger, 1982; Aspect, Grangier, & Roger, 1982.

p. 181: Bell wrote that requiring locality: Bell, 1964, p. 195.

p. 182: "Our world therefore does *not*": Rosenblum & Kuttner, 2006, p. 143.

p. 182: a group of physicists in Vienna published a study: Gröblacher, et al., 2007.

p. 182: "Quantum physics says goodbye to reality": http://physicsworld.com/cws/article/news/2007/apr/20/quantum-physics-says-goodbye-to-reality.

p. 182: "highly counterintuitive": ibid., p. 875.

p. 182: first proposed by Costa de Beauregard: See Jammer, 1974, pp. 238–239, and Costa de Beauregard, 1987, particularly p. 252.

p. 185: Stephen King dispensed: King, 2011, p. 61.

p. 185: "It is wrong to think of [the] past": Wheeler, 1983, p. 194.

p. 185: He wrote that since equipment operating in the present: ibid., pp. 194–196.

p. 185: "in some strange sense this is a 'participatory universe'": Wheeler, 1977, p. 6.

p. 185: "there is a sense in which what the observer will do": ibid., p. 3.

p. 186: "'observership' is a prerequisite": ibid.

p. 186: "acts of observer-participancy" could give "tangible 'reality'": Wheeler, 1983, p. 209.

p. 186: "You may ask whether the universe": Folger, 2002, p. 48.

p. 186: If some of the physical constants or initial conditions of the universe had been different: Wheeler, 1977.

p. 186: the odds of a low-entropy universe with formed matter: See Davies, 1983, chapters 12 and 13.

p. 187: the existence of God: See Collins, 2006.

p. 187: strong anthropic principle: Carter, 1974, and Barrow & Tippler, 1988.

p. 187: "Unless the blind dice of mutation": Wheeler, 1977, p. 28.

pp. 187–88: "It is well known that carbon": Dicke, 1961.

p. 188: thermonuclear combustion is required: Wheeler, 1977.

p. 188: " 'consciousness' has nothing whatsoever to do": Wheeler, 1983, p. 196.

p. 188: Though he only hinted at a consciousness-created reality: Herbert, 1985, p. 25.

p. 188: Wigner's friend: Wigner, 1962.

p. 189: "the being with a consciousness must have": ibid., p. 294.

p. 189: "it is the entering of an impression into our consciousness . . . unavoidably and unalterably": ibid., p. 289.

p. 189: He has written books: Stapp, 1996, 2007.

p. 189: "I do not know any sense": Folger, 2002, p. 48.

p. 189: "The universe begins to look more like a great thought": Jeans, 1933, p. 186.

pp. 189–90: "The doctrine that the world": d'Espagnat, 1979, p. 158.

p. 190: Everett's many-worlds interpretation: Everett, 1957. See also Herbert, 1985, for a discussion.

p. 190: Wheeler's stated reason: Wheeler, 1983.

pp. 190–91: "Brain function"—the mind—"will someday be explained": ibid., p. 207.

p. 191: "the observer is as essential": Wheeler, 1977, p. 27.

p. 191: Consciousness does not exist because the physical world does: This is similar to a statement by astronomer Bernard Haisch (2006): "It is not matter that creates an illusion of consciousness, but consciousness that creates an illusion of matter." I would not go so far as to say, however, that matter is purely an illusion, only that it only comes into existence out of consciousness.

p. 193: lucid dreams: See LaBerge, 1985.

p. 193: Gertrude Schmeidler: Schmeidler, 1943, and www.parapsych.org/members/g_schmeidler.html.

p. 193: This finding has since been confirmed: Palmer, 1977.

CHAPTER 9

p. 195: Near-death experience (or NDEs). Much of this review of NDEs comes from Poonam Sharma: Sharma & Tucker, 2004.

p. 196: Allan Kellehear reviewed: Kellehear, 1993.

p. 196: Satwant Pasricha likewise found: Pasricha, 1995.

p. 197: Todd Murphy collected: Murphy, 2001.

p. 197: Yamatoots (the messengers . . .): Pasricha & Stevenson, 1986.

p. 197: Author Sam Harris recently made this argument: http://www.samharris.org/blog/item/science-on-the-brink-of-death.

p. 197: *Proof of Heaven*: Alexander, 2012.

p. 197: *Heaven Is for Real*: Burpo with Vincent, 2010.

p. 198: Poonam Sharma, a medical student: Sharma & Tucker, 2004.

p. 202: Burmese children who have talked about being Japanese soldiers: Stevenson & Keil, 2005.

p. 203: Only one systematic survey: Barker & Pasricha, 1979.

p. 204: Tibetan Buddhists: See Rinpoche, 1993, chapter 14.

p. 205: Mediumship, the idea: For an overview, see Gauld, 1982.

p. 207: deceased relatives on the other side: Kelly, 2001.

p. 207: deceased relatives they hadn't known were dead before they had their NDEs: Greyson, 2010.

p. 210: hypnotic regression proponents suggest: For ideas along these lines, see Weiss, 1988, and Newton, 1994.

p. 210: This seems similar to how species: The analogy to natural selection developed during a stimulating conversation I had with filmmaker David Sauvage.

p. 212: concept of synchronicity: Jung, 1952/1970.

p. 212: three types of synchronistic events: ibid., p. 526.

p. 212: Bernard Beitman: Beitman, 2011.

p. 213: another factor in nature: Jung, 1952/1970, p. 485.

p. 213: a man who was intensely studying: Main, 2007, p. 12.

p. 216: a single nerve cell in one large nervous system: Sir James Jeans made the same analogy: *The Observer* (4 January 1931).

p. 217: islands as William James suggested: James 1909/1986, p. 374.

References

Alexander, E. 2012. *Proof of Heaven: A Neurosurgeon's Journey into the Afterlife*. New York: Simon & Schuster.

American Academy of Child and Adolescent Psychiatry Staff. 2000. *Your Child: Emotional, Behavioral, and Cognitive Development from Birth Through Preadolescence*. Edited by D. Pruitt. New York: HarperCollins.

Arndt, M., O. Nairz, J. Vos-Andreae, C. Keller, G. van der Zouw, and A. Zellinger. 1999. "Wave-Particle Duality of C_{60} Molecules," *Nature* 401:680–682.

Aspect, A., J. Dalibard, and G. Roger. 1982. "Experimental Test of Bell's Inequalities Using Time-Varying Analyzers," *Physical Review Letters* 49:1804–1807.

Aspect, A., P. Grangier, and G. Roger. 1981. "Experimental Tests of Realistic Local Theories via Bell's Theorem." *Physical Review Letters* 47:460–463.

Aspect, A., P. Grangier, and G. Roger. 1982. "Experimental Realization of Einstein-Podolsky-Rosen-Bohm *Gedankenexperiment*: A New Violation of Bell's Inequalities," *Physical Review Letters* 49:91–94.

Barker, D. R., and S. K. Pasricha. 1979. "Reincarnation Cases in

Fatehabad: A Systematic Survey in North India," *Journal of Asian and African Studies* 14:231–240.

Barrow, J. D., and F. J. Tipler. 1988. *The Anthropic Cosmological Principle*. Oxford: Oxford University Press.

Bartlett, J. 1968. *Familiar quotations*. Edited by E. M. Beck. 14th edition. Boston: Little, Brown and Company. Original edition, 1855.

Beitman, B. D. 2011. "Coincidence Studies," *Psychiatric Annals* 41:561–571.

Bell, J. S. 1964. "On the Einstein Podolsky Rosen Paradox," *Physics* 1:195–200.

Blatter, G. 2000. "Schrödinger's Cat Is Now Fat," *Nature* 406: 25–26.

Bowman, C. 1997. *Children's Past Lives: How Past Life Memories Affect Your Child*. New York: Bantam Books.

Bowman, C. 2001. *Return from Heaven: Beloved Relatives Reincarnated Within Your Family*. New York: HarperCollins.

Burpo, T., with L. Vincent. 2010. *Heaven Is for Real: A Little Boy's Astounding Story of His Trip to Heaven and Back*. Nashville, Tennessee: Thomas Nelson.

Carter, B. 1974. "Large Number Coincidences and the Anthropic Principle in Cosmology," *Confrontations of Cosmological Theories with Observational Data*, edited by M. S. Longair. Dordrecht, Netherlands: D. Reidel.

Cho, A. 2010. "The First Quantum Machine," *Science* 330:1604.

Collins, F. S. 2006. *The Language of God: A Scientist Presents Evidence for Belief*. New York: Free Press.

Collins, G. P. 2000. "Schrödinger's SQUID," *Scientific American*, October.

Costa de Beauregard, O. 1987. "Time, the Physical Magnitude," edited by R. S. Cohen and M. W. Wartofsky. Vol. 99, *Boston*

Studies in the Philosophy of Science. Dordrecht, Netherlands: D. Reidel.

Costa de Beauregard, O. 1995. "Macroscopic Retrocausation," *Foundations of Physics Letters* 8 (3):287–291.

Davies, P. 1983. *God and the New Physics.* New York: Touchstone.

D'Espagnat, B. 1979. "The Quantum Theory and Reality," *Scientific American* 241 (5):158–181.

Dicke, R. H. 1961. "Dirac's Cosmology and Mach's Principle," *Nature* 192:440–441.

Dictionary of American Naval Fighting Ships, vol. 5. 1970. Washington: Defense Department, Navy, Naval History Division.

Dirac, P. A. M. 1958. *The Principles of Quantum Mechanics.* 4th ed. London: Oxford University Press.

The Double-Slit Experiment. 2002. *Physics World.* September, 15.

Ecklund, E. H., and E. Long. 2011. "Scientists and Spirituality," *Sociology of Religion.* 72:253–274.

Einstein, A., B. Podolsky, and N. Rosen. 1935. "Can Quantum-Mechanical Description of Physical Reality Be Considered Complete?" *Physical Review* 47:777–780.

Everett, H. 1957. "'Relative State' Formulation of Quantum Mechanics," *Reviews of Modern Physics* 29:454–462.

Feynman, R. P., R. B. Leighton, and M. Sands. 1963. *The Feynman Lectures on Physics.* 3 vols. Reading, Massachusetts: Addison-Wesley Publishing.

Fine, A. 2011. "The Einstein-Podolsky-Rosen Argument in Quantum Theory," *The Stanford Encyclopedia of Philosophy* (winter 2011 edition), edited by E. N. Zalta. http://plato.stanford.edu/archives/win2011/entries/qt-epr/.

Folger, T. 2002. "Does the Universe Exist if We're Not Looking?" *Discover,* June, 44–48.

Foll, C. V. 1959. "An Account of Some of the Beliefs and Super-stitions About Pregnancy, Parturition and Infant Health in Burma," *Journal of Tropical Pediatrics* 5:51–59.

Friedman, J. R., V. Patel, W. Chen, S. K. Tolpygo, and J. E. Lukens. 2000. "Quantum Superposition of Distinct Mac-roscopic States," *Nature* 406:43–46.

Gauld, A. 1982. *Mediumship and Survival: A Century of Investiga-tions.* London: William Heinemann.

Gilder, L. 2008. *The Age of Entanglement: When Quantum Physics Was Reborn.* New York: Alfred A. Knopf.

Greene, B. 1999. *The Elegant Universe: Superstrings, Hidden Di-mensions, and the Quest for the Ultimate Theory.* New York: W. W. Norton.

Greyson, B. 2010. "Seeing Deceased Persons Not Known to Have Died: 'Peak in Darien' Experiences," *Anthropology and Humanism* 35:159–171.

Gröblacher, S., T. Paterek, R. Kaltenbaek, C. Brukner, M. Żu-kowski, M. Aspelmeyer, and A. Zeilinger. 2007. "An Ex-perimental Test of Non-Local Realism," *Nature* 446:871–875.

Hackermüller, L., S. Uttenthaler, K. Hornberger, E. Reiger, Brezger B., A. Zeilinger, and M. Arndt. 2003. "Wave Na-ture of Biomolecules and Fluorofullerenes," *Physical Re-view Letters* 91:090408-1–090408-4.

Haisch, B. 2006. *The God Theory: Universes, Zero-Point Fields and What's Behind It All.* San Francisco: Weiser Books.

Haraldsson, E. 1995. "Personality and Abilities of Children Claiming Previous-Life Memories," *Journal of Nervous and Mental Disease* 183:445–451.

Haraldsson, E. 2003. "Children Who Speak of Past-Life Experiences: Is There a Psychological Explanation?" *Psy-chology and Psychotherapy: Theory, Research and Practice* 76:55–67.

Haraldsson, E., P. C. Fowler, and V. Periyannanpillai. 2000. "Psychological Characteristics of Children Who Speak of a Previous Life: A Further Field Study in Sri Lanka." *Transcultural Psychiatry* 37:525–544.

Henry, R. C. 2005. "The Mental Universe," *Nature* 436:29.

Herbert, N. 1985. *Quantum Reality: Beyond the New Physics.* New York: Anchor Books.

Jacques, V., E. Wu, F. Grosshans, F. Treussart, P. Grangier, A. Aspect, and J. Roch. 2007. "Experimental Realization of Wheeler's Delayed-Choice Gedanken Experiment," *Science* 315:966–968.

James, W. 1896. Presidential Address, *Proceedings of the Society for Psychical Research* 12:2–10.

James, W. 1909/1986. "Confidences of a 'Psychical Researcher,'" *Essays in Psychical Research.* Cambridge, Massachusetts: Harvard University Press.

Jammer, M. 1974. *The Philosophy of Quantum Mechanics: The Interpretations of Quantum Mechanics in Historical Perspective.* New York: John Wiley & Sons.

Jeans, J. 1933. *The Mysterious Universe.* Revised ed. New York: Macmillan.

Jung, C. G. 1952/1970. "Synchronicity: An Acausal Connecting Principle," trans., R.F.C. Hull, *The Structure and Dynamics of the Psyche,* edited by G. Adler, M. Fordham, and H. Read. Princeton, New Jersey: Princeton University Press.

Kellehear, A. 1993. "Culture, Biology, and the Near Death Experience: A Reappraisal." *Journal of Nervous and Mental Disease* 181:148–156.

Kelly, E. F., E. W. Kelly, A. Crabtree, A. Gauld, M. Grosso, and B. Greyson. 2007. *Irreducible Mind: Toward a Psychology for the 21st Century.* Lanham, Maryland: Rowman & Littlefield.

Kelly, E. W. 2001. "Near-Death Experiences with Reports of Meeting Deceased People," *Death Studies* 25:229–249.

Khaing, M. M. 1962. *Burmese Family*. Bloomington: Indiana University Press.

King, L. S. 1975. "Reincarnation," *JAMA* 234:978.

King, S. 2011. *11/22/63*. New York: Scribner.

Klarreich, E. 2001. "Stamp Booklet Has Physicists Licked," *Nature* 413:339.

LaBerge, S. 1985. *Lucid Dreaming*. Los Angeles: Jeremy P. Tarcher.

Leggett, T. 2000. "New Life for Schrödinger's Cat," *Physics World*, August, 23–24.

Leininger, B. and A. Leininger, with K. Gross. 2009. *Soul Survivor: The Reincarnation of a World War II Fighter Pilot*. New York: Grand Central.

Main, R. 2007. *Revelations of Chance*. Albany: State University of New York Press.

McLaughlin, M. 1998. *Sierra Stories: True Tales of Tahoe*. Carnelian Bay, California: Mic Mac.

Mills, A., and K. Dhiman. 2011. "Shiva Returned in the Body of Sumitra: A Posthumous Longitudinal Study of the Significance of the Shiva/Sumitra Case of the Possession Type," *Proceedings of the Society for Psychical Research* 59:145–193.

Moody, R. L. 1946. "Bodily Changes During Abreaction," *Lancet* 2:934–935.

Murphy, T. 2001. "Near-Death Experiences in Thailand," *Journal of Near-Death Studies* 19:161–178.

Myers, F. W. H. 1903. *Human Personality: And Its Survival of Bodily Death*. 2 vols. London: Longman's, Green.

Nairz, O., M. Arndt, and A. Zeilinger. 2002. "Experimental Verification of the Heisenberg Uncertainty Pprinciple for Fullerene Molecules," *Physical Review A* 65:032109-1–032109-4.

Newton, M. 1994. *Journey of Souls: Case Studies of Life Between Lives*. St. Paul, Minnesota: Llewellyn.

Nissanka, H. S. S. 2001. *The Girl Who Was Reborn: A Case-Study Suggestive of Reincarnation*. Colombo, Sri Lanka: Godage Brothers.

O'Connell, A. D., M. Hofheinz, M. Ansmann, R. C. Bialczak, M. Lenander, E. Lucero, M. Neeley, D. Sank, H. Wang, M. Weides, M. Wenner, J. M. Martinis, and A. N. Cleland. 2010. "Quantum Ground State and Single-Phonon Control of a Mechanical Resonator," *Nature* 464:697–703.

The Oxford Dictionary of Nursery Rhymes. 1952. Edited by I. Opie and P. Opie. London: Oxford University Press.

Palmer, J. 1977. "Attitudes and Personality Traits in Experimental ESP Research," *Handbook of Parapsychology*, edited by B. B. Wolman. New York: Van Nostrand Reinhold.

Pasricha, S. 1995. "Near Death Experiences in South India: A Systematic Survey," *Journal of Scientific Exploration* 9:79–88.

Pasricha, S. K., J. Keil, J. B. Tucker, and I. Stevenson. 2005. "Some Bodily Malformations Attributed to Previous Lives," *Journal of Scientific Exploration* 19:359–383.

Pasricha, S., and I. Stevenson. 1986. "Near-Death Experiences in India: A Preliminary Report," *Journal of Nervous and Mental Disease* 174:165–170.

Putnam, F. W., K. Helmers, and P. K. Trickett. 1993. "Development, Reliability, and Validity of a Child Dissociation Scale," *Child Abuse & Neglect* 17:731–741.

Radin, D. I., and R. D. Nelson. 1989. "Evidence for Consciousness-Related Anomalies in Random Physical Systems," *Foundations of Physics* 19:1499–1514.

Rinpoche, S. 1993. *The Tibetan Book of Living and Dying*. New York: HarperCollins.

Rosenblum, B., and F. Kuttner. 2006. *Quantum Enigma: Physics*

Encounters Consciousness. New York: Oxford University Press.

Sabom, M. 1998. *Light & Death: One Doctor's Fascinating Account of Near-Death Experiences*. Grand Rapids, Michigan: Zondervan Publishing House.

Schmeidler, G. R. 1943. "Predicting Good and Bad Scores in a Clairvoyance Experiment: A Final Report," *Journal of the American Society for Psychical Research* 37:210–221.

Schmidt, H. 1993. "Observation of a Psychokinetic Effect Under Highly Controlled Conditions," *Journal of Parapsychology* 57:351–372.

Schrödinger, E. 1935. "Die Gegenwärtige Situation in der Quantenmechanik" [The present situation in quantum mechanics] *Die Naturwissenschaften [The Natural Sciences]* 48:807–812, 823–828, 844–849.

Seife, C. 2001. "Microscale Weirdness Expands Its Turf," *Science* 292 (5521):1471.

Sharma, P., and J. B. Tucker. 2004. Cases of the Reincarnation Type with Memories from the Intermission Between Lives. *Journal of Near-Death Studies* 23:101–118.

Shroder, T. 1999. *Old Souls: The Scientific Evidence for Past Lives*. New York: Simon & Schuster.

Shroder, T. 2008. "A Good Question," *Journal of Scientific Exploration* 22:115–116.

Stapp, H. P. 1996. *Mind, Matter and Quantum Mechanics*. Berlin: Springer.

Stapp, H. P. 2007. *Mindful Universe: Quantum Mechanics and the Participating Observer*. Berlin: Springer.

Stevenson, I. 1958. "Scientists with Half- Closed Minds." *Harper's Magazine* 217:64–71.

Stevenson, I. 1974. *Twenty Cases Suggestive of Reincarnation*. 2nd rev. ed. Charlottesville: University Press of Virginia. (First published in 1966 in *Proceedings of the American Society for Psychical Research*, vol. 26.)

Stevenson, I. 1977. *Cases of the Reincarnation Type, vol. II: Ten Cases in Sri Lanka*. Charlottesville: University Press of Virginia.

Stevenson, I. 1978. "Some Comments on Automatic Writing," *Journal of the American Society for Psychical Research* 72:315–332.

Stevenson, I. 1983. *Cases of the Reincarnation Type, vol. IV: Twelve Cases in Thailand and Burma*. Charlottesville: University Press of Virginia.

Stevenson, I. 1984. *Unlearned Language: New Studies in Xenoglossy*. Charlottesville: University Press of Virginia.

Stevenson, I. 1993. "Birthmarks and Birth Defects Corresponding to Wounds on Deceased Persons," *Journal of Scientific Exploration* 7:403–416.

Stevenson, I. 1997. Reincarnation and Biology: *A Contribution to the Etiology of Birthmarks and Birth Defects*. Westport, Connecticut: Praeger.

Stevenson, I. 1999. "Past Lives of Twins," *Lancet* 353:1359–1360.

Stevenson, I. 2000. "The Phenomenon of Claimed Memories of Previous Lives: Possible Interpretations and Importance," *Medical Hypotheses* 54 (4):652–659.

Stevenson, I. 2001. *Children Who Remember Previous Lives: A Question of Reincarnation*. Revised ed. Jefferson, North Carolina: McFarland.

Stevenson, I. 2006. "Half a Career with the Paranormal," *Journal of Scientific Exploration* 20:13–21.

Stevenson, I., and J. Keil. 2005. "Children of Myanmar Who Behave Like Japanese Soldiers: A Possible Third Element in Personality." *Journal of Scientific Exploration* 19:171–183.

Stevenson, I., and S. Pasricha. 1980. "A Preliminary Report on an Unusual Case of the Reincarnation Type with Xenoglossy," *Journal of the American Society for Psychical Research* 74:331–348.

Stevenson, I., S. Pasricha, and N. McClean-Rice. 1989. "A Case of the Possession Type in India with Evidence of Paranormal Knowledge," *Journal of Scientific Exploration* 3:81–101.

Stevenson, I., S. Pasricha, and G. Samararatne. 1988. "Deception and Self-Deception in Cases of the Reincarnation Type: Seven Illustrative Cases in Asia," *Journal of the American Society for Psychical Research* 82:1–31.

Stromberg, G. 1942. "Coherence in a Physical World," *Philosophy of Science* 9:323–334.

Terr, L. C. 1981. "FORBIDDEN GAMES: POST-TRAUMATIC CHILD'S PLAY," *Journal of the American Academy of Child Psychiatry* 20:741–760.

Tillman, B. 1979. *Corsair: The F4U in World War II and Korea*. Annapolis, Maryland: Naval Institute Press.

Tucker, J. B. 2000. "A Scale to Measure the Strength of Children's Claims of Previous Lives: Methodology and Initial Findings," *Journal of Scientific Exploration* 14:571–581.

Tucker, J. B. 2005. *Life Before Life: A Scientific Investigation of Children's Memories of Previous Lives*. New York: St. Martin's Press.

van der Wal, C. H., A. C. J. ter Haar, F. K. Wilhelm, R. N. Schouten, C. J. P. M. Harmans, T. P. Orlando, S. Lloyd, and J. E. Mooij. 2000. "Quantum Superposition of Macroscopic Persistent-Current States." *Science* 290:773–777.

Vedral, V. 2011. "Living in a Quantum World," *Scientific American*, June, 38–43.

von Neumann, J. 1955. *Mathematical Foundations of Quantum Mechanics*. Translated by R. T. Beyer. Princeton, New Jersey: Princeton University Press.

Wälder, R. 1933. "The Psychoanalytic Theory of Play," *Psychoanalytic Quarterly* 2:208–224.

Weiss, B. 1988. *Many Lives, Many Masters: The True Story of a*

Prominent Psychiatrist, His Young Patient, and the Past-Life Therapy That Changed Both Their Lives. New York: Fireside.

Wheeler, J. A. 1977. "Genesis and Observership," *Foundational Problems in the Special Sciences*, edited by R. Butts and J. Hintikka. Dordrecht, Netherlands: D. Reidel.

Wheeler, J. A. 1983. "Law Without Law," *Quantum Theory and Measurement*, edited by J. Wheeler and W. H. Zurek. Princeton, New Jersey: Princeton University Press.

White, S. H. 1977. *Sidney Howard*. Boston: Twayne.

Wigner, E. P. 1962. "Remarks on the Mind-Body Question," *The Scientist Speculates: An Anthropology of Partly-Baked Ideas*, edited by I. J. Good. New York: Basic Books.

Wright, D. 1999. *The Battle for Two Jima 1945*. Stroud, England: Sutton.

READING GROUP QUESTIONS

1. Have you ever known a child who reported memories of a past life?

2. After James Leininger had nightmares of dying in World War II, his father resisted the possibility of a past life for a long time. How would you react if your child showed signs of remembering a past life?

3. If you had a child who cried about missing previous parents, how do you think you would feel?

4. Has something ever led you to think you had a past life yourself?

5. Is there a time or place in history that particularly interests you, one you wish you could remember having a past life in?

6. If you could choose the circumstances of your next life, what would you choose? Is there a specific place you would want to live? Are there particular talents you would want to have?

7. If you come back in another life, what would you most want to remember about this one?

8. Would you want one of your grandparents to come back as your child? Would you want to come back as the son or daughter of one of your children or grandchildren?

9. What were your feelings about reincarnation before you read the book? What are your feelings now?

10. What did you hear about reincarnation when you were growing up? Did your parents believe in it?

11. How do the cases fit with your religious beliefs? Do you

think it's possible to have traditional Judeo–Christian beliefs and also believe in past lives?

12. Do you think we have all had past lives even if most of us don't remember them?

13. The author gives a couple of examples of children who said they remembered being an animal in a past life. Do you think that's possible? Would you want a future life as an animal? If so, what animal? Do you think our pets reincarnate?

14. The book describes how physicians and psychologists have investigated past-life memories. Do you think this is an appropriate topic for research? Why or why not?

15. Which cases in the book impressed you the most? Why?

16. Do you think that birthmarks and birth defects can come from trauma in a past life? If not, how do you explain the cases in which the children were born with ones that matched wounds the previous person suffered?

17. Some of the children said that before they were born they watched their parents' activities. Do you think that's possible?

18. The author expresses doubt about past-life hypnotic regression. What do you think about it? Have you ever tried it yourself?

19. Do you think it's possible that the children have memories of a past life because of ESP, not because they actually experienced that life? The author explains in Chapter 3 of *Life Before Life* why he thinks ESP is a weak explanation for the cases. Do you agree?

20. The author argues that consciousness is the primary force of existence and it creates the physical world. Do you agree? If this is true, what would it say about life after death?

ABOUT THE AUTHOR

Jim B. Tucker, M.D. is the Bonner-Lowry Professor of Psychiatry and Neurobehavioral Sciences at the University of Virginia. He is the director of the UVA Division of Perceptual Studies, where he is continuing the research of Ian Stevenson into children's reports of past-life memories. His work has been featured on *NBC Nightly News, CBS Sunday Morning, NPR Weekend Edition,* and numerous other programs. He lives in Charlottesville with his wife.